EMP

ip @ £55 -

^^7.50

Men, Women and Property in England, 1780–1870

This is an innovative study of middle class behaviour and property relations in English towns in Georgian and Victorian Britain. Through the lens of wills, family papers, property deeds, account books and letters, the author offers a new reading of the ways in which middle class families survived and surmounted the economic difficulties of early industrial society. He argues that these were essentially 'networked' families created and affirmed by 'gift' networks of material goods, finance, services and support with property very much at the centre of middle class survival strategies. His approach combines microhistorical studies of individual families with a broader analysis of the national and even international networks within which these families operated. The result is a significant contribution to the history of the middle classes, to economic, business, urban and gender history, and to debates about the place of structural and cultural analysis in historical understanding.

R. J. MORRIS is Professor of Economic and Social History at the University of Edinburgh. He was President of the European Association of Urban Historians in 2000–02.

Men, Women and Property in England, 1780–1870

A Social and Economic History of Family Strategies amongst the Leeds Middle Classes

R. J. Morris

University of Edinburgh

CAMBRIDGE UNIVERSITY PRESS

PUBLISHED BY THE PRESS SYNDICATE OF THE UNIVERSITY OF CAMBRIDGE
The Pitt Building, Trumpington Street, Cambridge, United Kingdom

CAMBRIDGE UNIVERSITY PRESS
The Edinburgh Building, Cambridge CB2 2RU, UK
40 West 20th Street, New York NY 10011-4211, USA
10 Stamford Road, Oakleigh, VIC 3166, Australia
Ruiz de Alarcón 13, 28014 Madrid, Spain
Dock House, The Waterfront, Cape Town 8001, South Africa

http://www.cambridge.org

First published 2005

Printed in the United Kingdom at the University Press, Cambridge

Typeface in 10/12pt Plantin system Advent 3B2 8.01 [TB]

A catalogue record for this book is available from the British Library

Library of Congress Cataloguing in Publication data

Morris, R.J. (Robert John)
  Men, women, and property in England, 1780–1870: a social and economic
  history of family strategies amongst the Leeds middle classes / R.J. Morris.
    p. cm.
  Includes bibliographical references and index.
  ISBN 0 521 83808 8 (hardback)
  1. Middle class–England–Leeds–History. 2. Middle class families–
  England–Leeds–History. 3. Property–Social aspects–England– Leeds.
  4. Leeds(England)–Social conditions–18th century. 5. Leeds
  (England)–Social conditions–19th century. I. Title.
  HT690.G7M674 2004   306.3′2′086220942–dc22   2004049688

ISBN 0 521 83808 8 hardback

Contents

List of figures

List of tables

Acknowledgements

A book which has been as long in the making as this one has benefited from the help and inspiration of many people. It is impossible to thank them all. Amongst colleagues at Edinburgh University, Michael Anderson, Graeme Morton and Stana Nenadic deserve special mention, as do Ann McCrum and Jim Smyth amongst past and present postgraduate students. There have been many cross-currents of university life in the past couple of decades. Amongst those I value most has been developing and teaching in the social science computer laboratory and the experience of taking part in the ESRC-financed SCELI (Social Change and Economic Life Initiative) led by Frank Bechofer at Edinburgh. Listening to sociologists devising a questionnaire and analysing its results is something no historian should miss. Outwith Edinburgh the activities and meetings of the Urban History Group and the European Urban History Association have been especially formative, as were those of the Association for History and Computing. Saying thank you so far covers a couple of hundred people, but amongst those who have been especially helpful and supportive are Geoff Crossick, Lee Davidoff, Simon Gunn, Catherine Hall, Liam Kennedy, Helen Meller, Richard Rodger, Ric Trainor and Brian Young. Dozens of other friends and colleagues have given specific advice and help.

Especially important over the years have been the librarians and archivists of the West Yorkshire Archives Service at Sheepscar in Leeds, in the Brotherton Library at the University of Leeds, the Thoresby Society in Leeds, the Borthwick Institute in the University of York, the National Library of Scotland and the library and special collections of Edinburgh University. Without them the work of being an historian would be impossible.

During the course of this work I have benefited from the funds and research leave schemes of the University of Edinburgh and the Nuffield Trust.

As ever my greatest debt is to Barbara Morris for support and criticism of the best kind, but given the topic of this book, the dedication should be to family, all of them, parents, grandparents, wife, children, sister, cousins, nephews, nieces, even a great-niece, uncles, aunts, in-laws, their in-laws – they know who they are.

1   Joseph Henry Oates: a world of madeira and honey

Sometime towards the end of January 1825, Joseph Henry Oates, merchant of Leeds in the West Riding of Yorkshire, had a dreadful day. On the 31st he wrote to his brother in London.

The day I received your letter of Monday, say on Wednesday last I was under engagement to Mr Cass to have an operation performed – I had prepared a written order to Beckett's complying with your request, but unfortunately had omitted to give it to our Clerk and the future events of the day put all out of my head – I submitted to the operation of having my bottom <u>mangled</u> and have been in bed and on the sofa ever since – I write this lying down.[1]

January 1826 was even worse. On 1 February he told his brother,

The fact is simply this and as true as it is simple. We owe Beckett's so much money that without putting a bill of some description into their hands I dare not ask a renewal of credit at Glynn's – I assure you I have not had it in my power to pay a Clothier one penny during the last month, but the very first remittce I receive shall go immy to Beckett's accompd by a request to renew yr credit at Glynn's for £400 – we have received only one remittance since this year came in and after looking with confidence for something handsome from J S Smithson there arrived a line from him yesterday without a penny.[2]

Beckett's were Joseph Henry's bankers, who held his balances both positive and negative and transmitted funds to London when needed, just as they did for a large part of the trading and manufacturing community of Leeds.[3] A week later the alarm was even greater.

But really money is not comeatable – I have actually suspended what? payment? no! not exactly, but I have suspended purchases of every description except bread,

---

[1] J.H. Oates, Oatlands to Edward Oates Esq., 12 Furnival's Inn, London, 31 January 1825. Oates O/R. [All letters were addressed to Furnival's Inn unless otherwise stated.]
[2] Oates, 1 February 1826.
[3] *Select Committee on the Bank of England Charter*, Parliamentary Papers (House of Commons), 1831–32, 6, evidence of William Beckett, Q. 1237.

meat and potatoes, and I have driven Clothiers away with a 'can't you call again next month?'[4]

These two incidents were buried in a bundle of letters which the Leeds merchant sent to his brother during the mid-1820s. Reading them is rather like listening to one side of a telephone conversation. They were written and kept because the merchant and his lawyer brother were settling matters of family business raised by their father's death and the probate of the will. There is no way of finding out if Joseph Henry got any sympathy for his financial problems or the discomfort of his piles but, as the business of settling their father's estate went forward, the letters show that energy was diverted from business by the insecurities of both middle-aged health and an uncertain economy.

Joseph Henry was partner in one of the leading merchant firms in the woollen textile trade of Leeds. He seems a fairly ordinary sort of individual, perched upon the higher ground of Meanwood, above the smoke of Leeds, surrounded by neighbours who were also part of those commercial and professional elites which dominated the provincial towns of England. He was unusual in that his family had been merchants since the late seventeenth century and was distinctive in his dissenting Unitarian religion and Whig politics.[5] There were many like him who could trace their origins back into the merchant, manufacturing and landowning families of the north of England. Others had within a generation come from craft, retailing and petty manufacturing families. In the 1820s they drew their income from a variety of sources in trade, manufacturing, land and the professions. As Joseph Henry went backwards and forwards to his counting house in the commercial centre of Leeds, just behind the chapel where he worshiped on Sunday, he saw a town which was growing rapidly in size and complexity.[6]

The letters between the two Oates brothers went to the heart of the family economy because their major concern was the transfer of property between generations after their father's death. The need for equity and certainty in this process opened up the family to the historian's gaze with a directness that few other life cycle events can offer. The brothers' willingness to fill their letters with the chatter of family and business life created a sense of context for this transfer, which was rare in probate

---

[4] Oates, 9 February 1826.
[5] R.G. Wilson, *Gentlemen Merchants. The Merchant Community in Leeds, 1700–1830* (Manchester, 1971).
[6] R.J. Morris, *Class, Sect and Party. The Making of the British Middle Class: Leeds, 1820–50* (Manchester, 1990), pp. 1–85.

documents. The major characters emerged slowly but clearly from the letters, as did the objectives which each participant had in mind.

Joseph Henry, the writer of the letters, was probably in his late thirties.[7] He was the active member of the Leeds firm of Oates, Wood and Co., merchants. He was second son of Joseph Oates of Weetwood Hall, who died in 1824 aged 82. Joseph was one of eight children and his father one of eleven, hence they were called the Weetwood Hall Oates to distinguish them from a number of cousins and uncles who headed other successful merchant and professional families. Joseph Henry was an active and industrious man, anxious to do what was right, whilst at the same time to get what was due to him. He was the one who undertook the probate of the will and negotiated the division of the estate. He also tended to be rather cautious,

I know to my sorrow that I am one of the most procrastinating chaps in the world

He was always worried about his health,

I am a poor timid mortal – particularly since the Piles have made such a formidable attack upon me.[8]

For him the family inheritance brought political and religious loyalties as well as the merchant business. Family involvement with old dissent made them an important part of the elite of Mill Hill chapel as it developed into the major Unitarian centre of Leeds, as well as making them members of the local Whig elite. Joseph Henry was not an activist. He was not an Edward Baines, founding editor of the Whig newspaper, or a John Marshall, wealthy flax manufacturer and MP after his successful challenge to the landowners' dominance of West Riding politics. But Joseph Henry paid his pew rent and his politics were clear enough to affect his social and business activity in times of conflict such as the 1826 county election. This election saw a hard fought contest for the West Riding seat at Westminster in which fellow urban capitalist and co-religionist, John Marshall, took a seat from the landowning Tory interest.[9]

The election sends us all to loggerheads and there is scarcely a blue mercht in the town who wd at present admit me within his doors – and perhaps the great bulk of our merchts are blue . . . With respect to this election, you will learn more from

[7] R. Thoresby, *Ducartus Leodiensis* (Leeds, 1816) edited by T.D. Whitaker. This was a substantially augmented version of the work of Ralph Thoresby, the early eighteenth century antiquarian, and included a number of genealogies of 'older' Leeds families.
[8] Oates, 14 May 1826.
[9] F.M.L. Thompson, 'Whigs and Liberals in the West Riding, 1830–60', *English Historical Review* 74 (1959).

Baines's paper, which I send by this post, than I can tell you, never having been beyond the Countg ho since this stir began – of course the mortification has been great – George is in the thick of it . . . Monday must show what is to be done – but I think there is every appearance of a hard contest – My vote and interest you may be sure are pledged to Milton and Marshall – George is on the York committee[10]

Joseph Henry wanted a well run business and a quiet family life, but family and chapel drew him into politics whether he liked it or not.

The Wood of Oates and Wood was George William Wood of Manchester who had married Sarah, eldest daughter and fourth child of Joseph. George William was the eldest son of the marriage between Joseph's sister Louisa Ann and Rev. William Wood. He had been the minister of Mill Hill Chapel who had followed Joseph Priestley and consolidated the position of the chapel as a leading Unitarian congregation.[11] Another crucial relationship in this puzzle was the marriage of George William Oates, a younger brother of Joseph, to Mary Hibbert, daughter of a Manchester merchant. These marriages, often involving cousins like GWW and Sarah, were important for many middle class elites. They consolidated family links and family capital. Such marriages also consolidated chapel links. Men like Rev. William Wood were not just leaders of a religious congregation. They developed and consolidated the ideology that sustained the religious faith, family values and political loyalties of families like the Oates. Joseph Henry Oates followed a rational God and guided his politics by calls for 'civil and religious liberty' against the monopolistic pretensions of the established Church of England. He also looked to his minister to justify and explain the family relationships which were crucial to his life style and economic fortunes.[12] Joseph Henry devoted substantial time and resources to sustaining these relationships and men like the Rev. William Wood provided him with motivation and legitimation.

George was the eldest child of Joseph. He was the 'awkward squad'. Considering the character of brother George explains why a little motivation and support from the likes of the Rev. William Wood was often needed. When difficulties arose over the settlement of their father's estate it was always George who was the target of Joseph Henry's letters of despair,

[10] J.H. Oates, Oatlands to Edward Oates Esq. at John Philips Esq., Heath House, nr. Cheadle, Staffordshire, 10 June 1826.
[11] W.L. Shroeder, *Mill Hill Chapel, 1674–1924*, (Leeds, 1925).
[12] J. Seed, 'Theologies of Power: Unitarianism and the Social Relations of Religious Discourse, 1800–1850', in R.J. Morris (ed.), *Class, Power and Social Structure in British Nineteenth Century Towns* (Leicester, 1986), pp. 107–56.

He declines to act . . . but he has every disposition to act in many ways – and does act – he receives rents and gives orders and makes payments at his pleasure.[13]

A foundry, which their father had financed, proved especially difficult to settle. George first wanted to break it up and sell, then to run it himself. The bulk of the property had been left to the brothers as 'tenants in common'.[14] This meant that if the individual items like Carr House and the 'mill' were to be controlled by an owner who had sole rights over them, and hence had the certainty needed to make investments and other dispositions regarding that property, then the brothers had to go through a complex operation of mutuality. This forced them to act and negotiate as a family if the property was to be released into the world of capitalist accumulation, risk and disposition. Such mutuality placed considerable stress on the brothers' ability to co-operate, yet co-operate they must if they were to get sole and unrestricted access to a fair share of their father's property. The difficulties with a character like George in the negotiation were clear.

I do not suppose we shall make any exchange of property; he wishes only to rent my portion of Carr House and receive interest for the sum due him on account of the Mill; this plan however will not suit me – I cannot pay 4% Intt for example on the £2600 (which is the sum we had in great measure settled six months ago as the price to be paid by me for his share in the Mill, Land and Improvemt at the Cottage) and receive £50 per an rent from a farm worth a full £2600. I must sell part of my acres at least.[15]

The foundry, which no-one really understood, and the fact that Edward in London was entitled to a share, and that all the brothers had property in their own right, which they might be tempted to sell and exchange, only added to the complications. They were still arguing a month later. The tangle of personalities, properties and calculations was intense.

You may be very sure I am equally anxious with George to arrive at a settlemt of accts. At the time Brown was about purchasing this place we made a sort of settlemt it is true, but I am by no means agreed with him in his statement to you that it was at a low rate – the rate was such as I was willing to sell for myself, and this under an impression that I could replace it for even less by building again – nothing but a good price was calculated to induce me to sell, and in case I had ever come to close quarters with Brown and actually fixed him a price, that price was to have been twice the sum fixed by George (as his share) for what was our joint interest – £400 per acre for the original land with something added for the

13 Oates, 17 January 1825.
14 Oates, 26 February 1825.
15 Oates, 17 January 1825.

house ... The idea of a sacrifice quite amuses me – giving up the Mill whch pays $7^1/_2\%$ in exchange for land which will only pay 3 – an exchange is not necessary – it will suit me equally well to pay him in money though I might have to sell my land to enable me to do it, but that would be no matter of his – still he might call it a sacrifice to give up the Mill paying $7^1/_2$ for money which will pay only 4% – what I can say is that I considered it a very excellent thing for him when I consented to take the whole burden of the mill upon myself and release him from so cumbersome a clog – nothing but my very strong desire to release him from the dilemma which the circumstances of my father's deed of gift brought him into could have led me to take such a step and had I ever dreamed that the affair would have gone so long unsettled I should not have agreed to take his share at all

Beneath all this good will was a manoeuvre designed to get sole control of a vital piece of capital, the mill. In order to achieve this Joseph Henry was willing to give up some of the land he owned in north and northwest Leeds. The deed of gift, which was dated 1819, together with the will, had given the brothers a tangle of joint control and obligations from which each was trying to negotiate his way out with the maximum of advantage. These arguments took place within the close confines of family politics. After yet another set of arguments about what had been agreed regarding the foundry, Joseph Henry wrote,

I wonder at this (the misunderstanding) as George seldom spends Sunday elsewhere than with us.[16]

George was to die on 17 October 1832 at the age of 52.

The object of all this letter writing was Edward, the third son of Joseph, an enigmatic figure. He was based in London practising as a lawyer with his address at a respectable 12 Furnival's Inn. He was to return to Leeds in 1836 to marry Susan, the daughter of Edward Grace of Kirkstall. Late marriage was characteristic of the Oates. His letters were full of concern for his books, pictures and drawings, many of which he had purchased on a trip to Italy in 1819. Joseph shared some of this interest but without the same commitment as his younger brother. The Oates were not major patrons of the arts in Leeds but, like many of the elite, their houses contained small and valued collections.[17] Edward carried out all the legal business of the family. He had an interest in the firm of Oates and Wood as well as in the estate of his father. His demands were less complicated than those of George because all he wanted was to get his

[16] Oates, 25 November 1825.
[17] R.J. Morris, 'Middle Class Culture, 1700–1914', in D. Fraser (ed.), *A History of Modern Leeds* (Manchester, 1980), pp. 200–22; J. Woolf and J. Seed (eds.), *The Culture of Capital: Art, Power and the Nineteenth Century Middle Class* (Manchester, 1988), esp. pp. 45–82.

interest out in cash and have it transmitted to London to support a consumption and investment pattern hinted at in his letters. Edward was the listener of these letters, the London link for the family and, although he stood a little apart from day-to-day family politics, he was still very much part of the Weetwood Oates.

The most vulnerable of all Joseph's children who grew to adulthood was Mary, his youngest daughter. Mary played a vital part in maintaining the family structure on which the Oates depended. It was she who kept the links between Manchester and Leeds working smoothly. About a fifth of the letters note that Mary was in Manchester, going to or just returned from Manchester. Mary was the late child of a late marriage. Her mother had died in 1798, about the time of Mary's birth. By the early 1820s, Mary had become housekeeper companion to her father. George thought of her in the same role but she would have none of that. The failure of his bargaining with Mary lay behind some of George's prevarications with Joseph Henry.

I think he changed his mind the moment he found Mary did not intend to take up her quarters with him at Carr House.[18]

Mary herself was very uncertain of her position. The debate over the fate of the various properties continued.

Rest assured we shall have stranger doings before that day comes – Mary is apprehensive that she will never be allowed to go again to the house to pack up even what is her own – the most charitable construction which I can put upon his conduct is that it must be the result of derangemt, whether temporary or permanent time only will shew[19]

Mary's major asset in the delicate and ill-balanced negotiations of family politics was the income she drew from a property in Call Lane in the centre of Leeds. Even here she had to rely on the goodwill and help of both Joseph Henry and Edward in the management of that property. She escaped from George's plans to recruit her as housekeeper but in the end her role as carer and maintainer of the family network caught up with her. It was the role frequently allotted to unmarried adult women in the family structures of the elite middle class. Mrs Headlam of Thorpe Arch, a female relative, frequently mentioned in the correspondence, was ill and off Mary went.

[18] Oates, 26 February 1825.
[19] Oates, 19 March 1825.

Mrs Headlam has had an attack of cholera morbus at Thorpearch which has left her in a very debilitated state – Mary had scarcely been returned from Manchester 12 hours before she was sent for to Mrs H – she is gone this morning.[20]

It proved a harrowing experience. Joseph Henry quoted some of his sister's letter.

Her (Mrs Headlam's) head was a little confused last night and I (Mary) hoped she might be released from all her sufferings . . . I wish you would request Dr Hutton's prayers for her on Sunday. I shd say for her release but I almost fear lest there shd be any selfish feeling in it and that I may wish myself to be released from my situation for it really is more wretched than any one can imagine who does not witness it.[21]

A letter later in the year claimed 'Mary was no worse for the shaking she got.'[22] When Ann Headlam died in July 1834, Mary received a legacy which included the linen, books, wine, wearing apparel and ornaments as well as a half share of the residual estate which amounted to £145.[23] Mary's role in the family was certainly not one of leisure. Banging backwards and forwards across the Pennine Hills in the pre-railway days was probably less restful than crossing the Atlantic in a 747, and then she had to listen to all the family ills and property disputes before coming back to George's designs for a housekeeper and Mrs Headlam with her fevers and bed sores.

There was a large supporting cast of uncles and aunts. Uncle Smithson was in Harrogate in 1825 and planned to winter in Bath or Brighton the next year. More important, he had a substantial sum of money invested at 4 per cent on a more or less permanent basis in Oates and Wood.[24] J.S. Smithson traded with Oates and Wood and was a trustee for Mrs Headlam who was related through marriage and chapel. She had money in the firm and was expected to leave property to Mary. Uncle Robinson was executor for Uncle George's will. Thomas Robinson had married Joseph's youngest sister and was a third Manchester link. Aunt Robinson seems to have died in 1826 adding to Joseph Henry's worries as nobody could find Uncle George's will. And so it goes on. Some of the

---

[20] Oates, 15 July 1826. This cholera could not have been the epidemic Asiatic Cholera of 1831–32. The label *cholera morbus* was often given to any savage stomach infection which produced diarrhoea, vomiting, cramps and dehydration – dangerous and painful enough to need care and strength to survive many attacks; R.J. Morris, *Cholera, 1832. The Social Response to an Epidemic* (London, 1976).
[21] Oates, 5 August 1826.
[22] Oates, 29 September 1826.
[23] Legacy Receipt on account of the personal estate of Ann Headlam, 13 April 1835, Oates Papers.
[24] Oates, 22 January 1825.

links, such as the Smithson one, went back three generations before finding a common ancestor.

This detail showed that each set of family relationships increased the density of other social and economic relationships. The investment of capital in the firm and the Manchester links reinforced one another. There were other more general patterns. The comfortable old age and independence of Uncle Smithson and Mrs Headlam depended upon the fortunes of Oates and Wood. When they went to Brighton or Bath, the economies of those leisured towns[25] depended upon the fortunes of the wool textile industry of the north of England.

The main protagonists in this family story were:

George, the eldest brother, unmarried;
Joseph Henry, the letter writer, married with young children;
Edward, younger brother, unmarried, seeking professional life in London;
Sarah, who had 'escaped' to a marriage in Manchester which served to deepen a variety of family and business links;
Mary, young and unmarried, always busy in keeping family networks and domesticity in good order.

Their life style was privileged, circumscribed by a variety of half specified rules and duties and threatened in often ill-defined ways. It was a life of substantial urban mansions on the northern and northwestern edges of Leeds away from the smoke. It was a life of madeira and honey, of books and pictures and fine wine, with the time to visit and dine at family tables covered with plate. As Joseph Henry tidied up Weetwood Hall, he packed up many of the things which Edward had left there after going to London. In April 1825 the plate was packed. Next week it was the books and pictures. Many of these had been acquired in the long tour Edward had undertaken in Italy between 1819 and 1821. These tours were not limited to gentry and aristocratic culture but were common to many of the established elite families of Leeds. Some of the books had to stay in the warehouse for a few months but Edward got two dozen bottles of madeira after complaining that he felt melancholy. In November, jars of honey were sent to London to remind him of home. In March 1826, the distribution of property began again in earnest. First the spoons were sent and then it was the turn of the pictures; hunting scenes and father's portrait. Joseph Henry was offended that Edward thought the pictures had been thrown about at Carr House. George, awkward as ever, had refused them space whilst others had been damaged in the canal trip from

[25] R.S. Neale, *Bath. A Social History, 1680–1850* (London, 1981).

Liverpool. He would complain to Rathbones, the agents in Liverpool. In May it was back to the subject of wine.

The wine promised to you long ago is now bottled – it is the wine alluded to by my Uncle S when we were last at Heath – it is Madeira and I think of a very fair quality – price to you 36/- per doz exclusive of bottles – indeed you drank of it at Oatlands the Sunday George dined with us.[26]

The next lot of pictures were going by carrier. The Oates were consumers in that limited consumer society which had grown in the eighteenth century. Objects, which may have been acquired in response to fashion and novelty or to demonstrate taste and status, were now invested with family meaning. The nature of the transaction varied. There were gifts of honey and madeira at special prices, but plate, pictures, spoons and tableware were carefully documented and accounted for.

In many ways this was a privileged and contented life but it was also insecure, and threats to health were prominent in that insecurity. Enough has been said about Joseph Henry's troubles. He was fortunate compared with his wife. In November 1825 at the end of a long letter on family business and property matters he told Edward,

I am very sorry that it is not in my power to send you a favourable report of my wife's health – She has not derived the benefit from sea bathing which I hoped was in store for her – she looks well but is so weak in the back as to be unable to sit up for a quarter of an hour at a time – there is a decided tendency to inflammation but Mr Cass states decidedly that the spine itself is not diseased – it is ascribed to child bearing and God grant that it may be nothing worse – and no more such labours I trust are in store for her and henceforth we are to occupy separate beds – indeed we have done long – Mary and children all well.[27]

It was not clear exactly what was wrong, a prolapse, some persistent infection or maybe damage to the base of the spine. His wife's health became a constant topic of the letters. Rest and sea bathing were tried but she never regained her energies. In late 1826 he wrote,

If the Almighty saw fit to restore strength to my dear wife I should be happy.[28]

With care neither were burdened with life threatening conditions but for both of them, fully active adult life was at an end. In assessing the economic histories and strategies of the middle classes, it must be remembered that for many of them medical conditions, which would form brief if sometimes unpleasant episodes in the lives of their counterparts in the late

---

[26] Oates, 19 May 1825.
[27] Oates, 22 November 1825.
[28] Oates, 29 September 1826.

twentieth century, could become the basis for a permanent reduction in the quality of their life and in their ability to sustain to the full the management inputs required by business. The wise medical man might advise a winter in Bath or a little good wine, perhaps risk some minor surgical intervention or prescribe a truss or strap to relieve the discomfort of hernias and the like. Many sufferers turned from the professionals and scanned the advertising pages of newspapers and magazines that recommended gallons of patent medicines. Others kept faith with a variety of traditional and folk remedies. Families like the Oates had all the resources available to meet these hazards, but they still had to assume that sometime in middle age, unless they were very fortunate, some medical condition would rapidly reduce their energy and mobility. This was not the drama of death but a slow nagging wearing away at energy and contentment. This is one of the meanings of middle age, and its importance for investment and gender was profound.

As if piles and prolapses were not enough to deal with, Joseph Henry was faced by a set of economic structures which were a source of irregular periods of instability. Like most businesses in this period, Joseph Henry Oates relied on major elements of credit on both sides of his balance sheet. His accounts were a complex structure of countervailing obligations. He had obligations to partners, to family depositors, to bankers and above all to the clothiers who supplied him with cloth and to the warehouse and mill labour involved in finishing that cloth. On the other side of the balance were assets. His warehouses were full of very material assets, his stock, the cloth ready for dispatch and in process of preparation. In addition he held obligations from those to whom he had supplied cloth. Such obligations took the form of bills of exchange or simple book debts.[29] In normal times the flow of obligations across the accounts was a smooth and regular one with a suitable surplus for household and personal spending (another 'obligation'). The process was helped by his bankers granting credit, discounting bills and holding balances. The banking structure was dominated by local and regional banks like Beckett's, with their London 'corresponding banks'.

This process could be disrupted in two major ways. The price of commodities was determined by national and international markets. When these prices fell, the cash value of stocks held in the warehouse also fell. The price of wool, for example, dropped by a quarter between 1825 and 1826.[30]

[29] P. Hudson, *The Genesis of Industrial Capital. A Study of the West Riding Wool Textile Industry c.1750–1850* (Cambridge, 1986).
[30] B.R. Mitchell and P. Deane, *Abstract of British Historical Statistics* (Cambridge, 1962). pp. 494–5.

Second, the flow of obligations was disrupted by the failure and inability of key members of the chain of obligations to pay. If this was a matter of one or two individuals, the system was able to cope, but late 1825 and 1826 was one of those semi-regular intervals at which failure to pay was widespread. The trigger for such failures varied, a poor harvest, war or the end of an investment boom. The origins of the 1825–26 crisis lay in a joint stock company promotion boom, which started in 1822. This was dominated by government bonds from a series of newly independent South American countries as well as commercial and mining companies designed to operate in the region. The majority of the bonds were to be subject to default by 1829 and the commercial and mining shares rarely paid dividends, except in the early years when dividends tended to come from capital.[31] These shares tempted funds from familiar markets such as mortgages and government stock. As long as credit expanded that mattered little. When confidence in the stock and in the continued prosperity of the national economy began to diminish in later 1825, then the rush to cash began. The failure of the London bank, Pole, Thornton and Co, in mid-December intensified the anxiety and the Bank of England, desperate to sustain sterling as a gold standard currency, stepped in as lender of the last resort, discounting bills, printing bills and digging deep into the vaults for minted coin. The peak of the crisis came in December 1825 and January 1826.[32] Although Pole, Thornton had few corresponding banks in the woollen areas, Joseph Henry's anxiety was intense as expected obligations to himself were unpaid or delayed. This anxiety was only increased by his distance from London where the vital action was taking place. In London he had one agent he could trust to put family interests first, namely young Edward who had money invested in the firm.

The smooth working of family and business was disrupted by events well outside Joseph Henry's control. In April 1825, he had been full of confidence, telling Edward that he could withdraw money from the firm as and when he wanted. At the start of November, when early signs of problems were beginning to appear in London, Leeds was still in the grip of a property speculation boom. George sold 'his joint property at Mill Hill – the whole was valued at abt £1450 (I think) – sold for £2500 .... – Leeds is going mad'.[33] The careful Joseph Henry quoted several other prices

[31] F.G. Dawson, *The First Latin American Debt Crisis. The City of London and the 1822–25 Loan Bubble* (Yale, 1990).

[32] J.H. Clapham, *The Bank of England. A History*, 2 vols. (Cambridge, 1944), vol. II, 1797–1914, pp. 94–109.

[33] Oates, 15 November 1825.

which he considered inflated and seemed very ill at ease and pressured by all this activity. A week later he asked,

I am going to take a great liberty, but such is the state of the times that I deem it imprudent to lose a day in sending for acceptance two bills received this morning... If all goes right please to return them at your earliest convenience, or if refused acceptance you will have them protested by a notary[34]

Edward in his turn put pressure on Joseph Henry to get the matter of the foundry settled quickly fearing that the liabilities of that firm would 'ruin' the family. By January the effects were evident in Leeds. Edward was not getting his normal income from the firm. 'I do hope to get enough to pay your interest very shortly, but really I cannot say when as the scarcity of money here is excessive'.[35]

Then came the two letters quoted at the beginning of this chapter. At the start of February Edward got £100 instead of £500 promised. This was a bad month for Leeds. 'I really have not time to send you any mercantile news – numerous failures are taking place but none yet that affect us in point of property – of course you may be sure that I feel exceedingly for the Stansfelds – they may eventually pay all but it is not in my opinion probable'.[36] Stansfeld's was a firm and family equal in rank to the Oates so that the news was an indication of how unstable the economic environment of their family prosperity had become.

It was a privileged life style, this life style of madeira and honey, but it was a life style which needed to be defended and maintained. Central to this defence and maintenance was the need to sustain an adequate flow of income. Amongst the male leaders of such families, the strategies devoted to this end had two major features. Income sources and hence risk were spread over a variety of activities, but each individual, family or household tended to focus on one particular source. Thus elder brother George, although he had money in the firm, was more interested in income from his land. 'All his property is real and he must want capital at his farm – cattle are not to be had on credit'. He had 'smokey houses' and was enthusiastically involved in the property boom in late 1825, looking for gains from the urban expansion of Leeds.[37] At one time he looked to be interested in taking over the foundry but it was not clear if this idea came to anything. This foundry, which caused so much vexation was itself an

[34] Oates, 20 November 1825.
[35] Oates, 14 January 1826.
[36] Oates, 2 March 1826.
[37] Oates, 31 January 1825; M.W. Beresford, 'East End, West End. The face of Leeds during urbanization, 1684–1842', *Publications of the Thoresby Society*, LX and LXI, nos. 131 and 132, (Leeds, 1988).

attempt on the part of their father to diversify his sources of income. It was a business of which they knew little. It involved partners from outside the family circle and caused endless problems.[38] Joseph Henry had substantial amounts of land. He was the only one for whom there was any estimate of value; the Intake at £2500, Woodside at £1000 and the Oakes at £2060. Despite this considerable total, Joseph Henry was still the merchant. During the crisis of January 1826, he was 'exceedingly busy of late at the mill'[39] and the counting house featured in many letters. In the bargaining around his father's estate, he was the one who wanted control of 'the mill'. He was prepared to sell or exchange land in order to get that control. Like many merchants, he had some manufacturing capacity in the preparation and finishing ends of the woollen textile processes. Edward had money in the firm and he owned land in Leeds. He was always corresponding on the topic of developing a property called 'Snow's', usually with the notion of developing it as a 'gentleman's residence'. Edward's central aim was a professional income for himself based in London. He continually withdrew money from the Leeds firm in order to sustain the life style necessary to this end. For the sisters, the strategy was less obvious because they had so little direct control over their resources. The property in central Leeds depended on the brothers for management and was probably held by them in trust for the sisters.

Each of the brothers had an array of different resources before him. They were aware that each had different qualities and the choice would depend upon the mixture of risk, expected income and expected demand for management input which was required, as well as the relevance to the experience, expertise and taste of the individual. Joseph Henry was well aware of these choices as he bargained with George. Land paid 3 per cent and money 4 per cent, whilst he thought the mill could deliver $7^{1}/_{2}$ per cent. Investments which promised high returns and originated in London he regarded with grave suspicion. He warned brother Edward,

London is full of spies and informers you cannot be too careful – another thing is I fear you will look out for something great some 8 or 10% and lose your principal altogether – whenever anything out of the way is offered rest assured it is a catch and I fully expect to hear of your being caught.[40]

Investment in land and housing played a major part in their correspondence. They owned a series of large peri-urban mansions and their associated estates to the northwest of Leeds, Weetwood, Oatlands and

[38] Oates, 27 November 1825.
[39] Oates, 14 January 1826.
[40] Oates, Xmas 1821.

Carr House, as well as other blocks of land and a variety of urban housing, warehousing and industrial properties. This real estate had a number of advantages. It was regarded as stable in value. It was local and embedded in an economic and social environment that the Oates brothers believed they understood. Although its immediate value depended upon the fluctuations of the local land market at any given time, the type of property which the Oates were buying had a variety of economic meanings. Owners might transfer a property from one meaning to another according to need and opportunity. The estate bought as a gentleman's residence might become a farm and then the base for speculative gains at periods of urban expansion. But the notion of merchants becoming landowners cannot be evaluated in any simple or direct way. At times land was simply a store of value which could be liquidated when the need to consolidate or defend merchant and manufacturing capital arose. William Beckett, the banker, claimed that he always extended credit to the merchants on personal security but, in times of economic crisis like 1826, the existence of a large block of real estate must have considerably extended creditworthiness. Real property had two disadvantages, a relatively low expected rate of return and high and often irritating management demands. Repairs, leases, damage done by tenants and countless petty or major legal matters were all added to Joseph Henry's worries and to Edward's legal income. In January 1825 Edward was told that Jos Todd (Mary's tenant in Queen's Court) was quitting on 1st March and had done considerable injury to the buildings,

by getting planks in and out of the windows from the room which he had let to the Thespians (the mayor wisely dispersed these gentlemen and ladies some weeks ago) what are the proper steps to be taken to compel him to repair the slates and repoint them with lime.[41]

In November, he was asking about rights of way and access to the property in Call Lane.

The firm of Oates and Wood was important to the whole family. Although the bulk of the money invested in this firm was tied and directed to the firm by family links, the relationship was still structured by the same world market forces that linked Beckett's to the Bank of England. Edward was treated with great preference when it came to extracting money from the business. He was told that he could have whatever he wanted at a few days notice, but when he asked for a higher than market rate of interest his brother replied,

[41] Oates, 17 January 1825.

It is quite unreasonable to expect more than the current rate. – we do not owe Beckett's a farthing and can have whatever we like on the underside of £10,000 at 4%. We shall pay Tennant only 4% and that perhaps only for twelve months longer – your money as I have always told you is at your service on a very short notice say a month or six weeks for instance free of Banker's commission or on an hour's notice on payment of quarter percent bankers commn. We considered it a favour to you allowg 5% – Beckett's then charged us 5%. when the proposal comes from us to lower interest to what is now the current rate (all the Bankers in this place have reduced their charge to 4%) you cry out as though you were hurt – my Uncle S whose money with us is more permanent has received only 4% last year.[42]

Thus the capital of the firm was made up not only of the partners' capital but also of family money resulting from shares of father's estate and of deposits from members of the older generation like Uncle Smithson. Some capital came from beyond the immediate family circle. It all added to the complexity of financing and managing.

Messrs. Tennant and Banks have called in their money in my hands, at least one of the annuitants is dead and they will want a £1000 of the money in six months – the remr may continue or not as most agreeable to me – but would be wanted on the death of a second old lady now between 70 or 80, I believe.

How far it would be desirable for me to pay off the whole and borrow more I hardly know at present – mortgaging seems so expensive a job that I wish I could avoid it but my real estate will not serve as capital for business, and I do not see that selling Woodside to George and Oaks to you wd immy raise anything for me in the shape of actual money, but transfers in our books only.[43]

The financing of the firm was bound in with the needs and pressures of family outside the immediate kin group, notably the needs of old age.

Beyond the various ways in which the family and associates related to the firm there were a variety of stocks and shares. Involvement in such assets affected the Oates in the 1820s at three levels. Joseph Henry, ever cautious and mistrustful of metropolitan ways, stuck to what he knew in the local economy. He, like George, bought shares in the Leeds and Yorkshire Insurance Company. In February 1826 they bought some Leeds Water Works shares, and had earlier subscribed to the projected Leeds and Hull Railway, but such items were a small part of his assets.[44] There was government consolidated stock paying 3 per cent on its face

[42] Oates, 22 January 1825.
[43] Oates, 29 September 1826.
[44] E. Parsons, *The Tourists Companion: By the Railroad and Steam Packet from Leeds and Selby to Hull* (London, 1835); R. Pearson, 'Taking risks and containing competition: diversification and oligopoly in the fire insurance markets of the north of England during the early nineteenth century', *Economic History Review* 46:1 (1993), 39–64.

value, but in the Oates circle these seem to have been for women. Joseph Henry was executor for Mrs Headlam and the papers of her estate show that she had £900 in 3 per cent consols. In a different league was Edward who, despite the warnings of his brother, was investing in the South American Stock boom. In November 1825 Edward made a list of his assets on the back of one of Joseph Henry's letters. In addition to the

Anglo American Mines	£299.10s
Columbian Mines	£20
Peruvian Mines	£57
Mexican Bonds	£407.9s.10d
Columbian Bonds	£485
British Iron	£298.15s
John McKerrelen	£75
Mrs Fitzsimmons	£350
Portable Gas	£208
Mexican Mint	£20
Protector Insurance	£11.5s
Total	£2237.4s.10s
Adds (presumably cash)	£400
To give a grand total	£2637.4s.

South American stock there were a public utility, an insurance company and two names, probably loans on personal security. This was a very different strategy from that of his older provincial brothers.

It was likely that his insistent demand for money was based upon his need to finance these purchases and the calls upon the shares for which he subscribed.

In all these strategies, the firm served the purposes of the family and the family the purposes of the firm. The capital of the firm depended upon the shares and deposits of the family. They in their turn used it as a 'bank'. The savings upon which their old age was financed were placed there at interest. It was a temporary store of value for brief surpluses. Uncle Smithson took his 4 per cent and went off to winter in Bath or Brighton. Edward's legal fees were simply entered into his account with the firm, along with the interest on his capital. When money was sent to London, a credit was opened for him at Glynn's, which was Beckett's corresponding bank in London, and the firm's account at Beckett's was debited like any other transaction. The firm was the medium through which Leeds money was transmitted to London. The family had their money with someone they knew and could keep an eye on, whilst in return they might be asked to wait for their 'interest' at times of crisis like January 1826. Although Edward's money seems to have been technically at interest, he often had to wait for payment during the crisis, thus suffering some of the irregularity of income of those who took the profit directly. This mixture of family and company accounts could cause awkward liquidity problems. In February 1826, a payment from Smithson's was made as a transfer in the books, which was no good for making external payments to people like clothiers and Edward; very useful for the Smithsons but useless for Oates.[45] All this was carefully accounted for and, as has been shown, all at market rates.

There was the same insistence on equity within the family that appeared in the distribution of property under their father's will. Gifts of honey were distributed in a tangle of polite disputes over who had the spoons and the tableware.

With respect to the spoons AR, there were only two – they had been my Uncle Rayner's and Mrs Headlam I know has more of ye same. The Castors to which you refer are in Mary's possession as your property and mine that is if your property I want a third of their value from you and a third of the value of a waiter from George – the castors and waiter having been adjudged of equal value . . . They (the castors) would go exceedingly well by waggon and shall be sent immdy together with two pots of honey.[46]

The middle class elite of which the Oates were a part was the social group, which in the 1820s was at the centre of the processes which were re-making the public and private values and actions of the middle classes of Britain. To live within that middle class was to be aware of a tangle of interests linking family to economy. It was to be aware of a spreading geographical network along which news, and people and resources could travel. These processes located the middle classes in the town and the family but also bound these towns and families together across a widening area. The processes of accumulation of property had a central place in understanding the dynamics of that varied and wide-ranging group who were becoming known as the middle classes.

The world of Joseph Henry Oates was a prosperous and well appointed world, a world of madeira and books and pictures; as well as silver spoons and honey. To sustain this structure in working order in a world of economic opportunity and insecurity needed close attention to the matters of trade, investment, capital, property, age, gender and family.

---

[45] Oates, 7 February 1826.
[46] Oates, 21 March 1826.

The vignette of the Oates family around 1826 established three things; the main actors within the family, the ever present importance of economic and demographic insecurity, and the importance of middle class family networks.

In search of the British middle class

Labels, languages and discourses

The experience of Joseph Henry and his siblings in the 1820s was an important one but it was part of something much bigger. The Oates family were members of one of the urban elites which were growing in prominence and which shared experience with a wide range of profit-seeking, fee-earning, property-owning people. People of middling status have been identified in the populations of British towns and cities since at least the emergence of the early modern economy. The composition of this group varied and relationships with other social groups changed but trade and the control of manufacturing and professional positions and of the middle ranks of government authority had always been vital.[1] The 1820s and 1830s were the years in which this group came to label itself and be labelled as a self-aware social group, 'the middle classes'. The label was nearly always plural, suggesting an ambivalence regarding the homogeneity, if not coherence of the group. This was an accurate reflection of the wide range of economic status positions and the variety of 'interests' encompassed by the label. It was also a group often bitterly divided by religious and political faction.

The growing use of such labels has been seen as a response to the structural changes associated with industrialisation and economic development, together with the associated political experiences.[2] Others have seen the growing language of class as an autonomous development related to political claims, notably those associated with the reform of parliament in 1832.[3] In some ways the claims of the 'middling classes'

---

[1] H.R. French, 'The Search for the "Middle Sort of People" in England, 1600–1800', *Historical Journal* 43:1 (2000), 277–93; K. Wrightson, *English Society, 1580–1680* (London, 1982), pp. 18–37.

[2] A. Briggs, 'The Language of "Class" in Early Nineteenth-century England', in A. Briggs and J. Saville (eds.), *Essays in Labour History* (London, 1960), 43–73.

[3] D. Wahrman, *Imagining the Middle Class. The Political Representation of Class in Britain c. 1780–1840* (Cambridge, 1995).

were a response to the self-aware actions of other social groups, notably the radical leaders of the labouring classes.[4] It would be wise not to be dazzled by semantic change. Those of middle status had claimed and been attributed various labels throughout the eighteenth century.[5] None the less, the claim to be 'the middle classes' gained a widespread response in the late 1820s and 1830s. It spread to all corners of social and political discourse, from platform to pamphlet and from parliament to newspaper. It gained powerful agency to mobilise across boundaries of faction and status and made sense of the situation and experience of many in the middle status range of British society, despite the evident differences within the group.[6] Such labels gained power in this period, despite the many alternatives available, such as 'true Britons', Protestants or Christians.[7] There were many near synonyms like 'respectable', 'independent', or 'opulent' but here the boundaries of reference were usefully blurred. There were others like 'the people' or 'citizens of...' which had varied and contested meanings and references. It was a label which had been available since around the 1790s, making an important appearance in the literature of some of the more intellectual of the nonconformist religious groups. 'Middle classes' was also a label which had to compete with other claims for identity and action. Radical popular leaders sustained an eighteenth century tradition of appeal to 'the people' within a programme of dealing with social problems and injustice through representative political action. The radical and Chartist leaders of the 1830s and 1840s were as likely to use this rhetoric as they were to talk of the labouring and working classes.[8] The claims of 'the people' were a more subtle challenge to those of middle status than the claims of the 'working classes'. The latter implied conflict, whilst the former threatened to incorporate the profit-seeking and property-owning in a much wider group. It was a threat that blurred boundaries and questioned the leadership of the urban elites. At the same time, the public leaders of that elite would mount the platform and talk to the 'middle classes', 'the

---

[4] E.P. Thompson, *The Making of the English Working Class* (London, 1965); John Foster, *Class Struggle and the Industrial Revolution. Early Industrial Capitalism in three English Towns* (London, 1974).

[5] P.J. Corfield, 'Class by name and number', pp. 38–61; J. Seed, 'From "middling sort" to middle class in late eighteenth and early nineteenth-century England', in M.L. Bush (ed.), *Social Orders and Social Classes in Europe since 1500: Studies in Social Stratification* (London, 1992), pp. 114–35.

[6] R.J. Morris, *Class, Sect and Party. The Making of the British Middle Class: Leeds, 1820–50* (Manchester, 1990).

[7] L. Colley, *Britons. Forging the Nation, 1770–1837* (Yale, 1992).

[8] G. Stedman Jones, *Languages of Class. Studies in English Working Class History, 1832–1982* (Oxford, 1983), pp. 90–178.

respectable' and to 'the people', demonstrating a tension between the desire to draw boundaries and the desire to incorporate and lead on different terms to the radicals.

Contemporaries, like historians, faced a repertoire of systems of social description. Choices were made because they made sense. They enabled contemporaries to respond to the regularities of social and economic experience and behaviour. Such choices could never be totally autonomous.[9] Choices and judgements were influenced by the labels and language available. Such labels were appropriated and contested. 'Gentleman' turns up in nineteenth century property documents in ways which would have surprised the sixteenth century people who fashioned the term. Other choices were made as part of an assertion or claim – for votes – or simply in Weber's term 'social honour'.[10] Once attributed and accepted, these notions of identity gained their own agency, influencing choice and judgement. Property identified the middle classes just as a middle class identity affected the ambitions and strategies of property. At the same time the deep structures of distribution, claims, ownerships and markets, of death, birth and survival enabled and restricted the application of these languages and the agency of the ambitions they generated in ways which could be both cruel and exhilarating. For the middling ranks it was the strategies of family and property which brought the agency of language and culture into sharp and sometimes disturbing relationships with the opportunities and limitations of the parameters of demographic, social and economic structure.

These labels were claims and attributions identified with behaviour patterns as much as with social and economic position and achievement. They were claims for authority and influence. The legitimacy of such claims was in part based upon a key series of value systems that had emerged over the eighteenth century and were associated with that 'middling sort who live well'.[11]

'Politeness' was in essence a system of manners and conduct based upon conversation and social interaction designed to demonstrate taste

---

[9] R.J. Morris, 'Structure, Culture and Society in British towns', in M.J. Daunton (ed.), *The Cambridge Urban History of Britain, Volume III 1840–1950* (Cambridge, 2000), pp. 395–426; A. Jones, 'Word and deed: why a post-poststructural history is needed, and how it might look', *Historical Journal* 43: 2 (2000), 517–41.

[10] The phrase was used in Weber's discussion of economic power and social order, especially in his account of status as a position 'determined by...(the) social estimation of honour', see H.H. Gerth and C. Wright Mills (eds.), *From Max Weber. Essays in Sociology* (London, 1948), pp. 180 and 187, and Max Weber, *Economy and Society*, G. Roth and C. Wittich (eds.), (New York, 1968), vol. II, p. 932.

[11] Daniel Defoe, *A Review of the State of the British Nation, 25 June 1709*, quoted by Corfield, 'Class by name and number', p. 115.

and morality, especially in matters of the fine arts and imaginative literature. It was conduct designed to please, to promote social harmony and
ignore the bitter divisions of politics and religion. Such conduct required
an audience and display, although it should be said that 'self' was a key
member of that audience. Above all, politeness demanded the control of
strong emotions and passions and required that argument should be
based upon persuasion. In its eighteenth century form politeness as a
discipline originated on the social boundaries of the gentry and the
London urban middle class.[12] It was encapsulated in the writings of
Addison and Steele published in the *Tatler* and *Spectator* between 1709
and 1714. These essays were printed, reprinted, quoted and paraphrased
many times over the next two centuries. 'Politeness' was appropriated
and transformed by many generations of the middle ranks, especially in
its links with morality and improvement.[13] The merchant households and
public houses of the manufacturing towns were very different from the
coffee houses and tea tables of London, but politeness infiltrated and was
transformed.

Halifax was a major centre for the woollen textile industry of West
Yorkshire. By 1750 urban leadership was provided by some 60–70
families of merchants and major manufacturers, although, as the example
of the Oates showed, the merchant/manufacturer division was not a strict
one. Amongst these families household practice changed in ways which
created spaces for the disciplines of politeness. At the start of the eighteenth century, the wealthy yeoman clothiers led open households with
sleeping places for apprentices and servants and easy conversation with
tradesmen suppliers like the colliers. By 1750, the leading merchant
families had neo-classical mansions in the latest fashion. Servants and
workpeople were separate from the family and any workshops distanced
to the back yard and beyond.[14] In many towns spaces for politeness were
created in the form of walks, parks, promenades, assembly rooms and
subscription libraries, thus freeing assembly by the middle classes from
church, chapel, the public house and the street.[15] A wide range of urban
places saw the formation of a world of clubs, associations, and lodges.

---

[12] J. Brewer, *The Pleasures of the Imagination. English Culture in the Eighteenth Century*
(London, 1997), pp. 98–122; J. Dwyer, *Virtuous Discourse. Sensibility and Community in
late Eighteenth Century Scotland* (Edinburgh, 1987); L.E. Klein, 'Politeness and the
interpretation of the British eighteenth century', *Historical Journal* 45:4 (2002), 869–98.
[13] My broken run of *The Spectator* was printed in Glasgow in 1791.
[14] J. Smail, *The Origins of Middle Class Culture. Halifax, 1660–1780* (Cornell, 1994),
pp. 39–41 and 110–13.
[15] P. Borsay, *The English Urban Renaissance. Culture and Society in the Provincial Town,
1660–1770* (Oxford, 1989).

Here men and occasionally women debated, read books and periodicals, listened, talked about bee-keeping, gardening and other interests, played music or just drank and entertained each other, but they were disciplined by the chair and a growing number of rules against drunken behaviour and against topics of political and religious division.[16]

The evangelical understanding of religion had its origins in the mid-eighteenth century but did not become influential until the last twenty years of that century. Central to the evangelical world was a deep sense of sin and the opportunity of salvation offered to those who gained faith through personal conversion, a process achieved and sustained by Bible reading and prayer. The most important demonstration of faith was through 'works' and the most important work of all was the conversion of others.[17] In practice, this gave rise to a network of associations and campaigns, some prescriptive and repressive like the Proclamation Society (1787) and the Society for the Repression of Vice (1802), others liberating, often in a paternalistic manner, like the campaigns against the slave trade, cruel sports, harsh factory conditions and slavery itself. What linked all these campaigns together was the vision of countless immortal souls in danger. Everything from gambling and the theatre to plantation slavery and factory overwork were seen as barriers to faith and salvation.[18] In its nineteenth century form, evangelicalism owed its rising influence to groups on the borderlines of the gentry and middle classes, exemplified by the Clapham sect, an active group of bankers, lawyers and clergy, men like Henry Thornton, James Stephen, John Venn the rector, Thomas Clarkson and Zachary Macaulay, who edited their journal the *Christian Observer*.[19] They were linked with key members of the gentry like William Wilberforce and were active in publication and voluntary associations. Most provincial centres had evangelical groups such as the one gathered around the Hey family in Leeds.[20] Despite the emphasis on individual faith, this group had a clear sense of social hierarchy. They were keenly aware of the influence of the 'high orders' of society but this only made them more assertive in their demands for changes in the behaviour of the gentry.

[16] R.J. Morris, 'Clubs, Societies and Associations', in F.M.L. Thompson (ed.), *The Cambridge Social History of Britain, 1750–1950*, vol. III, (Cambridge, 1990), pp. 395–443; P. Clark, *British Clubs and Societies, 1580–1800* (Oxford, 2000).

[17] F.K. Brown, *Fathers of the Victorians: the Age of Wilberforce* (Cambridge, 1961); S. Meacham, 'The Evangelical Inheritance', *Journal of British Studies* 3 (1963–4), 88–104.

[18] C. Hall, *Civilizing Subjects. Metropole and Colony in the English Imagination, 1830–1867* (Cambridge, 2002); R.Q. Gray, *The Factory Question and Industrial England, 1830–1860* (Cambridge, 1996), pp. 38 and 53–8.

[19] S. Meacham, *Henry Thornton of Clapham, 1760–1815* (Harvard, 1964).

[20] J. Pearson, *The Life of William Hey* (London, 1822).

Let them instantly quit the dice box, the turf and the tavern; every wicked and trifling employment and repair each to his proper station...if every gentleman would reside on his estate, and every clergyman on his living, we should need no other reformation.[21]

The Clapham sect and those like them were essentially a pressure group within the established Church of England. They were also active in alliance with evangelical non-conformist sects, like the Congregationalists and Baptists, in associations which included the London Missionary Society (1785) and the British and Foreign School Society (1808). Their wealth they regarded as held in stewardship from God, which both legitimated and directed their privilege and excluded others from questioning that wealth.[22]

The spread of evangelical influence was closely linked to the insecurities and questionings raised by the French Revolution.[23] John Bowdler warned that in France

A vast number of persons of all ranks, men, women, and children, have been beheaded, shot, drowned and poisoned. Many have fled and dare not return; and of those who remain, a great part have lost their property, and all the comforts and conveniences of life. Religion, law, order, and good government, seem to be at an end amongst them.[24]

Wilberforce also held that religion was 'intimately connected with the temporal interests of society'.[25] For a couple of generations, evangelical influence was compulsive and innovative. Even religious groups like the Unitarians, who were certainly not evangelical, showed a new social dynamism.[26] In as far as religion was a symbol system reflecting and

---

[21] J. Bowdler, *Reform or Ruin, Take your Choice, in which the Conduct of the King, the Parliament, the Opposition, the Nobility and Gentry, the Bishops and Clergy, etc., is Considered, and that Reform Pointed Out which Alone can Save the Country* (London, 1797), p. 18. Bowdler was better known for his edition of Shakespeare (1818) in which he eliminated or amended as many of the profane and obscene bits as he could.

[22] W. Wilberforce, *A Practical View of the Prevailing Religious System of Professed Christians in the Higher and Middle Classes in this Country Contrasted with Real Christianity* (London, 1797).

[23] V.G. Kiernan, 'Evangelicalism and the French Revolution', *Past and Present* 1 (Feb., 1952), 44–56.

[24] Bowdler, *Reform or Ruin*, p. 3.

[25] Wilberforce, *Practical View*, p. 1.

[26] R.V. Holt, *The Unitarian Contribution to Social Progress* (London, 1938); J. Seed, 'Unitarianism, political economy and the antinomies of liberal culture in Manchester, 1830–50', *Social History* 7:1 (1982), 1–26; J. Seed, 'Gentlemen dissenters: the social and political meanings of rational dissent in the 1770s and 1780s', *Historical Journal* 28:2 (1985), 299–325; J. Seed, 'Theologies of power: Unitarianism and the social relations of religious discourse, 1800–50', in R.J. Morris (ed.), *Class, Power and Social Structure in British Nineteenth Century Towns* (Leicester, 1986), pp. 108–56.

interpreting experience of the social and material world, evangelicalism reflected the middle classes' sense of insecurity and helplessness, whilst at the same time leaving moral and metaphysical space for individual action and responsibility.[27] By the 1830s and 1840s, evangelical action was tending to formalise. At one level it was a minor nuisance with tract distributors and preachers everywhere, like those parodied by Dickens in the characters of Mrs Pardiggle and Mrs Jellyby in *Bleak House*. At another level it was a major social hazard, increasingly anti-Catholic, a huge source of moral energy restricting and directing women's activities, and a source of opposition to the opening of a wide range of facilities on Sunday when they might be used by working people.[28] They left a legacy of moral and religious seriousness and a deep sense of the individual before an Almighty God with only Christ as mediator. It was a practice which respected hierarchy and social position but contained little that could be called emulation. Evangelicals were as quick to call the gentry to account for their misdeeds as they were to lecture the working classes. It was a potent source of assertion for the middle classes, and bound them in to a growing and complex sense of race and nation.[29]

The late eighteenth and early nineteenth centuries were marked by a re-negotiation of the subordinations of gender. Family and household were identified with very specific ideas of gender and the creation of a home centred life style of domesticity based upon religion, morality and comfort. These developments have been given a central place in the creation of middle class identity.[30] There was an emphasis on the private roles of women as wife, mother, carer and moral guardian, the maker and manager of the home. The male role was a public one, dominated by the task of ensuring that the household had the necessary income to sustain domesticity. The ideal, and frequently the practice, involved the exclusion of women, especially married women from the income earning cash economy of business and the professions. Attempts by women to enter the public world of associational culture, political contest, petitioning and opinion formation were resisted and contested. Even apparent female participation in the public sphere was often an illusion. The Leeds Ladies

---

[27] C. Geertz, 'Religion as a cultural system', in M. Banton (ed.), *Anthropological Approaches to the Study of Religion* (London, 1966), pp. 1–44.

[28] *Evangelical Alliance. Report of the Proceedings of the Conference held at Freemasons Hall, London, 19th August to 2nd September 1846* (London, 1847); Anon., *Caste in the Evangelical World* (London, 1886); B. Harrison, 'The Sunday trading riots of 1855', *Historical Journal* 8:2 (1965), 219–45.

[29] C. Hall, *Civilizing Subjects*; S. Meacham, 'The evangelical inheritance'.

[30] L. Davidoff and C. Hall, *Family Fortunes. Men and Women of the English Middle Class, 1780–1850* (London, 1987).

Branch of the British and Foreign Bible Society was a busy and active organisation. Its annual meeting was chaired by Dr James Williamson and the report read by Rev Thomas Scales with the resolutions proposed and seconded by the likes of Mr Robert Jowitt, woolstapler, and Mr J.H. Ridsdale, sharebroker.[31] A strident ideology and increasingly refined social practice directed female activity to the creation of a domestic sphere which had a key place in the support of the middle class family, in material, educational and, above all, moral terms. Women were directed to a key place in the management of domestic consumption. Part of this process was the subordination of female economic interests to the support of male led economic enterprise.[32] This was accompanied by aggressive and insistent cultural direction in the form of poetry, sermons novels and advice manuals. Even by the 1850s, the middle class residential suburb had reached nothing like the scale and extent of the late nineteenth century, but places like Edgbaston in Birmingham and Headingley in Leeds were beginning to see such developments. The move to the suburbs was often part of the life cycle moves crucial to property strategy in general. Such moves intensified the increasing separation of workspace and domestic space which reduced female opportunity even for a subordinate place in income earning cash economy activity.[33]

Closer examination of the seventeenth and eighteenth centuries has shown that the ideals and adoption of separate spheres were neither new nor did they produce clear boundaries of practice. From the late seventeenth century onwards such practices can be found on the creative boundaries of the gentry and urban middle class elites.[34] At the same time various studies outlined the extent of women's economic activity throughout the period. They were both important property owners and retained significant niches in the business world. In part, this was because of the structural 'facts' of demography. Many women were widowed or never married and hence escaped the legal and social disciplines of marriage. Many men had daughters and no sons to whom they might leave property. In other cases law and practice offered women a variety of ways of escaping potential limitations placed upon them.[35]

---

[31] *Leeds Mercury*, 13 October 1832 and 21 October 1837.

[32] Davidoff and Hall, *Family Fortunes*, pp. 272–316.

[33] D. Cannadine, *Lords and Landlords. The Aristocracy and the Towns, 1774–1967* (Leicester, 1980); F.M.L. Thompson (ed.), *The Rise of Suburbia* (Leicester, 1982).

[34] A. Vickery, *The Gentleman's Daughter: Women's Lives in Georgian England* (Yale, 1998); A. Erickson, *Women and Property in Early Modern England* (London, 1993).

[35] M.R. Hunt, *The Middling Sort. Commerce, Gender and the Family in England, 1680–1780* (California, 1996), especially pp. 125–71; M. Berg, 'Women's property and the Industrial Revolution', *Journal of Interdisciplinary History* 24 (1993), 233–50.

In practice, the division between public and private, between male roles and female roles proved to be both porous and varied. A limited number of women, such as the mid-eighteenth century Duchess of Devonshire, entered political life with enthusiasm, although the evidence suggests that such activity declined in the 1790s. Although the 1832 Reform Act quietly excluded female voters from the new franchises, this did not deter property owners like Anne Lister from informing her tenants how they should vote.[36]

From the 1760s onwards, an increasing number of women entered the public world through novel writing and other contributions to print media. These women linked one private activity, setting down individual thoughts in writing, with another private activity, silent reading, through a very public process, publication. This was one area in which the contradictions of the binary public/private could be exploited.

The domestic ideal itself created gaps in the public/private, male/female divide. By the 1830s, the ideal of manliness required that the public man should spend time at home.[37] It also attributed to women the responsibility of moral guidance for men and children as well as for the organisation of domestic comfort. Responsibility implied a degree of moral and social authority which appeared to challenge the absolute of male authority. It was a potent tension which puzzled many of the apologists for separate spheres domesticity.[38] Domestic and moral roles also gave women a legitimate basis for entry into public life.[39] In 1821, the Leeds middle classes had formed the Leeds Guardian Society to provide shelter and reform for those prostitutes who could be persuaded to come to its hostel. The management of property and money was for the male committee dominated by leading evangelical families including the Heys, but the supervision of the girls and the house was very definitely for a committee of women.[40]

The evidence showed no clear pattern of female loss of economic and social authority between 1700 and 1850. Areas of female activity, both contested and accepted as legitimate by the dominant value systems,

---

[36] L. Davidoff and C. Hall, *Family Fortunes. Men and Women of the English Middle Class, 1780–1850*, Second Edition (London, 2002), Introduction pp. xiii–l; K. Gleadle and S. Richardson (eds.) *Women in British Politics, 1760–1860: the Power of the Petticoat* (London, 2000); J. Liddington, *Female Fortune. Land, Gender and Authority. The Anne Lister Diaries and Other Writings, 1833–36* (London, 1998).

[37] J. Tosh, *A Man's Place. Masculinity and the Middle Class Home in Victorian England* (Yale, 1999).

[38] J. Hammerton, *Cruelty and Companionship. Conflict in Nineteenth Century Married Life* (London, 1992), especially his account of the writings of Mrs Sarah Ellis, p. 76.

[39] F.K. Prochaska, *Women and Philanthropy in 19th century England* (Oxford, 1980).

[40] *Tenth to 30th Annual Reports of the Leeds Guardian Society* (Leeds, 1831–51).

varied over the period. Even the strident assertion of male authority in the evangelical period, which began in the 1790s, left considerable areas of opportunity and contradiction. When Mrs Isabella Beeton summed up the experience of the period with the publication of the greatest of all manuals of practical domesticity, she chose the title with care, appropriating the word 'management' from the male world of business.[41] The opening words left no doubt, 'As with the commander of an army, or with the leader of an enterprise, so is it with the mistress of a house'.

The strict and internalised forms of gender subordination involved in separate spheres and the forms of 'domesticity', evident between 1800 and 1850, had origins which could be traced into the first part of the eighteenth century. The diffusion and dominance of such ideology and practice were uneven and by no means cumulative. Distinctions need to be drawn between origins and dominant diffusion. The arrival of such practices was not an 'event', although for many families and individuals it must have seemed so. Whatever the origins, extent and nature of diffusion might have been, the compulsive demands of this ideology and practice of gender and domesticity were absent from very few decisions in the years after 1800. There were material implications of this which must inform the argument of this book. Domesticity and separate spheres as practices had major economic costs. There was the opportunity cost of withdrawing a substantial portion of the potential adult labour force from the income producing cash economy. The story of the Cadburys, in which one generation contributed to the management of 'the shop' and the next did not, was a story which needs to be multiplied many times.[42] These practices also had a wide variety of direct costs. New and increasingly costly forms of housing needed to be created to separate home from work and provide the material base for domesticity.[43] Those houses needed to be filled with possessions from curtains to coffee grinders and served by domestic servants, who were now dedicated to the business of domesticity and were not shared with any income earning shop or workplace. Even if domesticity had been an ambition and practice evident amongst gentry and urban elites in the early part of the eighteenth century, its extensive diffusion had to wait not only upon the insistent moral intensity of the evangelicals and other internalised disciplines but also upon the

---

[41] I. Beeton, *The Book of Household Management* (London, 1861); S. Freeman, *Isabella and Sam. The Story of Mrs Beeton* (London, 1977).

[42] C. Hall, 'The butcher, the baker, the candlestick-maker: the shop and the family in the Industrial Revolution', in C. Hall, *White, Male and Middle Class, Explorations in Feminism and History* (Cambridge, 1992), pp. 108–23.

[43] Smail, pp. 164–87.

material means provided by sustained economic growth. This was a pattern of ideal and practice, with its contradictions and its apparently absolute prescriptions, which often proved impracticable and vague. This pattern was the basis upon which the men and women in this study, like so many others, took countless decisions regarding patterns of property accumulation and distribution.

There were other elements to the value systems available to the middling sort. There was a growing sense of romantic individuality – of the value of individual creativity and emotion. This built upon the more mannered notions of 'sensibility' which valued the individual emotional responses, not only to poetry, the novel and landscape, but also in more practical matters. In April 1788, one of the Oates network in Leeds wrote to his niece, Miss Fenton in Bristol, on 'so delicate a subject':

> Young ladies are in some instances too apt to think they ought not to marry except they feel a warm personal attachment, commonly called <u>love</u> or <u>desperate love</u>; that others on the other side, and, not being authorized by Custom to make the first Advances, dare not think of Love but hold themselves in readiness to take the first good offer without consulting their own particular Likings. A prudent lady will avow neither of these Sentiments. Where there is good Character, good Sense, a Similarity of Habits, not too great a Disparity in years, and a fair Prospect of good Provision in Life, a young lady may venture although she is not desperately in Love, and almost assure herself that an Intimacy will produce personal attachment founded on esteem, and prove a solid foundation for the most valuable enjoyments in human life.[44]

The subject of this was Mr Houghton of Norwich who had clearly made an offer of marriage which had been rejected by Miss Fenton, to the consternation of her sisters, friends and uncle. An earlier letter had recommended:

> However, a Gentleman of excellent Character, a Considerable Income, about £500 a year, a respectable Situation, and the offer he has made of a Settlement of £100 a year, (of all which Mr Houghton informs me) are certainly well worth your attention. And supposing there is not <u>personal dislike</u> I warmly recommend to you to consider seriously the Value of a <u>good Home</u> under the Direction of a worthy Character, in the Habits respecting general tenor of Life, Complexion of acquaintance and outward Profession respecting religious worship, agreeing so much with your own.[45]

Houghton appeared in later accounts of the Oates–Fenton network so Miss Fenton of Bristol must in the end have agreed to his proposal, but for a lady guided by a culture which taught her the instrinsic value of

---

[44] Leeds, 27 April 1788 to Miss Fenton, Jamaica St, Bristol. Oates Acc 1258.
[45] Leeds, 13 April 1788 to Miss Fenton, Bristol, Oates Acc 1258.

self-directed decisions guided by emotion and sensibility, such a decision was not easy.

There were many other strands of values and perceptions available to those who ordered and judged the worlds of the eighteenth and early nineteenth centuries. The rationality of 'science' emerged from the savants and associations of the gentry and elite to become an important and legitimate concern for the educated middle classes. The Lunar Society of the 1770s and the Unitarian networks of people like Joseph Priestley and William Turner were evidence of this.[46] The first formal Literary and Philosophical Societies were created in the 1790s and such associations had spread rapidly by the 1820s.[47] By the 1850s, scientific debate and education were an essential part of the power, authority and prestige sought by urban centres like Manchester, Newcastle and Birmingham.[48] Science, usually referred to by its gentlemanly name of natural philosophy, was only one aspect of the rationality of the enlightenment on offer. Adam Smith balanced the tensions of morality and political economy in *The Wealth of Nations* (1776) and his earlier *The Theory of Moral Sentiments* (1759). The many editions of the *Essay on the Principle of Population* (First edition, 1798 – Seventh edition, 1820) by Parson Malthus gave fuel to debates over poverty, philanthropy and population with a potent mixture of logic and fact. The authority of the rational appeared in new forms of public debate and public meeting which emerged in its ideal form from the coffee house and, by the late eighteenth century, was beginning to replace main force as the means for settling disputes and expressing political demands.[49] This had a philosophical expression in Adam Ferguson's *An Essay in the History of Civil Society* (1767).[50] The

---

[46] R.E. Schofield, *The Lunar Society of Birmingham. A Social History of Provincial Science and Industry in Eighteenth-century England* (Oxford, 1963), pp. 140–1; S. Harbottle, *The Reverend William Turner. Dissent and Reform in Georgian Newcastle upon Tyne* (Newcastle and Leeds, 1997).

[47] Sir W. Elliott, Presidential Address, *Transactions of the Botanical Society of Edinburgh*, 10 November 1870; List of Scientific Societies and Field Clubs, *Nature* 8, (23 October, 1873).

[48] R.H. Kargon, *Science in Victorian Manchester. Enterprise and Expertise* (Manchester, 1977); M. Berman, *Social Change and Scientific Organization. The Royal Institution, 1799–1844* (London, 1978).

[49] C. Tilley, *Popular Contention in Great Britain, 1758–1834* (Harvard, 1995); R.J. Morris, 'Civil Society, Subscriber Democracies and Parliamentary Government in Great Britain', in N. Bermeo and P. Nord (eds.), *Civil Society before Democracy. Lessons from Nineteenth Century Europe* (New York, 2000), pp. 111–34.

[50] A. Ferguson, *An Essay on the History of Civil Society*, F. Oz-Salzberger (ed.), (Cambridge, 1995); J. Habermas, *The Structural Transformation of the Public Sphere. An Inquiry into a Category of Bourgeois Society*, trans. T. Burger (Cambridge, 1992), first published in German 1962.

authoritative public meeting became a ritual which presented itself as argument, evidence and hearing all sides before reaching a decision.

What provided a common thread to this web of ideas and values was the growing assertion of individuality; the individual before God with prayer and faith and Bible reading; the individual in the market place taking decisions on price and purchase; the individual responding to the emotions be they of romantic love, or romantic scenery. After the Bible, one of the most frequently read books of the period was a seventeenth century book, *Pilgrims Progress*, the story of the individual's journey through trouble and temptation to salvation and content.[51] The nineteenth century saw a growing genre of moral and inspiring biography. Craik's *Pursuit of Knowledge under Difficulties* was characteristic of tales of moral and material triumph from self-directed individuals.[52] In the reports of many libraries like those of the Mechanics Institutions, biography remained the most popular of the non-fiction categories. In 1859, Samuel Smiles raised the genre to a household word with the publication of *Self Help*, as well as the associated biographies of people like George Stephenson and James Naysmyth.[53]

Those who took the decisions, expressed the opinions, and formed the strategies, which are the subject of this study, were informed by a wide repertoire of prescriptions and perceptions. The great supermarket of ideas which they inherited, developed and added to from the eighteenth century was bound together by a concern for the autonomy of the individual caught within a network of social and religious relationships and obligations. Discipline and control were part of the process; discipline and control for emotions; discipline and control brought by knowledge and the ability to organise knowledge of all kinds. For the individual decision and decision maker, choosing and using amongst this repertoire was rarely a matter of either/or decisions. Nor can generational change be seen as an evolution from decisions informed by one strand rather than another. The romantic might be one addition to the bundle of ideas and values which guided Miss Oates but this did not preclude other concerns. As the young lady took decisions about her marriage she was guided by romantic and by rational instrumental values. She demanded and

---

[51] R.D. Altick, *The English Common Reader* (Chicago, 1957), p. 127. It certainly solved the problem of what to read on Sunday. My copy was published by the Religious Tract Society in 1903 and was based upon manuscripts in the British Museum. The Society had first brought out an edition in 1826.

[52] G.L. Craik, *The Pursuit of Knowledge under Difficulties*, 2 vols. (London, 1833).

[53] R.J. Morris, 'Samuel Smiles and the genesis of self help: the retreat to a petit bourgeois utopia', *Historical Journal* 24 (1981), 89–109; S. Smiles, *The Life of George Stephenson, Railway Engineer* (London, 1857).

received a respect for the autonomy of her decision guided in part by emotion, but she was also anxious to take account of the wishes of the senior males in her family. Whether she got a patriarchal or a companionate marriage was not really an either/or question. She married into a world in which male power was dominant, and probably increasing, but with changing areas of female autonomy and agency emerging and surviving. Joseph Henry Oates was a patriarch who took his responsibilities seriously but still felt a deep concern for his wife's health that could only have come from many years of affectionate companionship. He was also both the protector and respecter of his unmarried sister's limited but very specific agency.

These values produced ideals around which strategies and decisions were taken. Within these ideals the tension between the subordinations of gender and the high value and authority, attributed to individual decision takers, provided a potent instability which occasionally exploded into public view before being bundled away. More subversive was the fact that these ideals simply did not fit the economic and demographic realities within which individuals took decisions. As individuals took decisions and formed strategies, not only were a large minority of them women, but many of the males had little of that control and ability to predict which was required if they were to exercise the authority and responsibility attributed to individuals.

This study is located at a point in time when British society was emerging from a long period of war and coming to terms with a sense of rapid economic change and urbanisation. There was a pervasive sense of moral importance coupled with material opportunity.

Structures of material resource

The Oates and those like them were living at the high point of an unprecedented demographic revolution. The relationships of family and property were embedded in a sustained period of demographic change. At one level, this change was simple. There were more people and the number was increasing. A period of population decline in the seventeenth century was followed by one of stagnation, which came to an end in the 1730s. Four decades of increases of around 5 per cent per decade preceded a period of accelerating increases, which culminated in decadal increases of around 15 per cent between 1801 and the 1820s. As a result, the English population rose from 5.2 million in the early eighteenth century to 11.5 million in 1821 and 21.5 million in 1871.[54] This increase

---

[54] E.A. Wrigley and R.S. Scholfield, *The Population History of England, 1541–1871, A Reconstruction* (Cambridge, 1989 (first edition 1981)) p. 529.

was the result of a growing gap between crude birth rate and crude death rate, which was well in excess of any loss of population due to overseas migration. Estimates made in terms of crude birth and crude death rates give a very direct account of the cultural and material impact of this change. By the 1820s, the decennial census and the writings of Parson Malthus had made British society vividly aware of the increasing population.[55] Debates over the treatment of the poor and moral arguments over improvident behaviour haunted decisions and judgements over marriage and the related family strategies of work and savings. The very fact of population increase and awareness of that increase produced a mixed reaction of heady enthusiasm and worrying threat.

This increase in population can be expressed in terms of a gross reproduction rate. A figure of two implied that, assuming zero migration, a population was replacing itself. In England the rate was just over two in the early eighteenth century and rose to a peak of 3.06 in 1816.[56] This indicated both significant demands and opportunities for family decision takers. Each generation, when planning for its children, needed to provide an extra social and economic 'slot' rather than a simple reproduction of previous economic and social relationships.[57]

These changes in population levels, birth, death, migration and marriage rates created important changes in the age structure of that population, which were a vital part of the environment in which family and property decisions were taken. The material implications of the changing age structure of a population are usually expressed as a dependency ratio, namely the number of those under the age of 15 plus the number of old people (in this analysis the over sixties) per thousand of the potentially economically active population (those between 15 and 60 years old). In England this ratio was around 730 in the early eighteenth century, fell to a low point of 673 in 1731, before beginning a fluctuating rise to a peak of 840/850 per 1000 between 1816 and 1826. The subsequent fall to 744 in 1851 came to an end with a slight rise in the 1860s. This consisted of two elements which have very different implications for this study. The number of children fluctuated at around 32/33 per cent of the population for the first 70 years of the eighteenth century. In the late 1770s there was a fluctuating rise to a peak of around 39 per cent between 1826 and the early 1830s. Falls left the figure at 36.5 per cent in 1871. The figures for

---

[55] J.R. Poynter, *Society and Pauperism. English Ideas on Poor Relief, 1795–1834* (London, 1969).

[56] Wrigley and Scholfield, pp. 229–34 and 530.

[57] M. Anderson, 'The social implications of demographic change', in F.M.L. Thompson (ed.), *The Cambridge Social History of Britain*, vol. II, pp. 1–70.

the old had a different pattern. Starting the eighteenth century at around 9 per cent, the percentage reached a low point of 7.9 per cent in 1746. A peak of 8.7 per cent in 1766 was followed by a low of around 6.5 per cent between 1821 and 1836. The 1860s marked a slight rise to just over 7 per cent in 1871. The material implications of changes in age structure for a population as a whole are usually analysed in terms of production/ consumption ratios, as children and the old consumed more than they produced.[58] For the analysis of the strategies of the property owning classes, there were additional implications. The late eighteenth century and, above all, the 1820s was a world full of children. The existence of children created additional motivation for the creation and accumulation of wealth. The proportion of old people followed a different pattern. The 1860s were marked by a rise in the over sixties, and, hence, of the over fifties, in the previous decade. As will be demonstrated in later chapters, the older population created a demand for very specific forms of asset.

Changes in the expectation of life at birth and the age and proportion of those who married were part of the environment in which family decisions were taken. There was an irregular improvement in the expect- ation of life at birth from the 1730s onwards, although this improvement was to stagnate in the 1830s and 1840s. This figure was a useful summary of many demographic insecurities but in itself the 'age' does not mean very much. It is a summary of high rates of infant mortality and changing rates of adult mortality.

For the population as a whole the mean age of marriage reached its lowest point in two centuries between 1800 and 1850 (Table 2.1).

The proportion of people who never married reached a low point in the late eighteenth century and was beginning to rise by the 1820s (Table 2.2).

These figures were estimates, indicators and summaries for a national population. They give a good picture of the demographic environment against which the middle class families of the first half of the nineteenth century took their decisions. But they are national summaries and conceal variations of behaviour related to status, to region, to urban/rural behav- iour and to the local economy. Amongst the six siblings from the Oates generation of 1826 in the case study, 40 per cent were never to be married. Even taking the small 'sample' size into account this was a long way from the 6–10 per cent of national experience.

Some indications of likely variations in behaviour between those of middle class status and the rest of the population can be gained from a thorough study of members of the Society of Friends in England and

---

[58] Wrigley and Scholfield, pp. 443–50 and 529.

Table 2.1 *Mean age of first marriage in England, 1600–1911*

	Male	Female
1600–49	28	26
1650–99	27.8	26.5
1700–49	27.5	26.2
1750–99	26.4	24.9
1800–49	25.3	23.4
1851	26.94	25.77
1861	26.39	25.39
1871	26.43	25.13
1881	26.60	25.30
1891	27.06	25.96
1901	27.31	26.27
1911	27.65	26.25

Note: The first part of the table comes from twelve parish family reconstitution studies. The second from Registrar General's demographic summaries.

Source: Wrigley and Scholfield, pp. 257–65.

Table 2.2 *Estimated proportion of people never married in England per 1000 of cohort aged 40–44 in the stated year*

1731	128	1801	68
1736	131	1806	72
1741	112	1811	65
1746	96	1816	63
1751	107	1821	71
1756	107	1826	78
1761	73	1831	75
1766	86	1836	82
1771	77	1841	96
1776	46	1846	102
1781	36	1851	110
1786	62	1856	119
1791	49	1861	107

Source: Wrigley and Scholfield, p. 260.

Table 2.3 *Mean age of marriage, 1650–1850. Society of Friends compared with twelve reconstituted parishes*

	Northern Britain		Urban		12 parishes	
	Male	Female	Male	Female	Male	Female
1650–99	28.79	25.89	29.75	26.35	27.8	26.5
1700–49	31.11	26.35	27.93	27.54	27.5	26.2
1750–99	31.25	28.25	28.47	27.86	26.4	24.9
1800–49	36.12	30.1	**29.83**	**28.46**	25.3	23.4

Source: Vann and Eversley, p. 103; Wrigley and Scholfield, p. 255.

Ireland.[59] The occupational composition of this group was heavily biased towards the middle classes. Between 1750 and 1850, the urban Quakers were dominated by commercial and retail people (about 75 per cent in the towns and 50 per cent in the countryside). Professionals made up about another 10 per cent and artisans another 10–13 per cent.[60] Demographic behaviour was partly related to this economic and social structure but also to the powerful cultural motivations provided by being a member of the Society of Friends.

The age of marriage was consistently later than in the twelve parishes and the gap increased in the late eighteenth century. The figures for those never married in this study were produced in a very different way (the information came directly from the records) from the national estimates given earlier and suggest very low rates. However, the study also gives high figures for cases with no direct information. If this group was assumed to contain a high proportion of unmarried then the 'never married' could be as much as 25 per cent of the over 50s.[61] The Quakers were very specific representatives of the middle classes with a highly developed family discipline. There is and was little systematic demography of the 'middling sort' but the indications were that they married later and they married less than the bulk of the population. This meant that any middle class family grouping was likely to have a greater number of adults who were not in the roles of husband, wife and

[59] R.T. Vann and D. Eversley, *Friends in Life and Death. The British and Irish Quakers in the Demographic Transition* (Cambridge, 1992).
[60] Vann and Eversley, pp. 70–1.
[61] Vann and Eversley, p. 108.

Table 2.4 *Estimates of national product. Percentage growth per year*

	National product	Per head
1700–60	0.69	0.31
1760–80	0.70	0.01
1780–1801	1.32	0.35
1801–31	1.97	0.52

Source: N.F.R. Crafts, *British Economic Growth During the Industrial Revolution* (Oxford, 1985), p. 45; J. Hoppit, 'Counting the Industrial Revolution', *Economic History Review* 43:1 (1990), 173–93.

children than other groups. Such people played a significant part in the social and economic relationships of family and property.

These massive and sustained changes were only one aspect of the material conditions which provided the structural framework for the decisions taken by the Oates and those like them. Evidence gathered in recent years by historians has shown that the eighteenth century was a period of sustained economic growth. Wealth accumulated and real incomes increased. The speed of this change varied but the long term direction was positive.

Giving an account of economic growth is at the best of times a black art. In the hundred years preceding this study any account depended not only upon that portion of production which was in the cash economy but upon that portion of the cash economy which was visible to historians through price series and indicators of output. The final result was equally dependent upon the manipulations chosen to produce the summaries derived from countless individual items of information. The most comprehensive recent investigation indicates accelerating growth in the availability of material resources.

The changing occupational structure of the population was often concealed by the changing labels and definitions of occupational categories employed by contemporary social tables, and their subsequent analysis, but two dimensions were crucial for the material background of the families examined here (Table 2.5).

A steady increase in urbanisation was accompanied by increased industrial activity in the countryside. One function of the towns was the organisation of the economic activity of the countryside through markets and commerce.

Recent re-working of the available information has concentrated upon the industrial sector, with the result that attention has been increasingly given to the experience of the generation involved in this study (Table 2.6).

Table 2.5 *Occupational structure of England and Wales, 1520–1801, as a percentage of the total population*

	Urban	Rural agricultural	Rural non-agricultural
1520	5.5	76	18.5
1600	8	70	22
1670	13.5	60.5	26
1700	17	55	28
1750	21	46	33
1801	27.5	36.25	36.25

Source: E.A. Wrigley, *People, Cities and Wealth* (Oxford, 1987), p. 170.

Table 2.6 *Industrial production, 1730–1830. Percentage change per annum*

	Industrial production	Industrial production per head
1730–40	0.3	−0.1
1740–50	0.9	0.5
1750–60	0.9	0.3
1760–70	1.3	0.8
1770–80	1.2	0.3
1780–90	2.3	1.4
1790–1800	1.9	0.8
1800–10	2.7	1.4
1810–20	1.9	0.4
1820–30	4.1	2.6

Source: R.V. Jackson, 'Rates of industrial growth during the Industrial Revolution', *Economic History Reviews* 45:1 (February, 1992), 1–23.

Some re-workings showed an even more substantial slow down in the last twenty or thirty years of the century than the series quoted here.[62] These accounts agree on two things. The people taking decisions in the 1820s and 1830s were experiencing unprecedented

[62] N.F.R. Crafts and C.K. Harley, 'Output growth and the British Industrial Revolution: a restatement of the Crafts–Harley view', *Economic History Review* 45:4 (1992), 703–30, esp. 712; N.F.R. Crafts, S.J. Leybourne and T.C. Mills, 'Trends and cycles in the British Industrial Revolution, 1700–1913', *Journal of the Royal Statistical Society* ser. A, 152 (1989), 43–60.

Table 2.7 *Urban hierarchy of England and Wales, 1700–1801. Population in thousands*

1700		1750		1801	
London	575	London	675	London	959
Norwich	30	Bristol	50	Manchester	89
Bristol	21	Norwich	36	Liverpool	83
Newcastle	16	Newcastle	29	Birmingham	74
Exeter	14	Birmingham	24	Bristol	60
York	12	Liverpool	22	Leeds	53

Note: The 1801 figures were taken from the Census. The 1700 and 1750 figures were estimated from a variety of sources. They provided a general order of magnitude rather than precise numbers.

Source: Wrigley, *People, Cities and Wealth*, p. 160.

increases in their material welfare, which contrasted sharply with the recent experience of the late eighteenth century. In addition they inherited memories of an eighteenth century of sustained growth with short run fluctuations.

The detail of the accounts of economic change indicated extreme unevenness. Between 1780 and 1830, woollen production nearly doubled and iron output increased eightfold, whilst cotton, starting from a very small base, increased thirty-five times. This meant that, even if overall growth slowed in the late eighteenth century, contemporaries would have been aware of spectacular gains in wealth in specific sectors of the economy, and often within specific regions and technologies within those sectors.[63] It was this as much as overall changes in national product which produced a sense of significant and often bewildering change.

This regional unevenness made its impact on both the urban hierarchy and on regional wage differentials.

Despite the change in hierarchy, one feature remained a constant. England was a metropolitan country dominated by its capital city. Any change in the relationship between London and its provincial cities was one of degree, not of kind. In 1700, London was some twenty times

[63] E.H. Hunt, 'Industrialization and regional inequality: wages in Britain, 1760–1914', *Journal of Economic History* 46 (1986) 60–8; P. Hudson (ed.), *Regions and Industries. A Perspective on the Industrial Revolution in Britain* (Cambridge, 1989).

Table 2.8 *Population growth of leading urban centres in England and Wales, 1700–1801*

	1700–50	1750–1801
London	17.39	42.07
Manchester	100.00	394.44
Liverpool	266.67	277.27
Birmingham	166.67	208.33
Bristol	138.10	20.00
Leeds	166.67	231.25
Norwich	20.00	0.00
Exeter	14.29	6.25
York	−8.33	45.45

Source: Wrigley, *People, Cities and Wealth*, p. 160.

Table 2.9 *Farm labourers' wages, 1767–1845*

	1767–70	1794–6	1833–45
Lancashire	6s 6d	10s 1d	12s 5d
Buckinghamshire	8s 0d	7s 4d	9s 10d

Source: E.H. Hunt, 'Wages' in J. Langton and R.J. Morris, *Atlas of Industrializing Britain, 1780–1914* (London, 1986), p. 68.

greater than its nearest rival. By 1801 this had fallen to ten times. Joseph Henry Oates was wise to value his family link with London.

The regional comparison of wages was difficult, not only because of the incomplete nature of the sources, but also because the organisation of work was different in different regions. The available evidence showed two dimensions. Between the 1760s and 1790s, the northern counties changed from being a comparatively low wage area to being a comparatively high wage area.

London remained the leading labour market, paying the highest wages in the building trade throughout the period. The dominance was so great that London wages provided the measure against which the regions were judged. In the late 1760s, both Manchester and Exeter paid carpenters around 64 per cent of the London wage rates. By the 1790s, Manchester had risen to pay 88 per cent of the London rates, whilst Exeter was still around 60 per cent.[64]

There was considerable contemporary awareness of some spectacular gains in wealth and income, often related to industrial enterprise. Those who gained became the 'heroes' of a moral and celebratory literature.[65] At the same time, rising rural poor rates and increasing urban concentrations brought the moral, political and physical threat of poverty into public debate. Overall judgements on the distribution of wealth and income were less easy to make and recent surveys of the evidence have produced accounts much less secure than those for population and national income. There were huge inequalities. Scattered information on Leeds showed that the elite professional and merchant households had an income of around £800–£1000 in this period,[66] whilst the stipend for the Vicar of Leeds was worth £1257 per year when Walter Hook was appointed in 1837.[67] In his social survey of Leeds in 1839, Robert Baker listed the wide range of wage earners' incomes. At the top of the list were millwrights and ironmoulders at 26 and 25 shillings per week, with weavers and woolcombers bottom with 13 and 14 shillings per week.[68] This inequality drove many of the political, social and material relationships of the town. Uncertainty arose from attempts to calculate overall measures of inequality, and to make judgements on the general direction of change.[69] The first account comes from a study of the average full-time earnings of key groups of wage and salaried workers.

Presented as index numbers based upon mid-century, these estimates showed that the greatest gains were made by the higher economic status groups. In real terms the greatest gains were made by the 'white collar workers' and the artisans, who had been the higher paid group at the start. The evidence also showed that inequality was greatest within the highest

---

[64] Hunt, 'Industrialization and regional inequality'.

[65] S. Nenadic, 'Businessmen, the urban middle classes, and the "dominance" of manufacturers in nineteenth century Britain', *Economic History Review* 44:1 (February 1991), 66–85.

[66] See the case studies of the Jowitt and Hey families in later chapters.

[67] His wife, Delicia, encouraged him by telling him that without a stipend of this sort, 'We have not the means of educating our children according to their condition'. W.R.W. Stephens, *The Life and Letters of Walter Farquhar Hook* (London, 1885), p. 195.

[68] R. Baker, 'Report upon the condition of the town of Leeds and its inhabitants, by a Statistical Committee of the Town Council, October 1839', *Journal of the Statistical Society of London*, 2 (1839), 397–424. [20 shillings equalled one pound.]

[69] A.B. Atkinson, 'On the measurement of inequality, in A.B. Atkinson (ed.), *Wealth, Income and Inequality* (London, 1973) for an explanation and critique of these measures, especially the Gini Coefficient.

Table 2.10 *Average full-time earnings for adult male workers, 1797–1851 (£ per year at constant prices, 1850)*

	Farm labourers	Middle group	Artisans	White collar
1797	21.6	27.8	35.1	60.7
1805	21.6	28.0	32.0	53.9
1810	19.5	27.3	32.1	51.7
1815	21.9	30.6	39.2	66.0
1819	21.4	28.8	37.8	71.9
1827	22.0	37.2	49.9	101.2
1835	26.6	45.5	59.1	172.2
1851	29.0	53.0	75.2	258.9

Source: J.G. Williamson, *Did British Capitalism Breed Inequality?* (London, 1985), pp. 17–18; P.H. Lindert and J.G. Williamson, 'English workers' living standards during the Industrial Revolution: a new look', *Economic History Review* 36:1 (Feb 1983), 1–250.

Table 2.11 *Trends in full-time earnings, adult male workers, 1797–1851. (1851 earnings = 100)*

	Farm labourers	Middle group	Artisans	White collar	All
1797	74.50	52.54	46.73	23.45	42.48
1805	74.51	52.96	42.55	20.82	40.64
1810	67.21	51.54	42.73	19.97	39.41
1815	75.51	57.81	52.18	25.49	46.71
1819	73.52	54.35	50.26	27.76	46.13
1827	75.86	70.18	66.39	39.10	58.99
1835	91.67	85.97	78.62	66.52	78.69
1851	100.00	100.00	100.00	100.00	100.00

Source: Williamson, *Did British Capitalism Breed Inequality?*; Lindert and Williamson, 'English workers' living standards'.

paid groups and that inequality was increasing. The results in this table must be treated with caution as the data on salaries was derived from those in government service and included some very high gains in the 'professional' group. The majority of the middle classes, including most professionals, took their income from the market economy of fees and profits. It is impossible to gain a direct view of the overall pattern of such incomes. The Gini Coefficient for the distribution within the professional classes rose from 0.488 in 1827 to 0.516 in 1851 before falling to 0.350 in

Table 2.12 *Indicators of income distribution derived from the Window Tax Assessment and Inhabited House Duty, England and Wales*

	Window Tax			Inhabited House Duty			
	Share of top 5%	Share of top 10%	Gini Coefficient	Share of top 5%	Share of top 10%	Gini Coefficient	Feinstein Revision
1777	42.61	52.32	0.524				
1781	42.91	52.59	0.532				
1823	43.80	52.50	0.457	39.51	47.51	0.400	
1830	47.07	55.18	0.515	39.44	49.95	0.451	0.607
1849	48.38	56.53	0.528				
1871				49.35	62.29	0.627	0.667
1891				45.71	57.50	0.550	0.601
1901				37.25	47.41	0.443	0.579
1911				29.65	36.43	0.328	0.553
1915				29.71	36.46	0.333	

Note: In general the Feinstein critique reduces the increase in inequality shown by the Wiiliamson figures for the first half of the nineteenth century and replaces the reductions in inequality of the second half of the century with indicators of a stable distribution.

Source: Williamson, *Did British Capitalism Breed Inequality?* p. 61; C. Feinstein, 'The rise and fall of the Williamson Curve', *Journal of Economic History* 48(1988), 699–729.

1881.[70] The period 1827–51 coincided with considerable anecdotal evidence for the existence of a substantial and insecure group of professionals. The imposition of professional organisation and discipline after mid-century was yet to come.[71] The same trend was noted for clerical workers.

Some compensation for the limitations of this can be derived from two taxes upon consumption, the window tax and inhabited house duties. The Gini Coefficient was a summary measure of the over-all pattern of inequality. Zero indicated everyone was equal whilst one would indicate that one person received the whole national income. These indicators suggested an overall pattern of change over time. During the war-time period from the 1770s until 1820, inequality remained stable and may have decreased. Between 1820 and mid-century, there was some increase in inequality, which then declined in the latter part of the century. The

[70] J.G. Williamson, 'The distribution of earnings in nineteenth century Britain', Discussion Paper, Department of Economics University of Wisconsin, December 1979, pp. 11 and 37.
[71] R.S. Neale, 'Class and class consciousness in early nineteenth century England: three classes or five?', *Victorian Studies* 12:1 (September 1968), 5–32.

Table 2.13 *Inequality and income shares from the principal social commenta-tors, 1688–1867.*

	Income shares					
	Gini Coefficient	Bottom 40%	40–65%	65–90%	Share of top 10%	Share of top 5%
King (1688)	0.468	15.40	16.70	26.00	42.00	27.60
Massie (1759)	0.487	15.80	14.10	25.80	44.40	31.20
Colquoun (1801/2)	0.519	13.40	13.30	28.00	45.40	29.80
Baxter (1867)	0.551	14.80	11.70	20.80	52.70	45.10

Source: Williamson, *Did British Capitalism Breed Inequality?*, p. 68; P.H. Lindert and J.G. Williamson, 'Revising England's social tables, 1688–1812', *Explorations in Economic History* 19 (1982), 385–408.

income tax returns of the 1800s and 1840s provide a tempting source of information, but these only contain information on the higher incomes within the economy and were in fact records of assessments, not incomes. In 1801, an examination of incomes assessed at over £130 suggested that 120,873 incomes (1.14 per cent of the population) earned 25.4 per cent of income, whilst in 1848, 236,000 incomes (1.18 per cent of the population) earned 34.9 per cent.[72] The implications of this and of other analysis of the income tax data were that inequality increased within the middle classes, providing a source of status and economic anxiety.[73] A confirmation that the most important tensions lay within the top third of the income earners came from a reworking of four of the most important 'social accounting' tabulations of the years between 1688 and 1867.

The Gini Coefficient suggested an overall increase in inequality, but the relative shares told a more important story. Here the 'battle' was not between the rich and the bulk of the labouring class (the bottom 40 per cent) but between the top 10 per cent and the next 25 per cent. The major redistribution indicated was within the top third, more evidence for a rise in economic status anxiety between 1800 and the 1860s.

The growth in population and economic output was accompanied by, and was the source of, considerable accumulations of wealth and capital. Such accumulations of capital were both causes and consequences of the increasing production of goods and services. The most comprehensive

[72] H.J. Perkin, *The Origins of Modern English Society, 1780–1880* (London, 1969), p. 135.
[73] Williamson, *Did British Capitalism Breed Inequality?* pp. 63–4.

Table 2.14 Gross domestic fixed capital formation, Great Britain 1761–1860. £m per annum, decade averages at 1851–60 prices

	1761–70	1771–80	1781–90	1791–1800	1801–10	1811–20	1821–30	1831–40	1841–50	1851–60
Dwellings	1.49	1.38	2.17	3.35	4.58	5.82	**8.91**	**10.28**	7.60	10.25
Public works and buildings	0.15	0.14	0.22	0.33	0.46	0.58	1.07	1.54	1.52	2.05
Agriculture	2.18	2.62	3.31	**4.26**	4.06	**4.45**	4.08	4.71	**6.16**	**6.90**
Industrial & commercial buildings	0.97	0.73	**2.13**	2.20	3.04	4.16	**6.81**	8.52	8.15	10.99
Industrial machinery & equipment	0.27	0.11	1.10	0.88	0.84	1.28	**2.65**	3.51	4.18	5.65
Mining and quarrying	0.08	0.04	0.08	0.16	0.12	0.25	0.28	0.63	0.88	1.17
Gas and water	0.00	0.00	0.00	0.00	0.00	0.19	0.23	0.45	1.05	2.32
Railways	0.00	0.00	0.00	0.00	0.00	0.10	0.10	**3.67**	**14.11**	**8.78**
Roads and bridges	0.53	0.52	0.53	0.49	0.47	0.78	1.15	1.19	1.02	1.01
Carriages and coaches	0.20	0.20	0.30	0.40	0.50	0.60	0.8	1.00	1.30	1.70
Canals etc	0.22	0.50	0.25	**1.04**	0.70	0.57	0.52	0.47	0.19	0.17
Docks and harbours	0.02	0.04	0.05	0.07	0.68	0.42	0.3	0.45	0.85	1.46
Ships	0.53	0.77	0.98	1.13	1.12	1.31	1.39	2.17	2.42	5.00
Total	6.64	7.05	11.12	14.31	16.57	20.51	28.29	38.59	49.43	57.99

Source: C.H. Feinstein, 'Capital formation in Great Britain', in P. Mathias and M.M. Postan (eds.), *The Cambridge Economic History of Europe,* vol. vii, *The Industrial Economics: Capital, Labour and Enterprise.* Part One. (Cambridge, 1978), p. 40.

survey and analysis of the evidence gave a complex and varied account of this accumulation. Capital is not, and was not, the same as wealth but the two concepts are closely related as the creation of capital provided many opportunities for the creation of wealth. In many cases, the relation was simply a matter of different ways of looking at the same asset. In the case study of the Oates family, the stock in trade, the warehouse and the mill were both wealth for the family and capital for the business. In other cases, capital provided opportunities for the production of assets such as agricultural mortgages, trade debts, personal loans and railway shares.

The survey of capital accumulation made by Feinstein in 1978 produced a comprehensive summary (Table 2.14). Presented at constant prices, there was a sustained increase in the annual rate of capital accumulation, but the structure of this accumulation changed over the period. The 1780s and 1790s were led by agricultural improvements. Canals were for the 1790s.[74] Between 1810 and 1830, domestic dwellings were the major form of investment followed by railways in the 1840s. During all these period, industrial and commercial buildings, as well as industrial plant and machinery, formed a significant portion of national capital formation.

This investment produced important changes in the structure of national capital (Table 2.15). Agriculture remained a major but declining portion of the whole (43–19 per cent) whilst domestic dwellings (39–26 per cent) became the largest portion. Industrial capital (7–27 per cent) gained in importance whilst the formidable accumulation of capital in the railways (12 per cent by 1860) was evident in the last cross section and changed the structure of wealth accumulating opportunities in ways which influenced every family in this study. This increase in capital stock kept pace with population up to the 1830s and not until then did capital stock show evidence of increases per head of population. For the middle classes, each of these accumulations provided different opportunities for the ownership of income-earning and marketable assets, in other words wealth and property.

The increase in economic output also created numerous and increasing opportunities for consumer spending. The change was not just one of quantity but also of quality. At one end of the scale was food. This benefited from the long-run increases in agricultural productivity, but food and the potential for shortage remained a major source of instability

[74] J.R. Ward, *The Finance of Canal Building in Eighteenth Century England* (Oxford, 1974).

Table 2.15 *Gross stock of domestic reproducible fixed capital, Great Britain, 1760–1860. £m at 1851–60 replacement cost*

	1760	1800	1830	1860
Dwellings	191	248	390	599
Public works and buildings	19	25	37	80
Agriculture	210	270	340	430
Industrial & commercial buildings	25	75	204	460
Industrial machinery & equipment	9	26	61	160
Mining and quarrying	2	4	8	35
Gas and water	0	0	4	42
Railways	0	0	2	268
Roads and bridges	15	28	47	66
Carriages and coaches	2	5	9	23
Canals etc	8	23	35	37
Docks and harbours	1	3	15	42
Ships	12	22	31	68
Total	490	730	1180	2310

Source: Feinstein, Capital Formation, p. 42.

and insecurity.[75] By the end of the eighteenth century, Britain had moved from being a food exporting to being a food importing country, thus intensifying the impact of years of poor harvest as it was no longer possible to pull back the surplus due for export into the domestic economy, either by the market means of rising prices, or the political means of threatened grain riots.[76] A series of poor harvests starting in the late 1790s created starvation, malnutrition and disorder. They were the material reference point for debates on population, poverty and the control of the grain trade. Insecurity for the individual family might take the form of the direct threat of starvation or the indirect threat of social disorder. Such threats were moral as well as physical. In as far as the middle classes shared and depended upon the power and authority of those who ruled

[75] M.J. Daunton, *Progress and Poverty. An Economic and Social History of Britain, 1700–1850* (Oxford, 1995), pp. 25–60; E.L. Jones, *Agriculture and Economic Growth in England, 1650–1815* (London, 1967), p. 18; B.R. Mitchell and P. Deane, *Abstract of British Historical Statistics* (Cambridge, 1962), pp. 94–5.

[76] E.P. Thompson, 'The moral economy of the English crowd in the eighteenth century', *Past and Present* 50 (1971), 76–136; E.J. Hobsbawm and G. Rude, *Captain Swing* (London, 1969); R. Wells, *Wretched Faces. Famine in Wartime England, 1793–1801* (Gloucester, 1988); Roger Wells, 'Dearth and distress in Yorkshire, 1793–1802', *Borthwick Papers* 52, York 1977.

British society, they sensed, as did many ruling classes, that the legitimacy of their authority depended upon their ability to ensure the supply of adequate food and welfare to the bulk of the population.[77]

At the other end of the scale, wealth and property came increasingly to include a growing quantity and variety of consumer goods. 'Things' were purchased and accumulated. Such possessions not only delivered daily use and value but were also sold, valued and inherited. 'Things' created the opportunities and stage sets upon which the values of politeness, domesticity and piety were acted out. They brought utility and status as well as fierce debates on the evils and benefits of luxury and fashion.[78]

Evidence from the period before 1760, when testamentary inventories were available for England, suggested that there was no specific consumer revolution but a process in which each generation identified and adopted new consumer goods or saw older consumer goods diffused to new regions and social groups.[79] There is some compensation for the silence of English sources in the form of Scottish inventories, which survived with some detail into the 1830s. Thus, in Glasgow, household goods were dominated by drinking vessels in the 1780s, as suited a generation for which decent hospitality involved sending guests home drunk and incapable. By the 1820s, it was the dining table and the furnishings of parlour and drawing room which dominated valuations.[80] This reflected a generation for which domesticity, rationality and evangelical self-directed actions were the objects of approval from the dominant value systems. These consumer patterns were reflected in the importance of wholesalers, shopkeepers and tradesmen in middle class occupational structures.

In terms of outcomes for the middle classes of the 1820s and 1830s, there were only glimpses from the sales which accompanied the processes of bankruptcy and inheritance. John Hebblethwaite's estate represented a top of the range Leeds gentleman merchant, active in the parliamentary

---

[77] Morris, *Class, Sect and Party*, pp. 204–26.
[78] J. Brewer and R. Porter (eds.), *Consumption and the World of Goods* (London, 1993); A. Briggs, *Victorian Things* (London, 1988).
[79] L. Weatherill, *Consumer Behaviour and Material Culture in Britain 1660–1760* (London, 1988); L. Scammell, 'Town versus country: the property of everyday consumption in the late seventeenth century and early eighteenth centuries', in J. Stobart and A. Owens (eds.), *Urban Fortunes. Property and Inheritance in the Town, 1700–1900* (Aldershot, 2000), pp. 26–49.
[80] S. Nenadic, 'Middle rank consumers and domestic culture in Edinburgh and Glasgow, 1720 to 1840', *Past and Present* 145 (1994), 122–56; S. Nenadic, 'The Victorian middle classes', in W.H. Fraser and I. Maver (eds.), *Glasgow, vol. II, 1830–1912* (Manchester, 1996), pp. 283–7.

50Men, women and property in England

Table 2.16 *Valuation of the property of John Hebblethwaite, Leeds 1840*

	£
Household furniture and effects	202
Silver plate	183
Linen	17
China and glass	21
Books and pictures	19
Wearing apparel	10
Jewels and ornaments of the person	6
Wine and liquors	139
Horse and carriage	20
Implements of husbandry	11
Total	629

reform campaigns and, like the Oates family, a member of Mill Hill Unitarian Chapel. The valuer gave a summary of an extensive and detailed account. For John Hebblethwaite, as for many others, value was stored in his furniture, silver and wine.[81]

This increase in economic opportunity for earning and for spending was associated with developments in both technology and trade. Awareness of the economic world was not simply a matter of steam engines, spinning and weaving machinery and the wonders of new iron smelting processes. Technology came to the middle class home as a new coffee grinder, a lawn mower and gas light.[82] The humble engraved print might serve as an example of what was happening. The print was a key part of the 'modern' experience, reproducibility making known a visual world beyond immediate experience and sharing that world in common with many hundreds and thousands of customers. Engraved prints had been around in some numbers since the mid-eighteenth century as both wood cuts and copper plates but the steel engraved process of the 1820s brought price down and quality up, so that the density of prints in homes and publications increased rapidly.[83] As with so many of the trends outlined here, this was not new but the number and richness of experience

81 Inventory and Valuation of the household effects and other personality of the late John Hebblethwaite Esq. of Woodhouse Lane, 6 June 1840. DB 43/10, Leeds City Archive.
82 Davidoff and Hall, *Family Fortunes*, pp. 357–88.
83 A. Griffiths, *Prints and Printmaking. An Introduction to the History and Techniques* (London, 1996), p. 39; R.T. Godfrey, *Printmaking in Britain. A General History from its Beginnings to the Present Day* (Oxford, 1978).

invited new responses and placed new pressures upon existing systems of relationships.

These changes were important because many of the patterns of social relationships identified in this study, especially patterns of family relationships, can be traced back to the early eighteenth century.[84] What happened in the late eighteenth and first fifty years of the nineteenth century was the development of these relationships in conditions of resource availability which were unimaginable for earlier generations. By the 1820s, a system of relationships and ambitions was responding to a richness of wealth and income flows that had never been available to such a sizeable portion of the population.

The generations between 1780 and 1850 experienced a period of heady and exhilarating change. All the evidence indicated that this pace of change increased in and after the 1820s as resources caught up in an economy at war were released to civil investment and production. To those who experienced it, this change would be evident both in the increase and in the redistribution of material resources. The redistribution took many forms. It took place between regions, between sectors of the economy, between rural and urban, as well as between socio-economic groups. Redistribution was in itself part of the processes involved in structural change in the economy. Differential rewards to labour and to capital in different sectors and regions were part of the mechanism which attracted labour and capital to transfer. In many cases the transfer took place between generations. Thus, in Leeds, the sons of handloom weavers became mechanics and machine makers and the sons of shopkeepers moved into the professions.[85] Inequality of reward increased as certain forms of human capital became more or less scarce in relation to demand. There was also a tendency to earn abnormal profits for those who innovated in terms of technology or the organisation of production, or were simply quicker to respond to changes in the market.[86] Institutional and social barriers also perpetuated differences of income and reward such as the control of certain types of human capital by skilled labour and

---

[84] R.B. Shoemaker, *Gender in English Society, 1650–1850* (London, 1998); A. Vickery, 'Golden age to separate spheres? A review of the categories and chronology of English women's history', *Historical Journal* 36:2 (1993), 383–414.

[85] Reports from Assistant Hand Loom Weaving Commissioners, Part III, *Parliamentary Papers*, House of Commons, 1840, 23, p. 583 evidence of James Whitaker of Armley, 'in our town there are at least 20 boys from 12 to 15, who have been put with mechanics; so that you see from this, that the weavers are most anxious to have their children away from that calling'.; T. Wemyss Reid, *A Memoir of John Deakin Heaton. M.D.* (London, 1883).

[86] For example, W.G. Rimmer, *Marshalls of Leeds, Flax Spinners, 1788–1886* (Cambridge, 1960); C.H. Lee, *A Cotton Enterprise, 1795–1840. A History of M'Connel and Kennedy, fine cotton spinners* (Manchester, 1972).

the increasingly organized professions.[87] Differential might also be perpetuated by lack of access to basic education in terms of literacy and
numeracy.[88]

All this presents far too benign a picture of the environment in
which Oates and others were taking decisions and forming strategies
for family and property. The economy and society of the 1820s was
one in which Britain was emerging from a long period of war. The
French wars of the 1790s and Napoleonic period had none of the
totality of twentieth century world wars but they produced deep
uncertainty, especially in trade. They created conditions in which
the military had a central place in national consciousness and society
and the more authoritarian aspects of governance were able to pros-
per. The 1820s saw the release of resources from war and, after a
short period of dislocation, these resources were devoted to other
uses such as the capital investment boom in woollen and cotton
textiles in the early 1820s.[89]

The years between 1780 and 1850 also saw a cyclical pattern of
economic activity establish itself, creating substantial swings in prices
and incomes.[90] The experience of 1826 was only one extreme example.
The tensions created were bewildering for those whose self esteem
centred upon work and responsibility for their own fate. There were

---

[87] T.J. Johnson, *Professions and Power* (London, 1972); D. Duman, *The Judicial Bench in England, 1727–1875* (London, 1982); A. Digby, *Making a Medical Living. Doctors and Patients in the English Market for Medicine, 1720–1911* (Cambridge, 1994), pp. 2, 7 and 37, shows that professional control was an uneven process and probably worked best in relationship to institutional positions with the state and charities; R.Q. Gray, *The Labour Aristocracy in Victorian Edinburgh* (Oxford, 1976); R. Price, *Masters, Unions and Men. Work Control in Building and the Rise of Labour, 1830–1914* (Cambridge, 1980); R. Colls, *The Pitmen of the Northern Coalfield. Work, Culture and Protest, 1790–1850* (Manchester, 1987).

[88] R.S. Scholfield, 'Dimensions of illiteracy in England, 1750–1850', *Explorations in Economic History* 10 (1973). 437–54. In his 1815–44 sample 3% of the gentry and 5% of those in retail were unable to sign their names on marriage, but the figures were 16% for textile workers and 66% for labourers and servants. R.D. Anderson, *Education and Opportunity in Victorian Scotland* (Oxford, 1983), pp. 125, 138–40 and 150–2 showed the importance of professional and commercial family background for entry into Scottish Universities in the 1860s; M. Sanderson, *Education, Economic Change and Society in England, 1780–1870* (London, 1983), pp. 15–19 gives evidence for a decline in literacy in the expanding textile areas of the 1810s and 1820s.

[89] D.T. Jenkins and K.G. Ponting, *The British Wool Textile Industry, 1770–1914* (London, 1982), p. 32 and *The West Riding Wool Textile Industry, 1770–1835, a Study in Fixed Capital Formation* (Edington, 1975).

[90] R.C.O. Matthews, *A Study in Trade Cycle History. Economic Fluctuations in Great Britain, 1833–42* (Cambridge, 1954); J. Parry Lewis, *Building Cycles and Britain's Growth* (London, 1965); Contemporary accounts were focused on London and often linked to financial policy developments. See D. Morier Evans, *The Commercial Crisis, 1847–1848* (London, 1849).

several series available for bankruptcy itself. The variations were caused by the different way in which each was constructed. Some came from cases published in the *Gentleman's Magazine* or the *London Gazette*. Others came directly from the records but referred to different stages in the complex process of bankruptcy. The story they told was consistent. The incidence of bankruptcy increased between 1780 and the 1820s, with sharp increases at times of crisis such as 1826. After 1826, the incidence decreased with the same points of crisis. Bankruptcy was a very specific form of business and financial failure. In theory, it was only open to those who were in 'trade', but that included all forms of trade, be it agricultural, manufacturing, commercial or retail. As each was processed by the courts, they were published in the *Gazette* and in the local newspapers. In the first four months of 1830, the *Leeds Mercury* listed some 27 names from across the status spectrum of the middle classes including:

John Summer – cloth dresser and common agent
James Bowes – flax spinner dealer and chapman
William Pays – coach maker
John Carber – saw manufacturer dealer and chapman
Thomas Thompson Metcalf – surgeon, apothecary dealer and chapman
Charles Robert – clockmaker
Thomas Wolrich Stanesfeld, Henry Briggs and Hamer Stanesfeld – merchants, co-partners, dealers and chapmen.[91]

This list was a cross section of the economically active property owning class of Leeds. They were mainly independent men and minor manufacturers, but included one professional and three of the merchant elite from the firm of Stanesfeld, Briggs and Stanesfeld. The Stansfelds were of the same social economic status as the Oateses and were mentioned in Joseph Henry's letters. They got into trouble in the 1826 crisis and had not been able to recover.[92]

The business records of Robert Jowitt, the elite Quaker woolstapler, showed him rather nervously keeping a list of all failures in the woollen textile industry between 1839 and 1848.[93] Bankruptcy was only the tip of an iceberg of business and financial failure. Many would be drawn into court as insolvents without the eventual protection of being declared bankrupt. The future earnings of a discharged bankrupt were protected

[91] *Leeds Mercury* January 1830 to April 1830.
[92] Joseph Henry Oates to Edward Oates, Oatlands, 2 March 1826, Leeds City Archives Oates O/R.
[93] Jowitt Papers, Bundle Five (old classification), 'Account of Failures in the Wool Trade, 1839–1848'.

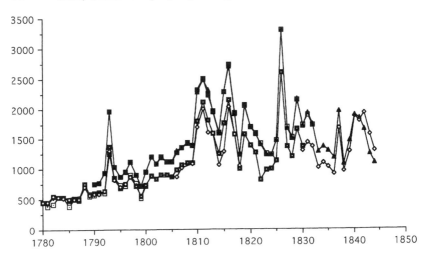

Fig. 2.1 Indicators of the number of bankruptcies in Britain, 1780–1844.

Source: S. Marriner, 'English bankruptcy records and statistics before 1850', *Economic History Review* 33 (August 1980), 351–66; V. Markham Lester, *Victorian Insolvency Bankruptcy, Imprisonment for Debt, and Company Winding up in Nineteenth Century England* (Oxford, 1995).

whilst those of an insolvent were not. Others would simply stop trading, unable to pay debts and with so little of value that it was pointless to pursue them through the courts. Evidence from later in the century, when trade directories became a little more consistent, demonstrated the short life and fragility of most businesses. A study of Edinburgh firms in the paper manufacture, printing, book binding, publishing and related trades such as stationers showed that of the firms for which evidence existed between 1862 and 1891, a third lasted one year only and only around 20 per cent more than five years.[94]

[94] S. Nenadic, 'The life cycle of firms in late nineteenth century Britain', in P. Jobert and M. Moss (eds.), *The Birth and Death of Companies. An Historical Perspective* (Carnforth, 1990), p. 181–95; E. Knox, 'Between capital and labour: the petite bourgeoisie in Victorian Edinburgh', PhD thesis, University of Edinburgh (1986), pp. 10 and 12 measured persistence in terms of Post Office Directory entries over five year periods (1850–55 and 1890–95). He found survival rates which varied between 40% for spirit dealers and 70/80% for drapers, ironmongers, grocers and booksellers. For selected trades rates again varied from 50% to 80%.

Table 2.17 *Male employment status and age, 1851*

Percentage in agegroup	<20	20–25	25–35	35–45	45–55	55+	N
Masters and employers of < 3	0	3	22	22	21	32	256
Journeymen	7	24	35	16	12	6	214
Apprentices	87	8	2	1	0	0	183
Manual occupations	24	14	21	16	13	14	2569
Total	19	14	22	17	13	14	7547

Note: This table was based upon the 2% duster sample of the census enumerators' schedules prepared by Michael Anderson; see M. Anderson, 'The Emergency af the modern life cycle in Britain', *Social History* 10 (1985), 69–87.

It was unlikely that the 1820s were any more stable than this. These fluctuations threatened and promoted a constant exchange of people between social classes. The occupational information in the census of 1851 showed that the movement from apprentice to journeyman to master was part of the potential life cycle for those who gave information on their status. Many more must have fallen back from the attempt to cross the barrier from journeyman to master (Table 2.17).

For many ventures, both large and small, survival and failure depended upon personal skill and ambition but, given the periodic economic blizzards like 1826, many of these failures took place in a manner which gave individuals little chance to exert control, thus creating a tension between the morality of individual responsibility and the experience of economic reality. Thomas Attwood was an elite Birmingham banker, known as a radical who campaigned, amongst other things, for a currency reform, which he believed would end the liquidity problems that caused so much grief and anxiety.[95] His writing was full of stories that illustrated the contradiction between morality and experience. There was the Norfolk farmer whose estate dwindled to nothing, 'without any want of prudence or industry, or the most strenuous exertions on his part'. There was the manufacturer whose mortgages and debts amounted to a fifth of his property who was insolvent because there were no bidders for his property, 'a very industrious and sober man, and who

---

[95] D.J. Moss, *Thomas Attwood. The Biography of a Radical* (Montreal and Kingston, 1990); A. Briggs, 'Thomas Attwood and the economic background of the Birmingham Political Union', *Cambridge Historical Journal* 9 (1948), 190–216.

Table 2.18 *Average age of death in selected towns and poor law unions,*
1837–40

	Professional persons and gentry	Those in trades	Labourers and artisans
Manchester	38	20	17
Liverpool	35	22	15
Leeds	44	27	19
Bolton	34	23	18
Rutland	52	41	38
Kendal	45	39	34

Source: E. Chadwick, *Report on the Sanitary Condition of the Labouring Population of Great Britain,* 1842, edited by M.W. Flinn, Edinburgh, 1965), pp. 219–39.

merely acted upon the principles upon which he and his father and neighbours had always acted and flourished before'.[96]

Added to this were the ever present demographic insecurities of death and morbidity. Life expectation may well have improved over the eighteenth century but this still left a massive slaughter of infants and high rates of premature death amongst adults. Amongst the public health surveys of the 1830s and 1840s was evidence that the higher status groups had higher life expectations. Chadwick summarised the findings and added his own analysis from the early figures of the recently established Registrar General's Office for Births, Deaths and Marriages (Table 2.18).

There was little to indicate directions of change over time and it can only be assumed that the direction of change was the same as for the bulk of the population. Even less can be guessed about morbidity and the toll of discomfort and debility brought by disease and injury, which medicine and better living standards might ameliorate but rarely cure.[97] There were some hints that the change in life style brought by 'politeness' and domesticity reduced some of the diseases of luxury like gout. As early as 1774, Dr Hayward, writing about Chester, had claimed that refined manners had banished gluttony and drunkenness.[98]

The insecurities of middle class existence were compounded by the fact that, despite all the evidence of wealth accumulation and economic

[96] T. Attwood, *The Remedy or Thoughts on the Present Distress* (London, 1819), pp. 15–16.
[97] I. Loudon, *Medical Care and the General Practitioner, 1750–1850* (Oxford, 1986); F.B. Smith, *The People's Health, 1830–1910* (London, 1979).
[98] J. Hayward, 'Observations on the population and diseases of Chester in the year 1774', *Philosophical Transactions of the Royal Society of London* (1778).

growth, many of the institutions and practices and forms of collective property through which the middle class would learn to mediate and distribute risk, hardly existed in the 1820s and 1830s, or existed in imperfect and little used forms. Life insurance was imperfect and marginal to the holdings of the minority who owned them. Estimates suggest considerable expansion of life insurance in the early 1800s and the 1850s and 1860s, but this was hampered by the imperfections of actuarial and medical science. Potential investors in life insurance were also deterred by the high failure rate of many companies founded in the first seventy years of the century. There was some evidence that they served specific groups within the middle classes. Evidence from the well-established Pelican Company in the 1860s showed that amongst those who used life insurance as a security for loans, 21 per cent were middle rank military men, 14 per cent gave commercial occupations and 21 per cent were professionals, of whom 9 per cent were clergy.[99] Indeed, life insurance tended to operate as a security for loans rather than as part of a life cycle savings strategy or premature death precaution. Evidence comparing assets listed in the Scottish testamentary records in the 1820s and 1870s showed that insurance only began to have importance in the later period.[100] The large industrial or commercial corporation with its salaried employment, pension fund and disciplined career structure did not exist.[101] Perhaps only the armed forces and the East India Company gave a hint of what was to come with the Banks and Railway Companies of the second half of the century.[102] Limited Liability had no regular basis in legislation and there was no well regulated stock market with transparent audited flows of information for investors.[103] The family was the only institution through which risk and insecurity could be effectively mediated and spread.

---

[99] B. Supple, *The Royal Exchange Assurance. A History of British Insurance, 1720–1978* (Cambridge, 1970), pp. 106–20; C. Trebilcock, *Phoenix Assurance and the Development of British Insurance, vol.I, 1782–1870*, (Cambridge, 1985), pp. 522–609; R. Pearson, 'Thrift or dissipation? The business of life assurance in the early nineteenth century', *Economic History Review* 43:2 (1990), 236–54.

[100] Work in progress by Ann McCrum for a PhD thesis at the University of Edinburgh. For an early report on this work see A. McCrum, 'Inheritance and the family: the Scottish urban experience in the 1820s', in J. Stobart and A. Owens (eds.), *Urban Fortunes*, pp. 149–71.

[101] L. Hannah, *The Rise of the Corporate Economy* (London, 1976); D. Lockwood, *The Blackcoated Worker*, (London, 1958).

[102] S. Pollard, *The Genesis of Modern Management. A Study of the Industrial Revolution in Great Britain* (London, 1965).

[103] T.L. Alborn, *Conceiving Companies. Joint Stock Politics in Victorian England* (London, 1998); R.C. Michie, *Money, Mania and Markets. Investment, Company Formation and the Stock Exchange in Nineteenth Century Scotland* (Edinburgh, 1981).

Thus, the middling classes, increasingly self aware both as individuals and as a group, faced unprecedented opportunities in material terms but did so in conditions of major economic and personal insecurity.

Stories, narratives and histories

Since the 1830s, the middle class, or classes, have always had an important place in the stories which the English, or British, tell about each other. At times the stories are told with fear and unease. At other times they are told with pride. They are addressed to themselves and to anyone else who will listen. These stories, overlapping, contested, competing and interacting with each other, have been told by both contemporaries and historians. The dominant narrative was one of a great nation with a history of growing wealth and progress moving to a future of democracy and the abolition of poverty. The emergence of a self-aware middle class was related to economic change. The individualistic, entrepreneurial spirit of this group led first to gains in trade and then in industrial production. The group appeared in the story challenging the warlike habits of the aristocracy, demanding the reform of parliament, the abolition of slavery and the creation of an effective civil service.[104] They faced enormous challenge and conflict from the working classes, but were able to achieve a viable class society through reform and negotiation. This stable, wealthy society was a product of the interaction of profit seeking and professional values amongst the middle classes. The story might appear in a right wing form essentially praising the English achievements around the process of industrialisation. In a left wing, or rather Fabian form the story drew attention to the widespread disruption and damage caused by industrial change and urban growth, but continued with reforms of factories, public health, and the poor law, and with the extension of education and parliamentary representation.[105] Whichever version was preferred, it was a story of moral and material progress centred upon an enlightened and educated middle class.

Running beside this was a tale of middle class 'failure'. It was told best by a United States visiting scholar and shared many of the elements of the success story.[106] The theme was taken up by a leading social scientist in

---

[104] A. Briggs, *The Age of Improvement*; Perkin, *The Origins of Modern English Society*.
[105] G.D.H. Cole and R. Postgate, *The Common People, 1746–1946* (London, 1938); J.L. and B. Hammond, *The Town Labourer* (London, 1917); G.D.H. Cole. *A Short History of the British Working Class Movement*, 3 vols. (London, 1925).
[106] M.J. Wiener, *English Culture and the Decline of the Industrial Spirit, 1850–1980* (Cambridge, 1981).

the 1981/2 Reith Lectures, a broadcast series which linked the intellectual world with the public sphere.[107] This story began with a middle class, entrepreneurial and risk taking, whose actions were the basis of massive and sustained economic growth. At some stage around 1850, this group lost its confidence. Risk taking was limited by ambitions for a safe but limited family income. Second generation family members 'retired' on investment incomes. They sent their sons to 'public school' where they learnt the habits of the 'gentry', which were antithetical to risk, profit and growth. They were drawn into the expansion and administration of an Empire providing a further drain on entrepreneurial talent and risk taking. In another form, imperial ambition provided expanding opportunities for overseas investment which further reduced economic expansion. This version of the story at one time became the basis of the Thatcherite political project of the 1980s and 1990s.[108] This 'failure' of the middle class was associated with reduced rates of economic growth and a growing overdependence on the state. There were more refined versions of this; many depended upon the analysis of economic motivation within family and gentry culture.[109] Ironically, there was a left wing version of the 'failure' story produced in the 1970s, in which a nascent middle class first challenged the aristocracy in campaigns such as that for the reform of parliament in 1830–32 and the repeal of the Corn Laws in 1839–45 but instead of carrying this through to a revolutionary destruction of aristocratic power, the middle class or bourgeoisie came to an accommodation with the gentry.[110] Important in this failure was the inability of British society to move from a bourgeois revolution to a working class revolution. Both these versions were seen as schematic and over simplified,[111] but lurking behind them were other stories which assumed a 'path' which advanced industrial societies ought to

[107] R. Dahrendorf, *On Britain* (University of Chicago for the BBC, 1982), p. 43–5.
[108] Department of Trade and Industry, *DTI – the department for enterprise* presented to parliament, January 1988, Cm 278, HMSO, *Parliamentary Papers*, LIV, 1987–8. 'The seeds of economic decline can be traced back over a hundred years ... The enterprise of the nation appeared to have been lost. The education system discouraged young people from working in business...' p. 1.
[109] P.J. Cain and A.G. Hopkins, 'Gentlemanly capitalism and British expansion overseas. I. The Old Colonial System, 1688–1850', *Economic History Review* 39:4 (1986), 501–25; P.J. Cain and A.G. Hopkins, 'Gentlemanly capitalism and British expansion overseas. II. New imperialism, 1850–1945', *Economic History Review* 401 (1987), 1–26.
[110] P. Anderson, 'Origins of the present crisis', *New Left Review* 23 (Jan–Feb, 1964), 26–53; this account is inseparable from E.P. Thompson, The peculiarities of the English (1965), reprinted in E.P. Thompson, *The Poverty of Theory* (London, 1978), pp. 35–91.
[111] W.D. Rubinstein, *Capitalism, Culture and Decline in Britain, 1750–1990* (London, 1993); M. Daunton, '"Gentlemanly Capitalism" and British Industry, 1820–1914', *Past and Present* 122 (Feb 1989), 119–58.

follow. Britain, first nation to experience industrialisation had certainly not followed a simple story of economic change, wage labour and capital producing class formation and class consciousness which formed the basis of class conflict and its revolutionary resolution.[112] Revolution was sidelined by the liberal accommodation of mid-century.[113] Nor had Britain followed a story in which 'industrial take-off' led to sustained economic growth. Economic growth had slowed in the 1870s. This was often linked to cultural change, some of it family based. Both the story of middle class progress and failure made significant assumptions about attitudes to risk, often referred to as enterprise. The late eighteenth and first half of the nineteenth centuries were identified as periods in which the middle classes took risks and responded to a disciplined 'work ethic', whilst the later nineteenth century was seen as a period when such direction was weakened. In these accounts, family based motivations and socio-economic processes were often assumed rather than examined.

Gender, usually present as an account of the fortunes and experience of women, was initially accommodated at the margins of this story. G.M. Trevelyan in his social history of England, completed during the 1939–45 war and dedicated to Eileen Power, Economic and Social Historian, included in his account of Cobbett's England, the women who went into the factories and 'lost some of the best things in life' as well as the young ladies who 'were suffering from too much leisure'.[114] This period provided the starting point from which women made 'progress' in education and legal rights but above all in claims for the parliamentary vote, political participation and a slow if heroic entry into public life.[115] By 1970, this marginality was tossed aside. Accounts of women's experience were more assertive, wide ranging and stood on their own rather than as part of those other stories such as the road to democracy, the rise of the trades unions and social reform.[116] This expanding curiosity regarding the nature of women's experience led to a focus upon gender, the socially defined relationship between men and women, and that relationship was given a central place in the formation and history of the middle

[112] R.J. Morris, *Class and Class Consciousness in the Industrial Revolution, 1780–1850*, London 1979.
[113] J. Foster, *Class Struggle*; R.Q. Gray, 'Bourgeois hegemony in Victorian Britain', in J. Bloomfield (ed.), *Class, Hegemony and Party* (London, 1977), pp. 73–94.
[114] G.M. Trevelyan, *Illustrated English Social History*, vol. IV. (London, 1942), pp. 23–4. M. Berg, 'The first women economic historians', *Economic History Review*, 452 (May 1992), 308–29, has pointed to the importance of a small group of women historians like Eileen Power who widened the scope of historical enquiry.
[115] Cole and Postgate, *The Common People* was an excellent example of this approach.
[116] S. Rowbotham, *Hidden from History 300 Years of Women's Oppression and the Fight Against it* (London, 1973); M. Ramelson, *Petticoat Rebellion* (London, 1967).

class.[117] The new accounts demonstrated that as the subordinations of gender were re-negotiated and re-enforced in years between 1780 and 1850, the public activities which women could legitimately undertake were reduced, and the division of a public male world and a private domestic world for women and men became clearer and deeper. The massive shift of the gender frontier was enforced by a vast cultural apparatus. This intensification of the separation of gender roles was crucial to class formation, not only because such subordination was central to many experiences but also because it underlay many other relationships crucial to middle class existence. Women in their domestic role reared and educated children, especially male children who would fulfil entrepreneurial and professional roles. Through the direct and indirect provision of capital and through the moral, emotional and material support services of 'a home', they sustained that day to day reproduction of labour which middle class males carried into the world of work and politics. Gender was also the basis of the middle classes as the builders and residents of suburbs, as the consumers of 'things' and as the employers of 'servants'.[118]

The middle classes of the eighteenth and nineteenth centuries retained and sustained a strong sense of place. The urban place was the location for their political and associational life. Here they achieved the critical mass for effective action in the public sphere. In the contests which both created and divided middle class loyalties in the first half of the nineteenth century, the stakes were predominantly the urban agencies of governance. The Vestry, the Municipal Corporation, the Improvement Commissioners, even on occasions the Water Company and the Cemetery were the base for exclusions, contests and challenges between party, religious grouping and faction.[119] In the 1840s and 1850s, status tensions between the merchant and professional elites and the shopkeeper lower middle class alliances were fought out in terms of rates increases and urban improvement schemes. Detail and timing varied according to the characteristics of each place.[120] The national campaigns for parliamentary reform and Corn Law repeal, which were a central part

[117] C. Hall, *White Male and Middle Class. Explorations in Feminism and History* (London, 1992), especially the Introduction, pp. 1–42.

[118] L. Davidoff and C. Hall, 'The Architecture of Public and Private Life. English Middle Class Society in a Provincial Town, 1780–1850', in D. Fraser and A. Sutcliffe (eds.), *The Pursuit of Urban History* (London, 1983), pp. 327–45.

[119] D. Fraser, *Urban Politics in Victorian England. The Structure of Politics in Victorian Cities* (Leicester, 1976); D. Fraser, 'The politics of Leeds water', *Thoresby Society* 53:1 (1970), 50–70.

[120] E.P. Hennock, *Fit and Proper Persons. Ideal and Reality in Nineteenth Century Urban Government* (London, 1973).

of middle class assertion, were identified with place, with Birmingham, Manchester and Leeds. Within each place the campaigns were led by factions which appropriated the identity of 'the middle classes' and of place for their campaign. Above all, the massive expansion of voluntary associational activity between 1780 and the 1850s was identified with place. Members and Subscribers joined associations that were identified with the urban place. These associations came in all shapes and sizes

Leeds Benevolent or Strangers Friend Society (1789)
Leeds Auxiliary Bible Society (1809)
Leeds Philosophical and Literary Society (1819)
Leeds Mechanics Institution (1825)
Leeds Temperance Society (1831)
Leeds Zoological and Botanical Society (1838)
Leeds Permanent Building Society (1849)

After the repression and violence of the 1790s, 1800s and 1810s, the leadership of a middle class in formation learnt to use the urban place as a stage set for their public meetings. Whilst the radicals were gathering in the open air on Hunslet Moor and St Peter's Fields, the middle classes were leading the way to the Court House, the Cloth Hall Yard, the Commercial Buildings, Music Hall, Philosophical Hall and Mechanics Institution. By creating and claiming these places, they identified with their town and not with faction, sect or neighbourhood, as they might have done in church, chapel or public house. Still less did they seek the ill disciplined marginality of the open spaces on the edge of the town. When they called these meetings they did so in the name of a place and a class.

'the inhabitants of the town and neighbourhood of Leeds' [to approve of the prudence and moderation of the late revolution in France] 18 September 1830

'the inhabitants of the Borough of Leeds' [to petition for parliamentary reform] 5 February 1831

'the owners of real property in the Borough of Leeds' [to petition regarding a proposed national property register] 19 February 1831

'a very numerous and respectable meeting' [to support James Buckingham's plan for a journey round the world] 9 April 1831

'inhabitant householders of the Borough of Leeds' [parliamentary reform] 12 May 1832

'merchants, manufacturers and other inhabitants of the Borough of Leeds' [to debate Belgian crisis] 24 November 1832

'the clergy, bankers, merchants, manufacturers and other inhabitants of the Borough of Leeds' [in favour of a bill for promoting the better observance of the Sabbath] 23 March 1833

And so it went on, 'respectable', 'leading', sometimes 'opulent' but always 'of Leeds'.[121]

Thus, in the late 1960s, as historical research began to focus on the middle classes, it was unsurprising that research design tended to take the urban place as an appropriate framework. Most attention was drawn towards places characterised as 'manufacturing', which again was natural given the importance of manufacturing in structural change and in the political and cultural dynamic of the period. What emerged was a varied and complex picture. In the major regional centres like Manchester, Birmingham, Leeds and Glasgow, the importance of 'the manufacturers' varied but, in general, political and cultural leadership was in the hands of an elite dominated by commercial and professional men.[122] Some studies emphasised internal conflict, sectarian and party, as was the case in Leeds, or between generations of capitalists, as in Bradford.[123] Others identified the assertion of independence and control against a regional aristocracy.[124] In some cases this was more a renegotiation of relationships with a dominant aristocratic landowner.[125] Less systematic attention was given to consumer and rentier towns like Bath or specialist towns like Portsmouth, where the state was the major employer.[126] These had a much less clear and stable elite leadership. Studies of the medium sized industrial towns showed that it was places like Rochdale and Bolton which were dominated and led by 'manufacturers'. The manufacturers were seen as the natural leaders in local government and, by 1850, many had asserted a paternalistic social and cultural dominance over their town.[127] Accounts of and significance attributed to conflict

---

[121] The quotes are taken from the *Leeds Mercury* at the dates given.

[122] V.A.C. Gatrell, Incorporation and the Pursuit of Liberal Hegemony in Manchester, 1790–1839, in D. Fraser (ed.), *Municipal Reform and the Industrial City* (Leicester, 1982), pp. 15–60; S. Nenadic, 'Businessmen, the urban middle classes, and the "dominance" of manufacturers'; Morris, *Class, Sect and Party*.

[123] T. Koditschek, *Class Formation and Urban Industrial Society. Bradford, 1750–1850* (Cambridge, 1990).

[124] R.H. Trainor, *Black Country Elites. The Exercise of Authority in an Industrialized Area, 1830–1900* (Oxford, 1993).

[125] Cannadine, *Lords and Landlords*.

[126] R.S. Neale, *Bath. A Social History, 1680–1850 or a Valley of Pleasure yet a Sink of Iniquity* (London, 1981); J. Field, 'Wealth, styles of life and social tone amongst Portsmouth's middle class, 1800–75', in Morris (ed.), *Class, Power and Social Structure*, pp. 67–106.

[127] J. Garrard, *Leadership and Power in Victorian Industrial Towns, 1830–80* (Manchester, 1983); P. Joyce, *Work, Society and Politics. The Culture of the Factory in Later Victorian England* (Brighton, 1980); P.J. Gooderson, *Lord Linoleum: Lord Ashton, Lancaster and the Rise of the British Oilcloth and Linoleum Industry* (Keele, 1996).

varied.[128] In general, a period in which an elite led middle class faced considerable change, growth and instability, was followed by a period of more stable and confident local leadership. In many cases, the formation of this elite led class had involved intra-class contest and negotiation for that leadership. Whatever variations and refinements were involved, there was a clear interaction between the formation and reformation of social group and the urban place.

Middle class formation and self awareness was derived from the public life of the urban place, but those spaces which were Manchester, Leeds, Glasgow, Preston, Oldham, Bath and the rest were not simply spaces which provided the theatre and stage set upon which the rituals of politics and civil society were acted out. When the middle classes as a social group looked upon urban spaces, and they frequently did so when they elected MPs, discussed the rates, petitioned on property laws or debated 'improvements', they looked upon an environment which they owned and had created. They owned the houses. They provided finance through mortgage and credit. They paid rent and collected rent. Property was local.[129] It was true that many towns had a dominant aristocratic landlord, but if these landlords did not deliver what the local middle classes wanted in both market and political terms, then their influence was marginal. Lord Calthorpe might collect his rents and assert the conditions of his covenants, as he was entitled to do under the laws of property and contract, but he was wise not to direct his Edgbaston tenants on how they might vote, quite different from Lord Durham and his landowning neighbours in rural and small town North East England.[130] The middle classes added the roads, the pavements and the lighting. They provided the drainage, gas and water works through improvement commissioners and joint stock companies. After the 1850s, they, as ratepayers, customers, members and audience were adding imposing and expensive town halls, concert halls, gentlemen's clubs

---

[128] Foster, *Class Struggle and the Industrial Revolution*; D. Gadian, 'Class formation and class action in North West industrial towns, 1830–50', in Morris (ed.), *Class Power and Social Structure*, pp. 23–66.

[129] R.J. Morris, 'The middle class and British towns and cities of the industrial revolution, 1780–1870', in D. Fraser and A. Sutcliffe (eds.), *The Pursuit of Urban History*; C. Bedale, 'Property relations and housing policy: Oldham in the late nineteenth and early twentieth centuries', in J. Melling (ed.), *Housing, Social Policy and the State* (London, 1980), pp. 37–72; M. Winstanley, 'Owners and occupiers. Property, politics and middle class formation in early industrial Lancashire', in A. Kidd and D. Nicholls (eds.), *The Making of the British Middle Class? Studies in Regional and Cultural Diversity since the Eighteenth Century* (Stroud, 1998).

[130] Cannadine, *Lords and Landlords*; T.J. Nossitor, *Influence, Opinion and Political Idioms in Reformed England. Case Studies from the North East, 1832–1874* (Brighton, 1975).

and department stores as they claimed the central business district as their own.[131] If there was any doubt, then local bylaws and police would discipline spaces and behaviour, which the cultural authority and self discipline of the middle classes had failed to control.[132] The family based strategies of this study played an important part in the creation of this urban landscape. The leading players still gaze down upon it, frozen in the bronze and marble of the statues which stand in many urban squares and parks, reminders of authority and power from a time when leadership and ownership firmly linked the local and the middle classes.

The urban story of the middle classes was closely related to the story of the middle classes as created by and creators of civil society. Gellner's instinctive definition of civil society as that element of social space between the tyranny of kings and the tyranny of cousins prevents some of the looseness often associated with the concept.[133] Civil society encompassed the non-prescriptive activities of self-directed, choice-making individuals. It was linked to the rule of law, the existence of a free market and, above all, to open and disciplined association. The outcome was a tolerant and pluralist society. Habermas presented these developments in a slightly different way as the creation of a public sphere in which public opinion was formed through the exchange of ideas and information. This was the world of newspapers, periodicals and books, of public meetings and petitions. Public opinion was formed through the disciplined argument of evidence and rationality. The outcome was the formation of what his translators call 'bourgeois society' which, in England, meant a society dominated in culture, values and practice by its middle classes.[134] Sennett located the rise of such a public in the coffee house culture of the early eighteenth century with its open exchange of information and debate.[135] This was part of a wider formation of associations in the growing number of clubs and lodges across English society.[136] By the late eighteenth century, such associations were more numerous and more open. After a brief period of repression between 1790 and 1820, they

---

[131] S. Gunn, *The Public Culture of the Victorian Middle Class. Ritual and Authority in the English Industrial City, 1840–1914* (Manchester, 2000).

[132] K. Cowman, 'The battle of the boulevards: class, gender and the purpose of public space in later Victorian Liverpool', in S. Gunn and R.J. Morris (eds.), *Identities in Space. Contested Terrains in the Western City since 1850* (Aldershot, 2001).

[133] E. Gellner, *Conditions of Liberty. Civil Society and its Rivals* (London, 1994).

[134] J. Habermas, *The Structural Transformation of the Public Sphere*; C. Calhoun (ed.), *Habermas and the Public Sphere* (MIT, 1994).

[135] R. Sennett, *The Fall of Public Man* (London, 1986 (1st edition New York, 1977)).

[136] P. Clark, *British Clubs and Societies*.

were to increase rapidly in both number and variety. Like many aspects of middle class culture and society, associational culture and public opinion can trace its origins back to the early eighteenth century but finds its full development between 1820 and 1850.[137] This was the period which saw the replacement of main force as the dominant mode of conflict resolution with the ritualised negotiation of meeting, debate and petition. By the 1820s, urban culture was a basis for an active, wide-ranging civil society. Practices of debate and transparency, which emerged in the late eighteenth century, provided an open and effective way of encompassing the varied cultural, political, religious and ideological ambitions of the middle classes, as well as providing a vehicle for exploring and expressing the 'interests' and implications of the overlapping structural situations in which they acquired their income, accumulated capital and property rights and organised their consumption of goods and services.[138] Analysis of the middle classes increasingly depended upon the identification of a public and private world, a public world of politics, the economy and civil society, and a private world of home, consumption and emotion.

This expansion of interest in the history of the middle classes coincided with a debate over the nature of the historian's task. There was an increasing self-consciousness about the manner in which historians crafted their 'stories'.[139] There was a growing awareness of the manner in which historians were guided by dominant narratives, of class, of economic growth and development and of the passage to a liberal democratic society. All these were usually packaged within a story of 'nation', itself seen as an historical product of a variety of cultural processes, one of which was writing history.[140] Accounts of structural features, such as class and status, were seen as products of intellectual activity imposed upon the past. There was a danger that this debate would result in the

---

[137] R.J. Morris, 'Voluntary societies and British urban elites, 1780–1870: an analysis', *Historical Journal* 26 (1982) 95–118.

[138] R.J. Morris, 'Civil society, subscriber democracies and parliamentary government in Great Britain', in N. Bermeo and P. Nord (eds.), *Civil Society before Democracy*.

[139] The 'story' is well told by R.Q. Gray, 'The deconstruction of the English working class', *Social History* 11:3 (October 1986), 363–73; Many pieces of the puzzle are brought together in P. Joyce (ed.), *Class* (Oxford, 1995); H. White, *The Content of the Form. Narrative Discourse and Historical Representation* (Baltimore, 1987), esp. pp. 1–57 sets out many of the issues whilst L. Jordanova, *History in Practice* (London, 2000) provides a clear statement of 'practice' for self-aware history writing; R. Price, 'Historiography, narrative and the nineteenth century', *Journal of British Studies* 35 (April 1996), pp. 220–56 provide the most comprehensive survey.

[140] E.J. Hobsbawm, *Nations and Nationalism since 1780* (Cambridge, 1990); A. Hastings, *The Construction of Nationhood. Ethnicity, Religion and Nationalism* (Cambridge, 1997); B. Anderson, *Imagined Communities, Reflections on the Origin and Spread of Nationalism* (London, 1983).

privileging of the cultural and the historian would focus on the analysis of signs and discourses from the past. In practice, this debate produced a writing of history which required the historian to be more self-aware and confident in the intellectual processes of shaping evidence from the past. Above all, it created an awareness of history, not as an account of some sort of a past 'reality', but as a disciplined account of the relationship between past and present.[141]

As a result, there was a growing lack of assurance amongst academic historians over the use of the concept of class for understanding both past and present. There was a suspicion of dominant narratives of all kinds and a preference for multiple narratives of gender, race, ethnicity and nation. There was a tension between approaches to understanding the past through analysis of its cultural products and that which relied on the identification and analysis of the structural elements of past society.

Social class was always more than a matter of labels. It was one means by which individuals and groups struggled to understand their experiences and to direct current loyalties, values and behaviour as well as future aspirations. At a cultural level, class was about the attribution of meanings to a complex of social relations and behaviours. These meanings often had powerful agency in the mobilisation of opinions and actions. Such mobilisation did not always involve the word 'class'. There were many codes to encompass the property owning profit takers. In 1839, the Mayor of Leeds called a meeting to collect funds for the relief of the 'unemployed poor'. He had no doubt that 'they will likewise find that the opulent part of the community sympathize in their sufferings'. In the words of the Whig MP, Edward Baines, 'it was the duty of the more opulent classes as it was in reality their interest'.[142] But in its various forms social class analysis was and is about the attribution of structure, in other words, of perceived regularities identified for purposes of analysis and explanation rather than simply the attribution of culturally constructed meanings. Such regularities were perceived as having an objective, often a material, reality independent of the cultural imagination and creativity of individual or social group.[143] The Leeds Political Union divided its council into 'middle class' and 'operatives'. The vice-chairman explained the distinction. 'Everyman who was obliged to maintain himself by the labour of his own hands should be considered as of the operative class and that all others should be taken as of the middle

---

[141] P.J. Corfield (ed.), *Language, History and Class* (Oxford, 1991), pp. 1–29.

[142] *Leeds Mercury*, 28 December 1839.

[143] Morris, 'Structure, culture and society in British towns', in Daunton (ed.), *The Cambridge Urban History of Britain*.

class'.[144] Such analysis appeared in the public health campaigns of the 1830s and 1840s. Here classes reflected different degrees and forms of access to material and cultural resources.[145] Older histories of class and histories, which accepted class as their dominant narrative, gave an emphasis to class as a relationship of conflict, which arose from changing relationships to the means of production.[146] Emphasis was given to organisation and ideologies generated around such conflicts. But, above all, class was about various forms of legitimate power and part of a complex system of subordinations. Class was about power and conflict. At its centre were distinctions of ideology, consumption and relationships of production and property as well as social and cultural style.[147] Social class and related notions have lost any monopolistic position in narrative and analysis but remain essential to the task of identifying inequalities of power, especially in matters of access to material resources. Class remains central to the task of debating and analysing the nature and impact of different economic positions on individual and group life chances, decisions, values, ambitions and experiences.[148] Social class was a 'claim' and a crucial part of the legitimisation of that claim was access to the means of disposing of material resources, goods, services, land, capital and labour.

One result of recent historiography has been a tendency to neglect the study of the structure of the middle classes. Interest in the middle classes grew in the 1970s at just the point when historians began to privilege the social and the cultural. There was little to compare, for example, with the intense debate which took place about the nature, and indeed the value systems of the 'labour aristocracy' in Britain, which not only examined the variety of economic and material experiences of the working classes, but also related this to social and cultural behaviour.[149]

The task of delineating the structure of the middle classes in this, or indeed in any other period, is a non-trivial one; even providing answers for apparently simple questions is contingent upon theoretical judgements, sources and historical practice. What portion of the population came from the middle classes? How did they relate to the various forms of power and status which structured class positions? How did they relate to

---

[144] *Leeds Mercury*, 17 December 1831.
[145] E. Chadwick, *Report on the Sanitary Condition of the Labouring*, Ed. M.W. Flinn, pp. 219–39.
[146] Morris, *Class and Class Consciousness* for a critical survey of this literature.
[147] D. Cannadine, *Class in Britain* (Yale, 1998); Patrick Joyce (ed.), *Class*.
[148] R. Crompton, *Class and Stratification. An Introduction to Current Debates* (Cambridge, 1993).
[149] G. Crossick, *An Artisan Elite in Victorian Society. Kentish London 1840–1900* (London, 1978); R.Q. Gray, *The Labour Aristocracy in Victorian Britain* (Oxford, 1976).

wealth distribution? The difficulties reflect the lack of assurance over the theoretical meaning of the concept of class and its place in story and analysis. This is compounded by the problems of generating an operational definition of 'middle classes' which can be related in a systematic manner to available sources. The value and comprehensibility of any decisions on such matters are compromised by the impact of age, gender and household and family relationships. In the example of the Oates family, Joseph Henry and George had clear and definable positions but Sarah's status was mediated by that of her husband, Mary's by that of her brothers and that of Edward partly by his public status as a lawyer and partly by his relationship with his brothers. Mrs Headlam had a direct public status as the owner and disposer of wealth.

The approach adopted here has been to locate the middle classes in terms of the forms of power and wealth which reflected the variety of relationships implying control over the means of production and consumption. This produced a number of qualitatively identifiable categories which related to groups recognised by contemporaries and which had economic status implications. Six of these groups contained 80 to 90 per cent of the urban populations which might be deemed to be middle class.[150] The operational definition or, to put it another way, the concept indicator relationship was based upon two sources appropriate to the period, the urban parliamentary poll book and the urban commercial and trade directory.[151] The parliamentary poll book provided a list of adult males who were qualified to vote in the parliamentary election on the grounds that they held property to the value of ten pounds per year. This figure had been selected as the level which qualified urban voters under the 1832 Parliamentary Reform Act. The choice had been made on the grounds that it included the bulk of the middle classes and excluded the bulk of the working classes.[152] Thus, in a borough like Leeds or Manchester, which was newly enfranchised and hence had no voters under the older franchise, the poll book provided a very practical definition of 'middle class'. Inclusion in the Commercial and Trade Directory implied an independent business or trade and/or an independent address to which mail might be delivered.

---

[150] R.J. Morris, 'Occupational coding: principles and examples', *Historical Social Research/ Historische Sozialforschung* 15 (1990), pp. 3–29.

[151] J.R. Vincent, *How Victorians Voted* (Cambridge, 1967); J. Sims (ed.), *A Handlist of British Parliamentary Poll Books* (Leicester and Riverside, 1984); J.E. Norton, *Guide to the National and Provincial Directories of England and Wales* (London, 1950 and 1984); G. Shaw and A. Tipper, *British Directories. A Bibliography and Guide* (Leicester, 1988).

[152] Morris, *Class, Sect and Party*, p. 132.

Table 2.19 *Estimates of the size of the Leeds middle classes, 1832–39*

	Total entries	Estimated population	%
Directory 1834 male	8117	31864	25.5
Directory 1834 female	984	36055	2.7
Poll Book 1832	3548	30105	11.8
Poll Book 1834	4669	31864	14.7
Poll Book 1837	5660	34502	16.4
Poll Book 1839	4484	36261	12.4

In the Leeds study two parliamentary poll books were used.[153] Those for 1832 and 1834. These were linked to the Commercial Directory for 1834. In order to compare like with like the totals were compared with the adult male population. The Directory included a small female population, mainly with an independent income or involved in retailing and education. Comparison with the adult female population indicated the small but significant number of women who entered the public realm as defined by the Directory.

The narrow definition of the poll books suggested that about 15 per cent of the adult males had a claim upon middle class status. The actual percentage varied with the state of trade, rising in years of relative prosperity like 1834 and 1837 and falling in years of difficulty. In part, this reflected the nature of a source that required the participant to pay poor rates to a certain value, and in part it reflected the experience of a trade depression in which many individuals lost status.[154] According to the broader definition represented by the Directory, 25 per cent of adult males had some claim on middle class status. Only 3 per cent of adult women were able to claim middle class status in the specific form of access to the public sphere described by the Directory.

As the middle classes left traces of their public life in nominal listings like the poll books and directories, they revealed details of their internal structure through claims to a variety of occupational titles. The quality of the titles in these two sources makes it possible to group the middling classes into a number of categories defined by status and by the type of relationship to capital and the means of production and consumption. Thus, the merchants controlled finance capital, the manufacturers

---

[153] Morris, *Class, Sect and Party*, pp. 134–5 for earlier presentations of these data.
[154] Fraser, *Urban Politics in Victorian England*, pp. 187–9.

Table 2.20 *Occupational and status structure of the Leeds middle classes, 1832 and 1834*

	Directory 1834	Directory 1834 male	Directory 1834 female	Poll 34 (Poll 34titles)	Poll 34 (Dir 34titles)	Poll 32 (Dir 34titles)
Distribution	23.60	22.00	37.10	21.30	32.20	31.60
Merchants and bankers	5.30	5.90	0.00	9.20	10.00	10.40
White collar	5.90	6.50	1.10	2.60	6.60	6.20
Manufacturing	17.60	19.20	4.60	16.40	13.90	14.20
Craft	28.90	30.70	13.90	12.70	17.40	17.30
Professional	2.30	2.60	0.00	3.30	5.10	5.10
Independent	8.30	4.90	36.40	25.70	5.90	6.50
N	9101	8117	984	5058	2871	2325

mainly capital in production and the professionals the human capital of their training and knowledge. These could be approached in one of three ways, through the Directory, through the Poll Book defined by the occupational titles included in the 1834 Poll Book, or through the Poll Book defined by the entries which could be linked to titles in the Directory. For Leeds in 1834 this produced three snapshots (Table 2.20).

This account of the occupational status structure of the middle classes of Leeds had several dimensions. The first depended upon the source chosen. The Directory being a wider and more inclusive source included a larger percentage of the lower status craft group. The second dimension was provided by the occupational title itself. This was not a description of occupation but an indicator provided either by the named individual (a claim) or by the document creator (an attribution). The nature of the choice of title depended upon the purpose of the source. The Directory was, amongst other things, about getting business and hence the title was about announcing the services and products on offer while the Poll Book tended to be about the status associated with occupation. The purpose of the latter was to recognise the claim to the status of being a parliamentary voter. Thus, the population of the Poll Book, the more restricted listing, appeared differently, when described by titles from linked names from the Directory, from when it was described by titles from the one Poll Book that had occupational titles, namely 1834. The Directory titles had more shopkeepers and fewer of independent income (those who had no title or claimed to be 'gentlemen').

Avoiding excessive claims for precision, the major features of middle class occupational structure can be identified through the lenses of contested definitions, qualitatively varied sources and differences in historians' practices in the allocation of occupational titles to categories. Whichever account of the middle class occupational status structure is preferred, several features emerge. In quantitative terms, the middle classes were dominated by shopkeepers and independent craft businesses. There was a significant group of manufacturers and small groups of merchants and professional men (where the Oates family would go). The manufacturers created the public reputation of towns like Leeds. The shopkeepers and craft businesses would dominate when numbers mattered, such as at the time of elections or in the creation of demand in the property market for housing and workshops, but investigation demonstrated that urban leadership, in politics, culture and voluntary associations came predominantly from the small groups of professionals, merchants and, to some extent, the 'gentlemen'.[155]

The Directory gave a glimpse of the structures of gender. Women were not absent from the public sphere but, even in the less demanding listings of the Directory, those who claimed and gained a public identity were only 11 per cent of total entries. Those who did appear were located in the lower status groups (distribution, crafts and services). Even here they appeared in specific areas of activity. Of the 137, in the craft sector, 55 were dress makers and 32 were straw bonnet makers. There were some who claimed 'male' occupations such as Sarah Kilburn, the millwright, and Maria Briggs, plumber and glazier. There were 353 female entries in the retail sector but of these 78 were milliners and dress makers of some sort, 68 were general shopkeepers and 50 kept lodging houses. Another important group of women appeared in the independent income section. They offered no occupational title but had sufficient status and independence to offer an independent address attached to their name in this public listing.

Other urban studies offer material for comparison. As it is important to compare like with like, comparisons will be offered only for appropriate parts of the Leeds table. The Manchester study was based upon a sample of the Poll Book.

Even allowing for differences in categorisation, the results were remarkably similar except for the greater importance of manufacturing in Manchester. The Manchester study included no white collar section of agents, travellers, clerks and bookkeepers (Table 2.21). Comparison with a study of Glasgow in 1832 produced the same sort of conclusions (Table 2.22). Shopkeepers and, to some extent, tradesmen were numerically dominant with proportions very much the same as those shown by

---

[155] Morris, *Class, Sect and Party*, pp. 318–31.

Table 2.21 *Comparative occupational status structures of the middle classes of Leeds and Manchester, 1832 and 1834*

	Manchester Poll 32 (Directory titles)	Leeds Poll 34 (Directory titles)
Distribution	28.00	32.20
Merchants and bankers	10.00	10.00
White collar	0.00	6.60
Manufacturing	30.00	13.90
Craft	13.00	17.40
Professional	6.00	5.10
Independent	8.00	5.90

Source: V.A.C. Gatrell, 'Incorporation and the Pursuit of Liberal Hegemony in Manchester, 1790–1839', in D. Fraser (ed.), *Municipal Reform*, p. 42.

Table 2.22 *Comparative occupational status structures of the middle classes of Leeds and Glasgow, 1832 and 1834*

	Glasgow Dir 32	Glasgow Poll 32	Leeds Directory 34	Leeds Poll 34 (Poll titles)
Distribution	28.30	20.30	23.60	21.30
Merchants and bankers	16.30	17.40	5.30	9.20
White collar	3.00	2.80	5.90	2.60
Manufacturing	9.80	8.10	17.60	16.40
Craft	22.10	19.40	28.90	12.70
Professional	10.80	9.30	2.30	3.30
Independent[a]	2.50	10.40	8.30	25.70

Source: S. Nenadic, 'The structure, values and influence of the Scottish urban middle class', PhD thesis, University of Glasgow (1986), p. 69.
[a] Nenadic separated the 11.5% with no occupational title

comparable sources and methodologies. The balance of manufacturing and commerce was very different. As a port city and service centre for the west of Scotland, Glasgow had larger commercial and professional sectors in its middle classes.

An analysis of the trade directories of two Black Country towns, which used only five categories, showed no evidence of a significant merchant class, but service centre functions were reflected in the number of professional men (Table 2.23).

Table 2.23 *Comparative occupational status structures of the middle classes of Leeds, West Bromwich and Bilston, 1834*

	Leeds 1834	W. Bromwich 1834	Bilston 1834
Merchants	5.30	3.00	1.00
Manufacturers	17.60	16.00	18.00
Professional	2.30	7.00	7.00
Shopkeepers	23.60	47.00	52.00
Tradesmen	28.90	19.00	18.00

Source: Trainer, Black Country Elites, p. 83.

One important approach to the study of middle class structure was the examination of those whose probate valuation (gross value of personal estate) was £100,000 or more. This strategy of representing the middle classes through the wealthy identified two distinctive dimensions. Throughout the nineteenth century, over 50 per cent of these estates were derived from commerce whilst only some 20–30 per cent came from manufacturing. In addition, there was a small but significant group of professions in the early part of the century who gained wealth mainly from their relationships with government. The geographical distribution of these estates was equally distinctive. In the first half of the century 60–70 per cent were London based falling to around 50 per cent after mid-century.[156] The same sort of result came from an examination of the distribution of Schedule D (tax on profits from business and the professions) income tax paid. In 1812, 38 per cent came from London and only 11 per cent from the six northern counties of England. By 1879–80, London still dominated, paying £26.30 per head of population. The nearest competition was Manchester with £24.92 per head. Leeds was down at £8.03. This confirmation of the metropolitan nature of Britain led to the claim that the disparity and difference were the basis for the creation of two middle classes.[157] There were a number of very wealthy manufacturers, like Arkwright, Crawshay and Peel, but their impact upon contemporary and later consciousness was the newness of this wealth. In Leeds in the 1820s there were spectacular manufacturing fortunes made by Benjamin Gott, woollen manufacturer, and John Marshall the flax

[156] W.D. Rubinstein, 'The Victorian middle classes: wealth, occupation and geography', *Economic History Review* 30 (November 1977), 602–23.
[157] W.D. Rubinstein, 'Wealth, elites and the class structure of modern Britain', *Past and Present* 76 (August, 1977), 99–126.

spinner. They were leading members of the local elite, one Tory Anglican, the other Unitarian Whig. Other major accumulations of wealth like the Becketts and, to a lesser extent, families like the Oates were merchant wealth. They were the latest of several generations of merchant wealth. Only in the small and medium sized industrial towns did manufacturers truly dominate.

The clarity of structural identity, which at one time dominated debates on social class in Britain, has been considerably blurred by recent study. The relationships of production involved a variety of structural positions. An individual's ability to command an income flow of middle class status might depend upon the ownership of a 'firm', or a professional status, or the ownership of rentier assets, or a marriage or family relationship. For some individuals 'class' might run through their life as they sold labour, managed capital and purchased housing on mortgage.

Central to all these stories was the individual embedded in a network of family relationships. It was the individual in the family who owned and controlled the firm, gained and utilised professional knowledge, and gathered together those resources which formed the basis of the production of home and domesticity. Central then was the individual as the owner of property. Property, the claims upon goods and services, might appear as land, houses, as capital, as wealth, as purchasing power, as the means of consumption and investment. Property may be considered as an element in the structural relationships of capital, or as a cultural construct essential to power relationships. Few enquiries into the nature and importance of the middle classes can proceed without attention to property. The link between the individual in the family and property as an economic, social and cultural relationship was central to eighteenth and nineteenth century society. It was the property owning individual which linked family objectives and relationships to the wider economy.

For the middle classes of Britain in the 1820s and 1830s property was that set of relationships within which culture and structure met, where the public and private worlds overlapped. There were several important locations where this conjunction was played out, but the most important was that network of social and economic relationships which intellectuals and nonintellectuals alike have called the family. Property was tied to the cultural definitions and practices of the law. Decisions were circumscribed by the moralities, expectations and legitimacies of gender and family relationships. Decisions were guided by the insights and enthusiasms of the political economists and the moralities of politics, religion and social understandings. The decision takers related to their property in a world of the ideals of culture, ideology and discourse, but their decisions were always limited by the parameters of structure. In this study the structures of the market were central. Culturally driven decisions were continually limited and upset by price levels and changes, by the cyclical nature of the market and by the interventions of the liquidity crisis, both global and individual. Ambitions and strategies were subject to the joys and cruelties of demography and morbidity. The complexity of the growing towns provided a range of 'externalities' from epidemic disease to changing land and housing prices. These had both negative and positive influences on the opportunity for decision taking.

The vignette of Joseph Henry and his family showed them sorting the affairs of family following the death of his father. The Oateses represented and were deeply embedded in one of the urban elites which provided political, social and cultural leadership to the increasingly self-aware middle classes. The merchanting and manufacturing leadership of the coalfield regions of England were the dynamic element of those middle classes. The Oateses were Unitarian and Whig in their religious and political loyalties but this group was one of the most active in the creation of the self-awareness and the dynamic interventions in civil society of the middle classes. The Oateses represented several generations of families which were powerful, successful and influential in the management and direction of the commercial and manufacturing economy of Britain. Those who seek to understand this period as a period of success, to be compared favourably with later generations, and who see this as a period worthy of admiration and perhaps emulation based upon enterprise, self reliance and family values must look at the processes which tied the family to the economy and the economy to those families who held manufacturing, commercial and professional power.

The story of the Oateses settling their affairs has identified the major dramatis personae of the story of family and property, namely:

The married adult male with his wife and children.
The unmarried brother.
The married sister.
The unmarried sister.
And a network of uncles, aunts, cousins, nephews and nieces.[158]

Only man, wife and children were recognised in the 'ideal' of contemporary discourse. They were the subject of sermons, poetry, advice manuals and legal guidance. Joseph Henry Oates was the 'ideal type' of the middle class decision taker for both contemporary culture and for much later academic and intellectual analysis. Surviving documentation does

---

[158] L. Davidoff, M. Doolittle, J. Fink and C. Holden, *The Family Story. Blood, Contract and Intimacy, 1830–1960* (London, 1999).

indeed show such men at the centre of action and decision for family networks. The relationship was often one of responsibility and bargaining rather than authority. This situation of the 'ideal type' was very different from the lived experience of a large portion of the actors in such relationships. Part of the 'story' was the tension and often contradiction between this ideal and the experience of the many and varied actors.

The story of the Oateses showed the prospect and occasion of death prompting a review of the holding, meaning and strategies associated with property. Although much of this study will focus on case studies, which exploit the depth of information in bundles of family papers, a broader base of information needs to be established through the analysis of a series of wills from the Parish of Leeds. This will establish the nature and strategies for the disposal of property at death and, by implication, throw light on wider strategies related to the life cycle and positions within family status structures.

The decisions of family and property were taken in the face of considerable economic and demographic insecurity. Premature adult death and the sudden death of children and adults were common. For those who escaped, debilitating illness and other medical conditions were a major hazard. Bankruptcy or simply the periodic reduction of income and property values was a hazard, even for those who exercised all the virtues of diligence and prudence recommended by the advice manuals. To be part of the middle classes was to be part of a group which, in terms of economic, social and cultural authority, had enormous and growing power but, for the individual, the position was one of great vulnerability in the face of the insecurities of the body and the insecurities of those structures called 'the economy'. Such anticipated vulnerabilities were a key feature of any individual's decision taking and strategy making.

The vignette of Joseph Henry Oates in the mid-1820s also showed that many decisions and strategies were taken and made with reference to that tangle of relationships loosely called the family. The concerns, the social processes and the social structures which emerge from a careful reading of family papers direct attention to the need to identify the mechanisms which linked public and private roles. Death and the remaking of family and property relationships that follow death was a key moment at which decisions were made and strategies revised and, above all, became visible to the historian. The text of wills and testaments provided an insight, not just into the few families for whom personal documents survived, but for a wide range of the property holding classes of Leeds. Probate and the text of the wills lack the self aware language of politics and petitions but they give access to key moments of reflection for property holders. They provide access to one moment in a life cycle pattern of decision and strategy making as they gather in the ambitions and subordinations of age, gender and ownership. The prospect and occasion of death prompted a review of the holding patterns, meanings and strategies associated with property. The wills were a record of roles and expectations, of cultural assumptions and structural constraints on key decisions and situations.

3   Reading the wills: a window on family and property

The Leeds probate cohort, 1830–34

Between January 1830 and December 1834, 374 estates were brought from the Parish of Leeds for probate at the Prerogative Court of York and the subordinate Court of Ainstey. Three hundred and sixty-two of these probates concerned the transfer of adult property at death.[1] In 74 per cent of them the transfer involved the directions of a written will. The rest were administrations for those who died intestate.

Over a quarter of the estates were female, with women having a slightly lower propensity to make a will than men (Table 3.1).

An estimated 10 per cent of adult male deaths resulted in a probate, as did 3.5 per cent of adult female deaths.[2] For women, this was the same as the proportion (3.5 per cent) who had appeared in the Directory of 1834. For men, the proportion was much lower than the 15 per cent who appeared in the Poll Book and very much lower than the 25 per cent of adult males in the Directory. This was an indication not only of the exclusion of women from the listings of the public sphere but also the great instability of male participation in the listings of property and entrepreneurship.

The wills provided two items of information which help describe the nature of this limited and selective population, the occupational title and the sworn value of probate. Both need to be read with care.

Males were attributed an 'occupational title'. In this most private of documents written in anticipation of a carefully scrutinised entry into the public domain of the law courts, women were attributed a civil status,

---

[1] At this stage in the analysis twelve cases were removed, leaving 362. Ten of these cases were Limited Administrations. These were incidental upon court cases involving the distribution of property, usually in the Courts of Equity. They often involved the passing of disputed property from one estate to another as it rattled its way around family networks battered by premature death and ill-drafted wills. The other two were minors whose brief lives had carried property rights requiring the attention of the probate process.

[2] This estimate was made by attributing the death rates and age structure of Leeds in 1841 to the population of 1831.

Table 3.1 *Estates brought for probate from the Parish of Leeds, 1830–34*

	Male		Female	
		%		%
Wills	204	76	63	24
Administrations	62	65	33	35
Total	266	73	96	27

N = 362

spinster, wife or widow. In the few cases in which their occupation could be derived from the will, they tended to be in some form of retail distribution.

The male occupational structure can be compared with that in the Directory and Poll Book of 1834 (Fig. 3.1 and Table 3.2).[3] Probate men were, overall, of higher status than those in the other property-holding middle class listings. Merchant and professional were over represented and craft and shopkeeping underrepresented. A distinctive feature of the probate population was the large number of 'property' related titles, namely yeoman and, above all, gentleman.

The importance of the title 'gentleman' bore little relationship to any respect for or ambition to join the lower ranks of landed or aristocratic society. The title was related to the nature of the last will and testament, a document produced in many cases by men at the end of their life cycle, who had retired from active business and lived on an independent or rentier income.

There were nine who held mostly small amounts of rural property. There were three professionals, including one who acknowledged that his father had transferred a small parcel of land to him, 'so as to qualify him to shoot game'. A group of fourteen included two merchants, one of whom had £21,000 in $4^1/_2$ per cent consols and might just be included in a traditional high status definition of gentleman.

The next group consisted of four who, in at least one of the 1820s trade directories, had been manufacturers and five others with craft or retail occupations. There was one clothier and a cloth dresser. Some acknowledged their occupation in 1822 but by 1825 called themselves 'gentleman'. For the eleven in this group, the term gentleman is best understood to

---

[3] This and subsequent references are to *The General and Commercial Directory of the Borough of Leeds* (Leeds: Baines and Newsome, 1834) and *The Poll Book of the Leeds Borough Election, 1834* (Leeds, 1834).

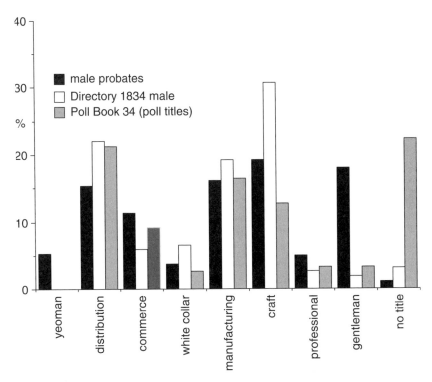

Fig. 3.1 Occupational status and male probate, Leeds 1830–34.

Table 3.2 *Occupational status and male probate, Leeds 1830–34*

	N	male probates %	Dir 1834 male	Poll 34 (poll titles)
yeoman	14	5.26	0.00	0.00
distribution	41	**15.41**	**22.00**	**21.30**
commerce	30	**11.28**	**5.90**	**9.20**
white collar	10	**3.76**	**6.50**	**2.60**
manufacturing	43	**16.17**	**19.20**	**16.40**
craft	51	**19.17**	**30.70**	**12.70**
professional	13	**4.89**	**2.60**	**3.30**
gentleman	48	**18.05**	**1.79**	**3.32**
no title	3	**1.13**	**3.11**	**22.38**
total	266	266	8117	5058

mean 'retired on rentier income'. Many listed the property, usually urban cottages, houses and warehouses from which they drew their retirement income. For them, 'gentleman' was a life cycle stage rather than an indicator of social status.

The last group consisted of four individuals linked to the building trades, including a joiner and a stone mason. One, John Dufton, was a major owner of working class housing, including the notorious Boot and Shoe Yard in central Leeds, which was already being pointed to by public health reformers as a source of disease.[4] He had a large number of cottages in Richmond Hill, York St and the Boot and Shoe Yard, as well as a tenement in Marsh Lane, 'where I now live'. In 1822, he was a furniture broker in Marsh Lane; in 1825, a general broker, at 9 Dufton's Court, Marsh Lane. His son, George Dufton, was listed as a bricklayer living at 43 Bridge St, Lady Lane. These 'gentlemen' were property developers.

The term 'gentleman' had begun its life in the sixteenth century with a fairly strict legal definition. By 1700, its meaning had already widened.[5] By the 1830s, it still implied someone who had an independent income or an income from property, but this claim had lost all meaning in terms of links with traditional society. The gentlemen of Leeds ranged from a lawyer with a game licence and retired merchants to a slum landlord whose property entered Leeds history by way of every public health report produced between 1832 and 1850.

The sworn value of probate was a product of a specific part of the probate process. Used with care and an understanding of the process which produced it, sworn value provided an indicator of socio-economic status and structure.

Amongst the most important obligations of executors and administrators was the payment of probate and legacy duties. These were required by laws consolidated in the Stamp Act of 55 Geo. 3. Executors and administrators were 'required by the Stamp Act to swear to the gross value of the personal estate without any deduction for debts'.[6] This had

---

[4] R. Baker, *Report of the Leeds Board of Health* (Leeds, 1833); R. Baker, Report upon the condition of the Town of Leeds and of its Inhabitants, by a Statistical Committee of the Town Council, October 1839, *Journal of the Statistical Society of London* 2 (1839), 397–424; R. Baker, *On the State and Condition of the Town of Leeds in the West Riding of the County of York* (Leeds, 1842). This was reprinted in the *Local Reports on the Sanitary Condition of the Labouring Population directed to be made by the Poor Law Commissioners* (London, 1842), no. 23, pp. 348–407.

[5] P. Earle, *The Making of the English Middle Class. Business, Society and Family Life in London, 1660–1730* (London, 1989), pp. 5–12; Chapters by K. Wrightson and G. Crossick in P. Corfield (ed.), *Language, History and Class* (Oxford, 1991), pp. 30–52 and 150–78.

[6] J.C. Hudson, *The Executors Guide* (London, 1838), p. 21.

to be done within six months of death or a penalty of £100 was due. If property was held in both provinces then two sets of sworn values and probate duty must be provided. Sworn values in the York records did not include property held in the province of Canterbury. This was an important omission because property held in the funds and shares in companies with head offices in London were theoretically counted as being in Canterbury. An examination of the Death Duty records suggested that, in practice, there were very few estates which were 'sworn' in both prerogative courts.[7] Sworn value included only personal property. All freehold of land and buildings was excluded. This was important as many amongst the Leeds middle class had substantial holdings of freehold urban housing and cottage property. Hudson reminded executors that personal estate included all leasehold property and any freehold real estate that was contracted to be sold. The position with partnership capital was complex.

If the testator were a partner in any house of trade, his share in any real estate belonging to the firm, as having been purchased with partnership property is to be included. But in the case of partnership, the executor is not to include the whole gross amount of the testator's share of the partnership property, but must obtain from the surviving partners a balance sheet, exhibiting both the property and liabilities of the firm, and the sum to be included in the estimate of the testator's property will be his share of the net balance only.[8]

Any fixtures were real estate but Hudson added helpfully,

Manure in a heap, as usually laid up preparatory to its being spread upon the land, is personal estate . . . (as were crops and timber) when severed from the land.[9]

Once the sworn value had been notified, probate tax was charged under an irregular series of tax bands. The sum actually entered in the probate was thus not the estimated value but the upper bound of the tax band within which the executor believed the estate would fall. When the full estate had been gathered in and debts paid then the executors could claim a rebate from the tax office or pay extra together with a penalty if they had under-estimated. Sworn value was not a direct measure or valuation of an individual's assets, even at the time of death. The relationship was,

Net value of assets at time of death = Sworn value in province of York – Liabilities + Value of real estate + Value of personal property held in province of Canterbury.

---

[7] This statement was based on an examination for the sample years of IR 27, The Indexes to the Death Duty Registers and IR 26, The Death Duty Registers. See J. Cox, *Wills, Inventories and Death Duties* (London: The Public Record Office, 1988), p. 36.
[8] J.C. Hudson, *The Executors Guide*, p. 21.
[9] J.C. Hudson, *The Executors Guide*.

Table 3.3 *Occupational status and average sworn value of probate, Leeds 1830–34*

Occupational status	N	Mean	Median	Coefficient of variation[a]
Commerce	34	4842	1500	1.30
Gentleman	51	2427	450	1.69
Professional	13	2077	800	1.25
Manufacturing	46	1443	100	3.29
No title	71	1235	450	1.92
Distribution	51	985	200	2.22
Miscellaneous	8	740	325	1.80
White collar	12	720	200	1.53
Yeoman	15	611	100	2.09
Craft	56	460	100	2.12
Wage labour	5	162	50	1.52
Total	362	1575	300	2.25

[a] Standard deviation/mean

Despite this, sworn value remained a useful indicator. When compared with that other indicator of socio-economic status, occupational title, the mean of sworn value produced the same sort of rank order as other evaluations, such as participation in the poll book listings and contribution to charitable subscription lists. Commerce led, followed by professionals and gentlemen. Within occupational categories, sworn value showed the same distribution as with other indicators. The manufacturers had by far the greatest spread of status, as they did with other measures.[10] The comparison of the mean and median showed massive skewed inequality in all groups, as in the sample as a whole. There was a large number of modest sized estates, together with a few large estates which affected the mean.

Two hypothetical examples illustrate the difficulties. In the first a manufacturer dies prematurely with an active business. He has substantial working capital and large liabilities to his suppliers, no partnership and has just begun to purchase real estate. His older brother dies aged sixty, a gentleman, retired from business with considerable household furniture, cash in the bank and extensive real property from which he draws income. The merchant has a sworn value of £10,000, his gentleman brother £3,000, but once the merchant's executors have paid his trade

---

[10] Morris, *Class, Sect and Party*, pp. 134 and 220–1.

debts (£8,000) even with the addition of the net worth of his real estate (£2,000), the net worth of the merchant will be only £4,000, whilst his retired older brother, sworn value £3,000 had few debts (£1000) and real estate with a net value of £10,000, net worth £12,000. The relationship between sworn value and net worth changed with life cycle stage. It also varied with the propensity to invest in real rather than personal property. If this was a matter of personal preference then there would be little problem about estimating the relative economic status of groups, but some groups, notably shopkeepers and craftsmen, had a higher preference for real property. In some areas of the country the prevalence of leaseholds meant that a real property preference would be recorded in sworn value whilst in other areas it would not.

Sworn value provided an account of the distribution of economic status across the death cohort of Leeds in the early 1830s (Table 3.4). The overall distribution was typical of income and wealth distributions across capitalist commercial and industrial societies. Even amongst property holders, a minority of the adult population, the distribution of wealth was very unequal. The distribution was skewed with a substantial number of modest accumulations of wealth and a long tail of small numbers in the larger categories (Fig. 3.2).[11] The 1829 Stamp Duty receipts for 1829 were published for the whole of Great Britain.[12] The distribution was very much the same shape although Leeds lacked the very large estates which were present on the national scale.

Although women had only 27 per cent of the probates involved in the sample, the average sworn value of each probate was not very different from that of the men (Table 3.5). The difference between male and female sworn values lay in the spread of the distribution. Women had a greater tendency to have estates of middle value (sworn value £2,000–£3,000 upper limit) whilst men had a greater percentage of their estates in the very large and the small categories. Evidence presented later suggested that men had a greater propensity to own real estate but also had higher debt levels.

Those whose estates were brought to probate between 1830 and 1834 were a minority of the death cohort of Leeds in those years. They were male dominated but included an important minority of women. Compared with other listings of property holders, the group who came to probate had some

[11] A.B. Atkinson, *The Economics of Inequality* (Oxford, 1975); Royal Commission on the Distribution of Income and Wealth, chaired by Lord Diamond. *Report no.1, Initial Report on the Standing Reference* (London: HMSO Cmnd 6171, 1975), for accounts of income and wealth distributions.
[12] Stamp Duty received in the year 1829, *Parliamentary Papers* (1830), 25.

Table 3.4 *Distribution of sworn value of probate, Leeds 1830–34*

Sworn value (upper limit)	Male		Female		Total	
	N	%	N	%	N	%
20	32	11.8	14	13.6	46	12.3
50	9	3.3	7	6.8	16	4.3
100	62	22.9	15	14.6	77	20.6
200	41	15.1	10	9.7	51	13.7
300	8	3.0	8	7.8	16	4.3
450	26	9.6	9	8.7	35	9.4
600	10	3.7	6	5.8	16	4.3
800	12	4.4	6	5.8	18	4.8
1000	9	3.3	2	1.9	11	3.0
1500	12	4.4	5	4.9	17	4.6
2000	4	1.5	9	8.7	13	3.5
3000	12	4.4	5	4.9	17	4.6
4000	5	1.9	1	1.0	6	1.6
5000	5	1.9	1	1.0	6	1.6
6000	4	1.5	0	0.0	4	1.1
7000	3	1.1	0	0.0	3	0.8
8000	2	0.7	1	1.0	3	0.8
9000	3	1.1	0	0.0	3	0.8
10000	4	1.5	0	0.0	4	1.1
12000	0	0.0	2	1.9	2	0.5
14000	2	0.7	2	1.9	4	1.1
16000	2	0.7	0	0.0	2	0.5
18000	2	0.7	0	0.0	2	0.5
25000	1	0.4	0	0.0	1	0.3
30000	1	0.4	0	0.0	1	0.3

bias towards high status commercial and professional people and an under-representation of shopkeepers and craftsmen. The prominence of 'gentlemen' was a product of the end of life cycle nature of the probates.

Law, custom and practice

In essence, the wills in this sample were lists of instructions prepared within a framework of law, custom and practice. The law was crucial as wills could be challenged in the courts of equity and common law and needed to be validated in the ecclesiastical courts. The manner in which the wills were signed and witnessed and the inclusion of certain key

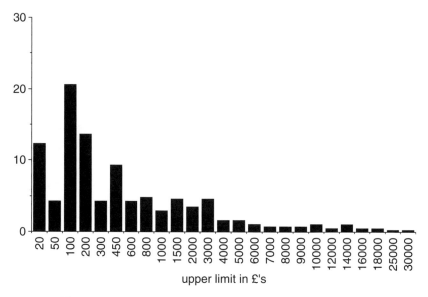

Fig. 3.2 Percentage distribution of sworn value of probate, Leeds 1830–34.

Table 3.5 *Average value of male and female sworn probate, Leeds 1830–34*

	Mean	Median
Female	£1267	£300
Male	£1624	£200

phrases were a product of this awareness of law. The law itself imposed key limitations on the type of instruction which could be included. Secondly the wills were framed within the custom of the ecclesiastical courts. With slight variations between the provinces of York and Canterbury, the custom of the ecclesiastical courts required that a third of the estate should be devoted to the care of the children, a third to the care of the widow and a third was the dead's part. In other words there was a freedom of choice here. The legal force of this custom had been abolished by statute at the start of the eighteenth century. None the less, the majority of the wills followed this type of formula very closely. Lastly, the will maker was influenced by the practices available within the middle classes. These can be identified through content analysis of the wills.

English law had two important features for the will maker. The law recognised the implementation of a will as being about intentions. Unlike all other property deeds, the courts attempted to give priority to the intentions of the testator rather than the strict interpretation of the language used. The debates surrounding the mild reforms of the law regarding wills in 1838 were centred upon the need to improve the courts ability to implement the 'intentions of the testator.'[13]

English law insisted on due process but, within that, gave considerable freedom to the testator. This freedom had emerged in the sixteenth century and had been completed by the legislation of the early eighteenth century.[14] Some commentators imagined the return of a Saxon freedom abolished by the military feudal tenures of the Norman conquest. Samuel Gale of Lincoln's Inn imagined a middle class version of the Norman Yoke,

> The nation seems to have undergone a relapse into barbarism at the Conquest, and to have had to retrace many stages in the way of recovery, in order to arrive at that degree of wholesome enjoyment of property which they had attained in Saxon times.[15]

The English discussed the law and practice of their will making and inheritance with general satisfaction. It was an aspect of advancement, improvement and civilisation. The experience of other nations, especially the French and the Irish, was regarded with pity and scorn. Reforms needed were minor and designed to make the system work better.

This freedom under the law meant that reading the text of these wills makes it possible to watch individuals making choices guided only by opportunity, custom and practice. What was remarkable was the degree to which those in the same sort of situation made the same sort of choices. The wills were one of the few life cycle decision points which were documented in the courts of England at this period in a reasonably systematic and consistent manner. Unlike many court documents, they were not created in the process of expressing, mediating and settling

---

[13] H.J. Stephens, Sergeant at Law, *New Commentaries on the Laws of England*, 4 vols. (London, 1841), vol. I, p. 544; Thomas, *A Treatise on Wills*, second edition by E.P. Wolstenholm and S. Vincent, 2 vols. (London, 1855), vol. I, p. 12; Inquiry into the Practice and Jurisdiction of the Ecclesiastical Courts of England and Wales (1831–32), *Parliamentary Papers*, House of Lords (1856), 36, p. 36; Second Reading of the Wills Bill, House of Lords, *Hansard Parliamentary Debates*, 3rd series, 36, 23 February 1837, cols. 964–9.

[14] H. Swinburne, *A Treatise of Testaments and Last Wills*, 7th edition with annotations of the late John Joseph Powell. (London, 1803), vol. I, pp. 300–2.

[15] First Report by the Commissioners appointed to inquire into the Law of England respecting real property, *Parliamentary Papers*, House of Lords (1830), 269, p. 109.

conflict, but were part of the process of reaffirming order through the recreation of key sets of social relationships after the death of a principal actor. In doing this, the maker of the last will and testament identified and affirmed key features of social reality, expressed values and affections, sustained life cycle strategies but, above all, would endeavour to lay down the terms for reestablishing order after death.

Given the privileged nature of this window on the relationships of property, family and the individual, it is important to ask and to understand the nature of the action involved in making a will. The will was not simply a document giving information on such relationships. It was a part of those relationships.

There was surprisingly little contemporary debate on the nature of will making given the central importance of will making, inheritance and their related legal processes to the orderly reproduction of middle class social and property relationships, and given the considerable potential for confusion in the legal arrangements. Most saw these matters as aspects of law and morality, a duty and part of maintaining the social order but went no further than that.[16] The most coherent statements came from the lawyers with a variety of contributions from political economists, philosophers and moralists. Even this discussion tended to be partial, uncritical and, at times, perverse for anyone, contemporary or historian, seeking guidance as to what was in the minds of the middle classes or their legal and ideological advisors when they made their wills.

In part, the answers can be derived from context, both the specific context of the urban commercial industrial society that was northern England in the 1820s and 1830s as well as the generic context of the individual contemplating death and, in part, from the behavioural evidence embedded in the text of the wills.

Another commentary was provided by the novels of the period, but this was a commentary of a very specific kind. The novel as a cultural form reached its full development in this period. Inheritance and the making of wills formed a recurrent theme, second only to the big themes of relationships between men and women, between parents and children, marriage, property and social class. The importance of wills and inheritance in the novel was one sign of underlying middle class anxieties on these matters. The novels need to be read with care. They were not social rapportage. In novel after novel, from *David Copperfield* (Charles Dickens, 1849–50) and *Dombey and Son* (Dickens, 1847–48) to *Middlemarch* (George Eliot,

---

[16] W. Paley, 'Moral and political philosophy', in *The Works of William Paley, DD, Archdeacon of Carlisle* (London, 1851), book 3, ch. 23.

1871–72) and *The Woman in White* (Wilkie Collins, 1860), wills and inheritance were central to the tension of the narrative. These novels were not textbooks or accounts of how the middle classes behaved. In fact they were usually accounts of how NOT to behave. The novels were social parables indicating the chaos which followed an ill made, ill intentioned, perverse or negligently made will. What then was an individual doing when they made a will?

There was considerable potential for making a will to be a quasi religious action, a sort of secular sacrament, especially in a period when evangelical thought was dominant. Despite the involvement of the ecclesiastical courts and the nature of early modern wills, with their complex, if often opaque and formulaic religious declarations,[17] the English wills of the early nineteenth century were intensely secular documents. The *Christian Observer*, the leading evangelical periodical, urged the sacred nature of the task.

A man draws up a deed, emphatically termed his last will and testament; that is, the last expression of his mind; the final act of his life; the final act of being, who, at the very moment it becomes of force, is himself in eternity; far out of the reach of all worldly considerations.[18]

The periodical urged that a will should start with the words 'In the name of God …'. Only ten in the Leeds sample took any notice of this. Thomas Gill, labourer, was exceptional, 'In the name of God Amen … being somewhat indisposed of body but of a sound and disposing mind memory and understanding … I recommend my soul to Almighty God who gave it and my body to the earth from whence it was taken to be decently interred'. William Atkinson, senior, fishmonger made his will 'By permission of God', whilst Thomas Barker, yeoman, declared 'In the name of God Amen … being of sound mind but considering the uncertainty of this life'. A much larger number took care like George Austin, butcher, to declare that they were 'in full possession of all my rational faculties, of sound memory and clear understanding'.[19] This was wise as one of the grounds for challenging the validity of a will was a claim that the testator

---

[17] C. Marsh, 'In the name of God? Will-making and faith in early modern England', in G.H. Martin and P. Spufford (eds.), *The Records of the Nation* (Woodbridge, 1990), pp. 215–50; C. Cross, 'Wills as evidence of popular piety in the Reformation period. Leeds and Hull, 1540–1640', in D. Loades (ed.), *The End of Strife* (Edinburgh, 1984), pp. 40–50; M. Spufford, *Contrasting Communities. English Villagers in the Sixteenth and Seventeenth Centuries* (Cambridge, 1974), pp. 320–44.

[18] *Christian Observer* (April 1811), p. 230.

[19] These wills are all in the Borthwick Institute of Historical Research in York. The Leeds wills were all in the Prerogative Court or the Court of Ainstey. The dates given are the

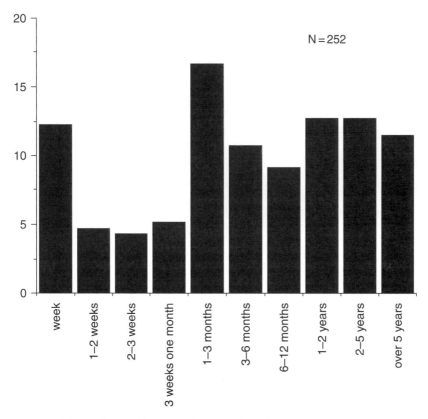

Fig. 3.3 Interval between the date of a will and the date of death, Leeds, 1830–34 (% of total).

was not fully rational at the time of making it.[20] For most, the prose was stark and utilitarian.

This was despite the fact that many wills were made close to death, and the drama of death, especially for evangelicals, was important to religious life. Of the 252 wills for which both date of death and the date of the will were known, 36 were made within ten days of death, 83 within 50 days. Just over half were made within six months of death.

---

dates on which these wills were brought for probate. Thomas Gill, 25 June 1832; William Atkinson, 11 April 1832; Thomas Barker, 3 February 1832 and George Austin, 9 February 1831.

[20] Sir W. Blackstone, *Commentaries on the Law of England*, 18th edition with the last corrections of the author and copious notes by Thomas Lee, Esq. 4 vols. (London, 1829), vol. II, pp. 375 and 489–510.

This was a matter of great concern to some contemporaries. Will making was often left to the last minute. Great confusion could be caused by the 'agitation of mind commonly attendant on death bed scenes'. As Lord Langdale put it in the House of Lords, 'moments too often of agitation, debility and destitution, when a man may not be able to procure the assistance which, at another period, he might have commanded and when he may be surrounded by interested and artful persons, willing, if they safely can, to withdraw the testator's estate from the proper objects of his bounty'.[21] The *Christian Observer,* with evangelical directness, attacked 'procrastination' when,

Sudden deaths are not unknown. Health, as well as life, is continually in danger: and in the last sickness the powers of the mind are not unfrequently so much enfeebled by the weakened state of the body[22]

There were, as the Lord Chancellor recognised in 1837, good legal reasons for making, or at least remaking, a will close to death. Under English law as it then stood, a will was only valid for real property which was seized or possessed at the time of making the will. Thus, any real property purchased between the date of the will and death was treated as if the individual had been intestate.[23] For a woman, any will she made was made invalid by marriage, but widowhood might, as in several cases in the Leeds sample, create a need for a new will. For a man, marriage, at least before 1838, did not invalidate his will, but marriage and the birth of a child did.[24] For some, an awareness of the complexities of the law and an evangelical preoccupation with death meant that the strategies for family and property embodied in a will were being continually reassessed as real estate was accumulated and the family advanced from one life cycle stage to another. The reasons, like the prose, were secular and utilitarian.

All wills were in the first place a settling of accounts. William Mawson of Burmantofts Grove, aqua fortis manufacturer, was one of many who began, 'I will and direct that all my just debts, funeral expenses and the charges of proving and registering this my will be in the first place fully paid and discharged'.[25] In his advice manual, J.C. Hudson gave careful

---

[21] J.C. Hudson, *Plain Directions for Making Wills in Conformity with the Law* (London, 1859), p. 13; Inquiry into the Practice and Jurisdiction of the Ecclesiastical Courts, p. 32; Second Reading of the Wills Bill, *Hansard,* 23 February 1837, col. 968.

[22] 'On the duty and mode of making a will', *Evangelical Magazine,* July 1811, 419.

[23] Lord Langdale, Second Reading of the Wills Bill, col. 983.

[24] Fourth report by the Commissioners appointed to inquire into the Law of England respecting real property, *Parliamentary Papers,* House of Lords (1833), 316 (56 of 1833), p. 13; Second Reading of the Wills Bill, cols. 966–8.

[25] Will of William Mawson, 11 March 1831.

instructions to executors, for the law required a strict order of priorities for the payment of debts. Debts to the Crown came first, then money owing to the parish or a friendly society. Next were debts due under judgements in the Court of Chancery and then at the Assize. Debts under bond or mortgage followed, whilst last, and usually most numerous, were debts under simple contract. The wages of servants and labourers had priority.[26] It was one of the oddities of English probate law that only personal property was liable for debts of simple contract.[27] If the residue of an estate was inadequate, then the executors took money from the specific legacies, but they could not dispose of real estate to pay debts of simple contract unless the will specifically empowered them to do so. On the settling of accounts the *Christian Observer* was as didactic as ever.

The payment of just debts ... should be provided for in the amplest manner. By the laws of England, real estates are not liable to the payment of debts incurred by simple contract, that is, those by oral evidence, or by notes that are unsealed. But if a man willfully omit this direction in his will, with a view to prevent his creditors from receiving their right, it has been justly said, he dies with a deliberate fraud in his heart, and leaves an indelible stain on his character.[28]

In some wills, arrangements were made to complete land purchases or to settle mortgage debts.[29] In others, instructions were given that specific debts were to be forgiven or to be taken as part of an individual's share in the estate.

One thing upon which the advice manual writers and the mainstream evangelicals of the *Christian Observer* were agreed upon was that making a will was a duty. Making a will should be done in good time to avoid confusion and to 'afford the best possible chance of avoiding litigation'.[30] At one level, the purpose and function of the will making and probate was very simple. It was a means of organising the transfer of property and authority at death within the law and according to the wishes of the testator. At a more general level, making a will was to ensure order in social and property relationships following a death. This notion of duty was closely related to the notion of the right to make a will. Blackstone, the jurist, and McCulloch, Professor of Political Economy at Edinburgh University, both rejected the notion that

---

[26] J.C. Hudson, *The Executors Guide*, p. 43.

[27] First Report by the Commissioners appointed to inquire into the Law of England respecting real property, *Parliamentary Papers*, House of Lords (1830), 269, p. 58.

[28] *Christian Observer* (July 1811), 421.

[29] For example James Furbank, gentleman, he whose father had conveyed a parcel of land to him so that he was qualified to shoot game.

[30] J.C. Hudson, *Plain Directions*, Introduction.

inheritance and the right to make a will had any basis in natural law or natural justice. The Real Property Commissioners saw the freedom to dispose of property at death as an aspect of the rights of property and McCulloch went even further.

The ability to make testamentary bequests, to transmit our property to those who occupy the chief place in our affections, or to who we have been under obligations is indispensable to the advancement of society in wealth and civilization.[31]

Like many of the lawyers, Lee in his commentaries on Blackstone, considered Locke's view that property rights originated with occupancy and the mixing of labour with natural resources and concluded that this had no part in justifying inheritance. Lee agreed with Archdeacon Paley that the right to make a will originated in the need for civil order.

Wills, therefore, and testaments, rights of inheritance and successions, are all of them creatures of the civil or municipal law...the legislature of England has universally promoted the grand ends of civil society, the peace and security of individuals, by steadily pursuing that wise and orderly maxim, of assigning to everything capable of ownership a legal and determinate owner.[32]

The real foundation of the right to make a will was the law.[33]

In both a legal and economic sense, the will was a contract of a very particular kind. A contract, by its nature, is a voluntary agreement of two or more parties whereby something is to be given or performed upon one part for a valuable and specific consideration present or future. The will had many of the properties of the contract. It had precision and involved exchange and enforceability. The will was a matter for the courts of law and had an important effect on property transfer, capital structuring and the maintaining of inequalities. However, the concept of contract applied to a will only in a partial fashion because, by its nature, the 'contract' became operational when one party to the bargain was dead. Enforceability was by proxy and demand and supply schedules of economic logic were hard to define.

There was some evidence of bargaining from beyond the grave. Four will makers were essentially bargaining with their sons to ensure a continuity of the income stream that would fulfil their obligations to a widow and younger children. Joseph Wood, gentleman, late of Smithfield Bars in London, but now living in Woodhouse, put the matter most directly. His eldest son was given several advantages. He

---

[31] J.R. McCulloch, *A Treatise on the Succession of Property Vacant by Death* (London, 1847), p. 10; *Eclectic Review*, new series, IV (1852), 187.

[32] Blackstone, *Commentaries*, vol. II, pp. 2 and 15.

[33] Paley, 'Moral and Political Philosophy', in *The Works*, book 3, ch. 4.

could borrow up to £1000 interest free from the trustees of the estate and he could purchase Joseph's real estate in Woodhouse for £500 under valuation 'to induce him to act and in the hope that he will act as a protector and friend to his younger brothers and sisters'. At the other end of the status scale, Edmund Craister, boot and shoemaker, devised his real estate in the Leylands to his eldest son, Edmund, and specified that his widow would either live with Edmund or have one of the ten cottages rent free plus £25 a year from the rents, so long as she remained a widow. In return, Edmund got the cottages and the business assets plus 'my silver pint'. The other brothers and sisters got a legacy of £80 each plus a share of the silver spoons. William Pawson, wealthy merchant manufacturer of Farnley, sworn value under £25,000, devised all his real estate to his only son, but left it heavily burdened with obligations to widow and daughters. These burdens were carefully phased so that the business and estate were not overstretched. The estate was liable for £9000 to be invested for the benefit of widow and daughters, but £3000 of this was to be paid after two years, and his son had the option to retain £6000 at interest if he thought fit. William Harrison, spirit merchant, sworn value under £7000, assigned his business to his wife and son Thomas as trustees, with instruction 'to continue and carry on my said trade of a spirit merchant until the youngest of my children shall attain the age of twenty one years'. Thomas was to have a quarter of the profits for the first seven years and half thereafter. William's widow was to have an annuity of £200 a year, reducing to £50 if she remarried. This annuity was a charge upon the 'rents and profits of the estate' to which the business as well as the sale of real and personal estate was to contribute.[34] These arrangements favoured one son, but always as part of an implicit bargain with the dead. This was an economic model of inheritance whereby one child gained an advantage in return for ensuring that the obligations of the dead towards widow and younger children were fulfilled.

There was sometimes a sense in which individuals were rewarded for services rendered during the life of the testator. This was more common in wills made by women. Thus, Isabel Dugdale, widow, with a sworn value of £800, directed that one nephew, William Holmes, should receive some named items of furniture and have the option to buy the silver spoons at cost 'as a small acknowledgement of his kindness to my late

---

[34] The wills and dates of probate were Joseph Wood, 4 June 1831; Edmund Craister, 5 December 1831; William Pawson, 31 December 1831 and William Harrison, 7 October 1831.

husband'.[35] When Ann Headlam died in 1834, her niece Mary Oates was duly rewarded for many visits paid to her Aunt when she was sick. Mary received a legacy which included the linen, books, wine, wearing apparel and ornaments as well as a half share of the residual, which amounted to £145.[36] George Eliot knew all about such implicit bargains. As Rosamund Vincy says in *Middlemarch*, '. . . I would rather not have anything left to me if I must earn it by enduring much of my uncle's cough and his ugly relations'.[37]

These transactions were not true contracts. There was no price or formal bargain. If Mary Oates had been left with nothing, no court of law could have intervened. The dominant feature of these transactions was that of the gift. In western capitalist society, the ideology of the gift suggests that such a transaction is a product of altruism, generosity and freewill. The sociology, anthropology and indeed practice of the gift is quite different. There is considerable and growing evidence that the growth of capitalist, money-based economic transactions over the past four centuries has been accompanied by the increasing importance of a gift economy. The gift economy has and had a number of key features. The gift has the immediate effect of creating a set of obligations and power relationships. In many cases a gift was met with a counter gift. Thus, the child's birthday present brings the thank you letter or phone call to granny. The gift of a dinner is met with the response of the bottle of wine. There is little about gift giving which is or was 'free'. Gifts are implied and required by key sets of social relationships and ritual, such as the child's birthday or the 'family' Christmas. The gift plays a key part in creating and maintaining social relationships. Indeed the family or a network of friends might be defined by the gift-giving network. At times the gifts have considerable value and substance. At other times, they are largely symbolic, like the Christmas card or the, usually male, circle buying alcoholic drinks for each other. Workplace relationships, professional and business alliances and neighbourly relations were and are all sustained in this way. Current evidence is that women give and receive gifts more than men and that this is related to their relative lack of power in the cash economy. Women do have a major culture of giving minor presents but many males probably fail to recognise their own gift networks, the drink with the lads or the mutual helping out with DIY. Gifts

---

[35] Isabel Dugdale, probate 17 September 1831.
[36] Legacy Receipt on account of the personal estate of Ann Headlam, 13 April 1835, Oates Papers.
[37] G. Eliot, *Middlemarch* (London 1871–2), Penguin Library Edition (London, 1965), ch. 11, p. 129.

need to be appropriate. What is given and not given is controlled and judgements passed in terms of the social structures involved and what is appropriate to maintain those key social structures. The grandparent who tried to compete for a child's affection by giving a present that is 'too expensive' will soon become the object of deep resentment. The politician or civil servant who accepted a costly gift from a potential contractor invited even greater trouble.[38]

This account of the gift comes very close to the transactions involved in the will and its related processes. As with the contract, the gift in the will is asymmetrical. One party by definition does not gain directly. This was true in the sense that the self-aware biological agent was dead, but the gift in the will could operate well beyond biological death. Obligations were created, identities affirmed. In the 1830s, the widespread use of trusts meant that the name and wishes of the testator lasted many years after death. Specific bequests often served to keep identities alive. 'My' picture was bequeathed to a son. The silver spoons marked with family initials were carefully distributed. 'My' music or a bible would be passed on with care. The skill with which a will was constructed affected the reputation of the maker for many years after death in exactly the same way as a gift created obligations and reputations. This showed in many of the novels. The ceremony of 'reading the will' was a ritual and a drama which had its own rules, like the opening of presents at Christmas or birthday. The fiction of the surprise had to be maintained. It was wrong to be 'openly reckoning on your property coming to them', said Mrs Maule as she tried to turn her brother against the Vincys when it came to will making in *Middlemarch*.[39] The will was judged by its ability to affirm and strengthen relationships. In the novel the will which did not meet expectations was a potent source of chaos. The 'second will' was a turning point in *Middlemarch*, not because it failed to reward worthwhile people like Mary Garth, but also in the failure of expectations of people like Fred Vincy. Fred must go into the church, he thought, and Mary seek another situation. There was an element of luck, which was ironical at the centre of a world ruled by an ethic of individuals rewarded for moral worth and hard work. Samuel Smiles and the evangelicals had a marginal place in such distributions.

Like gift giving, the making of the will took place within the law but was not directed by the law. It was directed by a sense of moral obligation, legitimacy and custom, and by an acute and dynamic sense of social

---

[38] M. Godelier, *The Enigma of the Gift* (Cambridge, 1999); A.E. Komter (ed.), *The Gift. An Interdisciplinary Perspective* (Amsterdam, 1996).
[39] Eliot, *Middlemarch*, ch. 12, p. 134.

structure. The interpretation of the will in terms of the sociology of gift giving fits with contemporaries' own versions of what they were doing.

Because of the freedom given to the English will maker, there were considerable opportunities for the expression of self and the imposition of authority and judgement. There was an opportunity to discipline children. Debate worried about the wisdom of this and the danger of failing to fulfil expectations. All commentators were aware that there might be an argument for a law which required individuals to take responsibility for widows and children.[40] The disobedient heir played a crucial part in the argument. Indeed, Blackstone saw this as one of the reasons for the growth in freedom.

At length it was found, that so strict a rule of inheritance made heirs disobedient and headstrong, defrauded creditors of their just debts, and prevented many provident fathers from dividing or charging their estates as the exigence of their families required.[41]

Lee quoted Paley with approval to the effect that it was quite acceptable to disinherit a son who was a waster even if this seemed to many to be against 'natural justice'.[42] Even the evangelical moralists of the *Christian Observer* gave cautious support to the view that freedom in will making had a useful and just potential for social discipline.

If one child by a long continuance in misbehaviour, have embittered a parent's life, and greatly marred his comforts; and if, in addition to this, no signs can be discovered of his returning to a right conduct, it must certainly be, both just and proper to make a difference between this child and others who have uniformly behaved dutifully and affectionately. But, even in the worst of these cases, an abandoned child is still a child, and some provision should, if possible, be made for him. His present or future wife, also, with such a family as may descend from him, should be remembered and provided for; the utmost care being taken to prevent the portion which is left to him, or to them, from being squandered or misapplied by his prodigality or imprudence.[43]

McCulloch admitted that there was some attraction in the argument that the law should require a father to make some provision,

for those he has been the means of bringing into this world . . . independently altogether of any considerations of personal merit, he is under the most sacred obligations.

[40] 'Considerations on the Law of Entail, London 1823', *Edinburgh Review* 40 (1824), 350–75.
[41] Blackstone, *Commentaries*, vol. II, p. 11.
[42] Blackstone, *Commentaries*, vol. II, p. 14.
[43] 'On the duty and mode of making a will', *Christian Observer* (July 1811), 423.

but concluded that anything but total freedom would 'render most people less anxious about the accumulation of wealth' and that

the securing some provision for children, without reference to their conduct, would in so far make them independent, and weaken that parental authority, which, though sometimes abused, is, in the vast majority of instances, exercised in the most indulgent manner, and with best effect.[44]

He concluded that 'The humanity of the law is but a sorry substitute for parental affection' and decided that 'the opinions and feelings of society' were the best guard against injustice to 'well behaved' children. In other words social and moral pressure should dictate the detailed arrangements of each will.

The evangelicals wanted to see more judgemental and discriminating will making. In April 1811, an executor made a direct attack on both primogeniture and 'share and share alike', in other words the practice of strict equality between all children. The will maker did not question this arrangement because 'he has only done what is perpetually done by others'. The writer claimed that,

injury grows out of an inconsiderate disregard to differences, in respect of health, talents, connections, and misconduct, which are so obviously perceptible among individuals of the same family.[45]

The moral will maker, it was suggested, would favour the sick, would favour daughters who had not married wealth and discriminate against sons who had wasted money; '"share and share alike" is, in reality, the sheet anchor of speculators and libertines'. The writer recommended that wives should have first call on the will maker, but that daughters in general should be more favoured than sons. 'Women are dependant and comparatively helpless'; daughters should be 'secure from the storms of the world', whilst sons should have enough to 'enable them to fight their own way . . . it is by no means to their moral disadvantage, if they are compelled to eat the bread of industry'.[46] Later that year, XYZ contributed some practical remarks on will making which reinforced the claims of wives and children. It was not until September 1814 that the case against discriminating between children was put. The original writer had admitted that many objected.

If you make a partial distribution among your children, you will infallibly create discord. They will hate each other; and your memory will not be blessed.

---

[44] McCulloch, *A Treatise*, pp. 11 and 13.
[45] 'On the moral construction of wills', *Christian Observer* (April 1811), 226.
[46] 'On the moral construction of wills', 231.

He acknowledged that 'family dissension is doubtless a great and a very great evil'.[47]

PARENS claimed that it was the responsibility of surviving brothers and sisters to look after any unfortunate members of the family and dismissed any thought of injustice to women on the grounds that they could marry above themselves.[48] This aspect of the debate had considerable relevance to middle class practice in will making.

The potential will maker's power was immense and contemporary debate around this theme was considerable but, in general, there is little evidence that such power was used. There were only two clear examples in the Leeds sample. A family row blew across the pages of the will of James Young, woolstapler, of White Cote in the out-township of Bramley.[49] His wife was to have 'furniture as she may think proper to select and chuse for the purpose of furnishing a room'. All the rest was to go to his son, John, but charged with the payment of £18 a year to 'my dear wife Sarah' and £18 'to my daughter Jane now the wife of Andrew Ferguson for her life or so long and such time only as she shall live separate and apart from her husband . . . '. Using a will in this way was normally a mistake and damaged reputations. In *Middlemarch,* Casaubon tried to limit his wife's freedom to re-marry through a codicil in his will. His action was condemned: 'there never was a meaner, more ungentlemanly action than this'.[50] The potential may well have been very effective. Crawshay, the Welsh ironmaster, told his sons, they could do as they liked when he was dead but whilst he was alive they did as he wanted.[51] In *Middlemarch*, Featherstone told Fred Vincy 'I can alter my will yet' as a direct way of disciplining the young man over debts and gambling.

The will and its text were a representation of a social world and those relationships of great importance to the will maker. As a text, the will presented an enclosed universe of men and women, adults and children. Their relationships were defined by carefully chosen attributes: my daughter, my dear wife, my friend. These relationships were developed by the instructions of the will as objects, income streams and property rights were being allocated. As a representation, the will had powerful agency. It was a symbolic description of a world but, taking the model of the gift as being central, it was a symbolic account designed to describe, strengthen

[47] 'On the moral construction of wills', 230.
[48] 'On equity in wills', *Christian Observer* (September 1814), 564–6.
[49] Probate 18 December 1832.
[50] Eliot, *Middlemarch*, ch. 49, p. 526.
[51] J.P. Addis, *The Crawshay Dynasty. A Study of Industrial Organization and Development, 1765–1867* (Cardiff, 1957).

Table 3.6 *Type of provision for widows by the male will makers of Leeds,*
1830–34

Condition	COUNT	%
Absolute	23	17.56
Natural life	62	47.33
Reducing	14	10.69
Widowhood	31	23.66
For children	1	0.76

N = 131

and reorder that world. Such reordering and remaking was especially
important after a death, especially the death of a property holder.

How did the will maker select and demarcate the universe of the will and
relate this to the wider universe of social relationships and identities? For 131
(65 per cent) of the 202 male wills, the central relationship was that between
man and wife. All the men who mentioned a wife in their will made some
provision for her. There was no evidence that such provision was ever less
than that which would have been required by the custom of the ecclesiastical
courts when that custom was law. The relationship of man and wife embodied
in the will was defined not only by the nature of the provision but also by the
conditions which surrounded that provision. There were four major types.

(1) Absolute. The widow had absolute access to the estate.
(2) Natural Life. The widow had the income from the estate for the rest
    of her natural life, but with no power to dispose of the estate at her
    death or to intervene except in an informal way with the manner in
    which trustees managed the estate on her behalf.
(3) Reducers. The widow had the income from the estate for her natural
    life but this was reduced if she remarried.
(4) Widowhood. The income from the estate was granted for widowhood
    only and was lost if the woman remarried.
(5) There was one case in which the trust was established directly for the
    children.

The frequency of each of these types of provision showed a strong
preference for a trust which provided an income stream for the remainder
of a widow's life (Table 3.6).

Joseph Rollinson, joiner and builder, gave a simple instruction,

I give and devise unto my friends, John Hobson of Leeds aforsaid wood dealer
and David West of the same place joiner, all my freehold dwellings houses and
cottages situated in York Street and in Marsh Lane in Leeds aforesaid and all my
other real estate whatsoever To Hold the same unto the said John Hobson and

David West their heirs and assignees Upon Trust to permit my Said Wife to receive the Rents of my said real estate for her life[52]

Richard Kemplay, gentleman, a member of the Tory Anglican elite of Leeds, sworn value £16,000, had more resources and was more aware of the pitfalls of the law. He instructed that the residue of his estate be 'turned into cash' and invested 'at interest upon Government or satisfactory personal securities'. He specified an annuity of £400 a year,

to my said wife during the term of her natural life ... free from all encumbrances whatsoever to be paid into her own hands for her own sole and separate use independent of and wholly exempt from the debts, contract or engagements of any aftertaken husband, her receipt alone being considered a good and effectual discharge to my said trustees[53]

There were two major variants on this form of provision. A small number of men specified that the provision for their widow would be reduced if they remarried. John Benson, woolstapler, had a substantial estate with sworn value of £10,000. He instructed his executors 'to permit and suffer my dear wife Judith Benson to use and enjoy' the dwelling house in Carr Place and 'also all my Household Furniture, Plate, Linen, China and other effects of Household for and during her natural life if she shall so long continue my widow ...'. In addition she was to have an annuity of £150 a year. If she remarried, then the house and contents were to be sold and the annuity be reduced to £100 a year. This he directed

was to be accepted and taken by my said wife in satisfaction of all Dower and Thirds to which she may be entitled out of my said real estates, and ... shall be for her own sole and separate use free from the debts control or intermeddling of any husband she may take

The third and extremely varied group of those who established trusts in this way specified that on remarriage the widow would cease to benefit from the estate. William Grayson, cooper, had a modest estate, sworn value £200, and some real estate. His wife was to have use of 'my household goods'. He asked that the rest of his personal estate be invested 'on good real or government securities' and that his trustees

pay the interest, dividends and annual produce thereof together with the rents, issues and profits of my said real estate unto my said wife for and during the term of her natural life if she shall so long continue my widow but not otherwise[54]

---

[52] Probate 8 June 1830.
[53] Probate 16 May 1831.
[54] Probate 14 November 1832.

He then included instructions for his estate in the event of his widow's death or remarriage.

Of the male wills making provision for a widow, 107 (82 per cent) used the medium of the trust. It is impossible to make more than a crude guess at the amount of property which was involved. Such wills involved 55 per cent of the 'sworn value' acknowledged in the sample as well as real estate.

The use of the trust was, as McCulloch had suggested, an exercise of 'power beyond the grave'.[55] The reason lay more in the nature of married woman's property law than in any psychological desire to assert influence and identity beyond death. The nature of that law was well expressed in the 18th edition of Blackstone's *Commentaries on the Law of England*, which had been published in 1829, as many of the wills in the sample were being made.

By marriage, the husband and wife are one person in law: that is, the very being and legal existence of the woman is suspended during marriage, or at least incorporated and consolidated into that of the husband, under whose wing, protection and cover, she performs everything; and is therefore called in our law french, a *feme covert*... under the protection and influence of her husband, her baron or lord; and her condition during her marriage is called her *coverture*.[56]

In short, a married woman had no legal personality at common law and was unable to make contracts, to buy or sell property or even make a will. The few residual rights which remained to a married woman could easily be overidden by her husband and his lawyers. Indeed, several of the wills included clauses to ensure that a widow had no rights of dower. In theory, the principle of dower entitled a widow to a third of the value of any real property which she had brought into the marriage and of any real property which had been purchased during the marriage. Eighteenth century conveyancing practice had long ago devised ways of getting around this and the Dower of Act 1833 made this even easier. Even so, 10 per cent of the 131 male will makers who provided for a widow thought it worth while to bar dower.

The trust was a device to protect a widow's portion from any future husband. There were two motives for this. Women who had money were believed to be vulnerable to fortune hunters. The exploitation of a woman for her money was a frequent theme of novels and periodicals. The story of Mr Jingle in *Pickwick Papers* (Charles Dickens, 1836–37) represented the feared runaway marriage as a threat to family property. In Wilkie Collins's novel, *The Woman in White*, the penniless aristocrat seducing

[55] McCulloch, *A Treatise*, p.43.
[56] Blackstone, *Commentaries*, p.441.

the honest bourgeois fortune provided the villain. The answer to both was the trust, free of the 'intermeddling' of any future husband, for both widows and daughters. Even a successful and affectionate marriage needed some protection against the misfortunes of trade. The insecurity of trade and monetary fluctuations was a major factor in middle class conduct. The threat of bankruptcy was an important factor in the social, legal and domestic arrangements of the middle classes. James Traill Christie, in his advice to those writing a will, urged that property should be settled by a father on his married daughters by trust especially if the husband was in trade, 'however wealthy and whatever confidence the testator has in him'.[57]

Despite this firm advice and the received wisdom of the middle classes upon which it was based, 18 per cent of the men who left widows did not bother with the protection of any trust mechanism and made an absolute grant of all or part of their property to their widow. Characteristic of this group was Frederick Appleyard of Bramley in the out-townships of Leeds, who instructed his executors,

all other my monies and securities for money, stock in trade, book debts, cattle, chattels, personal estate and effects whatsoever unto and equally between my dear wife Elizabeth and my son William Appleyard to and for their own proper use and benefit respectively absolutely for ever.

George Austin, butcher of Leeds, decided that the residue of his estate after debts and funeral expenses had been paid 'shall become the Bonae Fide absolute and exclusive property of my said wife Mary Austin'. The wording suggests that they knew that what they were doing was against the grain of normal practice and they wanted to make sure their wishes were carried out. This group had a number of distinctive features. A large portion of them (52 per cent) mentioned no children in the will. Most of them had a low sworn value, and that mean value of £1255 was inflated by the rather odd will of William Tetley junior, which was sworn at under £14,000, but the will was dated 1800, when Tetley's wealth would have been much less than at his death.[58] Without this the overall mean would have been £675. In terms of occupation, there was a slight bias towards the lower status groups, notably retailing, although judgement was made difficult by the small cell totals in this table. Retailers were important in the absolute gift group, possibly because women had more active roles in

---

[57] J.T. Christie, *Concise Precedents of Wills with an Introduction and Practical Notes* (London, 1849), pp. 14–15.

[58] E. Sigsworth, *The Brewing Trade During the Industrial Revolution. The Case of Yorkshire*, Borthwick papers, no. 31 (York, 1967).

such businesses.[59] There was evidence of trust in the business and practical abilities of women amongst this group of men. In thirteen out of twenty-three cases, their wives were amongst the executors for the will. Even when children were mentioned, the wording suggested a mutual confidence. John King, victualler, was 'sure' that his wife would look after their only son. One or two cases, like that of Anthony Fox, the bone merchant valued under £100, simply ignored conventional wisdom and left everything to his wife, including the minor children. Other cases had individual features which picked them out, such as Tetley who had not revised his will for thirty years, and Joseph Cooper, the joiner, valued at under £20, who felt obliged to ensure that his wife Ann had 'all the furniture she brought with her on marriage viz two beds, bed linen, one dining table, one tea kettle, one breakfast table, six common chairs, one large folio bible, one large chest of drawers with a drawer in it and other small articles'. Finally, there was the will of Joseph Bottomley, yeoman, under £100, who left the residue of his personal estate and furniture to Martha Green, singlewoman. This must have requited an important relationship for the real estate was set out for the benefit of 'my natural daughter Esther Green'. The will gives no further hints as to the history of this alliance but Joseph treated Martha and Esther with the same responsibility as the rest treated wives and children.[60]

These choices implied a variety of ideological perspectives. The absolute gift seemed to reflect trust and autonomy for the women. The other choices matched McCulloch's view that the will maker was seeking power beyond the grave in two very different ways. The grant for 'natural life' fitted the concept of marriage as a partnership from which the wife got a share when the partnership was dissolved by death, together with protection from her vulnerability under the married women's property law. The grant of property for widowhood represented a view of marriage in which the male head accepted responsibility for his widow but only until she remarried, at which point the responsibility went to someone else. The reducers had a position between these two. Such thoughts may have been in the minds of some will makers but situational evidence indicated that many were influenced by the tension between their responsibilities to children and their responsibilities to wives. The manner in which this tension was resolved depended upon resources and personal circumstances as well as the ideological position of individuals. Analysis was

---

[59] Hall, *White, Male and Middle Class*, pp. 108–23.
[60] Dates of probate, Frederick Appleyard, 15 June 1831; George Austin, 9 February 1831; William Tetley, 8 October 1831; John King, 12 May 1830; Anthony Fox, 21 April 1831; Joseph Cooper, 15 June 1831 and Joseph Bottomley, 28 November 1832.

Table 3.7 *Provision for widows and children in Leeds male wills, 1830–34*

	No children	Children	Minors	All
Nature of provision for widow				
Absolute	13	7	2	22
	52.00	12.07	4.17	16.79
Natural life	12	36	15	63
	48.00	62.07	31.25	48.09
Reducers	0	3	11	14
	–	5.17	22.92	10.69
Widowhood or	0	12	19	31
natural life	–	20.69	39.58	23.66
Trust to child	0	0	1	1
	–	–	2.08	0.76
All	25	58	48	131

Note: Column percentages are given below each figure.

hindered by the lack of contemporary discussion of these issues. On the content of middle class wills, contemporary discussion was at best peripheral and at worst misleading.

The best guide to the logic of the decisions, which these men took in the face of death and the responsibilities they accepted for the care of wife and children, was the context of the decisions they took. Context was represented by the resources each man had available and sworn value was the best indicator of this. Context was also represented by the children who were mentioned in the wills. The wills have been divided into three, those which mentioned no children, those which mentioned children and those which indicated that the children were minors, either by stating they were under 21 years old or by making provision for their education or an apprenticeship fee. There may have been minor children in the second group of wills and this needs to be borne in mind in analysis.

Although cell sizes were often small and the fit was by no means perfect, the presence of children, and especially minor children, was a major influence on the choices made. Over half those who made an absolute transfer to a widow mentioned no children and most of the rest had adult children. The 'natural life' group was dominated by those with no children or those who made no mention of minors. Those with minor children tended to choose the widowhood option or to be reducer on re-marriage people.

Amongst those who limited their wife's income to widowhood, 60 per cent acknowledged minor children. They indicated their concern in a variety of ways. Thomas Cowlam, painter and varnish manufacturer (sworn value £200), directed that his 'dear wife Eleanor' was to benefit from the rents and profits of his real estate and the interest and dividends of money placed at interest, 'during her life or widowhood for the purpose of maintaining herself and educating and bringing up such children as I now have and which may be born in due time after my decease'.[61] Thomas Wareham, gentleman, gave his trustees permission to use the income from the respective shares of any of his children 'for and towards their respective maintenance and education or for placing them out as apprentices or clerks to any business or profession until they shall respectively attain the age of twenty one years'.[62] As this group of men faced death, their major worry was for the welfare of their minor children in the event of their widows re-marriage. Although the nineteenth century was very aware of the fate of orphans, there was little public discussion of the fate of the children of a first marriage in the context of a second marriage. This had curious parallels in the late twentieth century. The widespread public debate on 'single parent families' was accompanied by little discussion of children of one marriage in a subsequent marriage, despite fragments of evidence that this group was often the subject of abuse and educational under-achievement. The best nineteenth century text on the subject was the novel *David Copperfield* by Charles Dickens. The novel was an especially nasty listing of the many ways in which men and women could make each other miserable. Amongst this was the fate of young David. David's father left a pregnant widow and thought he had fulfilled his responsibilities.

"Mr Copperfield ... was so considerate and good as to secure the revision of a part of it (his annuity) to me."

"How much?" asked Miss Betsy.

"A hundred and five pounds a year", said my mother.[63]

On this, his mother kept David, who was born six months after his father's death and a servant, Peggoty. She also had the house which David's father had bought. Re-marriage brought disaster. Despite his mother's annuity, David found himself with all the anticipated problems of the stepchild. Mr Murdstone married 'the pretty young widow'. David felt all the pangs of jealousy. His father's will gave no protection. No trustees appeared to care for his welfare. No income was available for his benefit when his mother remarried. He was first distanced from his

[61] Probate 11 August 1830.
[62] Probate 24 April 1830.
[63] C. Dickens, *David Copperfield* (London, 1849–50), ch. 1.

Table 3.8 *Provision (£) for widows and sworn value, Leeds male probates, 1830–34*

Nature of provision for widow	No children (Mean Median)	Children (Mean Median)	Minors (Mean Median)	Total (Mean Median)
Absolute	2126	115	150	1255
	200	100	150	100
Natural life	1750	1726	5167	2563
	200	200	450	250
Reducers		8373	4982	5709
		100	4000	4000
Widowhood		445	1565	1132
		200	600	450
Total	1946	1582	3391	2315
	200	200	800	300

N=130

mother, then beaten and sent away to school. The disaster was completed by his mother's death.

"The poor child's annuity died with her?"

"Died with her", replied Mr Murdstone.

"And there was no settlement of the little property – the house and garden – the what's– its name Rookery without any rooks in it – upon her boy?"

"It had been left to her, unconditionally, by her first husband . . . "

" . . . when she married again – when she took that most disastrous step of marrying you in short", said my aunt, " to be plain – did no one put in a word for the boy at that time?"[64]

The answer of course was 'No'. It was this type of situation which the male will makers of Leeds were trying to avoid when they made their conditions.

The second dimension of choice was available resources. These were indicated by the sworn value. The median is given to counter the impact of the occasional extreme value on the mean. The reducers and natural life group tended to have higher sworn values than the absolute gift and widowhood people. Setting up a trust both incurred management costs and limited potential income by the need to look for a secure investment. Those who had completed their life cycle of accumulation with adequate resources chose the natural life trust. The

[64] Dickens, *David Copperfield*, ch. 24.

Table 3.9 *Type of provision for widows by life cycle stage and socio-economic status, Leeds male probates, 1830–34*

	Socio-economic status	
Life cycle stage	Low	High
Early	Widowhood	Reducers
Late	Absolute	Natural life

strong preference of 'gentlemen' for this option confirmed its link to the later stages of the life cycle. Those who had more slender resources and no responsibility for minor children handed the capital to their widow, leaving her the option of higher income, higher risk activity in a shop or business. Those with slender resources but also minor children, fearing the Copperfield syndrome, chose the widowhood option. This would release capital when the widow re-married, and capital would be made available by the trustees to the children as they reached 21 years old and anticipated marriage or setting up in business. The reducers were wealthier and, hence, could respond to the needs of both widow and minors.

Men and children

The relationship between the male will maker and his children was the second key relationship in the wills. Children were mentioned in 144 (71 per cent) of the male wills. The quality of information made it possible to count the number of sons and daughters in 115 of those wills. The official discourse of law and public debate assumed that the will maker would give preference to an eldest son. Many were precluded from doing this by simple demographic circumstances. Of the 171 men in the sample, for whom there was adequate information, 84 had no sons. Thirty had only one son, but of these nineteen had daughters who might be discriminated against in any eldest male preference strategy. Thus, there were eighty-two men who might have operated some form of primogeniture in their inheritance strategy. This was 48 per cent of those for whom information was adequate and 57 per cent of those with children (Table 3.10).

Of the 131 for whom evidence was available, only nine gave preference to an eldest son and three gave preference to sons. Some form of equity between children was specified by 78 per cent of those for whom there was relevant information (Table 3.11).

For the middle classes, the dominant form of division between children was one of complete equity. J.C. Hudson in his *Plain Directions* spoke of

Table 3.10 *Numbers of children mentioned in male wills, Leeds 1830–34*

	mentioned	
	sons	daughters
no. of children		
unknown	2	4
none	84	78
1	30	39
2	33	27
3	17	16
4	8	9
5 or more	5	6

There was inadequate information in 23 wills.

Table 3.11 *Inheritance strategies and male wills, Leeds 1830–34*

	Inheritance strategies	N	percentage
1	Equity between children	78	38.61
2	Near equity between children	12	5.94
3	Equity in kind between children	12	5.94
4	Other division between children	5	2.48
5	Preference to eldest son	9	4.46
6	Preference to sons	3	1.49
9	Equity between other than children	12	5.94
10	No details	71	35.15
	Total	202	

'a long cherished design of making an equitable disposition of property by will'.[65] The male will makers of Leeds followed Adam Smith in the belief that an equitable division between children was 'the natural law of succession'.[66] The word 'natural law' were chosen with care because in an intestate succession, the law of England favoured the eldest son in matters of real property. Indeed, it might be said that the purpose of making a will was the prevention of what would have happened if no will had been made. In effect, this meant preventing primogeniture operating.

[65] J.C. Hudson, *Plain Directions*, Introduction.
[66] A. Smith, *An Inquiry into the Nature and Causes of the Wealth of Nations*, 5th edition. Introduction by J.R. McCulloch. (Edinburgh, 1849), book 3, ch. 2, p. 171.

Hudson warned against 'procrastination' in drawing up a will in case the 'cherished design' was defeated by death.

Joseph Rollinson, the joiner, made provision for his wife. On her death, the trustees and executors,

> shall by public sale or private contract sell or dispose of my said real estate for the best price that can be obtained and out of the money arising therefrom (after paying all lawful and reasonable expenses) to divide the same equally and amongst all my children . . . in equal shares and proportions share and share alike.[67]

The last phrase was repeated in wills drawn from the full status range of the middle class, from joiners and builders to merchants and professional men. Sometimes the instruction made no specific mention of children but seemed to have been included in anticipation or simply because a married man felt it was the right thing to do. The *Christian Observer* was a keen supporter of the strategy of equitable and partible inheritance. Unequal distribution, they warned 'will infallibly create discord . . . Family dissension is doubtless a great and a very great evil'.[68] In 1852, the *Eclectic Review* was repeating the message in comments on a new edition of Blackstone. Primogeniture involved 'building up one member of the family, by doing injustice to all the other members in each successive generation'.[69]

Equitable and partible inheritance was a practice rather than a rule of law but variations from strict 'share and share alike' tended to be either minor or directed by the same principle of equal treatment.

Some minor variations reflected shared interests and affections. Samuel Gilpin, bricklayer, asked that 'my pianoforte and all my other musical instruments' should go to his son James.[70] George Austin, butcher, sworn value £200, gave Scott's *Commentaries on the Bible* and his silver watch to his son John, 'as a token of my affection'.[71]

In many cases equity was not achieved through strict cash values but by allocating specific bundles of property to each child with the evident intention of achieving equity or near equity. John Hick, gentleman, sworn value £450, was very careful.

> To my son John Hick, my three mahogany tables, my best looking glass, my best oak chest of drawers, my silver spectacles and my three books intitled *Looking unto Jesus, God's Sovereignty* and *Lyric Poems* for his own absolute use and benefit. I give

---

[67] Probate 8 June 1830.
[68] *Evangelical Review* (April 1811), 230.
[69] *Eclectic Review*, new series (1852), 186–96.
[70] Probate 21 May 1830.
[71] Probate 9 February 1831.

and bequeath unto my daughter Mary the wife of John Wood of Leeds aforesaid painter for her own absolute use my mahogany clock, my silk umbrella, my large brass pan and the following books, that is to say my family *Bible*, *Village Dialogues* in two volumes, Herveys *Works* in eight volumes and Booth's *Reign of Grace*,

and so the list went on, with the blue and white teapot and the silver cream boat amongst items directed to other children.[72] This strategy of equity in kind was also operated by allocating specific bundles of real estate to individual children.

One important source of variation, which reaffirmed the principle of equity was the balancing of gifts which had been made during the life of the will maker. Samuel Gilpin, bricklayer, made an equal division between his seven children 'except my son George, to whom I have already advanced his fortune'.[73] James Mann, the maltster, who died in January 1830, willed that,

inasmuch as I have already given and paid to and on account of my son James and my daughter Ann Keating considerable sums of money from the payment of which I hereby release acquit and discharge them respectively and to the intent that I may make my other children's portions or shares in my personal estate as nearly equal to them as my circumstances admit[74]

These will makers followed the principles of the Statute of Distributions which required that, for intestate succession, a child who had had an inter vivos gift of land or cash during the lifetime of the testator must count this as part of their share.[75] Hudson advised that 'a proportionate deduction must be made from the shares of such as may have had advancements made to them by the Intestate in his lifetime'.[76] Such advancements included the purchase of a living in the church, an office under the crown, or a military commission, as well as a settlement or gift on marriage. The practice was known as 'Hotchpot'. Richard Kemplay, gentleman, directed that his sons and daughter should get equal shares and, like many, he directed that his grandchildren should have equal shares of their parents' share. There was provision for the trustees to use the capital for the 'maintenance and education' of any of them who were under 21 years of age but, if they did, they would get nothing from the final distribution 'without bringing his or her appointed share into hotchpot'.[77]

---

[72] Probate 17 April 1832.
[73] Probate 21 May 1830.
[74] See below, especially the case of John Topham.
[75] Blackstone, *Commentaries*, vol. II, p. 489.
[76] J.C. Hudson, *The Executors Guide*, pp. 117–18.
[77] Probate 16 May 1831.

This sense of equity was gendered in qualitative rather than quantitative terms. There was little evidence of greater cash sums going to sons, but sons got their portion for their own absolute use at the age of 21 years whilst many daughters received only an income stream from a trust which, like those of the widows, was controlled by trustees appointed by the will maker. William Wilkinson, merchant, set aside £1,000 to be invested 'upon real or government security' from which the 'income and dividends' would go to his daughter, Mary Ann, 'for the term of her natural life'.[78] This, he directed, 'shall not be subject or liable to the debts, control or engagements of any husband my said Daughter, Mary Ann, may happen to marry'. Thomas Wade, stone merchant, identified land and tenements at White Cote in Bramley township in the south of Leeds Parish; 'upon trust for my trustees or trustee for the time being under this my will to receive and take the rents and annual issues and profits for and during the natural life of my daughter Sarah'. The rents were to be paid to Sarah. On Sarah's death, she was empowered to instruct the trustees by will or testament as to who was to inherit the property and in what shares.[79] In twenty-nine of the wills involving fifty–one daughters there were instructions which provided them with an income stream but left the capital under the control of the trust. The practice was identified with the wealthier members of the middle classes. The average sworn value of the estates involved was £3411. Trusts for daughters were less common than for widows but they still involved around 10 per cent of the 651 daughters mentioned in the Leeds wills. As with widows, this practice protected daughters against the malice or ill fortune of husbands but also prevented them from investing in the higher risk, higher income activity of business. Comments in the *Christian Observer* showed that the morally aware middle classes were unsure of the practice.

The practical injustice arising out of the received construction of wills, is in the first place very seriously felt by females. From the constitution of civil society and from physical causes women are dependent and comparatively helpless. Consequently a daughter's fortune should be regulated so as to meet as far as fortune can meet, these unavoidable circumstances of dependence and helplessness. A female's portion is generally a determinate sum; either already funded, or to be paid by executors out of a certain estate. This sum when received is forwarded to a stockbroker. The interest and the interest only is her income. She cannot (except in peculiar cases) invest her capital in trade.[80]

[78] Probate 17 April 1832.
[79] Probate 29 August 1831.
[80] *Christian Observer* (April 1811), 226.

Many fathers and a small number of husbands wanted to leave daughters and widows with the option of investing in trade at the cost of leaving them without the protection of the trust in the event of marriage.

One group of variants showed that this practice of gendered equity marked a key cultural boundary for the urban middle classes with a clarity that few other forms of behaviour possessed. Edward Brooke, merchant, on the edge of the landed class, was one who favoured his son. Property relationships with his wife were governed by a marriage settlement. She was about to inherit land from a brother. His daughter had married John Gott, son of the wealthiest merchant-manufacturer in Leeds.[81] Richard Kemplay, gentleman, in the early 1820s, ran an academy for young gentlemen in north Leeds. His sworn value of £16,000 suggested wealth which owed itself to his links with land at Leavening in Yorkshire rather than to schoolteaching. He had a feeling for family continuity and identity through land and left his eldest sons £1000 more than the other three children with the option of purchasing his 'estate' in North Street at valuation.[82] Christopher may well have taken this up for he established himself there as a member of a leading firm of Tory solicitors, Bolland and Kemplay, in 1834. Edward Armitage, gentleman, lived at Farnley and under his father's will had the disposal of shares in the Aire and Calder Navigation. His eldest son got half of them whilst the other three got a sixth each.[83]

This boundary between the middle and upper classes was widely recognised. The *Christian Observer* identified primogeniture with aristocracy and feudal prejudice.[84] McCulloch, the Edinburgh political economist, defended the practice as a means of consolidating aristocracy which he felt was crucial to political stability.[85] He rejected Adam Smith's belief that large numbers of small fortunes were an essential spur to improvement. McCulloch pointed to the damage which he felt partible inheritance had done to the agriculture of France and Ireland.[86] Commerce and industry were identified with equitable inheritance. Blackstone was writing his law for a commercial society 'whose welfare depends upon the number of moderate fortunes engaged in the extension of trade'.[87] There was a cultural awareness that the reproduction of the middle classes was linked to the constant division of accumulations of wealth by the equitable

---

[81] Probate 1 June 1831.
[82] Probate 16 May 1831.
[83] Probate 15 February 1830.
[84] *Christian Observer* (April 1811), 225.
[85] 'Considerations in the Law of Entail, London 1823', *Edinburgh Review* 40 (1824), 350–75.
[86] Smith, *Wealth of Nations*.
[87] Blackstone, *Commentaries*, vol. II, p. 375.

inheritance practices used by the middle classes. Out of 202 male wills, 107 made some provision for widows which involved either dividing the estate or reserving a portion of it, usually around half, for the widow's lifetime. There were 137 wills, both male and female, with children present. Of these, 106 (77 per cent) involved dividing the estate. As Adam Smith and the *Christian Observer* anticipated, if the children in these two groups wanted to emulate their parents, they would have to work and to take the risks of profit seeking in the commercial and manufacturing economy.

J.C. McCulloch was Professor of Political Economy at the University of Edinburgh. He was not a great or original thinker by the standards of an Adam Smith or a Ricardo but he wrote with great clarity and directness. His work was a valuable guide to the contribution which political economy made to the consciousness and perceptions of the middle classes in the 1820s and 1830s. He wrote on inheritance to refute the views of Adam Smith. In a section of the *Wealth of Nations* devoted to agricultural improvement, Smith mounted a strong attack upon primogeniture. Equal division between children was

the natural law of succession... among all the children of the family; of all of whom the subsistence and enjoyment may be supposed equally dear to the father.

He believed that the practice of primogeniture and entail derived from a period when land was the basis for military power and protection. By the late eighteenth century it served 'the pride of family distinctions ... a right which in order to enrich one beggars all the rest of the children'. In Scotland (where the law was different from England), Smith claimed that between a third to a fifth of the land was under perpetual entail to the practice of primogeniture. This proved a great barrier to agricultural improvement.

It seldom happens however that the great proprietor is a great improver .... to improve land with profit; like all other commercial projects, requires an exact attention to small savings and gains, of which men born to great fortune, even though naturally frugal, are very seldom capable.[88]

McCulloch mounted a fierce attack upon this position and claimed

that entails form the only solid bulwark of a respectable aristocracy, and prevent generations being ruined by the folly or misfortunes of an individual.

He admitted that those with a life rent of their property were more secure than those depending upon trade or professional incomes, but he did not

---

[88] Smith, *Wealth of Nations*, book 3, ch. 2, p. 171.

see this as a barrier to improvement. The desire to build up property and emulate the aristocracy was a powerful stimulus. Entails

stimulate exertion and economy; that they hold out to industry and ambition the strongest and safest excitement, in the prospect of founding an imperishable name and a powerful family.

He claimed that sons who had the life tenancy of an entailed estate in a system of primogeniture had to save and accumulate to provide for a widow and younger children. In any case, such were the virtues of freedom, any individual who objected to the system of primogeniture could make a will to reverse the situation. It was also part of the 'perfection' of the English law that entailed primogeniture was limited to one life, which effectively meant one generation. It was the Scots who had let things go too far. The last thing that was required was a law enforcing partible inheritance after the manner of the French or the Irish gavelkind. In France, such laws, he claimed, had led to the loss of aristocracy so crucial to good government.

There is no class with that deep and abiding interest in the support of the existing institutions, that seem indispensable to protect a government against impulses, originating in popular prejudices and passions[89]

With the fervour of an Edmund Burke, McCulloch was anxious to remind his readers of the need for political stability and the value of an aristocracy to that end, but he saw primogeniture and entail as damaging to lower classes.

...as respects the estates of the commons, its operation is, on the whole very injurious. It fosters the growth of dissolute habits in the heirs of entail; it locks up landed property in the hands of those who would be glad to dispose of it; it prevents its acquisition by others; and fetters the application of capital to land.[90]

He refused to go as far as Adam Smith or Samuel Gale and condemn the system as fundamentally unjust. Hudson, in *Plain Directions,* saw equity as a matter of parental affections.[91] Jarman was prejudiced against entail because of the private need to provide for family and the public need to ensure the active circulation of property and capital, which was required for commerce, land improvement and industrial development.[92] The

[89] McCulloch, *A Treatise*, p. 133.
[90] McCulloch, *A Treatise*, p. 77.
[91] J.C. Hudson, *Plain Directions*, p. 2; 'The limits of testamentary bequests', *Eclectic Review*, new series 4 (1852), 191.
[92] T. Jarman, *A Treatise on Wills*, vol. I, p. 202.

general verdict was that the English had the right balance between political stability and the needs of commerce.

> In England families are preserved and purchasers always find a supply of land in the market. A testamentary power is given, which stimulates industry and encourages accumulation . . . property is allowed to be moulded according to the circumstances and wants of every family.[93]

This was a class conscious ideological debate between an aristocracy of primogeniture in the service of political stability and a middle class of partible inheritance crucial for a commercial capitalist society. If class was about the relationships of property and the means of production and distribution, then this aspect of property relationships, buried deep in the wills, needs to be marked with care. The landed aristocracy followed McCulloch and Burke and not Adam Smith or the middle classes of Leeds in the 1830s, although, in practice, the absolutes of primogeniture were mitigated by jointures for widows, portions for younger sons, dowries for daughters and the vagaries of demography.[94]

There was one small group of wills that broke the pattern of responsibility to widows and equity to immediate family. These household and community wills included servants, friends, business associates as well as family in the bequests. It was a choice available to the middle classes which, in the 1830s, very few were willing to take. Jabez Stead, merchant of Hunslet in the out-townships of Leeds, died in April 1831 with a sworn value of £14,000.[95] The 1834 Factory Survey found that he had established a woollen mill in 1830 powered by a modest 40 horse power engine and employed, under the direction of his trustees, at the time of the survey, 160 people.[96] The world which this manufacturing paternalist outlined in his will extended well beyond the nuclear family of wife and children. His real estate in Bramley was still subject to mortgage and he had minor children, indicating that death caught him in the middle of the life cycle. His trustees were a butcher, a merchant and an overlooker drawn from a friendship circle based upon the communities of the out-townships rather than status exclusivity. They were to stand possessed of his real estate, selling and disposing when they thought fit. They were to

---

[93] First Report of the Real Property Commissioners, p. 6.
[94] B. English and J. Saville, *Strict Settlement. A Guide for Historians,* University of Hull. Occasional Papers in Economic and Social History, no. 10 (Hull, 1983); J. Habakkuk, *Marriage, Debt and the Estates System. English Landownership, 1650–1950* (Oxford, 1994); B. English, *The Great Landowners of East Yorkshire, 1530–1910* (London, 1990), pp. 74–101.
[95] Probate 6 September 1831.
[96] Factory Enquiry Commission, Supplementary Report, part II, *Parliamentary Papers,* (1834) XIX.

be possessed of his capital and stock in trade, machinery, implements as well as household furniture, money and book debts. His property included a pew in St Paul's Church in Leeds. This was a new Anglican church established by private enterprise in the west end of Leeds. Had he lived, Jabez might have moved closer to the high status middle classes of Leeds. First care was his wife, Hannah. She was to have immediate access to food and drink plus £20, the characteristic acknowledgement of the initial powerlessness of women after their husbands' death. She was to select household furniture for her own use up to the value of £100. She was to have an income of £100 a year from the estate but, mindful of the minor children who remained, if she remarried, she lost the guardianship of the children, had to return the furniture to the estate and her annuity was reduced to £40.

Stead used his will to mark out his 'family' in a more extensive way than other will makers in middle class Leeds in the 1830s. A small legacy, £2 went to 'my aunt Sarah Brown'. Then small sums went to several named individuals 'if they shall be in my service at the time of my decease':

John Todd, my bookkeeper, £10

Samuel Brown

Robert Kenworth

Robert Walker, my overlookers, £5 each (Walker was also a trustee)

Reverend Joseph Wardle, cloth for a suit of mourning

Reverend Richard Foster, both cloth for a suit of mourning or £3 'as a small token of my remembrance'

John Holdsworth, handlesetter

John Armitage, coal leader

Joseph Mawson, carrier, all three sufficient cloth for a coat of mourning 'if they shall be in my service at the time of my decease'

John Willans, ironfounder, sufficient cloth for a coat.

The residue of the profits, rents and proceeds of the sale of his real and personal property was to be divided between his nine children 'as they shall severally attain their respective ages of twenty one years ... share and share alike'. Sarah, his fourth daughter and wife of William Casson, was to include in her share the £300 she had been given and the £150 which had been lent to her husband. The advantage given to his two sons was relatively small. They were to have £500 each in addition to their share, payable at the age of 21. Up to that point, the interest from these sums was directed to their maintenance and education. The out-township paternalist ensured that his sons had the sort of sum which would establish them in business when they reached majority. Benjamin Cromack, clothier of the out-township of Farnley, sworn value £5000, was another who made carefully graded bequests to servants, friends and business associates as well as family.[97] These wills represented a set of social relationships that were already disappearing in the late eighteenth century. The relationships embodied in the paternalistic open household, often containing servants and closely linked to work, had almost been obliterated in the long centuries of competition with the nuclear family household.[98]

In terms of reordering the social world, this was about family and not about civil society. There were very few bequests to charity.

Despite the importance of business of all kinds to middle class family income, there was very little reference to business continuity in the wills. Only twenty-four of the wills made direct reference to arrangements for such continuity, although another thirty-five mentioned 'stock in trade' in the categories of property being transferred. The transfer of property at death was not a major location for securing the continuity of business. Either such continuity depended upon arrangements made before death, or the reproduction of the middle classes did not depend in a direct sense on such continuities. The case studies based upon family papers throw some light on the mechanisms involved, but the wills reveal some of the features of such continuity. The small group concerned with business continuity when writing a will differed in two ways from the total population of will makers. There was a bias to those with minor children. Of the twenty–one males in the group eleven (57 per cent) had minor children compared with 29 per cent in the total male will making population. The number of children acknowledged in the will was also greater (Table 3.12).

Interest in business continuity was a feature of a life cycle stage. If mention of 'stock in trade' was regarded as an indicator of an interest in business continuity, then twenty-five of that group mentioned minor children, nearly half of the fifty-eight cases which mentioned minors in the total male will making population.

Instructions designed to secure business continuity were associated with a variety of tactics and situations. In almost all cases, provision for business continuity was designed to support a widow and/or minor children. James Tattersall, shopkeeper, made an economic bargain.

---

[97] Probate 6 May 1831.
[98] J. Smail, *The Origins of Middle Class Culture. Halifax, 1660–1780* (Cornell, 1994), pp. 39–41 and 110–13; J. Foster, *Class Struggle and the Industrial Revolution. Early Industrial Capitalism in Three English Towns* (London, 1974), pp. 25–7 and 177–82; P. Laslett, *The World We Have Lost* (London, 1965), pp. 1–22; K. Wrighton, *English Society, 1580–1680* (London, 1982), pp. 44–5; A. Macfarlane, *The Origins of English Individualism: the Family, Property and Social Transition* (Oxford, 1978); M. Chaytor, 'Household and kinship: Ryton in the late 16th and early 17th centuries', *History Workshop* 10 (Autumn 1980), 25–60.

Table 3.12 *Number of children and arrangements for business continuity in Leeds wills, 1830–34*

	0	%	1	%	2–4	%	5+	%	N
	Number of children mentioned in the will								
Mention of business continuity	5[a]	21	1	4	8	33	9	39	24
Male will makers with information on children		40		13		29		18	198

[a] Two of this group were women.

It is my request and direction that my said son and daughter should carry on my present business in partnership for their joint benefit, so long as my daughter shall remain unmarried but not longer and that my said wife should reside with them and assist them therein, and for such her assistance, I request and direct that they will provide her with Board and Lodging out of the Profits of the said business.

His widow was to get an annuity of £20 and the residue of the estate was to provide his children with the capital to run the business.[99]

George Metcalf, bricklayer, signed with a mark and asked that his trustees

allow my said son David in conjunction with my two daughters Mary and Elizabeth or either of them to carry on and conduct the business or respective businesses I am now engaged in[100]

They were to have possession of the relevant real estate and conduct the business 'as I myself would do if I were living'. He asked that the trustees take an inventory and 'at the commencement of every year inspect, examine and investigate the Books of Account, invoices and affairs connected therewith'. This arrangement was to come to an end when the two daughters married. Richard Clark, wharfinger, directed that his trustees should take possession of his 'ships, vessels and parts and shares of ships and vessels, money, securities for money, stock in trade implements of trade . . .' and that his son Richard should 'carry on my trade and business of wharfinger until the youngest of my children shall attain the age of twenty one'.[101] Sam Spence, innkeeper, who still had minor children, wanted to draw in his son in law and Richard Nicholson, saddler and harness maker, had his grandson in mind to take over the business, provided £5 a year was paid to his mother/my daughter.[102]

[99] Probate 8 May 1832.
[100] Probate 7 March 1831.
[101] Probate 7 December 1831.
[102] Probate 14 July 1832.

In several cases, a childless man established a link with a nephew to ensure that the business continued to supply the income for a widow. John Mawson, aqua fortis manufacturer, asked that his wife should have

full power and authority . . . in conjunction with my nephew John Mawson to carry on my said trade and business and transact all matters and things relating hereto and to retain the whole net profits arising therefrom to and for her own absolute use and benefit save and except a yearly sum of one hundred and fifty pounds which I hereby direct shall be paid and allowed to my said nephew John Mawson as and for a remuneration for his services in the management of the said trade and business.

On the widow's death, the nephew was then to inherit for his own 'absolute use and benefit'.[103] Samuel Raistrick, victualler of the Star in Mabgate End, wanted his wife to run the inn, but when she died or gave up the trade, his nephew Samuel Raistrick was to have

first offer of purchasing the Stock in Trade and other my effects and interest of and in the Public House occupied by me at a fair valuation.

One valuer was to be chosen by the nephew and the other by the executors.[104]

Other economic bargains could be embedded in the will to ensure continued support for widows and children. Thomas Bulter, the iron-master[105] and Charles Chadwick, chemical manufacturer[106] both arranged for a partnership to continue. William Farrar, another stone merchant in Bramley, anticipated the problem. He had entered articles of co-partnership with his brothers Thomas and John through which they agreed, in the event of the death of any of them, to continue the partnership and allocate the share of profits of the dead partner to his widow and children.[107]

Several sons who had been active in the business were given the option to purchase. The purchase was always to be done at valuation. In the words of Sarah Pickles, publican, 'so that one child may not be disadvantaged to the benefit of another'.[108] Thomas Wade, stone merchant, directed that his quarry interests should go to his son, but also allocated the income from specific pieces of land to provide an income for each of his daughters. The quarry was to be managed by his widow until Thomas junior reached the age of 21 years.[109] If one child was given an advantage,

[103] Probate 11 March 1831.
[104] Probate 16 December 1830.
[105] Probate 9 December 1831.
[106] Probate 21 March 1831.
[107] Probate 18 July 1832.
[108] Probate 19 October 1830.
[109] Probate 29 August 1831.

it was often stated that this was in return for a contribution to the business. John Pawson, cloth manufacturer and merchant' gave his eldest son George £1000 over and above his share 'as a reward for his diligent attention to business during my lifetime'.[110] John Clark, coachmaker, listed 'wages' owing to two of his sons as obligations of his estates. They were substantial sums. William was owed £900 and John £150, which must have been allowed to lie in the books of the business.[111]

Privilege for a family purchaser was not allowed to override equity between children. The most that would be allowed was a specified time to pay over the value of the business to the estate. Joseph Hallewell wanted his son Benjamin to continue the business of spirit and British wine dealer under the direction of the trustees. Benjamin took half the profits and the other half went towards an annual income for the widow and daughters. Benjamin was offered the real estate in Duncan Street at a fixed price of £6000. He had eighteen months to pay or longer, if the trustees thought fit. Robert Bullman, upholsterer, left the business to his son but with a variety of burdens in terms of income for his daughters. In a complex arrangement, Edward Bullman was allowed to retain a fifth share of this for fourteen years provided he retained the business. The instruction was so complex that it had to be taken to the Court of Chancery to be sorted out.[112] Easier to manage was the arrangement made by Josiah Teale, another upholsterer and cabinet maker, who directed the business to his son John and £1000 to his daughter but allowed his son to retain the legacy 'for the purpose of assisting him in carrying on his trade'. John was to pay the money in quarterly instalments over a four year period.[113] The will makers were aware that equitable division between children threatened the business by breaking up the capital required to run that business. Few businesses were able to sustain more than one middle class household, so careful arrangements needed to be made to ensure that the division of capital following death would not destroy the ability of a business to continue.

The concern for the continuity of the business was almost always linked to obligations to widows and children, usually minor children. In these cases the will maker judged that keeping the business going was the best way to ensure support for widow and minors and a fair portion for other children. In all cases the continuity of the business was subordinated to the need for equity between children. There may have been some sense of sentiment in

[110] Probate 28 July 1831.
[111] Probate 19 November 1831.
[112] Probate 16 February 1832.
[113] Probate 15 April 1831.

favour of a son or other relative keeping the business but this was always balanced by provisions to ensure equity. At the most the inheritor of the business was given time to pay, but the price was always a market one. When Charles Dickens wrote *Dombey and Son*, a novel about an obsession with handing down a business to a son, he provided a middle class moral fable and not a mirror of reality. For the bulk of the middle class, business continuity was one of several options for fulfilling obligations to widows and equity to children. It was an option suited to a minority of families.

The economic implications of the weak interest in business continuity were positive in terms of economic efficiency. The 'continuity' family firm locked up resources free of the discipline of any sort of open market, never mind the modern disciplines of a stock exchange or head office accountant. So long as the firm provided adequate income for family members and for the purchase of a minimal level of professional and technical expertise, and so long as any major liquidity crisis or market decline was avoided, then the firm continued on the momentum of the accumulated capital derived from its founding generation. This was the story of Marshalls of Leeds, of Armstrongs on the Tyne, and of Valentines in Dundee.[114] By the 1930s, the protection of Limited Liability Private Company legislation locked considerable resources into zero profit firms that existed to provide salaries for family members.[115] In most of the sample of wills, the outcome was quite different. On death, the assets were placed in the cash economy and subject to the discipline of the market. Viewed from the point of view of the family, two sets of assets were released. There were the material assets of home, business and investments, which could be reallocated to maximise the satisfactions of those involved. In addition, the human capital of the family was reallocated according to the abilities, potential and preferences of the individual members. This was not the insistent discipline of a public stock exchange and audited accounts but a situation in which once per generation 'the firm' and the human capital of the family were put to the market and reorganised. Economic discipline came not from the transparency of audited accounts and company law and only imperfectly from the price mechanisms of the stock and capital markets, but from the decision points of the life cycle and the reordering of assets at death.

---

[114] W.G. Rimmer, *Marshalls of Leeds. Flax Spinners, 1788–1886* (Cambridge, 1960); Benwell Community Project. Final Report Series no. 6, *The Making of a Ruling Class, Two Centuries of Capital Development on Tyneside*, (Benwell, 1978); R. Smart, 'Famous throughout the World. Valentine and Sons Ltd., Dundee', *Review of Scottish Culture* 4 (1988), 75–88.

[115] R. Mackie, 'Family ownership and business survival: Kirkcaldy, 1870–1970, *Business History* 43:3 (July 2001), 1–32.

Table 3.13 *Family and demographic situations of Leeds will makers, 1830–34*

Situation	No.	%	Percentage of male
Widow with children	15	5.64	
Widow alone	17	6.39	
Spinster	18	6.77	
Other women	14	5.26	4
Man with wife	24	9.02	11.88
Man with wife and children	59	22.18	29.21
Man with wife and minors	48	18.05	23.76
Man alone	34[a]	12.78	16.83
Man with children	27	10.15	13.37
Man with minors	10	3.76	4.95
	N=266		N=202

[a]Assuming that the percentage of childless individuals amongst widowed men was the same as that amongst men whose wives were still alive (22 per cent), then this group consisted of 8 men who were widowed and childless and 26 who never married, which was 4.1 per cent and 12.7 per cent of the male will makers.

Another surprising absence, given the importance of domesticity in middle class ideology, was the lack of concern for the family house. In one or two cases a son was given the option of purchase at valuation, but that was all. This lack of concern was another mark on the social boundary of the middle classes. There was none of the continuity of possession for house and estate characteristic of the aristocratic landed family. Nor was there any sense of the attachment, moral, emotional and economic, between family and land evident in many studies of peasant inheritance.[116] On death, the family house and the business became assets which were open to acquire new meanings or simply be turned into cash by way of the market. Family was a matter of a web of relationships and not of place or house. The importance which place and home undoubtedly had, was incidental and episodic.

The analysis so far has been led by the 'ideal' of contemporary debate, a man leaving property for the benefit of widow and children. This was the 'ideal' of the normative and didactic literature from advice manuals to law books. The 'population' of the wills showed that only 40 per cent of the sample found themselves in the situation defined by official discourse.

[116] E.H. Leyton, 'Spheres of inheritance in Aughnaboy', *American Anthropologist* 72:6 (December 1970), 1378–88; C. Arensberg and S.T. Kimball, *Family and Community in Ireland* (Harvard, 1940); D. Siddle, 'Inheritance strategies and lineage development in peasant society', *Continuity and Change* 1:3 (1986), 333–61; J. Goody, 'Strategies of heirship', *Comparative Studies in Society and History* 15 (1973), 3–20.

Just over half the male will makers fitted the model of the official discourse of responsibility to wife and children. Another 30 per cent fitted part of that model and had wife or children. A third of the men had no children alive at death whilst even amongst the ever married men 18 per cent were childless at death. These last two figures were a little less than those suggested by demographic models of high death rate/high birth rate stationary populations.[117] As the will makers came from the higher status ranks of the population of Leeds, they were likely to have high rates of survival for their children. Better nutrition and general levels of health would produce higher levels of marital fertility for their wives, which would counter the depressive effect of a later age of marriage on life time fertility levels. Thus it was likely that the 'population' of the wills gave a reasonably complete account of the family and demographic situation in which the will makers found themselves.

There were forty-nine women, 77 per cent of the female will makers, and fifty-eight men, 29 per cent of the male will makers, who mentioned no living children in their wills. They turned to the reserve army of cousins, siblings, nephews and nieces. At this point the middle class sense of extended family was very visible. Once the inheriting group had been selected, its members were usually treated with the same degree of equity as members of a nuclear family. The same strategies were used. There were clauses to cover the contingencies of death amongst potential legatees and to require 'share and share alike' amongst the legatees. Trusts and trustees were used to control female incomes and protect their property from husbands present and future. There were indications that sentiment and regard had a greater place in the decisions of bachelor uncles and childless couples. They were more likely than males with widow and children to choose specific items of property to recognise individual qualities, interests and affections. George Kemplay was an assistant schoolmaster, sworn value £200, with brothers in the woodworking trades. His will, made eight months before his death, showed a very specific regard for individuals within his extended family network.

James Hudson Kemplay, brother, linen and wearing apparel

Annabella, Caroline and Henrietta Kemplay, cousins, 'my three books called the *Souvenir for the Years 1824, 1825 and 1826*'

Richard Kemplay, uncle, 'all my pieces of writings and manuscripts consisting of prose and poetry'

---

[117] R.M. Smith, 'Families and their Property in Rural England, 1260–1800', in R.M. Smith, *Land, Kinship and the Life Cycle* (Cambridge, 1984), pp. 45–52.

James Kemplay, cousin, 'my watch with the appendages thereto belonging' plus half of his remaining books
  Christopher Kemplay, cousin, the other half of the books
  Elizabeth Kemplay, aunt, my silk umbrella
  Robert Wilson Kemplay, brother, ensure that he fulfils his part of a covenant in an apprenticeship agreement.
The residue was then divided equally between his two brothers.[118] James Gray, gentleman, after making provision for 'my dear wife' simply allocated a series of legacies to a variety of nieces and cousins.[119] These wills reflected the geographic scatter of the extended family. Thomas Westwood, confectioner of Leeds, made provision for his wife for her 'natural life' and then divided his estate into seven equal portions for his brothers and sisters.
  William Westwood, Church Fenton, farmer
  Robert Westwood, Saxton, tailor
  John Westwood, Selby, farmer
  Elizabeth, wife of George Mountain, Howden Clough, farmer
  Ann, wife of John Lupton, Pateley, farmer
  Isabella, wife of Joseph Gaunt of Leeds, tailor
  Samuel Gibbons [no relationship stated], Heaton, cloth weaver.[120]
These were all places within a long day's journey in the 1830s.
Selected members of the reserve army could become especially important to the childless as they made explicit and implicit bargains from beyond the grave to ensure that obligations were fulfilled. John Mawson, aqua fortis manufacturer, and Samuel Raistrick, victualler of the Star Inn in Mabgate, both brought in nephews to ensure business continuity and the support of their widows. These were legal bargains, an economic exchange enforceable at law. Other exchanges had more the implicit quality of the gift. Nieces and other females often found themselves as part of a contract for care. This was the case with Ann Thompson. John Bickerdike, gentleman, a sworn value of £5000, provided each of his nieces with income from trusts of £400 each as well as absolute gifts to nephews. Ann was different. 'I give and bequeath unto my niece, Ann Thompson, my present housekeeper, as much furniture as will furnish a small house or cottage . . . ' plus £150 direct and the income from £300. In the same way, Thomas Craddock, stuff merchant, gave 'my said sister Eleanor, who now resides with me, such part of my household furniture, beds and bedding, plate, linen and china, goods, chattels and effects that

[118] Probate 15 June 1830.
[119] Probate 14 December 1832.
[120] Probate 4 August 1832.

may be in and about my dwelling house at the time of my decease as she may select for the purpose of furnishing her a house to reside in suitable to her station in life'. This was in addition to her portion of the residue of the estate after debts and expenses had been paid, which was divided between brothers and sisters 'share and share alike'.[121] The preferences were slight and the dominant practice was that of equity between family members.

The novels suggested that the relationships between the childless and the reserve army was an especially delicate one and could lead to situations of considerable tension. *Middlemarch* was a textbook on the involvement of the extended family. Mrs Vincy dismissed the claims of Mary Garth, niece of the first marriage and housekeeper for Mr Featherstone.

... there's justice to be thought of. And Mr Featherstone's first wife brought him no money, as my sister did. Her nieces and nephews can't have so much claim as my sister's.[122]

This incorporated a notion of coverture, in which a wife's property rights re-emerged after marriage. Mrs Waule was not presented as the most generous and kindly of people but her account of what was expected as social practice was very accurate. When she found that none of Mr Featherstone's money was going to kin, her criticism was direct.

And all the while had got his own lawful family – brothers and sisters and nephews and nieces – and has sat in church with 'em whenever he thought well to come.[123]

The wills demonstrated the relative importance of the nuclear and extended family in this period of economic development. Anderson and others have identified the centrality of the nuclear family, especially as a co-residential group, but recognised the continued importance of the extended family.[124] There was little sense in the wills and elsewhere of an extended family system being replaced by one dependent on the nuclear family. The preference of the will makers was for the nuclear family, but when this failed they turned to the reserve army of the extended family. Given the insecurities of premature death and childlessness, there was no-one who could ignore the possibility of needing cousins, siblings and others to help them with the tasks of leaving order and fulfilling obligations after death.

---

[121] Probate 30 August 1831.

[122] Eliot, *Middlemarch*, ch. 11.

[123] Eliot, *Middlemarch*, ch. 35.

[124] M. Anderson, *Family Structure in Nineteenth Century Lancashire* (Cambridge, 1971); MacFarlane, *The Origins of English Individualism*, pp. 140–5.

Within the triple framework of law, custom and practice, choices were not only influenced by the situation of the will maker and the resources of property and kin available but also by the manner in which the will maker conceptualised those resources and attributed meaning to them. The family house, the mortgaged cottages, the capital and goodwill of a business and even the silver spoons were endowed with meanings and purpose. As the world of property was prepared for re-ordering after death, such assets might express affection, fulfil responsibility or simply be turned into cash for orderly distribution. As they delivered equity for children or considered obligations to widows, as they twisted and turned in the face of demographic and economic fortune, the will makers viewed the world in three overlapping but qualitatively different ways. There were 'things' people, 'real estate' people and 'categories' people. These three ways of conceptualising the world of property were closely linked to qualitatively different strategies for delivering the central aims of care for a widow, equity to children and the orderly re-ordering of assets after death.

Amongst the 266 will makers, both men and women, there were 48 'things' people who named specific items and those who were to inherit them. John Hick, gentleman,[125] sworn value £450, came from Hunslet, a southern manufacturing township of Leeds. He had been listed in the 1829 directory as an engine fitter. He delivered equity by listing the specific items which his sons, daughters and servants were to receive.

to my son Benjamin my silver cream boat, two silver table spoons, half a dozen silver tea spoons, one pair of silver sugar tongs and two portraits of himself for his own use. I give and bequeath to my grandson Charles Hick, the son of my late son Thomas for his own absolute use my two shares or portions of fifty pounds each in the South Market in Leeds aforesaid, and also my silver watch, half a dozen silver tea spoons and one pair of silver sugar tongs

Silver items were frequently mentioned by things people. Twenty-four of the forty-eight 'things' people mentioned silver and eleven of these were women. Mary Mawson added a codicil to her will just after her husband died. She had been married before and wanted to direct specific items to members of her own family and the family of her first husband, called Russell. Hannah Greenwood, a niece, got 'the feather bed upon which I generally sleep together with the curtains, bedstead, bedding and sheets and pillows belonging thereto'. Her brother, John Clapham, got the 'bed in the kitchen chamber', whilst another niece, Elizabeth Ingleton got 'the large looking glass in the common sitting room and my silver tea pot and basin marked with the name of Russell'. Silver, especially silver marked

---

[125] Probate 17 April 1832.

with initials, was often a carrier of family identity. Beds and bedding were frequently specifically give. They were high value items amongst furnishing and associated with much valued bodily comfort. The recipients were predominantly women. Watches, another carrier of identity, were more male, given by and to men. Twenty-one of the 'things' people mentioned a watch but only six of these were women. Most 'things' people were women.[126] It was more characteristic of men to pick out one or two items of special meaning in terms of relationships with a child or sibling and then to turn to one of the other two strategies.

There were 120 wills which listed items of real property and allocated them in carefully chosen bundles to achieve their aims. This view of the world was closely linked with a property and life cycle strategy that may be called that of the 'urban peasant'. John Topham, currier, died in February 1830.[127] He had appeared in the trade directories of the 1820s as a currier, leather seller and hair dealer. The sworn value of £450, together with a substantial listing of real property, indicated successful life time accumulation. He had a son, a daughter and left a widow. He achieved equity, not by the precise numerical division of a cash sum, but by allocating categories and items of real property to specified functions within his strategy. His dwelling house at 45 Trafalgar Street, together with 'household goods, plate, linen and other articles of furniture', went to his widow, but only for her natural life or widowhood. His widow inherited a life interest in a house, outbuildings and two closes of land in Ripon to the north of Leeds, thus ensuring her of an income as well as a place to live. Son John got the 'stock in trade and all my utensils and implements used in and about my business' as well as the ready money and debts owing the business. He also received an interest in some land at Buslingthorpe. Thus John had a working business and a bit of real estate on which to raise credit if he wished. Daughter received ten cottages in Mabgate and ten shares in 'a building club or Society... known by the name of the Commercial Union Building Society'.[128] Thus son got the more active male capital with its potential for high risk and high profit whilst daughter got the more passive property, although Topham, like many 'urban peasants' chose not to protect her with a trust arrangement. Finally, on his widow's death, son John got the Ripon and Trafalgar Street property on condition he paid outstanding amounts on the building club shares, both rewarding John for managing

---

[126] See this volume, Chapter 6, 'Women and Things and Trusts'.
[127] John Topham, currier, probate, 8 June 1830.
[128] M.W. Beresford. 'East end, west end. The face of Leeds during urbanization, 1684–1842', *Thoresby Society* LX and LXI, nos. 131 and 132 (Leeds, 1988), 186.

this element of the estate and retaining some element of equity. There was no hint of using the market or a market based valuation. Equity was qualitative and functional.

The title 'urban peasant' was chosen because such men sought income and accumulation by mixing the product of their own land, labour and capital. The urban peasant centred life cycle strategies on the accumulation of real estate, located within their own immediate urban experience. The urban peasant, usually male, tended to depend upon small accumulations of business capital for income. The independent craftsmen or the shopkeepers were typical. The bricklayer or joiner who moved into property development or the innkeeper were characteristic. At death, they had the drive for responsibility to widows and equity to children, but they took much less trouble to sieve their property through the homogenising medium of the cash economy with its valuations, private sales and auctions. Exceptions from equity and responsibility were more likely to be found amongst this group. Their judgements and intentions showed that they saw their property, especially their real property, not simply as something which could be liquidated and turned into cash, but as something much more specific having properties beyond its cash value. Their respect for equity and responsibility towards widows was tempered by a desire to assert their authority from the grave in a way which would serve a wide variety of family objectives. They sought to enable the surviving family to utilise a combination of real property, business capital, good will, personal skills and resources to serve economic, social and psychological needs. Their wills express a greater sense of the specific nature of items of property, of real property and, amongst some, of specific items of household and personal property. The ambitions and strategies of this group imposed a very distinctive element upon the built environment of the growing towns.[129]

The dominant form of will making was that of the cash economy capitalist. They used the cash economy as the medium through which they achieved order and equity. They used the auction and the valuation. These will makers required the executors to 'sell and dispose of all and every my said household goods ... and stock in trade, and also receive and collect in as soon as convenient all such money as shall be out at interest ... '[130] The money resulting from this was to be divided 'equally between and amongst all my children ... share and share alike'. The whole range of goods, securities and property was to be sieved and homogenised through the cash economy in the interests of equity. There was no hint of

[129] See this volume, Chapter Five, 'Strategies and the Urban Landscape'.
[130] Will of Joseph Binks of Armley, probate, 11 February 1831.

favouring the eldest son, or even of treating sons and daughters differently. It was a world in which continuity of a business was an option and not a necessity. It was true that the cash economy and its economic fluctuations and liquidity crisis could destroy family relationships and strategies, but they used the cash economy for achieving the support and equity which they identified with family. The repertoire of the cash economy capitalist had enormous power and flexibility.

The pure cash economy capitalist strategy was a part of many wills which included 'things' and 'real estate' listings, but this strategy was expressed most directly in those twenty-three wills which were merely a bleak list of categories. A simple version was that of Joseph Binks, the common carrier of Armley, whose will of December 1830 came to probate two months later, sworn value under £200. His was the simplest of middle class male wills. He left four sons, a daughter and a widow. The only thing that made his will at all distinctive was the affirmation of his religious faith at the start. 'In the name of God Amen, I Joseph Binks of Armley... common carrier, being of sound and disposing mind and memory, praised be God for the same...'. Joseph was embedded in the local neighbourhood community of Armley. His executors were his eldest son, James Lupton, cloth manufacturer and Thomas Wood, clothier. His property categories were:

household goods, furniture, plate, linen and china
stock in trade
money out at interest
ready money and securities for money whether the same or any of them
are or is by mortgage in fee or in years
bond note or otherwise
all other of my personal estate.

Many of these were standard legal phrases and Joseph Binks probably copied them from samples in one of the advice manuals.

The full power and variety of these strategies to order a world disordered by death was demonstrated in the three interlocking wills of the Thackrey and Chadwick families. Michael Thackrey, Esq., gentleman, died in October 1829, having made his will in August 1827.[131] The probate was valued at under £10,000. His real estate in Park Square he valued at £11,000. Two of the houses were occupied by his son John and by his friend and executor, Henry Rawson. These, together with an adjoining warehouse occupied by Rawson and Co., were valued at

---

[131] Probate 16 February 1830.

£6000 and the remainder at £5000. He left a widow, Rachael, and six children. One daughter was dead (Table 3.14).[132]

Michael Thackrey was a prosperous and successful man at a mature stage of life cycle and family formation. He had a wife, property and adult children. His daughters were married into the high status ranks of retail, manufacturing and the professions. Michael left £50 to the treasurer of the Baptist Missionary Society, £100 to the treasurer of the Bradford Northern Education Society for training up pious young men for the Ministry in the Baptist Persuasion, and £100 to the minister for the time being of the Baptist Chapel at Leeds. He was unusual in making charitable bequests in his will. Charitable subscriptions were usually something which the middle class did whilst alive. Thackrey, his sons and sons-in-law were all contributors to most of the major charitable subscriptions of the late 1820s, for the Leeds General Infirmary, for the Irish Famine of the late 1820s and for the unemployed poor during the winter of 1829.[133] They did what was expected of high status people without being especially active in public life. Frederick Wigglesworth once signed a petition in favour of Sunday Observance and voted for the Whigs in the 1832 election, but that was all.[134]

The Leeds wills, like the vast majority of wills, were about family. The evidence of the directories showed that family life centred upon Park Square and the neighbouring streets and dissenting chapels. Family wealth originated in the stuff (worsted type cloth) trade. In the early 1820s, George had moved up the hill to Woodhouse[135] leaving his brother in Park Square handy for the business in nearby Park Lane.

When Michael Thackrey made his will, he had resources at his disposal and the security of knowing that his family were as established in adult life as the insecurities of economy and demography would allow. Michael Thackrey, like other middle class males who anticipated death with adult children and a widow, worked from the central principles of responsibility to a widow and gendered equity to his children, mediated by the cash economy. Several features of his will, with minor variations of phrasing, were common to many others.

After reserving some specific categories, his executors were instructed to take all his real and personal estate and

---

[132] The information on the family was compiled from the will itself and the three Leeds commercial directories published at the dates given.

[133] Morris, *Class, Sect and Party*, pp. 204–27.

[134] R.J. Morris, 'Petitions, meetings and class formation amongst the urban middle classes in Britain in the 1830s', *Tijdschrift voor Geschiedenis* 103 (1990), 294–310.

[135] Beresford, 'East end, west end', 298.

Table 3.14 *The Thackrey and Chadwick families in the Leeds commercial directories of 1822, 1824 and 1834*

Hannah was wife of Charles Chadwick, dyer

1822	Charles Chadwick	dyer	Bowman Lane, h. St Anne's Lodge, Burley
1825	Charles Chadwick	dyer	w. and co, Bowman Lane h. Burley
1834	Charles Chadwick and Co	Wool and woollen cloth dyers, Bowman Lane	

Mary was unmarried

George

1822	George Thackrey	stuff merchant	Little Woodhouse
1825	George Thackrey	stuff merchant	h. 31 Woodhouse Land
[1825	George and John Thackrey	stuff merchants	8 Park Lane

John

1822	John Thackrey	stuff merchant	Park Square
1825	John Thackrey	stuff merchant	h. 40 Park Sq

[1834, they had both gone from Park Sq. There was a John Thackrey, dyer Isle of Cinder with a home address in Wellington St]

Ann was wife of Frederick Wigglesworth

1822	Frederick Wigglesworth	wholesale and retail furnishing ironmonger	6 Market Place
1825	Frederick Wigglesworth	furnishing ironmonger	93 Briggate
1834	Frederick Wigglesworth	gentleman	Eldon Terrace

Sarah was wife of Reverend James Acworth

1825	Rev James Acworth	Baptist Minister	3 Park Square
1834	Rev James Acworth	Baptist Minister	2 Blenheim Sq

Rachel was dead leaving three children by her husband, Reverend Richard Winter Hamilton

1822	Reverend R. W. Hamilton	minister of Albion Chapel	h. Park Square
1825	Reverend Richard Winter Hamilton	Independent Minister	12 Albion St
1834	Reverend Richard Winter Hamilton	Independent Minister	9 East Parade

when and as they shall think it most expedient to sell and absolutely dispose of all my said real estate hereinbefore devised to them either by public sale or private contract together or in parcels for the best price or prices that can or may be reasonably had or gotten for the same.

The personal estate was to be turned 'into money'. The first charge upon this was the payment of debts and funeral expenses, as was required by law. Then the executors were to put or place or continue out at interest on real security or on the government security or securities of this Kingdom, or that of the United States of America so much of the said trust money as will be sufficient to raise one annuity or clear yearly sum of five hundred pounds . . .

This was to be paid in two equal six-monthly payments to Rachel. Such instructions were in forty-eight (37 per cent) of the wills by men leaving widows. Michael was the only one who mentioned the United States. Like a minority of men who left widows, he used the annuity to eliminate the traditional property rights which married women carried into the probate process. The annuity was to be 'in full bar and satisfaction of all dower or thirds'. Some 10 per cent (fourteen) of the wills made by men leaving widows made a provision of this kind. Michael Thackrey owned substantial real property. The rights married women had in their husband's real estate deals during coverture were uncertain. Thackrey did not want anything to encumber his executors' ability to deal in the property market.

'My dear wife Rachel' was also given 'the use and enjoyment of all my household goods and furniture, plate linen and china' but, to emphasise she was only a life tenant, the trustees were instructed to take an inventory if they thought fit. This was unusual. Only nine (7 per cent) of the wills included such a demand. Michael realised this was inappropriate for the late 1820s. In a codicil, 8 September 1828, he directed that the household contents should be 'for her own use and benefit absolutely for ever' and for good measure added 'my double horse carriage and my one horse carriage or gig'. He joined the 21 per cent (twenty-eight) of the men who left household contents to their widows.

Clauses of the type Thackrey included at the start of his will emphasised the economic dependence of the majority of married women,

I give and bequeath to my dear wife Rachel all the wines and spirituous liquors and other consumable articles of household in or about my dwellinghouse at the time of my decease for her own use and also the sum of two hundred pounds to be paid to her immediately after my death for her support until the first payment of the annuity hereinafter given to her.

A husband's death left a widow technically destitute and these clauses ensured her ability to continue with the basic gender role of household management and financing. Textbooks on wills often warned of this situation. Thirteen wills had such clauses. Immediate support, household contents and an annuity were thus secured for his widow.

Michael Thackrey had more resources at his disposal than most. He could afford to be a little more elaborate in his arrangements but his basic principles were common to the middle classes of Leeds. 'From and after the decease of my said wife', the residue of the trust and any interest that had gathered over and above the annuity payment was to be divided 'equally between and amongst for the equal benefit of all and every my children . . . share and share alike'. His dead daughter's children were to share equally the portion that would have gone to their mother. An elaborate web of survivorship clauses was added to ensure that these principles were observed if any more children died before their father. In such cases all 'lawful issue', in other words legitimate children, were to share equally the portion which would have gone to their parents. If there was no lawful issue, then the sum involved went back into the general residue of the estate.

Thus far, measured by the cash economy, all was equal: male, female, eldest, youngest, married, unmarried. The 'fortune' which each child inherited was equal in value but there were qualitative differences. The trustees were directed to retain £4000 from each of the portions to which the three girls, Mary, Ann and Sarah were entitled. This £12,000 they were 'to put and place or continue the same at interest' on the same sort of securities as their mother's annuity fund. 'The interest, dividends and annual proceeds' were to be paid to the three daughters

during their respective natural lives for their own respective sole and separate use and benefit and independent of the debts control or engagements of the husband or respective husbands of any of my said daughters.

On each daughter's death, whether she was

covert or sole and notwithstanding her coverture . . . (her share of the said trust money was to be divided) . . . equally amongst all and every her lawful children . . . share and share alike.

Thus at 4 per cent, the three girls would have an income of around £160 a year, just enough for an independent household with a servant or, if married, a small income independent of her husband within the economic and legal dependency of marriage. The seventh portion was to be invested for Rachel's children, and divided amongst them when they were 21 years old. Fifty pounds a year could be provided for each of them and spent or handed to their father, the Reverend Hamilton for 'the maintenance education and bringing up of my said grandchildren'. Such trusts for grandchildren were not as common as those for daughters but were often found where money was left for minors. The economic and legal power of these men as fathers reached out from the grave, limited only by the early eighteenth century statutes on strict settlement.

Usually the son's portion was made over to them or devised, to use the legal term, absolutely, but Michael Thackrey could not resist giving his sons a number of choices, which showed his view of the nature of male wealth and capital. Good bourgeois capitalist though he was with his 'sell' and 'into money' clauses, he still had some feeling for the real estate he had accumulated in Park Square, the first, and now increasingly smoke-filled, west end of Leeds. He gave them the option of taking this property as 'tenants in common' at a valuation of £11,000. If they did not fancy this, then they could take the property in separate portions. The eldest son, George, was given first option of the portion with the warehouse or business end of the property. If they took the real estate, then it was to be treated as a part of their seventh share. The sons were given preference in terms of access to their father's estate, not in quantitative terms.

it shall and may be lawful . . . to lend and advance any part of the said trust money, hereinafter directed to be placed out at interest for securing the said annuity for my said dear wife or of the said one seventh part of my personal estate hereinafter given to or for the benefit of my said grandchildren (not exceeding the sum of ten thousand pounds in the whole) to my said sons at lawful interest on their joint or several bond . . .

The trustees were empowered to lend up to £4000

to any husband, they my said daughters may respectively have on his own personal security all such last mentioned advances being made with the consent and at the request in writing of such of my said daughters respectively to whom the money so advanced shall belong or for whose benefit it shall be held in trust.

Finally the grandson was to be allowed up to £200

as a fee or premium with him as a clerk or apprentice in any profession or trade or in his education at one of the universities or at any other establishment.

Sons, sons-in-law and grandson were to be given privileged access to the capital of the trust funds but, except in the last case, always at market rates. The economic relationships of generation and gender within the family were mediated by the market. Michael Thackrey was unusual in spelling out these arrangements in such detail in his will but the case studies from the family papers showed that many trustees followed the practice of giving male business privileged access to the trust funds, but at market rates.

Michael's late codicil and his wife's death in February 1831 provided a rare chance to compare the opportunities and responses of husband and wife to the disposing of their property at death. Rachel's choices were more limited. The sworn value of her estate was under £450 and she could dispose only of those categories devised to her absolutely in the codicil. For Rachel there were female things, and family things and there was equity. The female things were 'my plate, linen, china, trinkets and wearing apparel' which were to be divided equally amongst her four daughters; the children of daughter Rachel 'taking equally amongst them their mother's share'. Then there were family things; 'my household goods, furniture, wines, spirituous liquors, books, pictures, maps, prints, money securities for money debts...'. These were to converted 'into money' and divided equally between her six living children and her son-in-law Richard Winter Hamilton, but before that happened 'an inventory and valuation' was to be made and

> if any of the persons who under the trusts hereinafter declared shall become entitled to any part of share of the said trust money shall be desirous of purchasing any part of such articles comprised in such inventory and valuation he or she shall be at liberty to purchase and take the same at the price or respective prices at which the same shall have been so valued, the same to be taken in satisfaction and discharge of the share or respective shares of the trust money to which he she or they may become entitled by this my will.

The family gained privileged access to their mother's possessions, but an access mediated by market values to ensure equity. Money going to grandchildren under the age of 21 was reserved for their 'education and maintenance'.

Despite their high social status, the troubles of the Thackrey children were not limited to the deaths of parents. When Rachel made her will her son-in-law, Charles Chadwick, was already dead. There was no indication of what went wrong but in December 1829 he signed his last will and testament with a shaking hand and died six weeks later. Charles had been in business since at least the early 1820s but he was caught by death before his plans for his family could mature in the way that Michael Thackrey's had done. Again, he was a wealthy man, sworn value under £30,000, but his anticipation of premature death left him with a number of problems to solve if he was to fulfil the crucial aims of responsibility to widow and equity to children.

Some of the provisions were almost the same as those of his father in law. 'My dear wife Hannah' was to have all the household contents 'except money' and she was to have a legacy of £100 immediately upon his death. To further ease the transition the trustees were instructed

> to permit and suffer my said dear wife to occupy for the use of herself and my dear children my messuage or dwellinghouse with the outbuildings garden and land thereto belonging situate at Burley aforesaid for so long a time not exceeding two years next after my decease as she may think proper without paying any rent or other consideration for the same my said wife keeping the same in tenantable repair and paying the assessments charged thereon.

She was also to have

> for her own use and benefit... so much of the said trust money as will be equal to the amount of all such sums of money (if any) as at the time of my decease I may

have received from my late father in law Michael Thackrey . . . on account or in discharge of the portion or fortune to which in right of my said wife I am entitled under or by virtue of the last will and testament of my said father in law.

Having done all this, his executors and trustees were to turn the residue of his personal and real estate into money and 'to place or continue . . . out at interest on real or government security or securities from time to time when and as they think proper'. From this fund his wife was to have an annuity of £500, 'for and during the term of her natural life'. This was again to be taken in bar of dower and thirds. He made no attempt to prevent her remarriage and indeed took care that she should have an independent income within such a marriage,

the said annuity . . . shall not be subject or liable to the debts control or engage-ments of any husband with whom she may intermarry but that the receipt of my said wife only shall be a sufficient discharge to my said trustees.

Such instructions were included in sixteen (12 per cent) of the wills of men with widows.

Unlike his father-in-law, Charles Chadwick had children who were still minors. Their age can only be guessed. An elder boy may have been well into his teens. Charles did not view his family as completed. He instructed his executors to divide the residue of his estate 'into as many parts or shares as I shall have lawful children, living at the time of my decease or born in due time afterwards'. They were to apply 'the interest and annual produce' of such shares in the education and maintenance of these children, and then pay them 'their respective shares' at the age of 21. The usual elaborate survivorship clauses redistributed the share of the dead to any lawful issue they might have, then to the other siblings and then to his late brother's children. So far everything was easy, but Charles had an active dyer's business involving a partnership with his nephew, Joseph Chadwick, and he wanted all the provisions of his will to be subject to that partnership agreement. The high sworn value of this will may have owed much to the partnership capital which Charles had in the firm. He had capital which needed active business management to maintain its value, and he had sons who would expect to be set up with a business or career but were not yet adults. He empowered his executors to bargain with his nephew.

I do hereby authorise and empower them to make and enter into any agreement contract or arrangement they may think advisable with my said nephew either absolutely or conditionally for the withdrawing of my capital and interest from the said copartnership with him or for the continuing of such capital and interest in his hands until my sons or either of them shall attain the age of twenty one years.

No agreement was to extend beyond the time at which his sons would be 21.

There was no way of knowing how successful these strategies were. Joseph continued the business and in 1834 lived besides the works in Bowman Lane, which was still listed as Charles Chadwick and Co. At 2 Queen Street lived William Chadwick, dyer. At the same address lived a 'Mrs Chadwick'. By 1845, Joseph and William Chadwick, cloth and wool dyers were in Bowman Lane. Joseph lived at Bowman Lodge and William in Hunslet Lane. The premature death of Charles had driven the family back to its base besides the works in south Leeds after a brief period in the high prestige domestic accommodation above the smoke at Burley. It looked as if the business had survived with the nephew in partnership with one of the sons. As for the Thackrey brothers, they disappeared from Park Square and the public life of Leeds leaving sister and brothers-in-law as successful dissenting ministers. Brother-in-law Frederick remained in the 1834 directory as a gentleman living in the privileged middle class space of the north west.

Occupational status had some influence on the choice of ways in which a will viewed the world of property, but in all the major status groupings the bias was modest (Table 3.15). Unsurprisingly, agriculture, which included those who called themselves 'yeoman', had a bias towards real property, as did those with independent income, a category which included those who claimed the title 'gentleman'. The craft group had a slight bias to real property. Retailers, commercial people and the professions had a bias towards the abstract and legalistic style of categories. The professions were more likely to gift specific 'things' and avoided real estate.

The bias of those with no title towards 'things' was accounted for by the large number of women in this group (Table 3.16).

The relationship to 'sworn value' showed some influences (Table 3.17). The 'real estate' people were over-represented in the lower sworn values, which was not surprising given that real property was not included in that sum. Real estate was also over-represented in the estates of the very wealthy, indicating that land began to play a more significant role in the property strategies of that elite. The counterpoint to this was the importance of 'categories' for the middle ranks. The mention of specific items was something which was over-represented amongst middle and high wealth rankings, but the influence cannot be said to be great.

The 'cash economy capitalists' can be identified by the presence or absence of the instructions to 'turn into cash', an instruction which might or might not be qualified (Table 3.18).

140

Table 3.15 *Relationship between 'views of property' and occupational status for the major occupational categories, Leeds 1830–34*

	Things (%)	Real property (%)	Categories (%)	N
Agriculture	7.14	78.57	14.29	14
Retail	11.11	52.78	36.11	36
Commerce	15.38	50.00	34.62	26
Manufacturing	27.27	50.00	22.73	22
Craft	22.86	60.00	17.14	35
Professions	40.00	20.00	40.00	10
Independent	18.42	68.42	13.16	38
No title	35.90	35.90	28.21	39
Grand Total	20.96	52.40	26.64	229

Table 3.16 *Gender and 'views of property', Leeds 1830–34*

	Things	Real estate	Categories	N
Male	17.51	55.93	26.55	177
Female	32.69	40.38	26.92	52

Table 3.17 *Sworn value of probate and 'views of property', Leeds 1830–34*

Sworn value	Things %	Real estate %	Categories %	Totals N
Under £100	16.7	66.7	16.7	20
£100	17.0	61.7	21.3	47
£200	22.9	57.1	20.0	35
£300 to 450	20.7	41.4	37.9	29
£600 to 800	20.8	37.5	41.7	24
£1000 to 1500	23.8	52.4	23.8	21
£2000 to £9000	25.0	47.5	27.5	40
£10,000 to £30,000	23.1	53.8	23.1	13
Total	21.1	52.4	26.4	229

Table 3.18 *Instructions to 'turn into cash' and 'views of property', Leeds 1830–34*

	Things (%)	Real (%)	Categories (%)	N
No	23.28	55.17	21.55	116
Yes	20.93	34.88	44.19	43
Part	26.32	52.63	21.05	19
Personal only	16.67	61.11	22.22	18
Contingency (usually wife's death)	7.69	65.38	26.92	26
Other qualifications	28.57	42.86	28.57	7
Totals	20.96	52.40	26.64	229

There was a strong relationship between the cash economy capitalists and the categories people, whilst those who qualified the instruction to turn into cash were likely to be real estate people. Many of them were those who reserved the real estate to support wives or minors but then instructed executors to sell when this job was done.

None of these tables showed strong and compulsive relationships between economic or occupational status and the various strategies and views. The picture was one of individuals selecting from a repertoire of strategies in response to a variety of pressures which produced biases and preferences in behaviour and strategies.

4   The property cycle

The wills with their lists of instructions and contingencies were snapshots of intentions and strategies frozen in time by the prospect of death. The intentions outlined in the wills can only be understood as part of long term life cycle strategies. For members of the middle classes, a key part of such strategies was the management of property, hence the appropriate name for this process was the property cycle, which was as distinctive and influential as the poverty cycle which shaped the lives of many working class people.[1]

Robert Jowitt, woolstapler

Robert Jowitt of Leeds, woolstapler, was in many respects a characteristic member of the Leeds merchant elite. He was successful in trade and active in public life. His comfortable private and domestic life depended on a household income of around £1000 a year. He was exceptional in two ways. His membership of the Society of Friends gave him a height-ened awareness of the importance of family and property which was a feature of the English Quaker family networks[2] He kept detailed personal account books throughout his adult life. These accounts were a very particular mirror of his world. They were the means by which Robert Jowitt made sense of his world. They were the means by which he endeavoured to assert control over the relationships of property, family and business. In these books he partitioned his world between family and business. He identified property, obligation, cash and commodities. The picture and understanding of the world he gained from the process of making these accounts enabled him to take the decisions upon which depended the survival of his business, the consumption patterns of his

---

[1] B.S. Rowntree, *Poverty: A Study of Town Life* (London, 1902), p. 17; John Foster, *Class Struggle and the Industrial Revolution*, (London, 1974), pp. 96–9, 255–8.
[2] E. Isichei, *Victorian Quakers* (Oxford, 1970); Wilfred Allott, 'Leeds Quaker Meeting', *Publications of the Thoresby Society* 50 (1965).

household and the progress of his journey through the property cycle. Among the many advice manuals on the keeping of accounts, George C. Oke urged the advantage of knowing the true worth of a business and Issac Preston Cory claimed,

It is advisable for every person, be his dealings ever so simple, thus, or in some manner to examine his accounts at the close of each year, at least; not only to see that he has actually received all the rent, interest or income, that he ought to have received, but also to bring before his eyes any particular items of expenditure in which he had been inordinately, and perhaps unintentionally extravagant.[3]

These documents make it possible to follow the development of the property cycle of the successful middle class male.

Robert Jowitt kept several types of account book. Each represented a different aspect of property, income, debt and expenditure. Each interacted with the other. The private ledgers of the firm mediated between RJ as a private individual and the firm which by 1831 carried his name in partnership with his son. The advice manuals were insistent that partners must be in account with the firm and not with each other.[4] The major entities within this book represented both stocks and flows of rights and obligations.

The central account was the trade account. The bulk of the inputs were sales, together with the value of the stock at the end of the period. The outgoings were purchases. This was shadowed by the running account, which recorded actual payments. The balancing item of the trade account represented profit or loss. These flows were linked to the stock account drawn up each year, which represented the claims and obligations of the company as an entity in itself. In the late 1820s, the stock account recorded as obligations outstanding book debts, RJ's capital and loans from various family sources, notably his father's estate. The assets were dominated by book debts and the value of stock in hand. It was characteristic of such firms that their prosperity was determined not only by the balance of profit and loss on trading but also by the security of the book debts.[5] In 1830, Jowitt's book debts were 66 per cent of assets and 25 per cent of obligations. This was a potent measure of the risk environment in which the family operated. RJ also had a general account with the firm. Each year, this account began with the value of RJ's capital in the

---

[3] I.P. Cory, *A Practical Treatise on Accounts, Mercantile, Partnership, Solicitors, Private* (London, 1839), second edition; G.C. Oke, *An Improved System of Solicitors Bookkeeping* (London, 1849).

[4] Oke, p. 15; Cory, pp. 20–8.

[5] P. Hudson, *The Genesis of Industrial Capital. A Study of the West Riding Wool Textile Industry, c. 1750–1850* (Cambridge, 1986), pp. 107–30.

firm, to which was added interest on that capital, together with the addition or deduction of profit or loss and the balance on his running account with the firm. Each family member had a running account with the firm. The most important was that of RJ himself and, after 1830, that of his son, John Jowitt. On the debit side, RJ listed his cash withdrawals from the firm, but he also paid directly for his stock market purchases as well as some of his taxes. On the credit side was his income, which included his share of profit but also other income from the firm, rent and dividend, which were paid directly into the firm's books. The father and son, partners, were not the only entities of this sort in the private ledger. Others included 'the executors of the late John Jowitt' and Ann Jowitt, RJ's sister who benefited from a trust under her father's will. The last important entity in this ledger was the 'profit and loss' account, which was mainly derived from the balance on the trading account. Behind this summary lay the working account books of the firm. These included not just expenses like travelling but accounts with the manufacturers and clothiers to whom the Jowitts supplied wool. Pim Nevins, manufacturer, related by marriage to one of RJ's aunts and a fellow Quaker, was a major customer. The most important account was that with Beckett and Blaydes, their bankers. There were also accounts with London agents. These accounts, in turn, were derived from the Day Books which listed the day to day transactions of the warehouse and firm. These transactions would then be 'posted' into their appropriate place in the double entry accounts, ready to supply the summaries upon which Robert depended for the all important control of his business and family relationships.[6]

As a private individual, Robert Jowitt kept two types of account book which regulated his relationships with a wide variety of entities. Some were people, some companies, many were legal entities like executorships whilst others were categories of expenditure. His cash book was a simple listing of all outgoings which were listed in a single entry account as 'disbursements', with a note that they were balanced by 'my debit in JJ and sons Cash book'. In other words, he drew cash from the firm for his domestic expenditure. The listing was very detailed from 2 shillings for 'a gardener with a broken leg' to a purchase of corn and beans for £10.15s.[7] After he married, the list included regular drawings of £5 and £10 for his

---

[6] John Jowitt and sons, Private Ledger A, 1806–1831, BAJ 10; Robert Jowitt and sons, Private Ledger, B 1831–1844, BAJ 17; Robert Jowitt and sons, Private Ledger C, 1845–1860, BAJ 18. The Jowitt papers are located in the Business Archives of the Brotherton Library, University of Leeds. They are fully described in P. Hudson, *The West Riding Wool Textile Industry: A Catalogue of Business Records* (Pasold Research Fund, 1975).

[7] Robert Jowitt's Cash Book, BAJ 1805–1828, BAJ 4.

wife Rachel. He also kept another personal account book, only partly double entry, which was a summary of his own stock of property and flows of expenditure.[8] Many accounts involved small loans or debts incurred from or to other family members for goods and services supplied and received. Others were accounts with the treasurers of the many charitable and religious organisations which RJ supported. Others related to the purchase of shares and securities. His expenditure was allocated to a variety of categories, including travelling, tax and assessments and household. By the mid-1830s, he included an annual 'Memorandum of Personal Property'. On the 30th day of the 6th month in 1838, the list comprised:

	£.s.d
To balance of general account with RJ and son	18938.4.1
To 3 shares in Leeds Gas Company	536.3.0
To 5 do. in South Market	125.0.0
To 30 do. in Leeds and Yorkshire Insurance Company	300.0.0
To 1 do. in Leeds Waterworks	70.0.0
To 1 do. in Leeds Baths	20.0.0
To 10 do. in Humber Union Steam Company	500.0.0
To Loan to. Stockton and Darlington Railway Company on Bond	3000.0.0
To Samuel Stears, lent money	42.10.0

Some of these accounts related to the private ledger of the firm but others were quite separate entities. Only a part of this was mirrored in the stock account of the firm.

The detailed structure of these accounts was not exactly the same for the long adult life of Robert Jowitt. In the 1810s and 1820s, the relationship between stock and the running account was mediated by a general account each for Robert and his father, and the listing of personal property started in the 1830s as the complexity of RJ's holdings grew. The overall structure of the accounts revealed the separation of himself from his firm, even when he had no partner. The involvement of family was mediated by careful accounting.

The quality, consistency and completeness of Robert Jowitt's accounts were exceptional, but the importance he attributed to the making of accounts was not. Jane Hey, whose affairs are treated in more detail in

[8] Robert Jowitt, Private Ledger, 1803–1845, BAJ 2.

a later chapter, recorded her deep anxiety when she found even minor inconsistencies in her accounts and delight when she caught out her solicitor, brother-in-law in the accounts he sent to her.[9] The fraught history of the Rider–Lupton network derived from fairly small failures in personal accounting and provides a reminder that the 'order' which the accounts offered had a very direct social reality.[10] There was a Foucauldian sense in which these accounts created governable facts, but they also represented a Weberian economic rationality. There was no evidence that they were used as the basis for analytical calculations which then directed economic decision making. There was no sense of calculating a rate of return on capital within the firm nor any sense of discounting assets over time. The Oateses, like Jane Hey, were very aware of the different rates of return on assets over time and the relationship of this to risk. Family money, like other money in the firm, both as credit and debit, was charged a 'market rate of interest'. The awareness of time was not represented by any discounting of assets but by a careful and precise charging of interest on deposits and due payments.

The internal logic of the accounts was about control. They were about attributing property, assets, income flows and debts. They were about controlling relationships within partnerships and within families. They were about rights and obligations. The world which was structured, conceptualised and visualised in these accounts was the world of the adult males who had the bulk of the legal, economic and social authority to create such accounts. The process of keeping these accounts was in a very real sense a process of creating knowledge. It was knowledge which could be used to legitimate claims and actions. At times this involved the formal environment of the courts. Cory warned that accounts might be called for in a Chancery action or in the processes of the Probate Courts. Less visible, but equally important, was the creation of 'governable persons', self, family members, partners, friends, customers and suppliers.[11] The orderly relationships of the Quaker networks were maintained by the double entry accounts kept by men like Robert Jowitt. Esther Crewdson was one of RJ's in-laws at Kendal. In June 1813 she was debited with £2.18 shillings 'to Robinson's note for 4 vols of Pennington's Works elegantly bound' and on the same day 14 shillings for William

---

[9] See this volume, Chapter 6, 'Women and Things and Trusts'.
[10] See this volume, Chapter 7, 'Life after Death'.
[11] P. Miller and T. O'Leary, 'Accounts and the construction of the governable person', *Accounts, Organizations and Society* 12 (1987), 235–65; C. Lehman and T. Tinker, 'The "real" cultural significance of accounts', *Accounts, Organizations and Society* 12 (1987), 503–22.

Alexander's note. Two months later, on the credit side, was £3.2 shillings 'by cash at Kendal'. Robinson and Hernaman where major booksellers in Leeds. Esther had done some shopping in Leeds and the cash had been collected on Robert's next trip across the Pennines to Kendal. There was no professional closure in keeping these accounts.[12] The advice manuals talked about the 'mystery' of the Italian system of accounts, but there was no sense of a professionally trained group of accountants being required for keeping valid accounts. Keeping accounts was the responsibility of every property holder.[13]

In the accounts which Robert Jowitt and others like him were keeping, three elements were important. The accounts were about identifying the flows and stocks of resources and obligations, about the value of wool stocks, about book debts and bank balances. These were men whose economic activity did not face the discipline of the stock market or the branch plant under the scrutiny of head office in which the rates of return on assets were being constantly compared. These men faced the related disciplines of sustaining liquidity, maintaining their credit-worthiness, maintaining an orderly and stable relationship with others, especially family members as well as supporting a viable level of consumption and status.

The accounts represented a clear division of public and private. The private male, who owned stocks, bought hay and corn for his horses, made allowances to his wife and children and subscribed to schools and congregational activities, maintained a separate existence from the public male, who bought and sold wool and received interest and profits. This conceptual divide was in all the accounts although, in legal terms, Robert Jowitt was owner of both accounts and the liabilities incurred in the firm could be requited through creditors appropriating his personal and domestic assets. In any case the division was never perfect. Maderia wine appeared in the accounts of the woolstapling firm and the partners seem to have used the firm as a private bank before re-affirming the public–private division when drawing up the accounts. The concept of public and private did not just divide the worlds of men and women, but also ran through the lives and experiences of the middle class male. This division was elegantly inscribed in the flowing cursive script of the account books.

Lastly, the accounts showed a division between interest and profit. Interest was paid by the firm for the use of capital. It was paid to partners and other family members who deposited cash in the firm. In this sense

---

[12] T.A. Lee, 'A systematic view of the history of the world of accounting', *Accounting, Business and Financial History* I, no.1 (1990), 73–107.

[13] B.F. Foster, *The Origin and Progress of Book Keeping* (London, 1852).

there was a market discipline for capital in the firm. It was liable for the market rate of interest. As the history of the Oateses indicated, family capital had privileges and liabilities. Family members might expect to be 'accommodated' by the firm but, in return, they were expected not to withdraw their money at awkward moments. The discipline of sustaining liquidity was blunted by family, although the family expected, and was attributed, market rates of return. Profit was the return to entrepreneurship. It was the return for risk and enterprise. This conceptualisation was reflected later in the century by Alfred Marshall who outlined four factors of production, land, labour, capital and management, with their respective returns, rent, wages, interest and profit.[14] This division was an important aspect of the relationship between generations in those firms which made a successful transition from father to son. Profit was, in a very real sense, a return for the 'work' of the counting house and of the travelling merchant. As the older generation withdrew from active participation in business, their income relied upon accumulated capital, the interest, whilst the younger members took a greater share of profit in return for doing most of the work.

The decisions, transfers, flows and accumulations represented by these account books were structured by the property cycle. The accounts did not directly represent the stages of the property cycle, but the major changes of that cycle were often signalled by changes in the formal structure of the accounts. The initial keeping of accounts was an early sign of a move towards adulthood. In the late 1820s, Robert Jowitt moved from keeping a general account in his private ledger with the firm to keeping a listing of his personal property in his own private ledger. This change in location for his annual summary of his personal worth was a signal that the time had come to accumulate rentier as distinct from trading assets.

There were six distinct stages in the property cycle of the successful middle class male.[15]

(1) Childhood – dependence on parents.
(2) Training (normally aged 14 to 21 years of age) – dependence on parents for financial support during professional training or apprenticeship.
(3) Adult – earned income and net payer of interest. The young adult typically sought an income well in excess of consumption. Many personal and business loans were outstanding. Property accumulation

[14] A. Marshall, *Principles of Economics*, 8th edition (London, 1920), pp. 60–9, 482–505.
[15] R.J. Morris, 'The middle class and the property cycle during the industrial revolution', in T.C. Smout (ed.), *The Search for Wealth and Stability* (London, 1979), pp. 91–113.

was often supported by mortgaged debts. This phase was often associated with marriage or setting up an independent household.

(4) Adult – earned income and net receiver of interest. Income was still dominated by earned income from trade, manufactures or professional activity but the balance of interest was now in favour of the individual as debts were paid off, capital accumulated in the form of stocks, shares, real property, mortgages and loans and the balance of trade debts moved in favour of the individual.

(5) Adult – unearned income. Capital accumulation slowed and income was dominated by unearned income from rents, dividends and interest. Profits and fees were less important as a man withdrew from business. The break with business was often partial and took place over several years, so this was not the sharp break of a twentieth century 'retirement'. The change often took place in the early to mid-fifties.

(6) Life after death. As the evidence of the wills indicated, an individual's property was rarely dispersed immediately after death but was handed over to the executors and trustees of the estate. In this form the legal personality of the 'executors of...' sustained the living standards of widows and daughters. Only after this phase was complete was the property divided between the living children, or their children. Such a division might contribute to Stage 4 of the property cycle of the next generation.

The quality of Robert Jowitt's account books enabled his property cycle to be followed with considerable completeness. His business had been established by his father, John Jowitt, Junior, who had begun as a clothier's son in Churwell, a village near Batley, in the woollen district of the West Riding of Yorkshire. John moved to Leeds and passed through several partnerships before joining with Robert, his only adult son, in 1806, when the boy came of age.[16] Robert married Rachel Crewdson of Kendal in 1812. She brought with her a substantial marriage portion, £3000, which was soon followed by a legacy of £3606 from her mother in 1814–15. The marriage portion remained in trust to provide Robert with a stable though minor part of his income until his wife's death in 1856. The inheritance, which under existing married women's property law, became Robert's own property was placed in the firm.[17] His father died late in 1814, leaving personal property valued for probate at under £30,000, a substantial house off Woodhouse Lane to the north west of the town

---

[16] Letters to John Jowitt, clothier, at Churwell near Leeds, 1775–76. BAJ 30.
[17] Robert Jowitt, Private Ledger, 1803–45, BAJ 2, f.3–4.

the town centre, and 'all my messuage, warehouse and other buildings and tenements in Albion Street, Leeds'.[18] Robert only had a one sixth interest in this. His share enabled him to purchase Carlton House from his father's estate for £3000 and released him from the £3000 debt to his father, which he had incurred when he had entered into the partnership in 1806. This sum was put into 'hotchpotch' when the division of the estate was made.

Like other middle class males, John Jowitt behaved with strict equity towards his children and set aside a portion of his estate for the care of his widow. This left Robert with a problem. He now had a business which, in terms of capital stock, was valued at £37,527 in 1814 but Robert was entitled to only £6653 of that sum. His father held £20,836. The rest were book debts and elements of interest and profit due to both men on that year's account. By the end of 1816, the capital was reconstructed so that Robert held £13,243, but the bulk, £17,281, was now held by a new legal personality, 'the executors of the late John Jowitt'. In other words, Robert Jowitt, as one of the executors and trustees under his father's will, had allowed this money to remain on loan to the firm of Robert Jowitt and in return provided income in the form of interest for his mother and sisters. The stock account of that year included £283 interest debited to sister, Susannah, and £561 to mother, Ann. Over the next 18 years, Robert steadily reduced the amount due to his father's estate.

Table 4.1 *The debts of the Jowitt firm to the executors of John Jowitt, 1816–42*

Year	Amount due (£)	Robert Jowitt's capital (£)
1816	17281	9509
1817	14156	12779
1818	14235	16396
1819	12612	15727
1820	12244	13561
1821	12173	13506
1822	12475	14601
1823	12353	14839
1824	13639	15409
1825	13539	19288
1826	12388	10795
1827	10883	10653
1828	10925	11423
1829	8726	10453
1830	6510	12919

[18] Will of John Jowitt, late of Leeds, woolstapler, Court of Ainstie, September 1815, Borthwick Institute of Historical Research, York.

Table 4.1 (*cont.*)

Year	Amount due (£)	Robert Jowitt's capital (£)
1831	5998	16080
1832	6118	16559
1833	5029	19348
1834	5218	20396
1835	1093	20548
1836	224	18939
1837	380	14638
1838	844	15541
1839	69	18853
1840	436	16353
1841	1833	14694
1842	1189	11143

Note: The firm continued to hold small amounts for the executors after 1842 but, as with the post-1835 totals, these were cash balances held for the convenient management of the trust, rather than being substantial investments.

Source: John Jowitt and Son, Private Ledger A, 1806–29, BAJ 10; Robert Jowitt and Son, Private Ledger B, 1830–44, BAJ 17 f. 40–9.

By this arrangement, John Jowitt, had ensured an income for his widow, equity between his children and adequate working capital for his son. His son could only gain access to that capital by paying interest. He could only do this by continuing the management and entrepreneurial risk-taking of the business or, to put it in more formal terms, by undertaking his part in the reproduction of the commercial middle classes. Equity and the need to keep the capital as a working unit were both possible.[19] As Robert sought to gain control of the interest flow from his own business, he steadily reduced his obligations to his father's estate, but access to this loan capital was important for some 14 years after his father's death, especially in periods of heavy trading losses.

Robert Jowitt's income, spending and investment patterns may be reconstructed for the whole of his adult life (Table 4.2). The main characteristic of the woolstapler's income was violent fluctuation. The changes between 1823 and 1826 involved a rise of 150 per cent, a fall of 390 per cent and another fall of 35 per cent. These fluctuations were reduced in the 1840s, when the dividends and interest from railway

[19] J. Goody, J. Thirsk and E.P. Thompson (eds.), *Family and Inheritance: Rural Society in Western Europe, 1200–1800* (Cambridge, 1976), p. 4 on the general nature of this problem in inheritance practice.

Table 4.2 *Robert Jowitt: income, consumption and savings, 1806–62*

Year(s)	Income (£)	Consumption (£)	Savings (£)	Firm's loss attributed to RJ's account (£)
1806–08	577	130	448	
1808–10	1676	209	1467	
1810–12	399	582	−184	169
1812–13	696	628	68	
1813–14	1744	702	1042	
1814–15	5390	785	4805	
1815–16	968	604	364	1139
1816–17	4086	833	3253	
1817–18	4451	850	3601	
1818–19	2838	664	2174	2844
1819–20	1050	700	350	2518
1820–21	814	653	161	215
1821–22	1775	680	1095	
1822–23	918	668	250	12
1823–24	1762	588	1174	
1824–25	4394	852	3542	
1825–26	1130	1127	3	8436
1826–27	736	673	63	200
1827–28	1344	625	719	
1828–29	1059	783	276	
1829–30	3006	692	2314	
1830–31	4325	1207	3118	
1831–32	970	972	−2	47
1832–33	4522	1002	3520	
1833–34	2080	988	1092	
1834–35	1686	955	731	
1835–36	2969	947	2022	
1836–37	1164	867	297	4161
1837–38	2525	857	1669	
1838–39	2275	1221	1054	
1839–40	1067	1386	−319	603
1840–41	2134	1116	1018	
1841–42	2578	2293	285	
1842–43	1776	1101	675	
1843–44	3043	1022	2021	
1844–45	1803	1113	690	n.a.
1845–46	2095	1391	704	n.a.
1846–47	2235	1832	403	n.a.
1847–48	2091	1368	723	n.a.
1848–49	8245	1183	7062	n.a.
1849–50	2272	943	1329	n.a.
1850–51	1546	915	631	n.a.
1851–52	1528	1102	426	n.a.
1852–53	3576	1084	2492	n.a.
1853–54	2130	1007	1123	n.a.

Table 4.2 (*cont.*)

Year(s)	Income (£)	Consumption (£)	Savings (£)	Firm's loss attributed to RJ's account (£)
1854–55	6955	1198	5757	n.a.
1855–56	2075	1130	945	n.a.
1856–57	3873	1094	2879	n.a.
1857–58	2021	970	1051	n.a.
1858–59	1707	955	752	n.a.
1859–60	1673	726	947	n.a.
1860–61	1649	747	902	n.a.
1861–62	1482	753	729	n.a.
1862–63	731	326	405	

Source: John Jowitt and Sons, Private Ledger A, 1806–31, BAJ 10; Robert Jowitt and Sons, Private Ledger, B 1831–44, BAJ 17; Robert Jowitt and Sons, private ledger C, 1845–60, BAJ 18.

shares and loan stock began to provide a more stable form of income than commercial profits. The stability of this later period would be even greater had it not been for the two unusual and extreme years of 1848 and 1854.[20] The high income of those two years was a result of a legacy of £6000 in 1848 following the death of Robert's son and the transfer of Rachel Jowitt's trust capital to her husband's account shortly before her death. Robert's average income was £2291, with a slight upward trend produced entirely by those two unusual years. Robert probably aimed for an investment income which was much the same as his normal earned income. This influenced the timing of his withdrawal from active commercial life, which took place between 1842 and 1844.

His consumption pattern was quite different. Fluctuations were minor. The exceptional totals of 1841 and 1846 were accounted for by the marriages of his two daughters. These events, and the other minor fluctuations, had little year on year relationship to his personal income. There were a number of influences on his levels of spending. His adult life can be divided into five periods, 1810–15, 1815–29, 1830–37, 1838–56 and 1857 until his death. Within each of these periods, spending fluctuated around a norm fixed by the current needs and ambitions of the household. The break points were marked by events in the life cycle of Robert's family and by his own accumulation of property. In 1810, he married. In 1815, his father died and he bought Carlton House. In 1829, he became a

[20] The mean income for 1806–42 was £2085, with a standard deviation of £1349, whilst that for 1843–62 had a mean of £2090, with a standard deviation of £773 (excluding the two extreme years).

net receiver of interest rather than a net payer. This change was directly related to the fortunes of the firm for the prosperity of the late 1820s made possible recovery from the difficult years of 1818 to 1826. The break in the mid-1830s marked the point at which he had cleared his debts and began to accumulate rentier capital. The final change came with the death of his wife. Within these norms, changes were related to changes in price levels. For each period, Robert fixed a normal standard of living which he could maintain by increasing spending in the face of rising prices. This happened in 1818–19, 1825, 1838–39 and 1846–47 and in the mid-1850s. Another influence was the sporadic and occasional demands specific to the needs of the Jowitt household, such as the replacement of the family carriage in the mid-1820s and the marriages of the two daughters.

The stability and security of the standard of living of the middle class household was based upon a disciplined strategy. Consumption levels were fixed to ensure a substantial surplus of income over consumption. The resulting savings ensured a substantial accumulation of assets. On the rare occasions when income failed to cover consumption, assets could be liquidated in order to maintain standards, or even increase them, as happened after Robert's marriage when his consumption rose in the face of the losses of 1812. In a situation where prices and income could fluctuate widely, this strategy protected family, household and that social status which was linked to consumption. It was a strategy which gave a practical content to the moral meaning which the middle classes attributed to concepts like foresight, prudence and savings.

The strategic skill of the middle class male head of household was to select a level of consumption which would enable savings to accumulate in a manner adequate to provide this stability. On a year on year basis, savings were the residual after the needs of a constant level of consumption had been satisfied. Hence, the level of savings was closely related to that of income.[21] The savings schedule changed very little during the life cycle. The influence of the life cycle was apparent in the nature of the assets which Robert acquired.

The years 1806–35 were dominated by a massive accumulation of capital in the firm. Robert's capital in the firm rose from £3000 in 1806 to £20,548 in 1835. Occasional allocations of capital to other forms of investment were trivial: a £60 loan to the Lancastrian School in 1812–13, a small personal loan in 1823–24, house purchase in 1815–16 and the

---

[21] When a linear relationship was sought between income and consumption the result was r = 0.3, whilst the relationship between income and savings was 0.97. The relationship between the savings ratio and income was r = 0.65, although it was only linear in the middle ranges between £1000 and £4000.

Table 4.3 *Robert Jowitt: acquisition of assets, 1810–60*

Period	To business assets (%)	To rentier assets (%)	Of which percentage to railways
1810–15	98	2	
1815–20	70	30	
1820–25	92	8	
1825–30	68	32	
1830–35	92	8	
1835–40	38	61	51
1840–45	9	91	74
1845–50	6	94	92
1850–55	25	75	71
1855–60	25	75	61

Source: As note 21.

Table 4.4 *Robert Jowitt: sources of income, 1806–62, annual average*

Period	Profit and interest from the firm (£)	All forms of rentier income (£)
1810–15	978	17
1815–20	1810	41
1820–25	1741	51
1825–30	1270	60
1830–35	2386	139
1835–40	1544	298
1840–45	1282	660
1845–50	389	1309
1850–55	87	1450
1855–60	50	1972

Source: As note 21.

purchase of some public utility securities from the firm in 1829. Capital transfers were made into the firm to cover losses. After 1835, the direction and size of capital transfers changed dramatically. This began with an interest in railway shares and the local gas company. Brief attention was paid to the firm in 1837–39 to rebuild capital after the losses of 1837 but after that the firm was only used for small cash balances. The changing pattern of asset acquisition was reflected in the changing sources of Robert Jowitt's income.

The switch from entrepreneurial income from the firm to rentier income marked the point at which Robert withdrew both his capital and attentions from the business and entered Stage 5 of the property cycle.

The change began in the mid-1830s and was signalled by changes in his accounting practice. He took out two life insurance policies of £1000 each for himself and his wife in the Friends Provident Society. In this period, the use of a life insurance as part of life cycle accumulation was unusual. There were only four cases amongst the listed assets of the 204 male will makers in the sample.[22] He already had shares in three local public utilities, the Leeds Gas Light Company, Leeds South Market and the Leeds Water Works, as well as shares in the Leeds and Yorkshire Assurance Company. These had been purchased from the firm and transferred to Robert's private account in 1829. His next moves were disastrous ventures into the Humber Union Steam Company, in which he lost £781 (1835–40), and into the Victoria Bridge in Leeds, in which he had lost £300 by 1840.

Success came with his ventures into the railway capital market, first into loan finance and then into the purchase of equity and debenture stock. Railway shares were accepted by the family as a sound investment as early as 1832, when the trustees under Rachel Jowitt's marriage settlement put £3000 into the Liverpool and Manchester Railway after the end of a mortgage. Robert waited until the capital of his firm had risen to a satisfactory level and been freed of obligations to his father's estate. Then he was drawn in on his own account. In 1836, he loaned £3000 at 4½ per cent to the Stockton and Darlington Railway after he had been approached by the Quaker Pease family. In the same month he began investing in the North Midland Railway, when he placed £131 with J.H. Ridsdale, one of the leading Leeds sharebrokers. The money was a deposit and premium on ten shares. Successive calls drew in more funds over the next four years. No new purchases were made until 1840 when he extended his holdings in the North Midland. The following year he bought shares in the York and North Midland, Hudson's company.[23] The next batch of investment came in 1844–45, when he bought widely in the railway stock of companies operating in the Midlands and North of England. With several of his early purchases, he sold about half his holdings in early 1845 as the share price boom mounted and used profits of 50–80 per cent to finance further calls and make deposits on other shares. Although the main aim was to secure the asset base for a rentier

[22] They were a joiner, a merchant, an organist and the iron master, Thomas Butler.
[23] A.J. Peacock, *George Hudson, 1800–1871. The Railway King*, 2 vols. (York, 1988–89); S. McCartney and A.J. Arnold, 'George Hudson's financial reporting practices: putting the Eastern Counties Railway in context', *Accounting and Business and Financial History* 10:3 (November 2000), 293–316; R.S. Lambert. *The Railway King, 1800–1871* (London, 1934).

income, he was not averse to taking a few speculative gains on the way. Robert rarely looked outside the North and Midlands of England for his purchases.[24] He began as a regional investor, perhaps working with information that came along the networks of the Society of Friends, many of whom, like the Pease family were active in early railways. In 1848, he began to deal through the London firm of Foster and Braithwaite and purchased shares in the Eastern Union and North British Railways. In 1853–54, he moved further afield with massive purchases of United States Railway stock.[25] By the 1850s, his investment was national and international and had lost most of its regional and national identity.

His investment strategy was revealed directly and by implication in a letter he wrote to his cousin in 1844.

I think when thou waste over, I mentioned that I had withdrawn from business – I am therefore rather seeking desirable investment for my money, rather than wanting to borrow, as my sons don't wish for spare capital in their business – such being the case I regret to say it will not be convenient for me to receive the £400 thou speaks of –

I would not venture to recommend an investment in Railway shares to my cousins as I did to my daughters when similarly circumstanced but I may say that I think it would be an easy matter to invest money so as to pay rather more than 4 per cent at present, with a strong probability that the dividends will not be less for some years to come.[26]

Robert took little interest in the major alternative investment, housing and real estate. In letting his sister's old house, which came to him after her death, he admitted that its rental value had fallen and showed irritation with the details of property management. Robert Jowitt wanted the minimum of management for his income. He wanted to pay attention to the philanthropic and educational work for both the town of Leeds and the Society of Friends, which filled so much of his time in the 1840s. At times, the management of a portfolio of railway stock proved equally tiresome. 'It will be well if some of us don't find that these concerns have too large a share of our attention', he told his brother-in-law in 1844.[27] Robert's correspondence became a turmoil of requests for scrip, remittance of calls and requests for information from sharebrokers and company secretaries. He demanded a report of the last general

---

[24] Robert Jowitt, Private Ledger, 1803–1845, BAJ (2), f.124 and 156–7.

[25] Robert Jowitt, Private Ledger, 1854–62, BAJ 3.

[26] To John Jowitt Nevins, 26 December 1844, from Robert Jowitt, letter copy book, Mar 1844 to Apr 1846, BAJ 32. All the letters cited in this section are from this source.

[27] To Dillworth Crewdson, 5 December 1844.

meeting of the London and Birmingham Railway 'to test the accuracy of the payment' of the last dividend. He upbraided his sharebroker for sending him shares upon which all due calls had not been paid, 'until that is done I cannot consider that thy duty as a broker can be terminated'.[28]

William Hey, surgeon: human capital and real estate

William Hey's economic history differed from that of Robert Jowitt in a number of ways. He was a professional man, a leading Leeds surgeon and member of the Tory Anglican elite.[29] His initial interest in rentier assets was in real estate. His account books were less complete. The surviving ones, 1827–28 to 1842–43 mark the later stages of the property cycle. The major threat to his property cycle strategy was demographic, the death of his son, and not directly economic. His overall strategy was much the same. He sought to move from active to passive sources of income by accumulating rentier assets. He sought to make his business available to his sons and to provide support for a widow and equity for all his children.

The receipts of the medical business varied between £3000 and £5000. Although fluctuations were more gentle than those in Robert Jowitt's accounts, these figures were influenced by the fortunes of trade in Leeds. Professional income was not insulated from the fluctuations of trade. There was nothing equivalent to the fluctuating prices of commodities in the warehouse or under contract which caused huge gains and losses to merchants and manufacturers but much of professional business was done on credit and bills were paid annually or at six monthly intervals, so the state of trade influenced the rate at which money due flowed into the accounts of William Hey and son. It may also have influenced the propensity of individuals to call upon the services of the firm. The long history of professionalisation had as yet had little influence on stabilising and protecting the income even of the leading professionals like William Hey.[30]

The 'profits' of the firm varied between 60 per cent and 80 per cent of receipts. Expenses were fairly constant and the proportion of profits rose

---

[28] To Henry Booth, Liverpool, 18 March 1846; to William Simpson, 21 July 1846.
[29] J. Pearson, FRS, *The Life of William Hey* (London,1822); the Hey family provided material for several chapters. The William Hey of the account books was William Hey II.
[30] A. Digby, *Making a Medical Living. Doctors and Patients in the English Market for Medicine, 1720–1911* (Cambridge, 1994); W.D. Foster, 'Finances of a Victorian GP', *Proceedings of the Royal Society of Medicine* 66 (January 1973), 46–50, traces a career which struggled from an income of £174 in 1854 to one of £576 in 1865, but only after a family loan of £1200 helped set up the practice. The debt and insecurity cycle was little different from many merchants and shopkeepers.

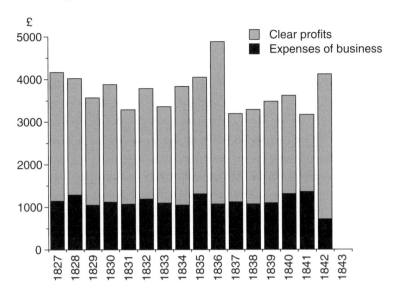

Fig. 4.1 Profits and expenses of William Hey and Sons, 1827–42.
Source: William Hey's Account book,1827–42. DB 75/20.

in good years. These were not profits in terms of formal returns to capital but represented the trading surplus available to pay the 'labour' of William Hey and his sons, who were the 'human capital' of the business.

The major items of expenditure were the 'expenses of the stable', between £500 and £600 in most years, the shopman's wages, around £50 to £60 pounds, as well as the general expenses of the shop, again around £500.

The 'profit' or trading surplus was divided between William Hey and two of his sons who were partners. The proportions varied as the terms of the partnership varied. The death of John in 1836–37 brought a major crisis to the firm and family which was reflected both in the figures and the response of the survivors.

William Hey II had been gradually easing his sons into a larger and larger proportion of the business. In 1827–29, his son William had 25 per cent of the profits, rising to 33 per cent in 1830–37. John had taken a sixth in 1829–30, then 20 per cent in 1831–33 and 25 per cent in the four years before his death. William Hey II's retirement from the honorary and prestigious post of senior surgeon to Leeds General Infirmary in 1830 was one signal of his intentions.[31] John's death in 1837 brought his father

---

[31] *Leeds Mercury,* 13 November 1830.

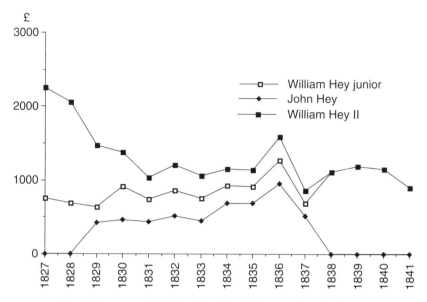

Fig. 4.2 Income of William Hey II and his sons from the firm of William Hey and sons, 1827–41.

Source: Same as Fig. 4.1.

back into the business in a 50–50 split with his surviving medical son. The loss of human capital to a professional business was as disastrous as the loss of finance capital to a merchant and in some ways harder to replace. John's death certainly denied the old man his 'retirement'.

Profits from the medical practice were only one part of William Hey II's income. Income from rents, interest on loans and earnings from stocks and shares were 50–60 per cent of his income in the early 1830s rising to 60–70 per cent by 1840. Family disaster meant that his withdrawal from active business was never as complete as that of Robert Jowitt.

By the 1830s, William Hey II's expenses were always in excess of his earned income. His life style and, in particular, his ability to contribute to the political, religious and charitable life of Leeds depended upon his unearned income. Even at this late stage in his property cycle, there was still a healthy surplus of total income over expenses in a normal year (Fig. 4.3).

His expenses were dominated by the household, with smaller sums for taxes and charitable donations. The increase in other expenses came from three sources. He provided an allowance and paid other expenses for his son Richard from 1830 onwards. John Hey's widow, Jane, had an allowance of £300 after John's death and, in the late 1830s and early 1840s,

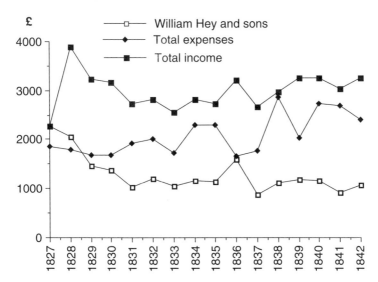

Fig. 4.3 William Hey II, expenses and income, 1827–42.
Source: Same as Fig. 4.1.

William II made a variety of political contributions to the revival of the
Tory party.

Choices

William Hey and Robert Jowitt made very different choices as they
accumulated rentier assets. As he entered the later stages of the property
cycle, William Hey re-organised, extended and developed holdings of real
estate which he inherited from his father and added a few public utility
shares and loans. All were based on the local economy. Ten years later,
Robert Jowitt showed a preference for railway shares which led him from
the regional to the international economy. As a cash economy capitalist,
the double entry account book was the perfect medium through which he
expressed his relationships with property and income. Such preferences
were a matter of timing, knowledge and opportunity. Robert Jowitt made
his move as large quantities of railway shares appeared on an increasingly
organised stock market.[32] He had access to relevant knowledge through
the family, religious and business networks of the Quakers, many of

---

[32] M.C. Reed, 'Railways and the growth of the capital market', in M.C. Reed (ed.),
Railways in the Victorian Economy (Newton Abbott, 1969), pp. 162–83.

Table 4.5 *John Jowitt, Junior: loans and mortgages, 1796–1814*

Nevins and Gatliff	1796, £1000
	1801, £350
	1802, £326
	(This seems to have grown as a trade debt. It was transferred to the executors of John Jowitt, Junior and helped support his widow and daughters.)
Leeds and Liverpool Canal	1796–1802, £2000
Sir Henry Carr Ibbetson	1799–1805, £1400
Walter Fawkes of Farnley Hall	1799–1814, £1500
	(This debt was also transferred to the executors.)
Pim Nevins	1801, £700
	1806, £2000 more was raised
	(The Nevins family were related to the Jowitts by marriage. In part this loan provided finance for the building of Larchfield Mill.)
Sam Elam	1804, £1500
	1808, £1000

Source: John Jowitt, Junior, ledger, 1775–1815, BAJ 38 and 39.

whom were leading players in railway development. William Hey II made his decisions some twenty years earlier. He had the opportunities provided by his father's real estate holdings. He was part of a dense Anglican social network which included John Atkinson, his solicitor. Both came from families of retailers and tradesmen, rising in status, whose establishments had fronted eighteenth century Briggate. They had a close understanding and knowledge of the opportunities and changes of the local real estate market.

Fragmentary knowledge of other cases, together with the account books of Robert's son John, make it possible to follow the influences of preference, opportunity and knowledge across generation and social status.

John Jowitt, Junior, Robert's father, was, like him, a woolstapler. He started business in or before 1775. His father was a clothier in Churwell who died in 1784, at which time his son owed him £883.12s11d and had recently received a gift of £1000.[33] Father was the major source of capital. The account books indicated a growing woolstapler's trade, purchasing wool in London and Norwich and selling to the clothiers of the villages to the south and west of Leeds.

In the 1790s John Jowitt began to place money on loan and mortgage.

---

[33] Will of John Jowitt of Churwell in the Parish of Batley, clothier, 8 January 1782, Court of Ainstie, September 1784.

There was also a small rent from an estate in Churwell and smaller debts from the clothing villages. One of these, to the Horsfalls of Gildersome, paid only 7 shillings in the pound when they went bankrupt in 1808. Many mostly small amounts were lent through the firm. These included £5000 to John Lister Kaye and £200 to the Leeds Water Works. High profits in 1793–95 and the break up of a partnership due to the death of his brother determined the timing of his move. The choice of investment was influenced by personal contacts and knowledge and the opportunities of the decade.[34] John provided loan finance to the canal boom and capital to the merchanting and manufacturing of wool textiles through links forged by family and religion. Finally, he contributed mortgage finance to the agricultural sector, in a period when rising food prices added to the value of land.[35]

John Atkinson was William Hey II's solicitor. He was part of that Anglican–Tory network of successful tradesmen, manufacturers and professional men, many of whom had their origin and spent part of their family life in Upper Briggate in the days when such people lived front of the street on the main street of Leeds and were happy that home and work were in the same building. John was son of a tallow chandler whose rented shop was in Briggate. In 1788, he qualified as an attorney. In 1796, he became sub-distributor of stamps, along with his partner Thomas Bolland. This required a bond of £500.[36] During his training and the building up of his place in the partnership, he relied upon his father's financial resources. When his father died in 1806, probate tax was paid at 'under £1500' valuation of personal property. Of the personal loans that were due to Thomas Atkinson, £500 was owed by John Atkinson himself.[37]

John's income came from a wide range of legal business, including property transactions, bankruptcies and executorships. By 1815, he began to build a substantial income from property in land. The rent book suggested that he began after the death of his father.[38] The property included a farm at Goole and several farms and closes of land at Pudsey, Bramley and other villages south of Leeds. The major purchases were made between 1818 and 1821. In 1822, he bought an estate at Little

---

[34] John Jowitt, Junior, ledger, 1775–1815, BAJ 38 and 39.

[35] J.R. Ward, *The Finance of Canal Building in Eighteenth Century England* (Oxford, 1974); D.T. Jenkins. *The West Riding Wool Textile Industry, 1770–1835* (Pasold Research Fund, 1975); B.A. Holderness, 'Capital formation in agriculture', in J.P.P. Higgins and S. Pollard (eds.), *Aspects of Capital Investment in Great Britain, 1759–1850* (London, 1971).

[36] DB 5/84 Professional papers of John Akinson.

[37] DB 7/71 Executors' papers for the estate of Thomas Atkinson, which include the receipts for legacy duty and the probate copy of the will.

[38] DB 5/54 Rent Account Book, 1810–15.

Table 4.6 *John Atkinson: rental and finance, 1815–32*

Year	Rent due (£)	Number of tenants	Interest from loans (£)	Cash due to Mary and Ann Dibb at the start of each year
1815				450
1816				850
1817				2000
1818	670	15	125	2300
1819	915	17	128	2770
1820	871	16	127	3570
1821	917	16	126	3800
1822	1116	20	141	4650
1823	1075	20	160	5250
1824	1081	21	158	5000
1825	969	23	147	5000
1826	1074	23	168	5000
1827	1097	23	153	5000
1828	1101	23	153	4100
1829	1088	22	163	
1830	971	24	156	
1831	895	23	148	
1832	848	23	132	

Source: John Atkinson's Rental, 1818–33, DB 5/58; John Atkinson in account with Mary and Ann Dibb, 1815–28, DB 5/57.

Woodhouse, which included the house in which he lived until the end of his life. Like his father, he had a small income from loans. The money on deposit from Mary and Ann Dibb, relatives of one of his partners, was likely to be only one of several sources of finance available to him. It was in the growing middle class suburbs to the west of the town centre that he laid out his property in lots for individual villas and for Woodhouse Square. The area experienced a slow and uneasy building development under the watchful eye of Atkinson himself.[39] In a period when much of the solicitor's work was involved with property development and finance, Atkinson had the knowledge and skill required to oversee the management of such assets in real estate.

Although William Hey II was deeply influenced by his father's investment in real estate, his son William Hey III was influenced more by

[39] M.W. Beresford, 'East end, west end. The face of Leeds during urbanization, 1684–1842', *Publications of the Thoresby Society* LX and LXI., nos. 131 and 132 (Leeds, 1988), 335–7.

Table 4.7 *William Hey II: shareholdings in 1844*

Leeds and Halifax Turnpike
Leeds and Homefield Lane End Road
Leeds and Liverpool Canal
Leeds and Selby Railway
Leeds and Yorkshire Assurance Company
Leeds Commercial Buildings
Leeds New Bath Company
Leeds Victorian Bridge Company
Leeds Water Works
Midland Railway

Source: Compiled from William Hey's Account Book, 1827–42. DB 75/20.

Table 4.8 *William Hey III: shares held in 1875*

Borough of Leeds		
Caledonian Railway	£3000 in 5% Preference shares	
East Indian Railway Company	£2000 registered in 1863	Sold for £2340 in 1875
East Lincolnshire Railway Company		
Gas Light and Coke Company	130 paid up shares plus £1000 Debentures	
Glasgow Barrhead and Neilston Direct Railway		
Great Eastern Railway Company		
Great Western Railway Company		
Midland Railway Company		
North Eastern Railway Company		
Leeds Club		
Leeds Library		
Leeds Philosophical and Literary Society		
Yorkshire Conservative Newspaper Company Limited		
Leeds Victorian Bridge Company		

Source: Probate of the Will of William Hey dated 30 June 1871. The probate was dated 13 July 1875. DB 75/2.

generation and behaved more like Robert Jowitt. Father's shares were local utilities and transport with one regional railway holding.

His son's holdings were very different. They were endorsed on the probate of his will. The shareholdings were British and imperial in range. His holdings of local shares represented recreational and political activities and not the investment in local infrastructure as his father's had been.

The mortgage men

By their nature, the wills provided only a glimpse of property strategies, usually late in the cycle. A minority of men were caught by death before the completion of their planned acquisition of assets. These wills revealed features of the cycle not always evident in surviving account books and family papers. The real estate strategists used a variant of the property cycle based upon the mortgage. In the early and middle parts of the cycle, finance would be borrowed on mortgage and then, if fortune favoured this group, the mortgage would be paid off and the rents provide an income for old age or for widowhood, and the capital value of the real estate provide inheritance for children. The supply side of the mortgage market might come from men in the later stages of the cycle but, in general, that finance, where it was linked to family property strategies, came from the operation of trusts set up for widows, daughters and minors.[40] On the supply side were many like William Naylor, gentleman,[41] who directed his trustees to sell his real estate and invest in government stock or place the money on mortgage. Several used both ends of mortgage finance. James Furbank, gentleman, described as solicitor in the directories,[42] was making provision for minor children and directed executors to pay off outstanding mortgages whilst he was also seized of tenements as mortgagee. Gervas Marshall, gentleman, whose daughter married the butcher, Joseph Rinder, was also 'seized' of a £300 mortgage on premises at Otley, a small woollen weaving town north of Leeds, but his property in Leeds, houses, brewhouse and land in Kirkgate and Briggate, was in turn subject to a mortgage of £2500.[43]

Another group gave instructions to ensure that a carefully planned process of property accumulation was completed after their death. James Canne, tailor of Nile St., east of Briggate, was making arrangements for the support and education of his daughter during her minority as well as for an income for his widow.[44] He directed that the mortgages of £400 a year on his Lady Lane estate and £400 on his Nile St. properties should be paid off at £100 a year. Thomas Barker, yeoman, required his executors to place the rents of his properties in Millwright St. into the bank until there was sufficient to pay off the mortgage.[45] Thomas

---

[40] R.J. Morris, 'The Friars and Paradise: an essay in the building history of Oxford, 1801–1861', *Oxoniensia* 36 (1971), pp. 72–98.
[41] Probate 13 March 1830. Sworn value £100.
[42] Probate 21 June 1830. Sworn Value £6000.
[43] Probate 17 February 1831. Sworn Value £100.
[44] Probate 17 February 1831. Sworn Value £100.
[45] Probate 3 February 1832. Sworn Value £20.

Crosland, cut nail manufacturer and grocer in Holbeck south of the river, who claimed the title of gentleman in his will, as did so many owners of small urban properties, directed that his sons should inherit their shares of his real estate in Holbeck providing they paid off the mortgage deed for £200 to his son-in-law, Matthew Dunderdale.[46] James White, flour dealer, wanted his executors to complete the process of buying land and cottages in Mabgate from Jonathan Lupton because the rents were designed to support his second wife.[47] Others like John Hardaker, clock-maker, simply wanted to ensure that the mortgage was paid off.[48] John Taylor, bricklayer and builder, made provision for some of his real estate to be sold in order to do this.[49] This was necessary because, under existing law, executors needed explicit authority to pay debts from real estate and their inability to do so might have led to the mortgage holder taking possession of the real estate.

Others used the mortgage as part of the intergenerational relationship. Henry Arnott, gentleman, raised £600 on mortgage to set his grandson up in business as a partner with his father, who was a dyer. This was not a gift for the account was to be settled at death in order to ensure equity. The sum was to be brought into hotchpotch and, if it proved greater than the shares of other children, then the grandson was to pay the excess.[50] John Reffitt, gentleman and one time cloth dresser, raised £1000 from the executors of Mr. Walker secured by mortgage on his property in Garland's Fold.[51] This was part of the £1900 loan to his son Joseph and Joseph's partner, John Scholfield, which had set them up in business as dyers in 1827. Again, this was not a gift and Joseph's debt was still part of the estate in 1831 so that there was equity between children. Reffitt gave his executors permission for the loan to remain with the business 'so long as my said trustees shall think proper'. He had a widow and minor children. Like Robert Jowitt, this sort of arrangement ensured both business continuity, equity and income for widows and minors.

The place which the ownership of housing had in the property cycle was recorded in the census tables of 1851. Although the occupational information was imperfect and generalised, there was one category 'house proprietor' which can be compared with those of merchant and

---

[46] Probate 6 May 1831. Sworn Value £200.
[47] Probate 18 September 1832. Sworn Value £200.
[48] Probate 2 May 1831. Sworn Value £100.
[49] Probate 3 September 1831. Sworn Value £100.
[50] Probate 6 May 1831. Sworn Value £200.
[51] Probate 21 November 1831. Sworn Value £2000.

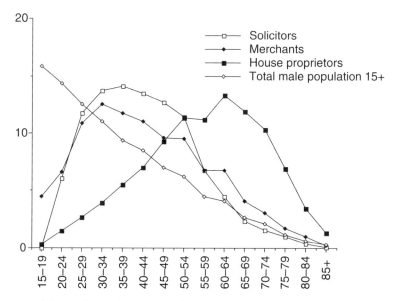

Fig. 4.4 Age and occupation for solicitors, merchants and house proprietors, Great Britain 1851.

solicitor. The house proprietors had a tendency to be in their 50s and 60s whilst the merchants and solicitors were in their 30s and 40s, indicating that the property cycle was spread across the British male population.[52]

John Jowitt's story

Superficially, the story of John Jowitt was very like that of his father. John's account books were kept with even greater care and consistency. They were even closer to the form outlined in the advice manuals of the 1830s. John joined the firm in 1832 with a capital of £1000, a gift from his father. The terms were fairly standard for a young partner, especially a son or nephew.[53]

John wrote the terms carefully into his first account book.

[52] *Census of Great Britain,* 1851.
[53] The information on John Jowitt, son of Robert, comes from John Jowitt, Junior, Private Ledger, 1832, BAJ 23, Brotherton Library, Leeds University and John Jowitt, Junior, Private Ledger, October 1848, BAJ 24.

2/3rd profits or loss belong to RJ; 1/3rd do. to JJ Jnr after allowing interest on their respective capitals.

That the firm RJ and son pay £100 a year rent of the warehouse in Albion St to RJ.

John was more of an accumulator than his father. In the first 20 years of his adult life, covering Stage 3 of the property cycle, John had a true income[54] of £44,774. His consumption measured by cash withdrawals from the firm was a modest £9047 for the 20 years, whilst measured by his household accounts it was £9211, suggesting that the firm was his only source of income at this time. In the first 20 years of his adult life, Robert had a true income of only £21,987 and a consumption total of £12,176, or £13,860 if measured by household spending. Thus, John spent only 20 per cent of his income, whilst his father had spent over 50 per cent. Even if Robert's withdrawals from the firm's capital were counted as income, which on a year to year basis it was in formal terms, then Robert still spent over 30 per cent of his income.

Despite his higher true income, John had a more modest level of household spending. Some of this may have been personality. Some may have been the habits of mind created by watching his father during the massive losses of the 1820s, together with his own modest profits in the 1830s. Some may have been due to the fact that his father was still alive. Robert was head of the family. He lived in Carlton House, a substantial villa north west of the city. John had no need to undertake the expenses of leading the family network and lived in the more modest terraced accommodation that was appearing in the fields around his father's house. John's spending pattern was marked by two features. There were three peaks which involved the purchase of furniture, one of them just after his marriage and the second probably related to his move from Blenheim Terrace to the more substantial housing of Beech Grove Terrace.[55] This move was related to progress from Stage 3 to Stage 4 of the property cycle. It was marked by a substantial increase in his 'normal' level of household spending. His became a well over £1000 a year household. This was also linked to his father's complete withdrawal from the business in terms both of claims of profits and share of capital. Robert was ageing and his household spending was in decline, so John was now taking over the leadership of the family and had the consumption pattern to match.

---

[54] 'True income' was defined as profits, plus interest, plus income from other sources, minus losses. It did not count withdrawals from the firm's capital as income.

[55] The year 1835–36 included a £664 furnishing account linked to his marriage, whilst that of 1850–51 also included £435 for furnishing. The directories of 1845 and 1853 showed his move.

In the 1850s, John moved into railway shares. He worked through the Leeds sharebroker, George Wise, and the London firm of Foster and Braithwaite. He bought and sold in a world capital market rather than building a stable portfolio of stock based upon local and regional knowledge as his father had done. He took preference stock from the United States, New York and Eire, Ohio and Pennsylvania, Chicago and Mississippi, often selling after two to three years and recording a loss. A few low paying shares in Leeds South Market[56] were his only local utility and the Leeds and Thirsk Railway a reliable and stable part of his funds. John's acquisition of a rentier income had little contact with the local economy. His father's death enabled him to move to Stage 5 of the property cycle as he began to establish his son Robert Birchall Jowitt with his capital in the firm. John was a cash economy capitalist. When his daughter married in 1860, his son-in-law got the marriage portion in the form of 89 Leeds Northern No.2 preference shares.[57] John was a railway man, but he was no longer tied by the networks and knowledge of the local and regional market in the way that his father had been. His learning process was through the semi-institutionalised world of his contango account with the local stockbroker working on the local Leeds Stock Exchange, rather than the cautious move from local to regional to national to international which his father had made.

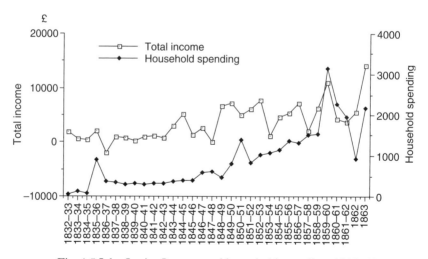

Fig. 4.5 John Jowitt. Income and household spending, 1832–63.

---

[56] Kevin Grady, 'The provision of markets in Leeds, 1822–29', *Publications of the Thoresby Society* 54 (1976), 122–94.
[57] John Jowitt Private Ledger, 1848–1863, BAJ 24, Property Account 1860, f.13.

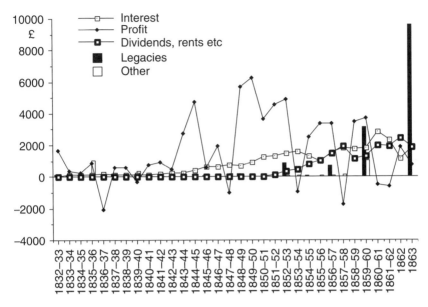

Fig. 4.6 John Jowitt, sources of income, 1832–63.

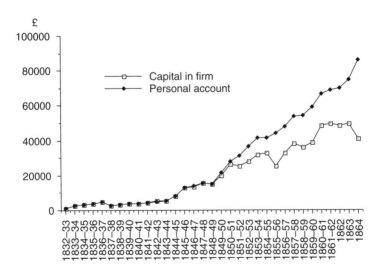

Fig. 4.7 John Jowitt. Capital structure, 1832–63.

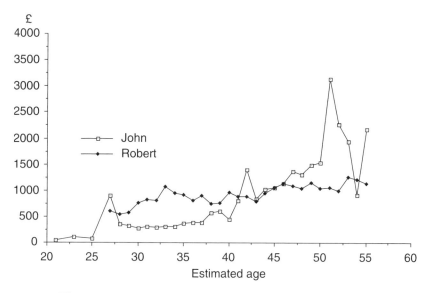

Fig. 4.8 Household spending of Robert and John Jowitt compared by estimated age.

The property cycle and the middle classes

Despite their differences in status and occupation, these men of the middle classes, merchants, medical men and lawyers, shopkeepers, manufacturers and builders, were united by the central structure of the property cycle. They all sought to eliminate debt and to move from active to passive forms of income. This was the equivalent of the mid- and late twentieth century career and retirement pension except that the men of the nineteenth century had few institutional intermediaries. Choice and the confrontation with each individual asset, an urban cottage with tenants and repairs, a railway share with fluctuating price and dividend, or the personal loan and mortgage with the judgement of character involved, were all raw and direct.

In the processes of the property cycle of the successful middle class male, there was a variety of choices of assets for the rentier phase, loans, government stock, railway and public utility shares, capital left at interest in a business, as well as real estate. This was very different from choices made earlier in the cycle when commercial, manufacturing and the human capital of a profession dominated choices. One effect of the property cycle was to partition the supply of capital into two streams. The first consisted of capital which accepted high risk in return for

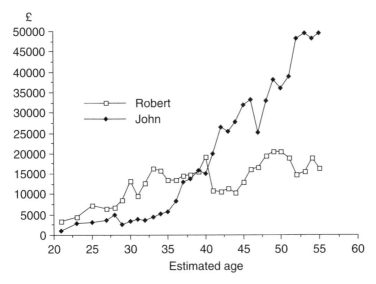

Fig. 4.9 Robert and John Jowitt. Capital in the firm by age.

potential high gains and required intensive and direct management input. The second stream sought a low risk with a stable income and minimal inputs of management from the holder. This was the capital of old age, of men like the Jowitts and Heys who wanted to spend less time in the counting house and more with the networks of family and the public life of church, chapel, politics and associational culture. There was a great hunger for suitable investments for such capital. Despite the importance of canals, turnpikes and local utilities, the market was still dominated by government stock and mortgages in the late eighteenth century. Many of these assets were not always as stable or as low risk as the owners would have liked. The shortage of suitable assets for the rentier phase of the property cycle explains some of the enthusiasm with which railway shares were greeted. The railway mania was not entirely a matter of speculative greed, but a product of the anxiety of men who saw a chance to move towards the rentier phase of their life without the troubles of real property management. Even here there were many losses. Men like Jowitt and William Hey III tended to buy high quality stock, loan stock, debentures and preference shares in established companies, but their account books record many losses and substantial falls in the capital value of their holdings.

The coming of railway shares, especially the huge quantity on offer in the late 1830s and the 1840s, had a major impact on the way in which the

Table 4.9 *The economic history of John Jowitt, 1832–63*

Year	Capital with RJ and son (£)	Interest (£)	Profit (£)	Legacies (£)	Other Dividends (£)	Dividends (£)	Income (£)	By cash (£)	Household spending (£)	Balance personal account
1832–33	1000	43	1695	90	0	0	1828	50	54	1100
1833–34	2778	124	388	45	0	0	557	110	116	2784
1834–35	3225	128	254	0	0	0	382	85	80	3225
1835–36	3522	142	873	0	1000	0	2015	732	903	3527
1836–37	4805	186	-2081	0	0	0	-1895	323	361	4807
1837–38	2587	110	587	197	105	0	999	326	333	2586
1838–39	3263	126	586	0	100	0	812	296	284	3252
1839–40	3779	147	-301	0	360	0	206	371	319	3779
1840–41	3613	160	749	0	35	0	944	271	294	3604
1841–42	4285	209	934	0	0	0	1143	291	315	4263
1842–43	5137	251	485	0	0	0	736	286	313	5107
1843–44	5587	273	2764	0	0	0	3037	393	374	5530
1844–45	8232	393	4725	24	0	0	5142	505	387	8191
1845–46	12869	621	599	36	3	5	1264	450	384	12926
1846–47	13682	656	1950	0	1	7	2614	539	582	13804
1847–48	15757	764	-996	0	197	6	-29	615	605	15836
1848–49	15114	703	5696	180	50	49	6678	497	458	15223
1849–50	19908	956	6238	0	42	46	7282	848	813	21439
1850–51	26345	1249	3630	0	50	46	4975	1182	1402	27870

1851–52	25468	1342	4543	0	50	149	6084	877	834	31319
1852–53	27744	1487	4909	850	60	385	7691		1032	36548
1853–54	31851	1620	-950	0	50	480	1200		1064	41313
1854–55	33049	1347	2538	30	0	805	4720		1140	41424
1855–56	25174	1007	3347	0	50	1031	5435		1370	43903
1856–57	32984	1537	3383	680	50	1470	7120		1305	47940
1857–58	38023	1842	-1723	0	87	1951	2157		1501	53727
1858–59	36062	1754	3462	0	0	1133	6349		1542	54362
1859–60	38948	1814	3701	3097	1000	1339	10951		3151	58921
1860–61	48179	2852	-510	0	0	1989	4331		2269	66889
1861–62	49423	2336	-606	0	0	1945	3675		1941	68619
1862	48213	1176	1888	0	0	2478	5542		921	70015
1863	49542	1866	766	9604	0	1908	14144		2176	74632

processes of inheritance and the property cycle operated in the economy, society and politics of England. Railways drew people like the Jowitts from a local to a regional to a national and then international market in rentier assets. For men like John Jowitt, Junior, and William Hey II, the comforts and freedoms of their old age depended upon the prosperity of the local and regional economy. This meant not just the urban economy but also the regional agricultural economy. John Jowitt, Junior, held mortgages on agricultural estates. William Hey I and II both held farms in the agricultural economy of the East Riding. Other links were less direct but the canal shares and turnpike trust holdings also depended at least in part on agriculture. The most immediate effect of the availability of railway shares was to break the link between the rentier property cycle strategies of the urban elite and the regional agricultural economy. One symptom of this was the readiness and enthusiasm with which the Anti-Corn Law League was accepted and supported in many urban industrial centres.[58] The Corn Laws had existed since 1815. There had been a small and ineffective criticism of them by radicals such as Ebenezer Elliott in Sheffield but they had gained little support from the urban elite leaders of middle class politics.[59] The Corn Laws were protecting investments like the mortgages of John Jowitt, Junior, secured on the agricultural estates of Yorkshire. The lower status portions of the middle classes, a small number of whom supported the radicals, were more likely to hold urban real estate and, hence, were less directly threatened by reductions in agricultural incomes, but Corn Law abolition had a low priority in a radical agenda that placed franchise reform high on the list. The Corn Laws were one of many monopolies attacked by radicals. In 1837, when the declining profit margins of Manchester cotton goods inspired a revival of anti-Corn Law politics from a powerful urban elite, there was a new generation much readier to listen, because rail shares meant they no longer depended on the regional agricultural economy.

The second effect of the coming of railway shares and a national and international market in shares took longer to have a significant impact. The holding of railway shares and loan stock brought about a slow disengagement from direct involvement with urban development on the part of key sections of the middle classes, especially elite sections of the

[58] D. Fraser, *Urban Politics in Victorian England. The Structure of Politics in Victorian Cities* (Leicester, 1976), pp. 237–51; N. McCord, *The Anti Corn Law League* (London, 1968); D.G. Barnes, *A History of the English Corn Laws from 1660–1846* (London, 1930), pp. 143–51, 202–16.
[59] *Ebenezer Elliott (Corn Law Rhymer), Centenary Commemoration* (Sheffield City Libraries: Sheffield, 1949); [Thomas Carlyle], 'The Corn Law Rhymes', *Edinburgh Review* (July 1832), 338–61; E. Elliott, *Chambers Papers for the People*, no. 8, (Edinburgh, 1850).

middle classes. By the 1860s, there was no longer any need to integrate urban development and the family and life cycle needs of key sections of the middle classes. This brought about a division of interest between high status middle class leaders who tended to promote urban improvements and public health regulation and the lower status tradesmen and shop-keepers who tended to be holders of urban cottage property. This was very evident in the political divisions of the last 40 years of the century.[60] The direction which that division of interest might drive policy was not self-evident. Urban improvement and regulation was not only a matter of adding cost to urban property, especially cottage property. It was also a means by which the 'externalities' of property,[61] especially of strategically placed holdings, might be increased.

The processes and practices of inheritance and the property cycle also had a generational effect, which played an important part in the repro-duction of the middle classes and their entrepreneurial activity. The practice of equity between children meant that in most demographic situations children would very rarely inherit a 'fortune' which enabled them to adopt a consumption pattern equated with that of their parents, especially that of their end of life cycle parents, unless the children concerned undertook the high risk, high gains, high management input activities of commerce, industry and the professions. This effect was only intensified by the tendency of most generational life cycles to overlap. Parents did not conveniently die just as children married and entered adulthood. What parents did was to withdraw partially from business, which enabled the hard working son to accumulate capital whilst paying 'interest' to his father. Not all followed father into the family firm, indeed this was a minority experience. Others took loans to support entry into professions or into businesses other than their parents. Successful parents offered credit and networks. Except in the case of an only surviving child, the next generation could not move straight into rentier leisure without first contributing to the entrepreneurial economy. Generational accumu-lation could be cumulative, as in the case of the Hey family, but this was a slow process and each generation raised its consumer level expectations and, hence, the necessity for an entrepreneurial phase of active income seeking.

---

[60] E.P. Hennock, *Fit and Proper Persons. Ideal and Reality in Nineteenth Century Government* (London, 1973).

[61] R.J. Morris, 'Externalities, the market, power structures and the urban agenda', *Urban History Yearbook* (1990), 103, quoting D. Harvey, *Social Justice and the City* (London, 1973), p. 58 quoting E.J. Mishan, *Welfare Economics* (London, 1969),' External effects may be said to arise when relevant effects on production and welfare go wholly or partially unpriced.'

5   Strategies and the urban landscape

In the Leeds wills of the early 1830s, 58 per cent of the men and 37 per cent of the women mentioned real property. In terms of the strategies of family and life cycle, these will makers had the same concerns as the others. They were embedded in the property cycle. They sought an income for old age which was less demanding in terms of risk and management. Many wanted to ensure the support and welfare of a widow and to treat their children, or their reserve army of siblings and cousins, with the equity which would ensure order and good relationships in the family. Others wanted to ensure that the upbringing and education of minors was completed. These objectives brought them into close relationships with the landscape and built environment around them. The bundles of property described in their wills and in the deeds and conveyances in their solicitors' deposit boxes acquired meanings linked to family and age. In turn the objectives of family and life cycle had a fundamental influence on the nature of that landscape and built environment. The creation of much of that built environment was made possible by the needs of age and family.

Contemporaries saw that urban landscape, growing in size and density and complexity, with both delight and alarm. Areas of the town became increasingly differentiated and acquired new social meanings. Concern was expressed for the perceived social segregation which this involved. Disraeli's novel *Sybil, or the Two Nations* was published in 1845 and paraphrased huge chunks from contemporary reports. The Leeds factory surgeon, Robert Baker, had dramatised this division with some innovative cartography in his report on the health conditions of the town produced in 1833 and 1842.[1]

---

[1] R. Baker, *Report of the Leeds Board of Health* (Leeds, 1833); R. Baker, 'Report upon the condition of the town of Leeds and of its inhabitants, by a Statistical Committee of the Town Council, October 1839', *Journal of the Statistical Society of London* 2 (1839), 397–424; R. Baker, *On the State and Condition of the Town of Leeds in the West Riding of the County of York* (Leeds, 1842). This was reprinted in the *Local Reports on the Sanitary Condition of the Labouring Population Directed to be made by the Poor Law Commissioners*, (London, 1842), 23, pp. 348–407; W.R. Lee, 'Robert Baker: the first doctor in the Factory Department, part one, 1803–1858', *British Journal of Industrial Medicine* 21 (1964), 85–93.

The area shading in the map divided Leeds into the healthy West End and the unhealthy East End and factory areas. Samuel Smiles, editor of the radical *Leeds Times*, certainly read the 1839 report in this way,

One half of the world does not know how the other half exists . . . many in this town will scarcely credit our statement that many of their fellow creatures are so reduced to a wretchedness and misery as to submit to occupy a loathsome dwelling and to herd with swine.[2]

Many features of this environment have been explained by the macro-economics of the building cycle, and by the microeconomics of the building plot and the geography of its location.[3] The ebb and flow of the market in property and capital certainly influenced the aggregates of building on a decade-to-decade basis but the aggregates of demand and supply were structured, in part, by the strategies of family and life cycle. On a plot-by-plot basis it was these which triggered decisions to build and finance. In part, the environment produced was structured by previous landscapes of burgage plots and field boundaries surrounding the growing town.[4] In part, it was produced by the economics of plot and location, but the nature of much of what was created can only be fully explained when seen through the lens of the strategies of age and family. This environment had a heterogeneity which was cursed by later planners and went against much contemporary ideology regarding domesticity. Houses were mixed with shops and workshops and factories. Substantial houses were built in the same plot as cramped wage earners' cottages. Family strategies were embedded in buildings and locations.

The poor and non-existent quality of institutional management and risk spreading for rentier investment made the local built environment an attractive and important source of potential income. Emphasis on the property cycle alone over-simplifies. Part of the attraction of the local built environment was not just the knowledge and understanding the individual decision taker might have but the flexibility of meanings which real property had in an uncertain world. The same bundle of property changed meaning as the circumstances of individual and family

---

[2] *Leeds Times*, 30 March 1839.
[3] J.W.R. Whitehand, *The Changing Face of Cities: A Study of Development Cycles and Urban Form* (Oxford, 1987); S. B. Saul, 'Housebuilding in England, 1890–1914', *Economic History Review* 15 (1962), 119–37; M.W. Beresford, 'Prosperity Street and others: an essay in visible urban history', in M.W. Beresford and G.R.J. Jones (eds.), *Leeds and its Region* (Leeds, 1967), pp. 186–99; J.P. Lewis, *Building Cycles and Britain's Growth* (London, 1965).
[4] M.W. Beresford, 'East end, west end. The face of Leeds during urbanization, 1684–1842', *Publication of the Thoresby Society* (1988), 5–19.

changed. Age and inheritance were important but they were not the whole story.

The papers of the Hey family were unusually complete and enable the aims and impact of the real property strategist to be followed through three generations. At the same time, social mobility and generation preferences pushed the Heys towards the strategies of the cash economy capitalist. A full understanding of what was happening can be gained by going back to a marriage contract of 1761 and then following the fortunes first of William Hey, the father of the account book William Hey, through a series of property developments until his death in 1818. The death of William Hey I enabled his son William Hey II to secure and increase the family real estate.

On 28 July 1761, a marriage contract was signed for the union of William Hey, apothecary and surgeon of Leeds, and Alice, daughter of Robert Banks of Knight Stainforth in the County of York, gentleman. 'In consideration of the said intended marriage', £700 provided by Robert Banks, and 'the natural love and affection which he the said Richard Hey hath and beareth towards his son', Richard settled three items of real estate upon William Hey I.[5] The first was two undivided third parts of property in Bridgegate in Leeds. There were two shops with a stable and another stable with a wash house, garden and a summer house. These properties were in the occupation of William Hey and three others. The marriage endowment also included two closes in Woodhouse Lane and two closes at a place called Black Bank on the east side of Leeds, which contained three acres and a barn.

This marriage contract and the properties which accompanied it was one basis of a very successful career which carried William Hey I to the elite of Tory Anglican Leeds. It was characteristic of many professional careers based upon successful tradesman's wealth. His father was a salter in the woollen weaving area to the south and west of Leeds. He probably made his money by supplying the chemicals required for the preparation, dyeing and finishing processes of woollen textiles. The properties with which he endowed his son provided the security needed for William to establish an elite medical business and enter into the public and intellectual life of Leeds at the highest level.[6]

William's success meant that by the time he signed his last will and testament on 9 January 1818 he had considerably augmented his holdings

[5] Marriage Contract of William Hey and Alice Banks, 28 July 1761. DB 75/5.
[6] J. Pearson, FRS, *The Life of William Hey* (London, 1822); R.V. Taylor, *The Biographia Leodiensis: or Biographical Sketches of the Worthies of Leeds and Neighbourhood from the Norman Conquest to the Present Time* (London, 1865), pp. 267, 371 and 403.

of real estate. His mother had added two more closes of land in east
Leeds, just to the east of Marsh Lane.[7] Like Black Bank, these were in the
growing hand loom weaving area, where new building was adding to
density. In addition, he had acquired three agricultural properties in the
immediate region. Most important of all, he used the Briggate property as
the base for a sustained campaign of land assembly, property ownership
consolidation and development. This property, together with the other
Leeds properties, then became the basis for the real estate accumulation
of his son William II. When William II died, the slow process of land
assembly and development over two generations was followed by an
equally deliberate but unhurried process of dispersal by William III.

    There were several social and economic processes which gave signifi-
cance to the details of this story. The first was the family property cycle.
Each William Hey wanted to accumulate some form of rentier income
and withdraw from active involvement in the business, thus leaving
himself free to take a full part in the public life of Leeds and the
domestic life of family. The business then passed to the son. On death,
the property thus accumulated was divided equitably amongst all surviving children. As the first two generations both had five children, or sets of
grandchildren, surviving, the accumulated property was divided in such a
way that no-one received enough to simply reproduce the retired rentier
phase of their father's life cycle. In order to achieve this, they first had to
accumulate profits from the business and to develop their real estate. In
other words, the practice of equitable inheritance was a key practice
through which the Hey family, like the people of the middle classes as a
whole, reproduced itself.

    The third major process, after the property cycle and inheritance
practice, was the expansion of Leeds itself. William Hey I had begun
marriage with a front of the street property on Briggate, the main trading
and residential street of the eighteenth century town. His father had
rented to him and then endowed him with one of the prime elite, residential and business sites in Leeds. Over the next 50 years, the growing
density of Leeds made such sites much less desirable as dwelling places.
The 'dispersal' of the Leeds elite involved, first, a preference for the west
side of the main street, for which William was well placed, and then for
specialist elite residential sites like Albion Street and Park Square. This
was linked to the building cycle. The detailed timing of the decisions
made by William Hey I and II was not simply a matter of property cycle

[7] This account was based upon a series of property deeds deposited in the West Yorkshire
Archives Service at Sheepscar in Leeds, DB 75/7.

strategy and the spatial re-organisation of Leeds, but also of the year-on-year changes in the opportunity cost of capital and the demand for residential and commercial properties of varying kinds. Lastly, there was a generational change. The strategy of rentier capital accumulation for later adulthood was a constant for all three generations, but each generation made changes according to different opportunities and preferences. William Hey III , married but childless, lived in a world with an active and highly organised market in stocks and shares, notably in railways and public utilities. His choices were very different from those of his father and grandfather. Thus, the story of three generations of William Heys was driven by the property cycle, inheritance practice, the expansion and spatial re-organisation of Leeds, the building cycle and the changing opportunities and preferences of the generations.

There was a direct logic to William Hey I's 1761 property disposition. The Briggate property was a prime front of the street central area elite site. Although such a socio-spatial structure has been identified in the literature with the pre-industrial city, the elite residential centre persisted into the early years of nineteenth century Leeds.[8] This site suited the strategies of the active and ambitious professional man. The formal layout owed its origins to the burgage plots of the fourteenth century borough, with the prestige frontage onto the main street and the narrow burgage plot behind. The house in which William I began married life provided a suitable site for family and business. He was surrounded by tradesmen and professional families like himself. Nearby in Briggate was Thomas Atkinson, tallow chandler, whose son John was to be the family lawyer for the Heys. A short walk down Kirkgate was the parish church, which was so important to William's political and social life. Next door were two other properties which were rented to others for a minimal management cost. On the burgage plot behind were lower status buildings, some residential, a public house, warehouse and stables. Behind that was open ground, a bowling green but mostly pasture land, long narrow properties stretching down from Burley Bar or the Upperheadrow, probably used as pasture or as tenter grounds for the finishing of cloth. It was not an environment which threatened the amenity of his family or business. The other properties at Black Bank and Woodhouse Lane provided a useful rent income, which would underpin the stability of his household income whilst he built up his medical practice.

---

[8] D. Ward, 'Victorian cities. How modern ?', *Journal of Historical Geography* 1 (1975) 135–51; D. Cannadine, 'Victorian cities. How different?', *Social History* 4 (1977) 457–82; R.J. Morris, 'Family strategies and the built environment of Leeds in the 1830s and 1840s', *Northern History* 37 (2000) 193–214.

William Hey I's control of his property was limited by its family nature and also by its urban nature. He only had two of three undivided parts of his Leeds property. One of his early acts of accumulation was to buy out this other third so he gained the full control of the Briggate property which he needed for development.[9] His disposal of the property was also limited by its involvement in the marriage settlement specifying that his widow retained a legal right to dower.

Although the narrow burgage lot provided an acceptable environment for family and business, William was anxious to gain as much control of the properties in the burgage as possible so he bought properties within it whenever opportunity arose. In his will he listed five purchases in what was then called the Slip Inn Yard but which was later renamed the Pack Horse Inn Yard. There was a piece of ground called the Garden 'situate near thereto' from the estate of Nathaniel Bagnall. This was at the rear or west end of the burgage. There were two purchases from Mrs Rose Rushworth and a garden previously owned by James Labron, whose business fronted Briggate. At about this time, Mrs Rose Rushworth, widow, appeared as a member of the St. James Street Building Club, which gathered its members between 1788 and 1795. She appeared to have used the money from Hey to buy her back-to-back pair of houses in a new street on the east side of Briggate.[10] Another building in the Slip Inn Yard was bought from Thomas Teale. William Hey I recorded that he had pulled down certain buildings and erected new ones: three houses with shops, a warehouse and other buildings, together with two other dwelling houses and two cottages. There were also a stable barn and middensteads.

The yards were becoming more crowded and, although there was little record of the day-to-day interactions within the burgage, a legal agreement of November 1797 gives a flavour of the difficulties and a very practical example of the meaning of an externality in a developing urban environment.[11] John Teale and William Hey noted they were tenants in common of the open and vacant parts of the Slip Inn Yard and of diverse tenements in that yard, and that William Hey was sole owner of the yard to the south, and Teale sole owner of the yard to the north. Teale owned a warehouse at the south west end of the yard. He had bought it from John Shule, who built it on garden ground. The warehouse had no rights of access to the yard but the occupier had recently formed a

[9] Will of William Hey, dated 9 January 1818, DB 75/2.
[10] Beresford, 'East end, west end', 484.
[11] R.J. Morris, 'Externalities, the market, power structures and the urban agenda', *Urban History Yearbook* 17 (1990), 99–109.

drain which discharged into the yard and had made several windows overlooking the yard. 'The waste water coming from the said warehouse or building is suffered to run into and upon the said Slip Inn Yard to the great nuisance of injury of the said yard'. Teale agreed that, on expiry of current lease, he would block up the hole or drain and lead water into a middenstead in the Slip Inn Yard, which he owned.[12] The waste water was one aspect of the deteriorating environment of the yard as building density increased. Although Hey insisted on his legal right to have the 'nuisance' removed, he did wait until the current lease was over, thus making life a little easier for Teale and suggesting that social as well as legal considerations influenced policy.[13]

Such attempts at consolidation were slow and, in 1823, when William I's sons and sons-in law came to consider their inheritance, the Hey family only controlled a part of the yard.[14]

By the 1780s, William Hey I's ambition lay beyond the boundaries of the 'ancient burgage' in Briggate. On 1 and 2 January 1782, William Hey, surgeon and apothecary, purchased from Jeremiah Dixon, Esq., 'all that close, piece, or parcel of ground known as the Bowling Green...at or near the bottom of...Lands Lane' together with a stable in the north west corner already in the occupation of Hey. It contained about one acre. He paid £400.[15] This was one of several sales which marked the moving out of the early mid-eighteenth century generation of Leeds merchant families. The Dixons, who had gained Red Hall and its associated closes through marriage, moved north to Gledhow and Mrs Wilson, widow, resident in York, was selling land to the west of Briggate to pay mortgage debts, although she had required an act of parliament to disentangle her estate from various legal entails and trusteeships. Surrounding estates has been bought by Edward Hinchcliffe, carpenter and coachmaker, and by Samuel Murgitroyd, tobacconist. The elite tradesmen of Briggate had moved in.[16]

The next change came in a series of purchases which William I made between 1793 and 1796. This flurry of activity was part of a wider national economic movement. The peak in the duty paid on bricks in 1793 was one indicator of the building boom of the early 1790s.[17]

[12] Agreement between John Teale, hosier, and William Hey, 20 November 1797. DB 75/5.
[13] Articles of Agreement between John Teale and William Hey, 20 November 1797. DB 75/5.
[14] Indenture 2 January 1823, between Rebecca Hey and William Hey and others, DB 75/5.
[15] Indentures 1 and 2 January between William Hey and Jeremiah Dixon, DB 75/5.
[16] This account was based upon a number of indentures for the sale of property in DB75/5 and on Beresford, 'East end, west end', esp. 168–70.
[17] B.R. Mitchell, *Abstract of British Historical Statistics* (Cambridge University Press, 1962), p. 235.

Imports of fir and deal were also at a peak that year, whilst the yield on government stock, one alternative investment, was at a low.[18] Perhaps this movement induced John Hinchcliffe to begin the break up of the property his father had purchased. John was about to go into partnership with Joseph Bowling as owner of a flax mill, so he wanted his capital out of real estate.[19] Such activity allowed countless transfers of capital across Leeds and between sectors. The sale drew in a series of developers and speculators. Although the archive record is partial, William Hey made at least four purchases.[20] As a result, he owned property stretching back from the old Briggate burgage to the newly laid out Albion Street, which provided a new north–south link west of Briggate. On this land he build a large eight-bay house for himself and two other houses, one of which was occupied by his son William II.[21] One purchase from John Hinchcliffe included the land upon which the new reservoir for the Leeds Water Works was being constructed. William had permission to build over this if he wished but it remained as part of the garden of his new house. This move was part of the expansion of Leeds westwards, which involved a progressive specialisation of land use. There was no separation of work and domestic and nearby properties still included warehouses, but the deeds involved in the laying out of Albion Street, to which William I was a signatory, gave an indication of changing views of the environment suitable for an elite surgeon's home. The houses on the new road were to have sash windows and not bow windows, which would obstruct the pathway. 'They shall be built of stock bricks, bastard stocks or stone'. The owners agreed to share the costs of the common sewer. But most important of all for the future environment of the street were conditions limiting the use of the new buildings. No building 'shall be made use of as or for a glasshouse, common brewhouse, slaughter house, place for melting tallow, or boiling soap, making candles, baking or refining sugar, baking pots or tobacco pipes, burning of blood, public bowling green, cock pits, tippling house, skittle alley, gin shop or other shop for retailing spirituous liquors, distillery drying house, steam engines, shops for blacksmiths, whitesmiths, pewterers, tinners, braziers, tanners, skinners or curriers...'[22] For the Hey family

---

[18] Parry Lewis, *Building Cycles and Britain's Growth*, p. 12.
[19] Beresford, 'East end, west end', 242.
[20] Indenture 5 July 1793 between William Hey and William Walker; Conveyance of ground in Albion Street, William Walker to William Hey, 6 July 1793; Indenture 7 July 1793 between Joshua Turner and William Hey; Indenture 2 July 1793 between Edward Hinchcliffe and William Hey; Indenture 1 January 1796 between William Hey and William Walker. All are in DB75/5.
[21] Beresford, 'East end, west end', 161.
[22] Indenture 11 July 1793 between William Hey, Joshua Turner and William Walker, DB 75/5.

this was very different from the Briggate yard and the house of 1761 which was within smelling distance of the Shambles in Briggate.

In part, this move was a response to the building cycle and, in part, driven by the family property cycle. William I was investing the gains of 30 years. He wanted space for his active political, philanthropic and cultural life. He wanted to provide William II with his own domestic establishment as his son took the most active part in the business.

Any account of the cost of this land assembly operation must be incomplete. The Bowling Green cost £400. The major rectangles of land which took him west cost £829.16s and £646.5s. A small extension was £403 and the land upon which the reservoir was built was £161.15s.6d. The house in which William I lived was insured in 1797 for £1000. In 1818, this assemblage was left to William II with an estimated value of £3000.[23]

The Bowling Green/Albion Street group was only part of a larger pattern of property accumulation designed to serve the family of William I. He had purchased a series of farms in the region and his will showed how each was designed to serve what he saw as the needs of his children and their children. The estate at Farlington went to Reverend Robert Jarratt for his natural life and then to the children of his late daughter, Margaret. Samuel got an estate at Clapham, whilst Mary, wife of Reverend Thomas Dykes, and his unmarried daughter, Rebecca, got the farm at Sutton in the East Riding as tenants in common. Throughout the will, he gave values for the estates and reminded his readers of intervivos gifts to his children to indicate that he was treating them with strict equity. They were each getting property to a value of about £4000. William II was getting the business but by that time he was the major active partner and probably held most of the business capital. He got the Albion St/Bowling Green property as a domestic/business base and

my share of the furniture of the shop and laboratory with the drugs and medicines therein. Also all my medical books and manuscripts and all my surgical instruments and anatomical preparations for his own use plus my share of the saddle horses and their furniture and also in the carriages and carriage horses belonging to the same and in the hay and corn remaining at the time of my decease.[24]

The property in the burgage plot was covered by the marriage settlement of 1761 and appeared to have gone to all four children plus Jarratt as tenants in common.

---

[23] This is based upon the deeds in DB 75/5 and the 1818 will of William Hey I in DB 75/2.
[24] Will of William Hey, 9 January 1818. DB 75/2.

There was no indication of how William Hey I had financed the accumulation of urban and rural properties which, at his death, fitted so neatly into his family obligations. There was no evidence of mortgage or borrowing. It seems likely that he was able to finance by the surplus of income over household expenses in good years and by withdrawing capital from the business as his son took over the active running of the medical practice.

William Hey I had been tied to the landscape of Leeds by his own knowledge, by the lack of any more attractive alternative form of rentier investment, and by the terms of his marriage settlement. When William Hey II took possession of his portion of the estate, he was aged about 50. The Briggate burgage plot, consolidated by his father's purchases, was to be held as tenant in common with his brother Samuel, two brothers-in-law and his unmarried sister, Rebecca. According to Blackstone, 'Tenants in common are such as hold by several and distinct titles, but by unity of possession; because none knoweth his own severality, and therefore they all occupy promiscuously...no man can certainly tell which part is his own'. Such a property right could be created 'by express limitation in a deed'.[25] But tenants in common could be compelled by statutes of Henry VIII and William III to make partition, and they need not make joint actions in terms of suing and being sued regarding the property. As an asset which held a strategic position in a part of Leeds which William depended upon for his business as a surgeon, his domestic comfort and now a major part of his rentier income, the burgage plot was an imperfect item of capitalist real property. William II did not have the full rights to use, exclude and alienate.

His first actions ensured that he had absolute control of the burgage plot property. The tenants in common first signed a deed to bar entail in 1822.[26] He, his brothers and brothers-in-law then bought out Rebecca's share of the tenancy in common for £1800.[27] She invested this money in consols to produce a steady income with few management problems until her death in 1841.[28] A division or buy out of interests with the others took place later that year. William II used his control of the south part of the yard to redevelop it as the north side of Commercial Street, confusingly called Bond Street for the first few years of its existence. In 1823–24, he

<hr>

[25] Sir W. Blackstone, *Commentaries on the Law of England*, 18th edition with the last corrections of the author and copious notes by Thomas Lee, Esq. (London, 1829), vol. II, p. 190.
[26] Deed between William Hey and others to bar entail, 12 October 1822, DB 75/5.
[27] Indenture between Rebecca Hey and William Hey and others, 2 January 1823, DB 75/5.
[28] Rebecca Hey's account book with Crompton and Co., 1830–1840, DB 75/3.

spent £4546.16s. building four shops and houses in Bond Street (Commercial Street).[29] Between 1825 and 1828, he invested £6504.3s.1d. in two new houses 'in my croft Albion St'. His next major investment did not come until 1837, when he built a warehouse in Wellington Road for £3226.6s.2d. The listing of real estate in William II's will in 1844, together with the listing of Hey family properties in Leeds in the Soke Rate, provided more evidence. The Marsh Lane estate disappeared from William's holdings. This was the property in the hand loom weaving area of east Leeds, which William I had inherited from his mother. Brother Samuel and the brothers-in-law had their own undivided properties in Commercial Street, suggesting that the building had seen a division of the tenancy in common. The rateable values indicated that William II had got two fifth's of the property and then invested more than the others in building.

Thus, in the 1820s, and in his own early 50s, William Hey II made a substantial investment in the properties which had begun with his father's marriage settlement. William was then able to live on the income from these properties, recorded in the surviving account book. But this was not the whole story. In addition to the rents, William II had a small income from loans on personal security. He also had income from the small number of local utilities and transport securities then available, including the old water works which had its reservoir on his land. In the 1840s, the coming of railway shares replaced some income from personal loans (Fig. 5.1).

The effect of these actions upon the landscape of Leeds was significant and incremental. The process had begun with part of the ancient burgage on the south side of the Slip in Yard, when Briggate was still home to the Moot Hall, the meeting place of the magistrates and the Corporation, and the Shambles. It was a place of the uproar of local politics and the nastiness of the butchering trade (Fig. 5.2).

By the time Netlam and Giles published their plan of 1815, the landscape had experienced considerable modernisation as streets replaced yards and crofts. William Hey I had a major part in this. In doing this, he not only served his own life cycle and family property strategies but also influenced the environment in which he lived and earned his living (Fig. 5.3).

The Hey family properties recorded in the Soke Rate Book of 1842 can be imposed upon the Ordnance Survey map of 1847, although the

[29] Account of the expenses of building four shops and houses in Bond Street in 1823–24, DB 75/19.

Table 5.1 *Property holdings of William Hey II and other family members in Soke Rate Book of 1841*

Tenant		Property	Address	Value
William Hey		Stable	Little Cross St	4.25
William Hey		Cellar	Little Cross St	8.25
William Hey		House and printing office	Trinity St	18.25
William Hey		House and shop	Commercial St	61.50
William Hey		House and shop	Commercial St	41.50
William Hey		Office	Commercial St	25.00
Samuel Hey		Beer house, shop, warehouse	Lands Lane	20.00
Samuel Hey		Shop and museum	Commercial St	41.50
Samuel Hey		Shop	Commercial St	24.00
William Hey, Snr		House and shop	Commercial St	62.50
William Hey, Snr		House and shop	Commercial St	58.25
William Hey, Snr		House and shop	Commercial St	66.50
William Hey, Snr		House and shop	Commercial St	66.50
William Hey, Snr		Shop	Commercial St	41.50
Samuel Hey		Shop	Commercial St	24.00
Rev Dykes		House and shop	Commercial St	50.00
Rev Dykes		House and shop	Commercial St	50.00
Rev Jarrat		House and shop	Commercial St	91.50
William Hey, Snr	Mrs Kinnear	House	Albion Place	88.75
William Hey, Snr	William Hey, Jnr	House	Albion Place	88.75
William Hey, Snr	William Hey, Snr	House and land	Albion Place	104.00
William Hey, Snr	Jeremiah Scott	House	Albion Place	35.00
William Hey, Snr	Thomas Powell	House	Albion Place	33.25
William Hey, Snr		Warehouse	Brittannia St	175.00
William Hey, Jnr		House	Wellington St	28.25
William Hey, Jnr		House	Wellington St	28.25
William Hey, Jnr		House	Wellington St	28.25
William Hey, Jnr		House	Wellington St	28.25
William Hey, Jnr		House	Wellington St	28.25

boundaries are approximate and the complex details of the property deals of the 1790s impossible to reconstruct (Fig. 5.4).

In effect, William Hey I burrowed his way out of the family base in the ancient burgage. He took advantage of the break up of the Dixon Red Hall estate in the 1780s and then of the laying out of Albion Street in 1792.[30] His purchases were opportunistic both in the old yard and in the meadows beyond. First, he built a fine house for himself. Albion Place was side on to the new street. Here he could entertain and hold meetings

[30] Beresford, 'East End, West End', 168.

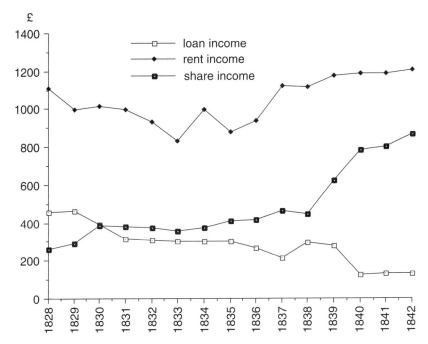

Fig. 5.1 William Hey II. Sources of rentier income, 1828–42.
Source: William Hey's Account Book, 1827–42. DB 75/20.

of the philosophical society he formed in the 1790s.[31] Then came houses for his two sons. After John's death, sadly, one was rented out. Meanwhile, the old yard was a source of rent income. Already, by 1818, William I had rebuilt two houses as part of the laying out of Commercial Street. William II added four more houses in 1823–24. These turned their back on the yard and faced the new street.

The outcomes for the material and social landscape can be traced through the fortunes of the Hey properties, especially those that once stood in the yard.

In 1822, there was still a great deal of vacant land. The full outcome for the Heys and for Leeds was evident when information from the 1834 Directory, the 1841 Soke Rate and the 1847 was collated (Figs. 5.5 and 5.6).

The Hey family interest built up by William I and II had modernised one portion of the built fabric of Leeds when the comfortable street turned its

---

[31] R.J. Morris, 'Middle Class Culture, 1700–1914', in D. Fraser (ed.), *A History of Modern Leeds* (Manchester, 1980), pp. 203–4.

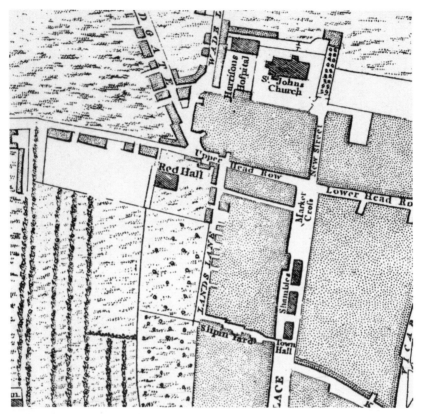

Fig. 5.2 William Hey's real estate. The Slip in Yard area in 1770.

Source: T. Jefferys. *A Plan of Leeds, 1770* (London, 1772). See K.J. Bonsor and H. Nichols, Printed Maps and Plans of Leeds, 1711–1900, *Publications of the Thoresby Society* 47, 106 (1960), 5.

back upon the narrow yard of the ancient burgage. The street was the base for businesses which supplied parts of the material and service fabric of middle class life, furnishing, clothing and books. The tenants were fairly stable. The list with the map (Fig. 5.6) was taken from the 1834 Directory. By the time the 1845 Directory was printed, Charles Lord, chemist and druggist had replaced the bakers at No. 5; John and J. Hopkinson, music professors, publishers and sellers, piano forte manufacturers, had replaced hair, perfume and toys at No. 6, and William and John Bickers, linen drapers and hosiers were at No. 8. with the remainder of Commercial Street having the same structure of ownership. Property was held in blocks of about four units and let to a variety of businesses serving middle class

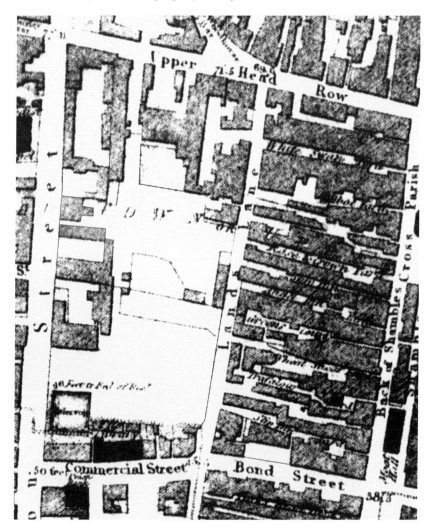

Fig. 5.3 William Hey II's real estate. The Commercial Street area in 1815.

Source: Netlam and Francis Giles, *Plan of the Town of Leeds and its Environs, 1815* (Leeds, 1815). See Bonsor and Nichols, 'Printed maps and plans of Leeds', 11.

needs. At least two groups were owned by executors and, hence, served the needs of life after death, supporting widows and minors. The two banks west of Lands Lane owned their own premises, but George Shaw, the butcher at No. 43, opposite the Hey family block, was the only true owner,

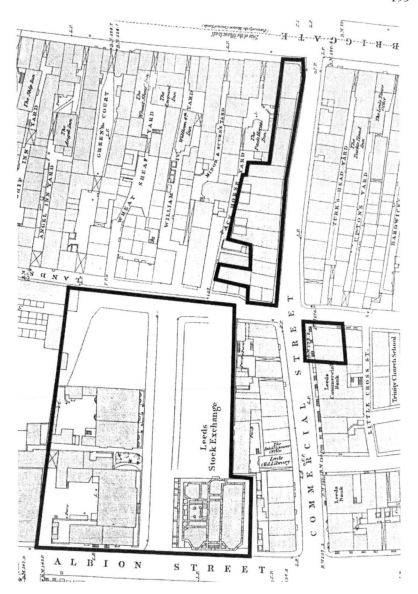

Fig. 5.4 William Hey II's real estate, 1782–1847.

Source: In addition to the deeds cited in the text, Ordnance Survey large-scale (1:1056) town plan of Leeds surveyed in 1847 and published in 1850. (Southampton, 1850).

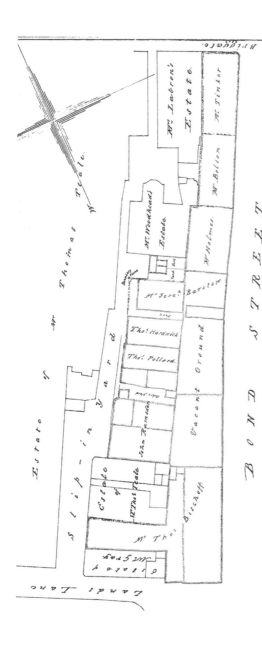

Mary Labron and son, furnishing ironmongers and lamp manufacturers, 55 Briggate.

Samuel Tinker, jeweller, gold and silversmith, watchmaker, h. Chapel Allerton.

James Bolton, Woollen draper and Cheshire cheese factor, 20 Bond St

Henry Woodhead, victualler, Pack Horse, Slip in Yard, back of Shambles.

John Holmes, auctioneer, appraiser, bookseller and dealer in Dunfermline woollens.

Jeremiah Barstow, tea dealer.

Thomas Hardwick, [no entry].

Thomas Pollard, [no entry].

John Ramsden, plumber and glazier.

Thomas Bischoff, Jnr, general commission merchant, corner of Commercial St and Lands Lane.

Fig. 5.5 Tenants and owners in the Slip in Yard/Bond Street area, 1822.

Source: The information on William Hey's tenants was taken from the Leeds section of Edward Baines, Directory of the County of York, vol. I, Leeds 1822, and from the deed of 1822 in DB 75/5, from which the map was also extracted.

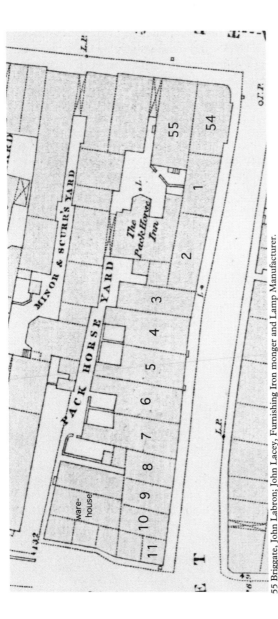

55 Briggate, John Labron; John Lacey, Furnishing Iron monger and Lamp Manufacturer.

54 Briggate, Rev Robert Jarratt; John Wilkinson, Working Gold and Silversmith, Jeweller, Watchmaker, Optician and Cutler.

1&2 Commercial St, Rev Thomas Dykes; 1. David Broadhead, Hat Manufacturer and agent for sale of London Hats; 2. John Cross, Bookseller, Stationer, Binder and Print Seller.

3 Commercial St, Samuel Hey; George Morton, paper stainer and hanger.

4–8 Commercial St, William Hey II [Jane Hey after 1844]; 4. J. Moorhouse and Co., tea dealers; 5. Smith, G. and Son, Bankers; 6. Edward Atkinson, Hair Cutter, Perfumery and Toy Warehouse; 7. Thomas Craister, Boot and Shoemaker; 8. John Craven, Cabinet Maker and Upholsterer.

9–11 Commercial St, Samuel Hey; 9 John Holmes, Auctioneer, Bookseller, Patent Floor Cloth and Dunfermline Table Linen Warehouse; 10. John Calvert, Animal Preserver and Dealer in Foreign Fancy Birds; 11. Calvert's Museum.

Fig. 5.6 Tenants and owners of the Hey family properties in the Slip in Yard/Commercial Street area, 1834–47.

Source: Compiled from the 1834 Directory (tenants and occupations), the 1842 Soke Rate (owners) and the Ordnance Survey large-scale (1:1056) plan (surveyed 1847, published 1850). The names of owners are given first and then tenants. The Hey family is in italics.

occupier, house and shop. William Hunt, gentleman, at No. 42 was an owner occupier rentier, renting out to Catherine Hall, Straw and Tuscan hat manufacturer, and Christopher Norfolk, laceman, hosier and glover. In 1822, William had been a straw hat manufacturer in Commercial Street and must have passed on the business and retired to live on the rents. The detail of the relationship was hidden but the influence of a successful property cycle on the landscape of central Leeds was evident.

The meaning of these actions was multiple. At one level, they were a simple response to trade, prosperity and the expansion of the Leeds economy. The years when the decisions to build were taken, 1823–26 and 1836–37, were years of commercial prosperity, years when the Jowitts and others were recording large profits. These decisions were also a response to life cycle and family needs. The shops in Commercial Street were built as William II entered his 50s and was looking for an increase in rentier income before turning more of the medical business to his sons. The warehouse investment coincided with the sudden death of John Hey and his father's wish to support John's widow, Jane. At that point, the Commercial Street shops must have taken on a new meaning, which was revealed in William II's will when he died in 1844.[32] They became one element of support for Jane Hey and her family. The will saw his property divided out into units, which would serve equity and the needs of his children. William III got the business and the associated property between Albion Street and Lands Lane while Jane and her family had the income from the Commercial Street shops. The estate in Pudsey, that had come with his father's marriage long ago in 1761, went to son Richard. Both cases were in the form of an income stream managed by trustees. The Sutton farm went to Samuel. Black Bank and the Wellington Street warehouse were to be sold, although William and son-in-law John Atkinson had first option of purchase at valuation.

Even before his death in 1844, William II was starting to move away from the urban peasant real estate strategy set by his father and grand-father. He had the selection of regional transport and utility shares listed in the previous chapter. His probate account showed that these were less than a third of his personal estate. The estimated annual value of William Hey II's real estate in Leeds recorded in the Soke Rate Book was £820. If the capital value was assumed to be between 14 and 20 years purchase, 5 per cent to 7 per cent returns, then his real estate would have been worth between £11,714 and £16,400.

---

[32] Will of William Hey of Leeds, 2 February 1841, DB 75/2.

Table 5.2 *Probate account of William Hey II, 1844–45*

	£	%
Cash in house	82.24	0.27
Cash at bankers	847.68	2.76
Rents due at death of deceased	526.70	1.72
Mortgages and interest at death	12542.40	40.86
Book and other debts	1621.51	5.28
Canal and other shares	8617.66	28.08
Reduced 3%s £1500 @ 98 7/8ths	1483.13	4.83
Consols 3% £5000 @ 99 5/8ths	4972.88	16.20
	30694.19	100.00

Note: This was an unsigned draft in DB 75/14.

The second sign of change was a deed concerning a road in Gledhow, which recorded that William II had recently purchased Plot 228 on the plan, one acre two roods and a perch for £200 from Thomas Benyon and John Dixon. Just before his death, William was preparing to move out of town and to add to and join the semi-circle of peri-urban villas, which had grown to the north and west of Leeds since the third quarter of the eighteenth century.

As soon as William III inherited his share of his father's estate in 1844, he accelerated these changes. In 1845, he sold two of the Albion Street properties to Samuel Dickson Marton, land agent, for £4999. In 1847, he sold some vacant ground to Jeremiah Sowry, pawnbroker, for £495 and a second to William Middleton, solicitor, for £575. Money was needed for building 'the villa' at Gledhow. The alterations and additions made in 1854 alone cost £727.[33] The earlier accounts do not survive. William III also bought stocks and shares on the national and imperial market. In 1863, his holdings of East India Company Consolidated Stock were registered with a face value of £2000.

The comfort and welfare of William Hey III was detached from the economy and environment of Leeds in a way which his father's had never been. The stability of the government of India was as important to him as the stability of the Leeds economy. Some holdings from the Briggate yard and its extension remained. William III had no children but the medical business was carried on for a while by a nephew, and the properties were increasingly let as offices. The garden was built over for the Leeds Stock Exchange

[33] These indentures and agreements are in DB 75/6.

(dealing mainly in railway shares). The detachment of the Hey family from their spatial commitment to both yard and street was almost complete.

East of Briggate, where Mrs Rushworth had taken her capital, was a different world. Here was the world of John Taylor, builder and brick-layer. His social and economic status was lower than that of the Heys but he shared the concerns of age, responsibility to widows and family equity. He also saw his world in terms of bundles of properties. The barriers between family and business meanings were even more porous than those in the perceptions of the elite professional who made Albion Street and the Bond Street shops. For John Taylor, as for most of lower status, the documentation is fragmentary. The wills, directories and poll books give only a glimpse of his strategies and influence. He made his will on 7 July 1831 and died eleven days later. His will was brought for probate to York, 3 September 1831.[34] The bulk of the social, economic and property relationships which mattered to him were in a fairly confined area, but not always contiguous. The sworn value of his estate was 'under £100', but that was only personal estate. The activities of John Taylor and his sons can be traced in the directories and poll books of the 1820s and early 1830s and then located on maps of mid-century Leeds (Table 5.3, Fig. 5.7).

John Taylor's will outlined a world in which the economic and envir-onmental fortunes of the petty capitalists and independent producers were tightly bound up with those of the wage earners who lived amongst them, paid them rents and, at times, worked directly for them. It was a world in which the mortgage and the building club provided credit and fragile accumulations of capital for a wide variety of economic and social activity. John Taylor was one of a significant group of men who had a distinctive view of this world as both producer and accumulator of real estate. He was described as a bricklayer in 1788 when he put his name down for two back-to-back pairs in the Crackenthorpe Building Club, which created Union Street.[35] In his will he was simply a builder. Although his activities combined both production and accumulation, his real estate involved a mixture of life cycle and family purposes, of providing a rentier income and a credit base, as well as a working entre-preneurial income. His holdings and family relationships lacked spatial compactness but, when located on the map, family, work and property were within a few minutes' walk of each other.

Under the will, his son, John, received a public house with the brew-house, pump and outbuildings, which he already occupied, together with

[34] Will of John Taylor, 3 September 1831.
[35] Beresford, 'East end, west end', 195, 200, and 203.

Table 5.3 *John and Robert Taylor, 1822–34*

1822	John Taylor, bricklayer and builder, 28 Union St
	John Taylor Jnr, bricklayer, Nelson St
	Robert Taylor, bricklayer, Coach Lane[a]
1826	John Taylor and sons, bricklayers and builders, 8 Cross St, Lady Lane[b]
	John Taylor Jnr, bricklayer etc, h. 32 Linsley Fold, Mabgate
	[no sign of Robert]
1832	Robert Taylor, house, Cross Street
1834	John Taylor, bricklayer, 3 Templar Lane
	Robert Taylor, bricklayer, 27 Union Street and 2 Cross Street
1834	(poll) Robert Taylor, Cross Street.

[a] Known as Charles St. by 1834, running north from St Peter's St. and intersecting with Line St
[b] Cross Street was Mill Garth Street on the 1847 survey. It ran from 39 George's St. and contained Ripley and Ogle (woollen cloth manufacturers and merchants), Gilyard Scarth and Sons (dyers) as well as Robert Taylor. The dye house and woollen cloth works were marked on the 1847 survey.

Source: 1822. Edward Baines, *History, Directory and Gazetteer of the County of York*, vol. I, West Riding. (Leeds, 1822); 1826. William Parson, *General and Commercial Directory of the Borough of Leeds* (Leeds, 1826); 1832. *Poll Book of the Parliamentary Election for the Borough of Leeds* (Leeds, 1832); 1834. *General and Commercial Directory of the Borough of Leeds*, Baines and Newsome (Leeds, 1834); 1834 poll. *Poll Book of the Leeds Borough Election, 1834* (Leeds, 1834).

two adjoining cottages, a vacant plot fronting the said house, another plot with a recent building occupied by a patten ring maker and a plot of land on the south end of the estate used as a limehouse. Despite its name, Line Street was a disorderly collection of back-to-back houses just south of Quarry Hill. Initially, the executors were to take the estate and use the income of the estate to pay interest on a mortgage of £200 and support the education of his son's children. It is not clear why John, Snr used a trusteeship. It was unusual to do so for a male offspring, but it would certainly have had the effect of protecting money intended for the grand-childrens' support from any economic misfortune on the part of his son. There were indications that John was the least economically secure of the two sons. He did not appear in the poll book of 1832 and had recently abandoned the public house business. John Taylor also got the horse and cart from his father's business. In the event John did move into building and by 1834 was found in Templar Street, just north of Lady Lane.

Robert Taylor got five cottages in Union Street and Nelson Street, where John himself was living. Robert also got 'all my scaffolding, tools and utensils in trade'. By 1834, he was established as a bricklayer in 21 Union Street.

200

Fig. 5.7 John Taylor's world. Property and family east of Briggate, 1822–34.

Note: The map base was taken from Map of Leeds published by John Tallis, London in the 1850s. Other information was taken from John Taylor's will and the sources cited for Table 5.3.

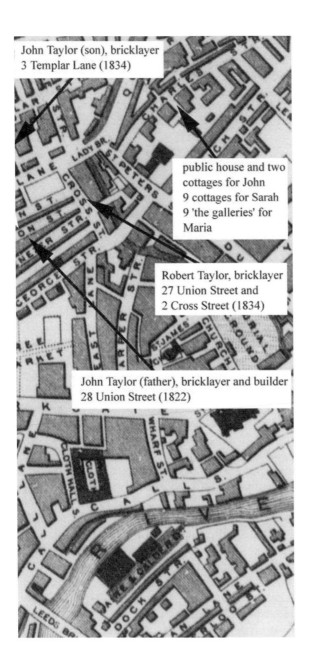

John Taylor (son), bricklayer
3 Templar Lane (1834)

public house and two
cottages for John
9 cottages for Sarah
9 'the galleries' for
Maria

Robert Taylor, bricklayer
27 Union Street and
2 Cross Street (1834)

John Taylor (father), bricklayer and builder
28 Union Street (1822)

There were four daughters who were tied into the neighbourhood by marriage and by the income they were to get from their father's estate. Hannah got eight cottages in Union Street/Nelson Street and was married to William Catlow, cloth dresser, 21 Union Street. Sarah got nine cottages in Line Street . There was no record in the directories. Elizabeth was dead. Her husband Robert Margereson, a butcher, had a house and shop in Lady Lane, just north of the Union Street/Nelson Street complex. John set aside £150 to be invested for the education and welfare of her daughter, also Elizabeth. Maria was the only one to escape a little from this tight spatial network of family and property. She got 'nine cottages called the Galleries (consisting of six cottages above and three below) situate in or near Line St'. Her husband, Lancelot, was a flour and provision dealer based in Kendell Row just off Hunslet Lane, south of the river.

John was an East End live-in builder who lived, worked, collected rents, accumulated property and saw his sons and daughters work and marry in a very small geographical area. The streets which he helped create were by no means the worst in Leeds, but they were dangerous places none the less. In 1833, Robert Baker, surgeon and public health reformer, found Union Street paved and sewered with many dirty yards and with two dead in the recent cholera epidemic. Nelson Street, which had been developed by the individual enterprise of speculative builders like Taylor, was badly paved and sewered, 'a very confined street', which had had seven deaths.[36] John, who had created and owned two important pieces of this landscape, saw a very different logic in those streets. He parcelled up his real property to ensure the continuity of a public house business and to ensure equal parcels for each of his children, carefully structured so that his daughters got independent income and his sons could continue the business if they so wished. One parcel was set aside to create a personal estate to pay debts and to support his grand-daughter.

The layout and logic of this built environment was related to family strategy. The outcome was a landscape, which can be understood in terms of blocks of property which took their logic from these strategies. The apparent heterogeneity and chaotic layout can be resolved. The block derived from the multiple needs of a family and a life cycle/property cycle strategy which was conceived in terms of relationships to real estate. This began with the need for entrepreneurial income from a business, a shop, or a commercial, professional or manufacturing establishment. This involved access to the relevant real estate, to capital and to inputs

---

[36] Baker, *Report* (Leeds, 1833).

of an appropriate mix of managerial, craft or professional labour. The
block also needed to include the potential for a later rentier income in the
form of domestic housing, shops or warehouses. The wills of those caught
by death in mid-property cycle showed that this accumulation was usually
financed by mortgage which, in turn, was the rentier income for someone
else's property cycle or for a widow and children support plan. The
property could have many meanings. It provided for the eventual need
to care for a widow and to provide gendered equity for children. The
property was often used to sustain business continuity across generations,
which was one of several options for securing this aim.

The owner-occupier-rentier structure, in which owners lived in the
block of property from which they derived their income, was a way
of reducing management costs and, above all, the management risks of
absentee ownership. The examples of the wills showed many variants of
this structure, linking a property block to family strategy via mortgage and
anticipated provision for widows and children. The wills also show, as in
the case of John Taylor, that the property 'block' was not always geographically compact and contiguous but derived its unity from a neighbourhood network of enterprise and family. The spatial logic of John Taylor's
world was tied together by the business interests of his sons and sons-in-law
and by the manner in which as an resident owner-manager, producer-
investor, he worked the area which he knew most about.

In the next example, John Rose created shapes upon the ground which
were clearer on the map and reflected the direct, if complex, nature of his
strategies. His world was that of School Close, south of Boar Lane and
north of the River Aire. The heterogeneous blocks of property which
served the real estate strategists, – the rentier republics of the urban
peasant – had been laid out in open ground in the years before 1820
and attracted several men of modest capital. John Rose, whitesmith of
Leeds, was one of them. He died on 1 January 1831, having made his will
on 13 June 1829 and added a codicil 17 December 1830. His will was
probated at York on the 17 February.[37] In 1822, John Rose was 'whitesmith, screwpress and machine maker, Neville Street, School Close'. By
1825, he had been joined by Thomas Rose, whitesmith, operating from
3 Rose Yard, Neville Street, School Close (perhaps a brother or cousin).[38]
In 1831, he was caught by death with his plans and ambitions for family
and property only part complete, John died leaving a widow, Ann, and
five children, two of whom were under 21 years of age, namely:

---

[37] Will of John Rose, 17 February 1831.
[38] Information from the same directories as for John Taylor.

Mary Ann, wife of John Richards
Sarah, wife of William Firth
William Rose
John Rose, a minor
Joseph Rose, a minor

The text of his will was a snapshot of his ambitions as he balanced the processes of capital accumulation, ageing and responsibilities to wife and children one against the other in an expanding but insecure economy. He saw his property, especially his real property, not simply as something which could be liquidated and turned into cash but as something much more specific, having characteristics and meanings beyond its cash value. Like most middle class males he sought equity between children and responsibility to his widow but he tempered this by a desire to assert authority from the grave in a way which would serve a wide variety of family objectives. He sought to enable the surviving family to utilise the combination of real property, business capital and good will, personal skills and resources to serve economic, social and psychological needs. Like that of John Taylor, John Rose's will highlighted the relationship between family strategies and the built environment of the early nineteenth century town.

John Rose left his affairs in the care of two executors, men who lived in the immediate neighbourhood, Marshall Hartley, Kerseymere printer, (stuff and woollen printer, home, Sandford Street, School Close) and Joseph Richardson, cabinet maker, (cabinet maker and upholsterer, 23 Mill Hill House, home, 11 Bedford Place) who had replaced Charles Lee, drysalter (Blayd's Court, Briggate home Wellington St).[39]

The instructions were carefully drawn up, 'My dear wife Ann' was to have £10 immediately on John's death. Such provision, common in many wills, indicated dramatically the direct day-to-day dependence of most women upon their husbands.[40] Ann was to have use of all 'my household goods, plate, furniture and effects in and about my dwellinghouse at the time of my decease'. But only 'during her life in case she shall so long continue my widow'. To ensure that these terms were strictly adhered to he required that 'an inventory be taken and held by my executors'. The executors were to invest the residual of the personal estate 'in government or real securities' and pay Ann an annuity of £20 a year from the income of this fund. This annuity was also to finish if she re-married. As in other

---

[39] Information from the Baines and Newsome, *Commercial Directory* (Leeds, 1834).
[40] See the discussion of Michael Thackrey's will in this volume, Chapter 3, 'Reading the Wills'.

wills, this limitation was related to the existence of minor children. In this case, John and Joseph Rose had the residual of the trust fund devoted to their maintenance and education.

On Ann's death or re-marriage the provisions of family equity operated. The fund was to be divided 'equally amongst my children ... or such of them as shall be living and the issue of such of them as shall be dead, such issue taking their deceased parents share'. The shares of those who died without issue were to be divided equally between the surviving brothers and sisters. This sense of equity between children was accompanied by a careful sense of potential mortality. Like many testators, John tried to cover every possible combination of death and survival whilst still preserving equity.

Death had caught John Rose half way through his life cycle. He had not yet established his family in adult life. Two daughters were married, but there were still two sons who were minors. He knew that an active business was worth more to the family than its value sold up and invested in government stock, so he gave William, the eldest son, the choice of continuing with the business.

I do hereby will and direct that in case my son William Rose shall be desirous and willing to purchase my said stock in trade and shop tools, it shall and may be lawful for my said trustees ... to sell the same to him, my said son William Rose by private contract valuation or otherwise and to take and accept his promissory note for the payment of the purchase money with lawful interest for the same.

John used the cash economy and its market mechanisms as a means of balancing his desire to provide for the continuity of the business and to achieve equity between his children. The business here was a means to an end rather than an end in itself. No preference was given to William other than first choice of purchase at valuation. He was to be offered credit but would pay interest and thus provide the income flow for his mother and siblings. William was to be protected from the hazards of a public auction but otherwise the normal processes of valuation and legal interest within the cash economy were to set him equal with his brothers and sisters. The result was that, in 1834, William Rose, whitesmith and weighing machine maker, was operating from 19 Neville Street, School Close. Thomas was now a shopkeeper at 16 Neville Street, School Close. By 1845, the relationships of the Rose family with Neville Street and the yard that carried the family name had changed again. John and Thomas Rose, whitesmiths, operated from 8 Rose's Court. Thomas lived in 7 Hopkins Yard, Neville Street whilst John was at 5 Rose's Court. William had left the scene and his younger brother now carried on the business.

The means by which this continuity was achieved becomes evident from the Soke Rate Book of 1840 (see Fig. 5.8). John Rose gave his

Table 5.4 *John Rose: real estate in Neville Street, from the Soke Rate Book of Leeds, 1840*

Owner	Occupier	Property	Address	Rateable value (£.s.)
Executors of Jno Rose		House	Neville St	15.15
Executors of Jno Rose	William Rose	Shop, yard	Neville St	16.10
Executors of Jno Rose	Mrs Rose	House, yard	Neville St	4.0
Executors of Jno Rose		House, yard	Neville St	6.10
Executors of Jno Rose		House, yard	Neville St	3.5
Executors of Jno Rose		House, yard	Neville St	2.0
Executors of Jno Rose		House, yard	Neville St	4.5
Executors of Jno Rose		House, yard	Neville St	3.15
Executors of Jno Rose		House	Neville St	7.10
Executors of Jno Rose		Millwright's shop	Little Neville St	17.10
William Hopkin	Thomas Rose	House and shop	Neville St	4.0
William Hopkin		Cellar and chamber	Neville St	4.0
William Hopkin		House	Neville St	4.0
William Hopkin		House	Neville St	4.0
William Hopkin		House	Neville St	4.0
William Hopkin		House	Neville St	4.0
William Hopkin		House	Neville St	4.0
William Hopkin		House	Neville St	4.0
William Hopkin		House	Neville St	4.0
William Hopkin		House	Neville St	8.5

executors power to 'sell and dispose of my said real estate ... as soon as convenient after the death or second marriage of my said wife'. The entries for the Rose estate and the neighbouring property of William Hopkin show that Ann was neither dead nor re-married.

Nearly ten years after his death, John Rose lived on in the shape of the legal personality of his estate. It provided a business for his eldest son, whilst his wife lived in one of the smaller houses in the yard, still entitled to her £20 a year and 'his' household furniture. The frontsides/backsides layout of property, the relationship of landlord and tenant and the mixture of residential and industrial property vilified by later urban commentators was the physical built embodiment of the family needs and strategies of John Rose and his like. It was home, business premises, widow's pension and housing as well as the basis of a broadly based entrepreneurial and rentier capital accumulation, all within a close geographical space for easy supervision. John Rose was another owner, occupier, entrepreneur, rentier of the type fundamental to the social and physical structures of urban Britain in this phase of development.

Linking the 1847 large-scale Ordnance Survey map with the 1841 Soke Rate Book revealed many cases like that of John Rose. The Soke Rate rate

was laid, 19 May 1841, as a result of the Act of 2nd Victoria for dischar-
ging or buying out an irritating feudal survival, namely the obligation of
the inhabitants of Leeds to grind corn at the old manorial soke mill.[41]
When School Close was laid out and sold for development somewhere
between 1810 and 1830, it produced a string of little urban estates. The
overall appearance was chaotic, but the internal logic of each plot was
related to the family republics which developed them. A walk around
Sandford and Neville Streets armed with the commercial directories of
1822, 1825 and 1834 and the Soke Rate Book of 1841, identified twelve
of these urban estates (Table 5.5).[42]

Thus, in the twelve properties visited along Sandford Street and
Neville Street, six operated as a family republic, supplying domestic
shelter, business or manufacturing premises and rentier income. In two
cases these little urban estates were operating to support widows.

The interaction of family and life cycle strategies with the built environment of Leeds produced a number of characteristic features. The first
was the heterogeneity of property bundles. The owners were not specialists in one form of property, domestic, commercial or manufacturing.
Even if the elements of these property bundles were not contiguous, they
were spatially compact. The owners tended to be resident owner-
manager rentiers. In some cases, the properties were bound up with or
intended for the support of widows and minor children.

The wills gave many snapshots of the changing meanings of bundles of
property. Henry Arnott, 'gentleman'[43] was a minor member of the Salem
Chapel network of Congregationalists. He was also part of the textile
network which spread across the southern townships of Leeds parish. He
had links with lowland Scotland and had married into the Nussey family
which included dyers and woolstaplers. One daughter had married a
packer, Peter Hindle, who, by 1834, was a cloth manufacturer in Isle
Lane in Holbeck, while the other married a clothier from Stanningley. His
trustees included George Rawson, a leading member of Salem Chapel.
This was a man of modest means, who was not a member of any elite, but
had links with the nonconformist leadership of Leeds. In the 1820s, he
had purchased a variety of cottage properties, five in Vine Street and five
in Grape Street just off the Hunslet Rd and close to the Larchfield Mills of
Pim Nevins (Fig. 5.9). These and twelve other cottages were to provide
an income for his daughter, Mary Hindle. He also had nine cottages in

[41] Leeds Soke Rate Valuation and Collection, 1841. Leeds Archive Service. DB 234.
[42] The supplementary sources are the three commercial directories already described,
together with William's Directory of the Borough of Leeds, (Leeds, 1845).
[43] Will for probate 6 May 1831. Sworn value £200.

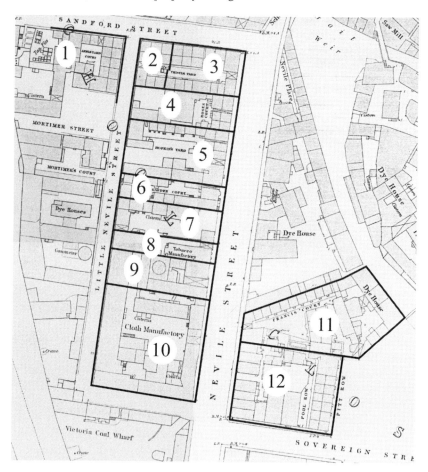

Fig. 5.8 The 'urban estates' of Neville Street, 1841–47.

Source: Based on O.S. plan (surveyed 1847). The information was taken from the Leeds Soke Rate valuation, 1841. DB 234.

Stanningley which he purchased from the assignees of Samuel Walton, his son-in-law. These and another eleven Stanningley cottages were to provide rent and profits for daughter, Ann Walton, for 'her natural life'. Finally, there were three dwelling houses in Meadow Lane. Arnott lived in one and Peter Hindle, still described as a packer, lived in another. The meaning of these cottages changed with family and economic circumstances. In 1827, they were rentier income for Henry Arnott, domestic space for himself and his daughter's family. They were also intended to provided a separate income for his daughters, very necessary given the

Table 5.5 *The rentier republics of School Close [Neville Steet], 1822–41*
1. Thomas W. Appleyard
(11 houses, 3 stables, one shop).
TWA occupied a shop on Sandford Street. He had a second block of property on nearby
Mill Hill; two warehouses and a beer house. He was a dyer who lived on Mill Hill looking
down on Sandford Street, where he developed his property. In the mid-1820s, he retired to
live upon the rents of his cottages and warehouses. By 1834, he was confident enough to
move out of the area up to Burley Terrace. By 1842/45, a relative, Thomas Appleyard, was
back on the estate as a tanner. It was not clear if he owned some of the property, as the rate
book was vague, just listing the owners as Appleyard. The republic had clearly served family
needs. The Appleyards and their like had access to markets to rent out surplus property.
Indeed, one of the objectives was to accumulate enough property to produce an adequate
rentier income before retirement. Thus, the meaning of the property changed as the family
developed. At the start, it was industrial capital, domestic dwelling house and a means of
accumulating and broadening the capital base to support an active business in an uncertain
and fluctuating economy. Then it became the rentier capital of retirement and finally, by
1840, the industrial capital and perhaps dwelling house for establishing another business for
another generation.

Directory

1822	Appleyard, Thomas Wade	Dyer	28 Mill Hill
1825	Appleyard, Thomas Wade	Gentleman	28 Mill Hill
1834	Appleyard, Thomas Wade	Gentleman	Burley Terrace
1845	TWA not listed but	Tanner and	11, 12 and 15
	Appleyard, Thomas[a]	currier	Sandford St

[a] No relevant Thomas Appleyards in earlier directories.

Soke Rate Book 1841

Owner	Occupier[b]	Property	Address	Valuation (£ decimal)	Ref.
Appleyard		Beer house	Mill Hill	16.5	179
Appleyard		Warehouse	Mill Hill	41.5	180
Appleyard		Warehouse	Mill Hill	41.5	182
Appleyard		House	Appleyard Ct	4.25	474
Appleyard		House	Appleyard Ct	6	475
Appleyard		House	Appleyard Ct	6	476
Appleyard	T.W. Appleyard	Stable	Appleyard Ct	4.25	477
Appleyard		Stable	Appleyard Ct	4.25	478
Appleyard		Stable	Appleyard Ct	1.5	479
Appleyard		House	Appleyard Ct	6.5	480
Appleyard	Thomas Appleyard	Shop	Sandford St	12.5	481
Appleyard		House	Appleyard Ct	6.5	482
Appleyard		House	Sandford St	8.25	483
Appleyard		House	Sandford St	8.25	484
Appleyard		House	Little Neville St	6.5	485
Appleyard		House	Little Neville St	6	486

Table 5.5 (*cont.*)

Soke Rate Book 1841					
Owner	Occupier[b]	Property	Address	Valuation (£ decimal)	Ref.
Appleyard		House	Little Neville St	6.5	487
Total				186.75	

Source: As tables 5.1 and 5.4.
[b]Only given if the occupier is clearly related to, or the same person as, the owner.

2. Robert Hardisty

1822. There were no clear links to the directories although there was a cattle dealer at 70 Briggate, and a Briggate shopkeeper in 1834 (glass and chinaware). This could be an absentee with a small estate.

Soke Rate Book 1841				
Owner	Property	Address	Valuation (£ decimal)	Ref.
Robert Hardisty	House	Little Neville St	7.5	532
Robert Hardisty	House	Hardisty's Yard	4.75	533
Robert Hardisty	House	Hardisty's Yard	4.5	534
Robert Hardisty	House	Hardisty's Yard	4.5	535
Robert Hardisty	House	Hardisty's Yard	4.0	536
Robert Hardisty	House and shop	Hardisty's Yard	4.25	537
Robert Hardisty	House	Little Neville St	5.75	538
Robert Hardisty	House	Little Neville St	6.25	539
Robert Hardisty	House	Sandford St	10.76	540
Robert Hardisty	House	Sandford St	8.25	541
Robert Hardisty	House	Sandford St	8.25	542
Total			68.75	

3. Fountain Brown

This was the property of a merchant who lived in the very different environment of Park Place, but still only a few minutes walk away from his business.

Directory			
1822	Brown, Fountaine	Merchant	Home: 1 Park Sq.

Soke Rate Book 1841					
Owner	Occupier	Property	Address	Valuation (£ decimal)	Ref.
Fountain Brown	Fountain Brown	House and land	Park Place	91.5	231
Brown		House	Sandford St	5.75	544

Table 5.5 *(cont.)*

Soke Rate Book 1841

Owner	Occupier	Property	Address	Valuation (£ decimal)	Ref.
Brown		House	Sandford St	5.75	545
Brown		House	Sandford St	5.75	546
Brown		House	Sandford St	5.75	547
Brown		House	Sandford St	5.75	548
Brown		House	Thistle Yd.	5.0	549
Brown		House	Thistle Yd.	5.0	550
Brown		House	Thistle Yd.	5	551
Brown		House	Thistle Yd.	5	552
Brown		House	Thistle Yd.	5	553
Brown		House	Thistle Yd.	4.5	554
Brown		House	Thistle Yd.	4.5	555
Brown		House	Thistle Yd.	4.5	556
Brown		House	Neville St	4.5	557
Brown		House	Neville St	15	558
Brown		House	Neville St	25	559
Total				203.25	

Then followed the estates held by the executors of John Rose and the neighbouring property of William Hopkin. Hopkin had no linkable entry in the 1822 directory but by 1832-34 he was recorded as a builder and joiner who also had property in George's Street.

4. John Rose (see Table 5.4)
5. William Hopkin (see Table 5.4)
6. Michael Thwaite

Directory

1822	Thwaites, Michael	Joiner	School Close
1832 and 1834	Thwaites, Michael	Joiner	School Close

Soke Rate Book 1841

Owner	Occupier	Property	Address	Valuation (£ decimal)	Ref.
Michael Thwaite		House	Little Neville St	6.5	514
Michael Thwaite		House	Garden Ct	2.5	515
Michael Thwaite		House	Garden Ct	5	516
Michael Thwaite		House	Garden Ct	3.75	517
Michael Thwaite		House	Garden Ct	4	518
Michael Thwaite		House	Garden Ct	4	519
Michael Thwaite		House	Garden Ct	4	521
Michael Thwaite		House	Garden Ct	2.5	522

Table 5.5 (*cont.*)

Soke Rate Book 1841

Owner	Occupier	Property	Address	Valuation £ decimal	Ref.
Michael Thwaite		House	Garden Ct	5	523
Michael Thwaite		House	Garden Ct	3.75	524
Michael Thwaite		House	Garden Ct	2.5	525
Michael Thwaite		Cellar	Garden Ct	2.25	526
Michael Thwaite		House	Little Neville St	5	527
Michael Thwaite	Michael Thwaite	Shop and house	Garden Ct	11.5	528
Michael Thwaite		House	Garden Ct	7.5	529
Michael Thwaite	Michael Thwaite	Beer house	Neville St	16.5	530
Total				86.25	

7. William Simpson

1822. There were no clear links. He was a plumber and glazier in 1832 and 1834.

Soke Rate Book 1841

Owner	Occupier	Property	Address	Valuation £ decimal	Ref.
William Simpson	William Simpson	House	Neville St	12.5	587
William Simpson	William Simpson	Shop	Neville St	21.25	588
William Simpson	Josh Simpson	house	Neville St	10.75	589
Total				44.5	

8. Thomas Boyne

1822. Boyne Thomas tobacconist, home Queens Square, (he was listed as Tobacco and Snuff Manufacturers and Dealer at School Close).

1825. Boyne Thomas tobacco and snuff manufacturer, 13 Neville St, home Virginia Cottage, Little Woodhouse.

1832–34. He was recorded living in Little Woodhouse with property still in School Close, but there was a William Boyne, tobacconist in Briggate suggesting that the business may have gone to another family member, maybe a son.

This was a clear example of an absentee owner who had separated home and work perhaps at retirement. He was the occupier but not of a domestic property.

Soke Rate Book 1841

Owner	Occupier	Property	Address	Valuation (£ decimal)	Ref.
Thomas Boyne	Thomas Boyne	Warehouse and mill	Neville St	37.5	590

9. Owner not clear from the evidence

10. Richard Bramley

1822. Hirst, Bramley and Co, merchants and woollen manufacturers, School Close.

1825. Hirst and Bramley, merchants and woollen cloth manufacturers, 12 Neville St

Richard Bramley was recorded as an owner of the mill in 1832 and 1834 but there was no evidence that he lived in the mill house which was on the other side of Neville St from the mill itself.

Soke Rate Book 1841

Owner	Occupier	Property	Address	Valuation (£ decimal)	Ref.
Richard Bramley	Richard Bramley with Thos. Hirst and others	Manufactory	Neville St	770.25	593
Richard Bramley		House	Neville St	8.25	595

11. Francis Strickland

1822. Strickland Francis, stone mason, Neville St, School Close.

The 1834 Directory had an entry for Elizabeth Strickland at 18 Francis Court, but no mention of a William in the Court. This looks like a family republic which was serving the purpose of supporting the widow and providing a residence for another member of the family. It was unusual in that ownership was attributed directly to the widow rather than being held in trust by executors.

Soke Rate Book 1841

Owner	Occupier	Property	Address	Valuation (£ decimal)	Ref.
Widow Strickland		Stable	Little Neville St	4	510
		Counting house, shop and wood yard	Little Neville St	27.75	512
Widow Strickland	William Strickland	House	Francis Ct	8.75	670
Widow Strickland		Beer house	Neville St	20.75	671
Widow Strickland		House	Neville St	8.25	672
Widow Strickland		House	Francis Ct	5.25	673
Widow Strickland		House	Francis Ct	4.75	674
Widow Strickland		House	Francis Ct	5	675
Widow Strickland		House	Francis Ct	5.25	676
Widow Strickland		House	Francis Ct	5.25	677
Widow Strickland		House	Francis Ct	5	678
Widow Strickland		House	Francis Ct	4.5	679
Widow Strickland		House	Francis Ct	4.5	680
Widow Strickland		House	Francis Ct	4.5	681
Widow Strickland		House	Francis Ct	4.5	682
Widow Strickland		House	Francis Ct	5.25	683
Widow Strickland		House	Francis Ct	5.5	684
Widow Strickland		House	Francis Ct	5.5	685
Widow Strickland		House	Francis Ct	5.25	686

214

Table 5.5 (*cont.*)

Soke Rate Book 1841

Owner	Occupier	Property	Address	Valuation (£ decimal)	Ref.
Widow Strickland		House	Francis Ct	6.5	687
Widow Strickland		House	Francis Ct	6.5	688
Widow Strickland		House	Francis Ct	6.5	689
Widow Strickland		Dyehouse	Pitt Row	62.5	691
Total				221.5	

12. William Clark

1822. No entry.

In 1832–34 he was a coach maker in School Close. This was a true family republic which mixed residential, business and rentier property on the one site.

He was an owner occupier rentier with his house, frontsides in Sovereign Street.

Soke Rate Book 1841

Owner	Occupier	Property	Address	Valuation (£ decimal)	Ref.
William Clark		Beer house	Pitt Row, School Close	20	655
William Clark		House	Pitt Row, School Close	4.75	656
William Clark		House	Pitt Row, School Close	4.75	657
William Clark		House	Pitt Row, School Close	4.75	658
William Clark		House	Pitt Row, School Close	4.75	659
William Clark		House	Pitt Row, School Close	4.75	660
William Clark		House	Pitt Row, School Close	4.75	661
William Clark		House	Sovereign St	6.25	662
William Clark		House	Pool Row	6.25	663
William Clark		House	Pool Row	4.75	664
William Clark		House	Pool Row	4.75	665
William Clark		House	Pool Row	4.75	666
William Clark		House	Pool Row	4.75	667
William Clark		House	Pool Row	4.75	668
William Clark		House and shop	Neville St	30	693
William Clark		House and shop	Neville St	16.5	694
William Clark		House and shop	Neville St	25	695
William Clark		House and shop	Neville St	29	696
William Clark		Shop	Neville St	25	697
William Clark		Shop	Neville St	25	698
William Clark		Shop	Neville St	33.25	699
William Clark		Warehouse	Sovereign St	104.00	700
William Clark		Warehouse	Sovereign St	66.5	701
William Clark	William Clark	House and shop	Sovereign St	18.25	702
William Clark		Warehouse	Bridge End	16.5	799
William Clark		House and shop	Bridge End	8.25	800

Table 5.5 (*cont.*)

Owner	Occupier	Property	Address	Valuation (£ decimal)	Ref.
		Soke Rate Book 1841			
William Clark	Sarah Clark	House	Bishopgate St	33.25	442
William Clark	William Clark	Warehouse, shop, counting house etc	Sandford St	133.25	457
Total				648.5	

economic insecurities of the textile trade which had already caught one
son-in-law. These houses could also be used to raise capital for family
advancement. In November 1827, he made a codicil to his will. He had
raised £600 from John Fretwell, secured on mortgage on the twelve
cottages in Hunslet Lane.

Such mortgage was made by me for the purpose of an advancement for my
grandson, Henry Arnott Hindle, the eldest son of the said Peter Hindle . . . to
enable him to commence business in partnership with his said father and with Mr
Abraham Holt as dyers and to form a capital in such business

Arnott directed that the mortgage should not be paid from personal estate
but that the rents and profits of the 'said premises . . . shall be applied in the
first place in keeping down the interest of the said mortgage debt and in the
insurance of the said mortgaged buildings'. The principal of the mortgage
debt was to be paid from the sale of the property as directed in his will.
Equity between children was still required. Henry Arnott Hindle was not to
receive anything further from the estate 'without first bringing into hotchpot the said principal sum of six hundred pounds and all interest which may
have been paid in respect thereof'. If that sum exceeded his share then
Henry Arnott Hindle was 'to pay and refund such excess'.

Thomas Crosland, Gentleman, was a man who worked on the edge of
the textile economy of Holbeck village.[44] His property was on Isle Lane in a
chaotic area of folds, yards, mills and back-to-back houses (Fig. 5.10).
Hindle's Fold was a neighbour. The Wesleyan Association Chapel backed
onto his 'estate'. The notion of the street was little understood when the
area was laid out. His family economy was only a partial success but was
surviving in a way which depended heavily on manipulating the meanings
of his real property holdings. Demography and economic fortune had
treated the Croslands unkindly. His eldest son William was dead, leaving

[44] Will for probate 6 May 1831. Sworn Value £200.

Fig. 5.9 The 'urban estate' of Henry Arnott, gentleman, 1831.
Source: Extract from O.S. plan (surveyed 1847, Published 1850).

a widow, children and the half share of the property, he had recently purchased with his father, in the hands of Perfects and Smith, bankers and holders of the mortgage. Thomas, Senior, bought it back. William had been a commission agent, an activity which required little capital, a great deal of credit and skill or good fortune. Frederic had gone to Montreal where he had died leaving six children, 'whose names I cannot mention with certainty'. John was a curate in Lincolnshire. The eldest daughter, Elizabeth, married Nathaniel Dunderland, clothier of Isle Lane. As in the case of Henry Arnott, father-in-law sought a means of turning real property into capital, although this time there was no evidence of bankruptcy or liquidity difficulties. Daughter Elizabeth was to have,

the amount of a mortgage deed, being the sum of two hundred pounds secured upon an estate situate at Holbeck in the Parish of Leeds aforesaid belonging once to Nathanial Dunderdale her husband with all the right title and interest in the same ... the said dwelling house and premises ... (free) of control debts or disposal of her husband.

Thomas described himself in 1829 as a cut nail manufacturer and grocer, a dual occupation which reflected the inadequacy and insecurity of the income he expected in either. The duality was also helpful in terms of family strategy because, by 1834, his two surviving sons in Leeds were described in the Parliamentary Poll Books as,

Charles Crosland, house, ironfounder, Bowling Green
Thomas Crosland, house and shop, grocer, Isle Lane

The business interests of father had been divided between them. There were indications that Thomas, Senior, was still living on credit. Elizabeth was to have the household furniture on condition 'a certain promissory note on interest due and owing to Mr. John Hutchison now or late of Rothwell near Leeds' as well as half of the funeral and probate expenses were paid. Real property again was not just a matter of a rent income for Thomas, Senior, but was a means of providing capital and credit for his sons and rescuing them when they got into difficulties. Equity was still part of the strategy, although the cash sums and property rights transferred by the will were certainly not equal. The will was trying to balance help already given to some of his sons during their father's lifetime.

Except those debts and sums of money due and owing to me from my sons herein before mentioned Charles Crosland, Thomas Crosland, William Crosland, Frederic Crosland and John Crosland for sums of money advanced to them at different periods, now I do hereby give, forgive and release the said sums

Thomas was trying to achieve so much in terms of family and life cycle purposes that there were bound to be tensions. The widow and children of

William were to be given £20 on condition they 'quit and deliver up peaceable possession of the house they now occupy and which I by this my last will and testament devise to my son Charles Crosland'. William's part of the family had presumably had their share as a result of whatever economic troubles led to the bank repossessing the mortgaged property. The cases of Arnott and Crosland had none of the neatness of Hey and Rose but they do show the complex and multiple meanings which produced the landscape of south Leeds. The chaos of Isle Lane was typical of many areas of Leeds and had a clear logic in the eyes of Thomas Crosland and those like him.

The general applicability of the findings derived from the case studies can be tested against information derived from the three surviving rate books of the Leeds Soke Rate of 1841. The three books covered about half the property of Leeds township and represented three very different types of area.[45] Book One included School Close, a densely built collection of mixed industrial and residential property between the mill goits, the river and the lower end of Briggate. This was the land of John Rose and his neighbours. Book Two included the yards west of Briggate, which provided the family commonwealth of the Heys, as well as the 'west end' development around Albion Street and Park Place. Book Three took the rate collector west along the Kirkstall Road to a newer, raw landscape of mills and back-to-back houses.

The property descriptions and valuations summarised the contrasting nature of these three environments (Table 5.6).

One of the most important groups of properties were those described as 'house and shop'. They not only represented the spatial integrity of home and business for many, but they were a touchstone of the different natures of the three areas (Table 5.7).

As was the case throughout Leeds, the mixed industrial area of School Close was dominated numerically by domestic property but, in terms of value, industrial and commercial premises were the most important. In the area west of Briggate there was a slightly lower proportion of domestic properties but they included the Park Square area and had a higher average value. This area included the warehouses of Basinghall Street and the yards behind the Park Square houses. Commercial property was important in terms of both numbers and value. Shop property included the front of Briggate and new developments like Hey's Commercial Street. They were superior in average value and in proportion to those

---

[45] These three rate books are held in the Leeds division of the West Yorkshire Archives service. DB 234.

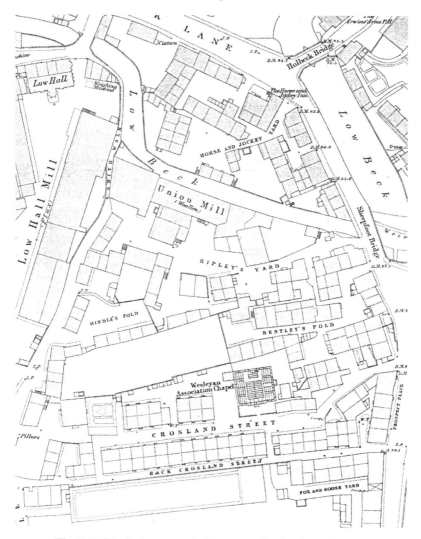

Fig. 5.10 The 'urban estate' of Thomas Crosland, gentleman, 1831.
Source: Extract from O.S. plan (surveyed 1847, published 1850).

of School Close. In this area manufacturing was trivial. The Kirkstall
Road area was quite different. It was dominated by huge numbers of low
value domestic properties. Their average value was a half to a third that of
the other two areas. The second feature was a small number of very large
mills with an average value nearly double that of the smaller mills around
School Close. This was the area of Benjamin Gott's Bean Ing Mill.

220

Table 5.6 *Leeds Soke Rate, 1841. Property valuations and descriptions*

	Mean value of cases £ decimal	Cases	Total value (£ decimal)	Value (%)	Cases (%)
School Close	**34.59**	**814**	**28160.25**	**34.64**	**21.89**
Domestic	14.21	445	6325.23	22.46	54.67
Commercial	50.70	159	8060.51	28.62	19.53
Shops	35.21	106	3731.75	13.25	13.02
Drink	63.46	28	1777.00	6.31	3.44
Manufacturing textiles	166.11	43	7142.75	25.36	5.28
Other manufacturing	39.01	23	897.25	3.19	2.83
Government and public	16.63	4	66.50	0.24	0.49
Land etc.	26.54	6	159.25	0.57	0.74
West of Briggate	**33.32**	**977**	**32549.54**	**40.04**	**26.28**
Domestic	19.71	439	8651.50	26.58	44.93
Commercial	43.95	307	13493.26	41.45	31.42
Shops	45.70	163	7449.00	22.89	16.68
Drink	53.25	27	1437.75	4.42	2.76
Manufacturing textiles	14.55	5	72.75	0.22	0.51
Other manufacturing	19.25	20	385.00	1.18	2.05
Government and public	67.80	15	1017.00	3.12	1.54
Land etc.	43.25	1	43.25	0.13	0.10
Kirkstall Road	**10.68**	**1927**	**20582.48**	**25.32**	**51.83**
Domestic	5.67	1752	9942.42	48.31	90.92
Commercial	13.00	6	78.00	0.38	0.31
Shops	13.00	82	1065.75	5.18	4.26
Drink	28.24	34	960.25	4.67	1.76
Manufacturing textiles	260.20	31	8066.25	39.19	1.61
Other manufacturing	50.95	5	254.75	1.24	0.26
Government and public	9.88	4	39.50	0.19	0.21
Land etc.	13.50	13	175.50	0.85	0.67
For total population	**21.86**	**3718**	**81292.26**		

Table 5.7 *Properties described as 'House and Shop' in the Soke Rate, 1841*

	Mean value £ decimal	Cases	Total value	As percentage of cases in area	As percentage of value in area
Total	**39.06**	**229**	**8945.50**	**6.16**	**11.00**
School Close	39.67	64	2539.00	7.86	9.02
West of Briggate	52.36	107	5602.25	10.95	17.21
Kirkstall Road	13.87	58	804.25	3.01	3.91

Table 5.8 *Ownership structure of properties in the Leeds Soke Rate of 1841*

	Mean	Cases	Sum value	Cases (%)	Value (%)
Total	140.62	578	81275.87		
Male	158.09	293	46320.31	50.69	56.99
Female	95.62	37	3538.00	6.40	4.35
Firm	194.55	28	5447.50	4.84	6.70
Institution	132.67	12	1592.00	2.08	1.96
Legal personalities	136.99	48	6575.75	8.30	8.09
No information	111.26	160	17802.30	27.68	21.90

These surviving rate books cover key areas of Leeds but several types of area were missing. The back-to-backs of east Leeds, of 'clubland' and the 'gentleman' urban peasant builders, and the hand loom weaving district of the Bank were missing, as were the villas of Little Woodhouse and the infilling of mixed domestic and industrial around the old eighteenth century merchant villas north of Briggate. There was enough left to show the varying degrees to which the owner-occupier-rentier flourished in different built environments, and to show the manner in which these environments related to family and life cycle property .

The relationship of the properties in the Soke Rate Book to these strategies can best be judged in terms not of individual properties but in terms of bundles of properties. Each bundle has been identified with a common owner. In most cases, these bundles were contiguous, although some were dispersed like those of John Taylor. In part, the findings are compromised by the partial coverage of the books but it is unlikely that the missing books would alter the direction and order of magnitude of these findings.

Overall there were 578 bundles of property identified by owners. The ownership structure was overwhelmingly male dominated.

The cases on which there was insufficient information were those with surname and perhaps initials. Given that in public documents like wills and directories, women were almost always identified by their civil status, it was likely that these cases were all male, as with property owned by a firm or partnership. Women owned less than 5 per cent of the property in the three books by value and only 6.4 per cent of the property bundles. The few who did own property had a lower mean value than the other categories. This was very different from the distribution of personal property in the wills where women had made 24 per cent of the probated wills and the mean sworn value had been male £1624 and women £1267. Female mean sworn value was 78 per cent of male, whilst the mean value of their

Table 5.9 *Property held by each individual or unit of ownership in Soke Rate books, Leeds 1841*

Value of property (£)	Frequency	%	Cumulative %
0–19	54	9.34	9.34
20–39	95	16.44	25.78
40–59	98	16.96	42.73
60–79	47	8.13	50.87
80–99	43	7.44	58.30
100–119	47	8.13	66.44
120–129	31	5.36	71.80
140–159	23	3.98	75.78
160–179	23	3.98	79.76
180–199	12	2.08	81.83
200–229	7	1.21	83.04
220–239	10	1.73	84.78
240–259	8	1.38	86.16
260–279	8	1.38	87.54
280–299	11	1.90	89.45
300–319	11	1.90	91.35
320–339	4	0.69	92.04
340–499	21	3.63	95.67
500–999	20	3.46	99.13
>1000	5	0.87	100.00
Total	578	100.00	

Soke Rate property holdings was only 60 per cent. Holding and managing real property was much more male than the holding of personal estate. When Rebecca Hey sold her share in the family real estate and bought government stock, she followed a widespread female property preference. A small number of institutions, like the Music Hall and the Court House, were important in the central area. The 'legal personalities' included a number of executors, administrators and trustees who held property on behalf of others, many as a result of the instructions of a will. These legal personalities represented 'life after death' as part of the property cycle. They were managing 8 per cent of the property of Leeds.

The distribution of property amongst these owners had the characteristic of many property distributions, namely a modest number of very small accumulations, a large number of modest accumulations and a small number of large accumulations. The results are presented here in terms of total value of property held by each individual or individual unit of ownership. Nearly 60 per cent of owners held less than £60 annual value of property while 25 per cent held less than £40 annual value. The

Table 5.10 *Property bundles. Leeds Soke Rate, 1841*

	Count	%
Domestic	215	37.2
Stable	2	0.3
Vicarage	1	0.2
Land	1	0.2
Domestic with warehouse	33	5.7
Domestic with offices	5	0.9
Houses and shops	76	13.1
Houses with manufacturing	32	5.5
Houses with services	8	1.4
Domestic cluster no manufacturing	64	11.1
Domestic cluster manufacturing	38	6.6
Warehouses	41	7.1
Offices	10	1.7
Offices with service	1	0.2
Warehouses and offices	4	0.7
Warehouses with manufacturing	9	1.6
Warehouses with services	4	0.7
Shops	7	1.2
Shops and offices	1	0.2
Shop and manufacturing	1	0.2
Public house	7	1.2
Manufacturing	8	1.4
Services	2	0.3
No domestic manufacturing cluster	7	1.2
Local government	1	0.2
Total	578	

'executors of John Rose' were just above this class with holdings valued at £81 for the Soke Rate. There was a small but important group of 61 (10.5 per cent) people who held property valued at over £300. William Hey II with £820 was in this group. At the top were the five men who held over £1000 of property. Benjamin Gott's complex at Bean Ing, valued at just over £2000, was top of the list. This was not an account of the total property holding of Leeds, but it was likely that if rate books had been available for east and north Leeds and for the industrial townships to the south, then the shape of the distribution would have been much the same.

There were several features of these property owning clusters. First, there was a dominance of heterogeneity and multiplicity in ownership patterns. The property clusters were classified in the following way. Just under half the clusters, 284 (49 per cent), were specialists and dealt in only one type of property and, of these, 215 (37 per cent) were domestic.

Another 37 per cent contained domestic property together with another type, usually shops. This heterogeneity reflected the multiplicity of the aims of most property owners as well as the very imperfect division of domestic and workplace space.

Only 19 per cent (111) of the clusters contained one unit of property of which forty-seven were houses. The majority of holdings were four or less units (54 per cent) while 80 per cent had ten or less. Most owners sought a modest rentier income as well as a variety of family objectives.

Leeds was not noted for major property holders. There were no dominant 'landowners'. The largest holdings in the Soke Books include few public figures. Size may be measured by total annual value or by number of properties. Each type of accumulation indicated a typology of relationships with the landscape and direction of change over time.

Thomas Prince owned fifty properties with a total annual value of £907. The nature of his holding and evidence of his life cycle trajectory in poll books and directory outlined a passage from an owner-occupier-rentier republic to a retirement phase in the growing suburban villages in the north of the borough of Leeds. Thomas Prince owned warehouses, a saw mill and a calender mill along Mill Hill as well as his own dyeworks on the adjacent Isle of Cinder. He had houses and warehouses in Albion Court and Buttons Yard behind what had been his family house in 1822. By 1834, he had moved out to Moor Allerton. There were many examples like this where early suburban villas were as much about life cycle stage as they were about 'social class' and environment.

Obediah Willans held thirty-one properties with a total value of £1728. These fell into three distinct groups. There were sixteen substantial middle class houses in York Place, part of the Park Square 'west end' development which had started in the smoke-free late eighteenth century. There was a block of warehouses in Brittania Street behind York Place. One of these was used by Obediah Willans and sons, woollen cloth manufacturers. Then there was the mill on Wellington Road, valued at £778, also occupied by the firm. Willans had a balance of property providing for the family business and rentier income.

John Howard, carpet manufacturer was slightly different. He held three groups of property which were functionally related by the needs of work, family and rentier income but were spatially divided. He owned and occupied a substantial house in Park Place, annual value £91, a warehouse in Greek Street and thirty-eight low value back-to-back houses in Howard Street and Back Hanover Street to the northwest of Park Square.

His relationship to the landscape had something in common with the majority of the specialists in low value back-to-back working class housing. Four held substantial blocks of such housing in the area between

Table 5.11 *Heterogeneous property bundles, Leeds Soke Rate, 1841*

Share (%)	Rentier republics	West of Briggate	N
All property bundles	25	36	578
Heterogeneity but no manufacturing	36	59	64
Heterogeneity with manufacturing	45	45	38

West Street and Wellington Street, north of Bean Ing and the other mills along the River Aire. These minor capitalists provided the housing for the workforce of the major manufacturing establishments. William Hardwick had a beerhouse on West Street close to his houses in Jerry Street, Henry Street and Charley Street. The other owner-occupier-rentier specialist was Joseph Mason, 'gentleman' of Wellington Place who lived amongst his thirty-six properties, total annual value £139. Nearby were the houses of Mr Howarth, who has left no trace of his dwelling place but he owned forty-one properties in Well Street, Cropper Gate and the Triangle Yard. Finally, there was a relic of the Paley property empire which had over-extended itself and collapsed earlier in the century.[46] The entity called 'Paley' was presumably being run by assignees or administrators in bank-ruptcy and held sixty-two houses worth £229 in all. Mr. Wheelwright had the same sort of specialist holding around Lower Hanover Street north of West Street.

These specialist holdings of back-to-back housing were a feature of the raw landscape west of Park Square. This was the area of Rate Book Three. Whilst Rate Book Three held 40 per cent of the property bundles, it included 65 per cent of the specialist bundles of domestic property. These bundles had a mean annual value of £51, considerably below that of the specialist domestic bundles in the other two areas. In the rentier republics of Book One, mean annual value was £68, whilst in the yards and streets west of Briggate it was £61. The other aspect of specialism in the raw landscape of Book Three was the mill owners who held only manufacturing property. The high status owners of these large mills did not hold their life cycle rentier investment as neighbourhood real estate or housing.

In the two other areas, the property types of maximum heterogeneity were considerably over-represented.

---

[46] M.W. Beresford, 'The Making of a Townscape: Richard Paley in the East End of Leeds, 1771–1803', in C.W. Chalklin and M.A. Havinden (eds.), *Rural Change and Urban Growth, 1500–1800*, (London, 1974), 281–320.

When the bundles were evaluated in terms of annual value a very different picture emerged. Only two people appeared in both groups. There were two groups of major property holders by value. Three held large blocks of manufacturing capital, Benjamin Gott at Bean Ing, William Sheepshanks, who held mills in West Street and Kirkstall Road, and Edward Hudson who had an oil and seed crushing mill and associated property on the Isle of Cinder. There were the two warehouse gentlemen. Charles Makin lived above the smoke in Woodhouse and collected rents from his warehouses in Bond Street, Russell Street and Basinghall Street. John Ellershaw's holdings resulted from a life cycle move from his business as drysalter, soap boiler and oil crusher in the Isle of Cinder. He had moved from Queen Square to retirement in Roundhay. His property included Bond Street warehouses but also warehouses in Sovereign Street adjacent to his business. In 1845, the business continued as John Ellershaw and Sons with John, Junior and Robert John living in Park Square and Park Place. High value bundles of property were related to manufacturing and warehouse property whilst bundles with a large number of properties usually contained low value back-to-back houses.

Specialism at both ends of the scale was a feature of the raw urban landscape of large mills and associated back-to-back housing. Heterogeneity was a feature of the older landscape of School Close and the developments of the yards and closes west of Briggate. This was the landscape of William Hey and John Rose and their family and life cycle based strategies of accumulation.

A key feature of landscape creation and social relationships was the owner-occupier-rentier. Very few houses were owned and lived in by the same person. Of the 3711 properties listed in the rate books, only 156 (4.2 per cent)[47] were lived in by their owners, but many houses were owned by people who lived in the same area or even in the same block. These were participant managers. Living in the same area or block increased control and knowledge and reduced risk. This owner-occupier-rentier structure of ownership was a product of the imperfect division or lack of division of domestic and workplace environments. Overall, 30 per cent of the properties and 27 per cent of the property bundles were in the hands of

---

[47] In 1839, Robert Baker calculated that of the 17,839 dwellings in Leeds township, 3.7 per cent were occupied by their owners. Baker, *Report* (1839), p. 410. J. Springett, 'Land Development and House Building in Huddersfield, 1770–1911', in M. Doughty (ed.), *Building the Industrial City* (Leicester, 1986), p. 40 calculated that in Hudderfield, c. 1850, 10 per cent of the houses were owner occupied but that this declined with the age of the houses. Other comparable figures varied from the 17 per cent in Durham City in 1850 to 4 per cent in Leicester in 1855, R. Dennis, *English Industrial Cities in the Nineteenth Century* (Cambridge, 1984), p. 143.

Table 5.12 *Owner-occupier-rentiers in the Leeds Soke Rate, 1841*

Owner-occupier-rentier	Properties (%)	Bundles (%)
West of Briggate (mature)	17	18
School Close (second generation)	34	27
Kirkstall Rd (raw urban)	36	35
Total	30	27

owner-occupier-rentiers. There was a sharp contrast between the three areas represented by the three rate books.

The more recent the development of the area, the higher the presence of owner-occupier-rentiers. In a new area individuals built around their family and business, including the business of property development but, as the area matured, life cycle and generational effects led to individuals, where possible, moving out to the villas which surrounded Leeds or passing their property through inheritance to other family members, who might not always continue to live on the family 'estate'. The relationship of the share of business occupiers to the three areas was the inverse, suggesting that many families retained 'business' links with their estate after they had moved away from the site of their workplace.

The 7 per cent of the properties in the three books which were owned by legal personalities were evidence of the relationships between social strategies and landscape. Here, the quality of property ownership was not absolute but limited by the conditions of a trust, executorship or assigneeship in bankruptcy. About half the properties affected were domestic, which meant that housing was under-represented.[48] Commercial property, like the warehouses, and the retail units, like the house and shop, were over-represented.

The wills provided a very different means of assessing the general character of the real property strategists. Individual wills provided an account of property and family context with a detail which the rate books could never do, but the English will was not and did not generate an inventory of property, and the information in each will varied according to the perceptions as well as the actual possessions of the individual testator. Any measure of real property ownership must be an imperfect indicator and without precision. An indicator of real property ownership was constructed from the number of units of real property mentioned in the text of the will. Wills which simply mentioned categories were entered

[48] See Tables 5.6 and 5.8.

Table 5.13 *Real property in Leeds wills, 1830–34*

	Not mentioned		Mentioned		
Real property	Absolute no.	%	Absolute no.	%	Total
Male	84	41.6	118	58.4	202
Female	40	62.5	24	37.5	64
Total	124	46.6	142	53.4	266

Table 5.14 *Occupational title and real property in Leeds wills, 1830–34*

	No real property mentioned		Real property mentioned	
Occupational title	Absolute no.	%	Absolute no.	%
Yeoman	5	33.3	10	66.7
Distribution	19	46.3	22	53.7
Commerce	12	52.2	11	47.8
White collar	4	66.7	2	33.3
Manufacturing	11	40.7	16	59.3
Craft	13	34.2	25	65.8
Professions	4	57.1	3	42.9
Other services	3	100		
Labour	1	33.3	2	66.7
Independent income	13	28.9	32	71.1
Others	5	55.6	4	44.4
No occupational title	34	69.4	15	30.6
Total	124	46.6	142	53.4

as zero unless a specific item of real estate was mentioned. Other wills mentioning a block of property were entered as one or two. Others listed cottages, shops and workshops in some detail. The numbers involved were too small for detailed analysis so the wills were divided into those which made mention of real property and those which did not, thus separating out those for whom real property strategy was important enough to warrant detailed consideration in their will.

The wills confirm the fact that a real property strategy was predominantly male. The contrast in female behaviour was explained by the widows. Of the thirty-two widows who made wills, only 25 per cent mentioned real property while of the thirty-two spinsters, 50 per cent mentioned real property. Occupational status had an important influence on the propensity to select a real property strategy. The 'yeomen' and

Table 5.15 *Sworn value, gender and real property in Leeds wills, 1830–34*

Sworn value	All wills				Male wills only	
	Real property not mentioned		Real property mentioned		Real property mentioned	
£	N	%	N	%	N	%
Under 100	31	40.3	46	59.7	39	63.9
Under 200	17	40.5	25	59.5	22	62.9
Under 450/300	21	56.8	16	43.2	13	52
Under 600/1000	21	58.3	15	41.7	11	44
Under 1500/2000	13	54.2	11	45.8	8	53.3
Under 3000/30,000	21	42	29	58	25	60.8
Total	124	46.6	142	53.4	118	58.4

those on independent income, mainly those who claimed the title of 'gentleman', had a high propensity to use real property, although the yeomen tended to mention one block of property and the 'gentlemen' to list substantial numbers of cottages. Next came those involved in manufacturing and in craft occupations. The manufacturers tended to mention one block of property while the craftsmen listed their cottages and workshops. The shopkeepers behaved very much as the overall population, but those involved in real property usually listed a number of units. Those with no occupational title had a strong aversion for the real property strategy but as this group was mostly women this was explained by gender. Others with a tendency to avoid the real property strategy were the professional men, white collar occupations and, to some extent, those engaged in commerce. Amongst the men, those who used real estate and fixed capital in their business were those who were most likely to involve themselves with real estate in the family strategies they outlined in their wills.

The relationship of real property strategies to the sworn value of probate, which in itself was an indicator of the value of personal property, was complex. The propensity to adopt a real property strategy was highest with low sworn values and fell as sworn value rose. For those with modest accumulations of property, and that was the majority of those who made a will, there was a choice between real property and personal property strategies. Higher levels of accumulation made it possible to move back into real property strategies without entailing a reduction in personal property, so that real estate becomes important amongst the top ranges of personal property valuations. In part, the low levels of real property preferences in the middle ranges of the sworn value measure can be accounted for by the tendency of women to appear in that range, but the same tendency appears when only the male population is considered.

Although the indicator is very crude because of the nature of the document and the need to avoid small numbers in the cell totals during the analysis, the results are consistent enough to suggest that gender, especially related to widowhood, and occupational status, especially when related to the nature of capital were the most important influences. Economic status was a complex influence. Judgement on these figures must be complex as one cause of a low 'sworn value' was a real property preference. Real property preference cannot be accounted for simply by low economic status. However, those occupational groups with low status according to other indicators were also those with real property preferences.

Through the documents of ownership and family, the landscape of Leeds in the first half of the nineteenth century resolved itself into a patchwork with several layers of social and economic meaning. Some elements of that patchwork can be placed on the map. Briggate was the central spine for the old burgage plots. These were densely built yards of heterogeneous properties: high value front of the street shops and a variety of workplaces, warehouses, public houses and cramped working class cottages at the back. There were a few owner-occupier rentiers but these yards provided the rentier income of investors like Mrs Jane Hey and second or third generation Leeds families, which had long moved from the area. Others belonged to life cycle accumulators like the Duftons, who lived east of the old centre. To the west, a proto-central business district was developing. The warehouses of Basinghall Street and the shops of Commercial Street were evidence of this, but it was still an area where owner-occupiers lived and domestic and workplace were linked by property and neighbourhood. West of that were the late eighteenth century elite houses of Park Square. The square itself was an elegant encapsulated space but behind were warehouses and access to mills and finishing shops to the south and west. East of Briggate the documents were less forthcoming and detailed. Here was another mixed landscape of the building clubs and the closely related family neighbourhood networks of men like John Taylor. North and northwest of the centre was a ring of peri-urban villas. Those along the streams of the Meanwood Valley were often linked to mills and workplace properties. Those of Woodhouse were usually true specialist domestic environments, to which the elite and those who gained a successful rentier retirement phase might retreat from the smoke below. Between Briggate and the peri-urban north were a series of old eighteenth century family commonwealths, which were rapidly changing and infilling. There were two other distinct environments. The rentier republics of School Close, finely developed heterogeneous blocks of property, had been built a generation before the Soke Rate Book recorded them. The mills and back-to-back housing along the Kirkstall Road were a raw urban environment, which attracted specialist ownership and development. Here, in an area dominated by the major accumulations of industrial capital and their demand for labour like Bean Ing, Airedale Mills and Brittania Mills, the division of ownership between industrial and domestic property was between very different types of owner.

There were several social and economic processes producing this landscape. The expansion of Leeds itself created a simple demand for more property and the appropriation of space around the original built up area but without any real improvement in urban transport. There was a division between different parts of the landscape in a spatially generational manner into old, recent and new developments, which had different implications for interaction with ownership. The economics of the building and trade cycle provided conditions in which adequate returns were expected from different types of property. Geographical position created different expectations of economic gain. There were the opportunities of School Close and the Kirkstall Road for smaller and larger units of industrial capital and, west of Briggate, between old centre and elite housing, for improved 'house and shop' units and the new middle class shopping of Commercial Street.

Central to the heterogeneity of the urban 'estates' were the family and life cycle strategies of their owners. These strategies brought workplace, dwelling place and cottages for rent together in the same block. The 'house and shop' units were one aspect of this. This variety spread risk and eased property management but, above all, it allowed for the changing meanings of these properties. They were a home, a base for the profits and returns to labour for a business. They were the base for the accumulation of capital. These houses were assets for sale or securities for a mortgage or loan at times of family and personal crisis or opportunity. Such properties might be the basis for further expansion or meet the needs of family, enabling a business stake for a son or son-in-law. The same houses could be the income for a daughter or a widow. Some were a dwelling place for widows and children. Above all, the successful accumulation of real property provided an income for the rentier phase of the property cycle. These rents provided the urban 'gentleman' with income and independence. They enabled the owner-occupier-rentier to move to the villas above the smoke and find a little distance from the noise of rentier republics and family commonwealths like School Close.

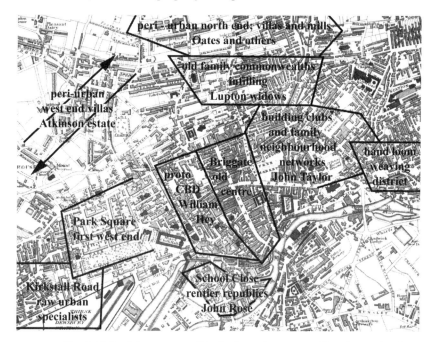

Fig. 5.11 Social economy of the built environment of Leeds, 1780–1850.

This landscape produced by the processes of family and space was not a transitional phase between a pre-industrial and an industrial city. It was a formation specific to a particular phase of capitalism and associated institutional and technological development. The balance between the different elements of heterogeneous rentier republics and specialist areas, between peri-urban villas and independent craft, petty capital neighbourhood networks varied with the economic structure of each urban place but there was a series of constant structural, institutional, technological and cultural features. The market for many rentier assets was unreliable, mistrusted by many and poorly institutionalised, so many chose a real estate strategy. The choice of local real property reduced risk because knowledge of opportunities and tenants was better. Such a choice eased management costs and problems. The heterogeneity of the real property choices was itself a product of the multiple aims and meanings, which were bound up with the accumulations recorded in the wills and family papers.

6 Women and things and trusts

Women

So far women have sat at the edge of the story. Their apparent passivity was both conditional and contingent. The relationships of property and family could not work without the active and influential intervention of women within the family network. This was especially true when the family economy and strategies were tested by the insecurities of demography and the economy. The ideal offered to the readers of law books and advice manuals was a matter of a man with wife and children but, in practice, that was an option available to around half the will makers. Whatever the books and the theory of domesticity might say, a significant number of women were involved in the decisions of family and property. The dominant elements in the historical literature have two dimensions. One mapped the exclusion and subordination of women in the world of property ownership and the market economy. This detailed the mechanisms of shutting out from the world of work and business, and suggested that this provided vital support for male economic activity.[1] The other strand of literature outlined the extent to which women held property and were able to enter specific areas of the market economy.[2] There was uncertainty as to whether the economic space available to women was increasing or shrinking in this period.[3] The relationships and tensions of gender were certainly asymmetrical, but they had a dynamic impact on the relationships of property and the flows of capital.

---

[1] L. Davidoff and C. Hall, *Family Fortunes. Men and Women of the English Middle Classes, 1780–1850* (London, 1987), especially pp. 198–316.
[2] M. Berg, 'Women's property and the industrial revolution', *Journal of Interdisciplinary History* (1993), 235–50; M. Berg, 'Small producer capitalism in 18th century England', *Business History* 35 (1993) 17–39; M. Berg, 'Women's consumption and the industrial classes of 18th century England', *Journal of Social History* (Winter 1996), 415–34.
[3] A.L. Erickson, *Women and Property in Early Modern England* (London, 1993); R.B. Shoemaker, *Gender in English Society, 1650–1850* (London, 1998).

Table 6.1 *Female probates. Average sworn value*

	Wills		Admin	Mean (£)	Median (£)	N
	No.	%				
Widow	32	72	14	1825	525	46
Spinster	18	72	7	769	300	25
Wife	7	39	11	643	100	18
Own title	6	86	1	2186	200	7

Table 6.2 *Female wills. Average sworn value*

	Mean (£)	Median (£)	N
Widow	1935	700	32
Spinster	666	250	18
Wife	1037[a]	100	7
Own title	2216[b]	150	6

[a] Sarah Arthington at £5000 raised the mean; [b] Catherine Elam at £12,000 raised the mean.

Women were responsible for 27 per cent of the probates. Women's probates involved around a fifth of the 'sworn value' of the property brought to the probate courts. The mean value of female property was £1267, while that of male was £1624, with a tendency for women to have more estates in the middle range of values than men. In the sample of probates as a whole men brought property with a sworn value of £440,190 whilst women brought £130,480, or 22 per cent of the total. These were somewhat fictional figures as they were derived from the upper bounds of the categories under which the estates were taxed, but they provided a useful indicator of women's control of around one fifth of the personal estate. Women had a lower propensity to own real property than men. Only 37 per cent mentioned real estate in their wills compared with 58 per cent of men and in the surviving rate books women had just under 5 per cent of the property by value. In terms of direct control, women held a minority but significant share. In terms of the functioning of the system of family and property relationships, this was important for two reasons. Women's behaviour and relationships regarding property was often different from that of men. In addition, closer examination showed that direct capitalist ownership was only one way in which women and property interacted in the family system.

Women's relationships to property could be better understood if they were differentiated by civil status. There were four groups: widows, spinsters, wives and those who claimed their own economic status titles. The sworn value of their probate showed considerable differences.

Despite the small numbers, there was enough evidence to suggest that the widows disposed of considerably more personal property than the spinsters, while the values for wives and women with their own economic status title were low, despite means raised by two relatively wealthy women. This evidence must be balanced by the greater likelihood that spinsters had real property. Amongst the spinsters, 50 per cent mentioned real property, only slightly less than males. Widows were distinctive in the way they presented their world for probate. They were much more likely than either spinsters or males to detail specific things and allocate them to specific friends and relatives. Where children were mentioned, widows treated them with the same equity as men, but children were mentioned much less than by males, and minors mentioned not at all, suggesting that widows went to probate later in the life cycle and, in any case, may well have been subject to a trust fund income and contingencies enabling them to dispose of less in their own right. Assuming that the widows were drawn from a death cohort very much the same as that which produced the probates of 1830–34, then the thirty-two widows (50 per cent of female will makers) was more than might be expected if they were simply a result of the 17 per cent (22 out of 131) who gained absolute control of their husband's property as a result of their husband's will. A widow's property was not a simple result of their husband's.

Blackstone's ponderous summary of the relationships of gender and property was a normative statement.[4] A statement of the dominant ideological doctrine. It was certainly not a description of practice and outcomes. Two small groups in the sample show why Blackstone's account was incomplete.

There were seven wives who made wills. The evidence of the text of the wills suggested two major reasons for a wife being able to make a will. Sarah Arthington, wife of a Quaker brewer in the southern townships of Leeds, began her will by setting out the terms of her marriage settlement.[5]

---

[4] Sir W. Blackstone, *Commentaries on the Law of England*, 18th edition with the last corrections of the author and copious notes by Thomas Lee, Esq, four vols. (London, 1829), vol. I, p. 441; J.E. Bright, *A Treatise on the Law of Husband and Wife* (London, 1849), p. 1; '. . .the husband and wife are one person in law. . .'

[5] Probate 25 August 1830.

Four others were disposing of rights they had under the wills of others. Maria Bewley had the right to dispose of items of real property under the wills of her brother and grandfather.[6] Sarah Broadhead disposed of a considerable estate under the will of her first husband.[7] Ann Chapman had just remarried, to a cabinet maker, and disposed of property under her father's will.[8]

A close reading of the legal textbooks showed that even in terms of common law married women were left with a scattering of fragmentary rights to property. There was the theoretical view that under couverture women's property rights were not destroyed but simply subsumed under her husband's rights for the period of the marriage. At a more practical level there were 'choses in action' (debts owing, rent arrears, legacies) which only went to the husband on condition he 'reduced them into possession' by some positive action such as giving a receipt for the property concerned.[9] This could be important if the husband died insolvent; '. . . the wife's legal choses in action will survive to her against her husband's assignees in bankruptcy, unless reduced into possession in his lifetime'. The wife's right to paraphernalia was another exception. These were 'such apparel and ornaments of the wife's as are suitable to her condition of life'.[10] This again could be important if a man died insolvent. In formal terms, a wife had right of dower in real property possessed by her husband during the marriage. For practical purposes, dower had been reduced by the development of eighteenth century conveyancing practice and under the legislation of 1833 could be eliminated with ease. Dower remained a source of uncertainty and some men took trouble to bar dower. Samuel Firth, blacksmith of Armley, had accumulated considerable cottage and warehouse property in the township and instructed his trustees,

to permit and suffer my wife Ann Firth and my daughter Hannah Firth to receive and take the rents issues interest and dividends and annual proceeds thereof and of every part thereof [the cottages] equally between them share and share alike for and during the natural life of my said wife, the same to be in full satisfaction and discharge of any dower or thirds to which my said wife would be entitled out of my real estates or any part thereof at common law or otherwise.[11]

---

[6] Probate 7 October 1830.
[7] Probate 21 November 1831.
[8] Probate 13 July 1832.
[9] Blackstone, *Commentaries* vol. III, p. 384; Bright, *Law of Husband and Wife*, p. 34.
[10] Bright, *Law of Husband and Wife*, pp. 72 and 286.
[11] Probate 2 February 1832. Sworn value £100.

Barring dower in this way was not a way of excluding the widow from benefiting from the property but it ensured that that benefit was on terms set by the husband and also ensured that there was clear title to the property in the event of a sale. The mean sworn value of those who chose to bar dower was raised by two or three high value estates, including those of Thackrey and Chadwick. There was a higher proportion of real property owners than in the sample as a whole. Nearly 90 per cent as against 58 per cent.

A husband might have 'allowed' a wife to make a will. There were good reasons why he might do this. As will be shown, many men left property in trust for women on condition that their husbands did not 'intermeddle' with either income or capital. Other men may have left a wife's claims alone because, by doing so, such property, say a debt or mortgage bond, would be safe from the claims of assignees in bankruptcy. Wives took much less care of their property than widows and spinsters. Many did not bother to make a will, two thirds as compared to one third for all female probates. Under administration the property went to any husband alive.

There were two examples of the wills of both husband and wife in the sample and these showed the power balance between husband and wife in matters of property. Michael Thackrey, the merchant, made careful provision for his wife under a trust fund established for her natural life.[12] His sworn value was £10,000. Rachel had a small number of household and personal things as well as her income. When she died just over a year after her husband, her estate had a sworn value of £450. Rachel was a woman who was 'allowed' property rights.[13] Mary Mawson died five months after her husband William, an aqua fortis manufacturer at Burmantofts.[14] His sworn value was £3000 and hers £1500 but Mary had £1300 , 'part of my own property and declared to be my money' invested in a trust fund under a marriage settlement. In Mary's case this was her second marriage. In other wills the women's authority seemed enhanced in a second marriage, as well as often being protected by settlements of various kinds. In two cases it was the husband's second marriage that was mentioned, but the women disposed of various amounts of property, often using it to mark their association with their husband's original family such as Elizabeth Garbutt[15] and Ann Paley.[16]

---

[12] Probate 16 February 1830. See Chapter 3.
[13] Probate 6 May 1831.
[14] William was brought for probate, 11 March 1831 and Mary Mawson, 21 November 1831.
[15] Probate 26 August 1830.
[16] Probate 29 May 1830.

A second group of women claimed their own economic status title rather than their civil status, sometimes adding their husband's socio-economic title. These were women who had places in the female niches of the market economy. In general, the sworn value was very low. Sarah Pickles, publican, sworn value under £100, gave directions for the disposal of the goodwill of the business, her stock in trade and other personal estate for the benefit of her children, some under 21 years of age.[17] Elizabeth Proctor, shopkeeper, also under £100, signed with a mark and divided her property between four siblings.[18] The brothers were all labourers. Aquilla Thomas[19] had a little more to divide amongst her daughters with a sworn value of £200 and some cottages in Halifax, whilst Cecilia Crowther, confectioner, had under £800 to divide between cousins and friends.[20] Very different was Catherine Elam, daughter of a leading Quaker merchant family.[21] She described herself as 'gentle-women'. In the under £12,000 class, she was an heiress who had retained her independence. Links between the wills and the trade directories showed that the titles, widow and spinster, could conceal participation in the market economy. Elizabeth Craven,[22] appeared in the 1826 directory as a furniture broker while Sarah Bayliffe, widow,[23] was partner in a Ladies Boarding School at 10 Skinner Lane and Dorothy Page[24] was listed in the 1834 directory as 10 Rockingham Street, Lodgings.[25]

The largest groups of female will makers were widows (32) and spinsters (18). Despite the differences between them, a number of characters and characteristics emerged from these two groups. Many behaved exactly as a man would have done under the same sort of circumstance. There were widows who identified property and instructed the executors to divide, 'share and share alike'. Ann Rinder, widow of a butcher, had a sworn value of £1500 and freehold property in Leeds, which she instructed should be divided between her two daughters.[26] Sarah Pickles showed that respect for equity, business continuity and choice amongst her children typical of many male wills. If any of the children

---

[17] Probate 19 October 1830.
[18] Probate 16 June 1831.
[19] Probate 19 August 1831.
[20] Probate 19 August 1831.
[21] Probate 28 November 1831.
[22] Probate 21 May 1830. Sworn value £300.
[23] Probate 17 April 1832. Sworn value £2000.
[24] Probate 17 April 1832. Sworn value £1000.
[25] Information of occupation and address not taken from the wills or otherwise acknowledged in this chapter was taken from *The General and Commercial Directory of the Borough of Leeds* (Baines and Newsome: Leeds, 1834).
[26] Probate 22 November 1830.

wanted to purchase the business, they were to have the option, but to pay full value. Like the males, those who were childless brought in the reserve army of siblings, cousins, nephews and nieces. Ann Clayton's estate, sworn under £450, went equally to brothers and sisters.[27] This was inevitably important for the spinsters.

Female wills rarely fitted the template of the characteristic male will. There was none of the dominating concern for widows and children, especially minor children. In a formal and literal sense the concern for widows was irrelevant, although several of the 'wives' directed the property under their control to husbands, but reading the will as a structure of relationships and instructions revealed a number in which a nominated individual, usually another woman, took the place of the widow. Priscilla Catlow, spinster, left her household furniture and her moity of their co-partnership in business to her 'dear friend Hannah Roberts' for her natural life.[28] The property was then to be divided between sister, brother and nieces. In the 1826 Directory, the business of Cattlow and Roberts, tea dealers was at 12 St Peters Street. Martha Shackleton gave a life interest in her household goods and real property to her sister Susanna before the division amongst other relatives.[29] They had lived together at 12 Claypit Lane. Two others were directed to married sisters, and Sarah Padgitt[30] gave a life interest to her mother, whilst Phillis Phillips chose her brother.[31] In some cases the limited records remain opaque. Others showed that, whilst there was not the same asymmetry of power as a husband and wife relationship, there was a recognition that sustaining a critical mass of domestic capital was vital to a partner's welfare, so the same 'natural life' device was employed as males used for widows before attention was given to a wider division of property. Concern for partners and the desire for control beyond the grave was not an exclusively male affair.

Women were much more likely to diverge from strict equity in their division of property between their chosen group of relatives, especially when these relatives were not their own children. They often showed female preference and an awareness of female things and male things when allocating property. Ann Fowwether was a 'things' person for her three daughters.[32] They divided up the silver tea spoons and the sugar

---

[27] Probate 24 January 1831.
[28] Probate 17 February 1831. Sworn value £100.
[29] Probate 20 July 1830. Sworn value £450.
[30] Probate 16 February 1830. Sworn value under £20.
[31] Probate 16 February 1830. Sworn value £100.
[32] Probate 11 January 1830. Sworn value £20.

tongs whilst the sons simply divided the residue. Ann Paley left money to siblings and the children of Paley's first marriage but sisters and step daughters got twice as much as the males. Amongst the widows, nineteen out of thirty two showed some form of female preference. Both Rachel Thackrey and Ann Jackson[33] gave the household goods to their daughters before dividing the residue equally between all children.

This was one aspect of a wider feature of the female wills. Although women in total and in general had much less power than men, where they did have power, they used it with much greater freedom. They showed much less regard for the constraints of custom and practice. They used their wills to mark out their social and emotional world. Compared to males their marked world was much broader. It contained a wider range of family, and more friends, including servants. There was a wider geographical spread. There was more recognition of charities, churches and chapels.

Mary Coldcall died on 3 January 1831 leaving an estate with a sworn value considerably above average at £8000 as well as real estate.[34] She was an old lady whose nephews and nieces were already married with their own children. She left no direct trace in the directories of Leeds and no evidence of children of her own, but she used her will to mark out her social world with care. The result showed how disorderly the meaning of family could be once the vagaries of fertility and mortality had done their work. The result did not fit into any pattern of nuclear, stem or extended family. Cousinage network was probably the best label.

First there were the children of her late husband's sister, Elizabeth Wigglesworth [£200 each]. Then there were the children of those children [£100 each]. Elizabeth's eldest (William) already had at least one married child. Two of Elizabeth's daughters were married and one dead leaving minor children. These had their money put in trust '...for their maintenance and education'. Mary used the trust with great deliberation. Another nephew of her husband's had the income from £200 for himself and his wife Ann. The capital was to be divided amongst their children on their death. This arrangement was a response to the insecurities of trade and the existence of minor children. In 1834, Ann appeared as a butcher at Woodhouse Carr with no sign of John. Then there was an assortment of nieces and nephews who got £10 each and, finally, John and Mary Ann Craven, children of a late nephew. These were probably from Mary's family of origin. John was a linen draper in nearby Otley.

---

[33] Probate 18 November 1830. Sworn value £450.
[34] Probate 16 June 1830.

One meaning of this network was Mary herself. The economic focus was Woodhouse Carr.[35] Here, Mary had a dwelling house with outhouse, stable, cowhouse and other outbuildings as well as several closes of land. John and Mary Ann Craven got this as tenants in common, with a charge of £12 a year to go to another cousin, Ann Richardson of Cookridge, spinster. Her tenant, Benjamin Chadwick, was farmer and ale and porter dealer who kept the Ridge Tavern. Ann was butcher there and the interestingly named Coldcall Wigglesworth (not mentioned in the will) was a cloth drawer. The rest had not gone far. Frederick was ironmonger in Briggate. Others were in Otley, Armley, Horsforth and Bramhope, nearby weaving and farming villages.

Mary's world was more complex than just a network of nephews and nieces. She was one of the few will makers who left legacies to charities in Leeds. The Leeds General Infirmary got £60 and the House of Recovery and the National School £19 each. The widows in Harrison's Hospital, a seventeenth century foundation on the edge of Woodhouse Carr, got five shillings each. Maybe Mary identified with old ladies. She mentioned monies out on loan and in the 'public funds of government' so, with a final value of £8000, it was likely that the residual was considerable. This went to Cadmans, Cravens and others. These were probably linked to her own family of origin so that, having marked out and acknowledged her husband's family, she directed the bulk of her property back to the family from which she had come.

The final part of her world was marked by the interest on £200 which was to be for the benefit of Mary Banks, widow, for her natural life. This money was to be managed by William Wigglesworth, her husband's nephew, and go to him once Mary's funeral expenses had been paid. This was to be an acknowledgement of companionship.

Fertility and mortality as well as the mixed and unstable economic fortunes of the middle ranks of the middle classes had provided Mary Coldcall with a disorderly set of relationships from which she built her 'family' with care and skill helped by her own considerable economic status within the clan.

Hannah Middlebrook died in July 1831 with a sworn value of under £12,000.[36] Like Mary, she was childless and relatively wealthy. Like Mary, she was concerned to be identified with her family of origin and asked to be buried in the family vault in Huddersfield Parish Church 'with

---

[35] In 1830, this was an open area of fields and scattered buildings near the north west edge of the built area of Leeds.
[36] Probate 6 September 1831.

suitable decency but without funeral pomp'. It was the Huddersfield and Upper Agbrigg Infirmary that got her charitable legacy.

Like Mary, the world which she identified in her will spilt out beyond family. She asked that mourning rings be bought for her friends 'as a mark of my esteem'. These were:

James Brooke of Huddersfield, merchant, an executor
William Hey, senior, the surgeon, another executor
Thomas Marshall of Thorpe in Aldmonbury, gentleman, an executor
Joseph Brooke
Mrs John Marshall
Mrs Martha Brook
Mrs Mary Guy
Mrs Hannah Shaw
Mrs Ann Clark.

Her servant and late servants also got small legacies. Like many of the childless, she adopted nieces and nephews. There were two groups in her will. Samuel and George Tinker got £50 each and also were to have an annuity of £50 a year purchased for them with strict provisions against anticipation. Another group, Thomas Marshall, Jeremiah Marshall, James Marshall, the elder of Bradford, Martha Downing and Mary Blackburn (wife of Abraham) were each to get a sixth share of the residue. The other sixth went to the children of the late Hannah Tetley with trusts for those under 21 years. This was fairly standard practice and it was not clear if the difference between the two groups was due to one being husband's side and the other Hannah's family or to differences in character and situation.

Mary Mawson (£1500) made her will when she was a wife and did so by the authority of her marriage contract. Her marriage with William Mawson, aqua fortis manufacturer of Burmantofts, in 1804 was her second marriage and she acknowledged this through a series of legacies of £100 to the brothers and sisters of her late husband, Benjamin Russell. Like many independent women, she left small legacies to servants and to her place of worship [£50 to the trustees of the Old Wesleyan Methodist Chapel]. In the original will she left 'wearing apparel and furniture belonging to me' to her nieces 'share and share alike' but her husband's death in January 1831 increased her power and she wrote a detailed codicil with instructions directing her possessions to named nephews and nieces. The feather bed, the bed in the kitchen chamber, the large looking glass and several items of silver were allocated to individuals. Her husband's will put this in context. In a careful bit of bargaining beyond the grave he arranged the continuity of his business through a complex arrangement involving his widow and a nephew. In exchange for supporting the widow for what turned out to be a relatively short period, John inherited the business, for it was his in the Directory of 1834 just as William's will directed 'after the decease of my said wife'. In these examples, the women recognised the relationships of earlier marriages, in one case her own, in the other her husbands.

Mary Marriott's authority originated in a marriage contract of 1792 and the early death of her husband in 1800.[37] She was part of the Quaker network of the North of England. The care which members of the Society of Friends took with family property relationships meant that many features of middle class practice were very fully developed amongst them. Mary's legacies mapped out a wide geographical network involving friends and relatives. The focus of her geography was Leeds and Marsden in Lancashire but included Sheffield, Bradford and Nottingham. The list of charitable legacies was a very full statement of her social and moral views. She may have been excluded from the public sphere in her lifetime but in death she made a determined statement.

The Anti Slavery Society, 18 Aldermanbury, London	£500
The Society in London for the Promotion of Permanent and Universal Peace	£200
Leeds General Infirmary	£50
Asylum for the Blind in Liverpool	£50
The Guardian Asylum, St James St, Leeds	19 guineas
Leeds Auxiliary Bible Society	£50
Institution at Doncaster for the relief of the Deaf and Dumb established by William Fenton	£50
To be distributed amongst such poor widows members of the Society of Friends of Brighouse Monthly Meeting	£50
To be distributed amongst poor widows in 'my own neighbourhood'	£50
For poor widows in the neighbourhood of Harewood near Leeds.	£50

Women were more likely to include servants in their wills. Alee Ingle not only gave to friends, cousins and the Methodist Chapel but also ' to my servant girl, whoever she maybe, five pounds for mourning'.[38] Mary Juliana Rawstorne provided her servant girl with an annuity of £20.[39] Charlotte Fawcett left 19 guineas for each of her two servants.[40]

[37] Probate 15 March 1832. Sworn value £14,000.
[38] Probate 6 August 1830. Sworn value £3000.
[39] Probate 16 October 1830. Sworn value £4000.
[40] Probate 6 April 1831. Sworn value £1500.

Women's use of their freedom meant that they were more likely than
men to fashion their will in a judgemental manner. Isabel Dugdale
selected her nephew William Holmes to receive 'my best bed, bedstock
and bed hangings...my best quilt and also my clock...as a small
acknowledgement of his kindness to my late husband'.[41] He was also to
be given the option of purchasing the tea spoons and silver plate at
valuation. Gratitude and equity were finely balanced. Judith, the daughter of Henry Wilcock, got £4, 'because she was named in compliance with
my request'. In many cases preference was a reward for companionship.
Grace Hagreaves favoured her niece Mary Atha 'with whom I now live'.[42]
Lucinda Wilson, spinster, sworn value £600, assigned legacies to a variety of nieces and nephews but specified that her real property, several
cottages at Quarry Hill in Leeds, should go to two of them, Mary Johnson
and Dinah Lucinda Johnson 'who reside with me' in what again appeared
to be preference in return for companionship.[43] Judgements could be
negative. Sarah Arthington, the Hunslet brewer's wife, a Quaker, was not
a widow when she made her will but had rights under a marriage settlement. She again made careful and considered judgements across a network of nephews and nieces, notably dismissing poor John William Elam
with £10 because he had already lost money loaned him in his firm's
financial crisis.

In some cases the very process of marking out the boundaries of 'family'
was itself an act of judgement. Sarah Horner was a resourceful though not
an educated woman.[44] She signed with her mark and patrolled a disorderly network of family, friends and neighbours. Her sworn value of
£1000 included £600 invested in the Leeds and Elland Turnpike Road,
and in addition she had 'four several cottages' at Stocks Hill in Holbeck.
This was above the average, the result of a successful property cycle. The
main property was a 'public house with brewhouse back yard and stable
and also my maltkiln and cottages in or near to Isle Lane in Holbeck'. Her
public statement was simple, £100 to Leeds General Infirmary and £100
to Mill Hill Chapel. She was a Leeds person and an Unitarian. The
property and residue went to her cousin, Joseph Horner, on condition
he paid a series of legacies which marked out family and friends in a broad
and very inclusive manner. It was not clear if John Horner was husband,
son or cousin but he had had a busy life and his illegitimate children were
not to be forgotten.

[41] Probate 17 September 1831. Sworn value £800.
[42] Probate 22 January 1831. Sworn value £100.
[43] Probate 31 October 1832. Sworn value £600.
[44] Probate 15 November 1832. Sworn value £1000.

Mary Burrough, Holbeck, widow of John Burrough	£30
Mary Clark, Holbeck, widow	19 guineas
William Hargreaves, Leeds, my solicitor	£50
Benjamin Haste, son of my late Aunt Sarah Haste	£60
Children of the late Richard Haste, son of a late aunt	£60 divided amongst them
Two daughters of cousin Joseph Horner	£5 each
Frederick Bashforth, illegitimate child of Mary Bashforth by the late John Horner	£5
Sarah Horner Smith, illegitimate child of Smith by the said late John Horner	£5
Mary, wife of William Alderson of Holbeck	£5
Betty Tillotson, my servant	£5

Sarah was an influential women. To be included in her definition of 'family' was well worth while. She was one of a small but significant number of women who made little impact on the public sphere but were important locations of power within the wider family network. They were childless, often widows. Their freedom to allocate property and support was much greater than their male counterparts constrained by custom and practice. Their importance comes into public view in many of the wills. Mary Coldcall was a source of loans. Indeed she stated in her will,[45]

I have lent at interest to some of my relations or to the husband or husbands of some of my relations and to the relations of my said husband Thomas Coldcall divers sums of money on bond and promissory notes or otherwise.

None of them were to get their legacies unless they first settled these debts. Mary was banker to the clan. The sums, less than £200, were not great, but such a sum, or the potential for such sums when seeking credit, was invaluable in the insecure world of the moderate and small sized businesses which dominated the directory entries. Sarah Arthington had the same sort of authority.

Such women were a source of loans for business capital but they were also a potential resource for rescue when things went wrong. At one level, this was a form of exploitation for female capital with nowhere else to go. In fact, there were plenty of alternatives: government stock, mortgages and personal loans, even for women who did not want to be involved in real property. In families like the Jowitts, such female capital was moved

[45] She did not give the pre name of Sarah Horner Smith's mother in the will.

into non-family locations as quickly as possible. This was what would have been expected if such capital was seen both as independent and a potential reserve. The assumption must be that such women were making choices. They were willing to sustain the family network in its wider sense. In return, the network gave them companionship, meaning and locations for the investment and deposit of capital. Any network which contained such women would be stronger than one which did not. These women were a powerful source of social discipline, especially the disciplines that involved family identity. These women had considerable status and authority which cut across the dominant authority structure of patriarchy. For this reason they were feared, derided and valued.[46] They were an active imperfection upon the face of male authority. This was the Betsy Trotwood syndrome. In his early novel, *David Copperfield*, Charles Dickens explored the cruelty of family relationships, but the click of the gate and the entrance of Aunt Betsy Trotwood with her small independent income was the source of rescue for young David.

The operation of woman as network 'banker' was most fully developed in the will of Hannah Middlebrook with its loans and the rescue of Mary Moon. The will outlined the material and financial importance of women like Hannah for these networks. Like Mary Coldcall, she had made modest loans to the nephews.

Jeremiah Marshall	£60
Thomas Marshall	£60
Samuel Tinker	£300

These were to be paid back before any of the legacies were paid out. The most remarkable element of the will was the story of the rescue of Mary Moon, Hannah's niece and wife of Frederick Moon, woollen merchant of Huddersfield. Care was taken to ensure that the rescue remained permanent. Mary was to have £200. She was also to have 'the goods, household furniture, which I purchased of the assignees of the said

---

[46] M. Anderson, 'The social position of spinsters in mid Victorian Britain', *Journal of Family History* 9, 4 (Winter 1984) 377–93; S. Jeffreys, *The Spinster and her Enemies. Feminism and Sexuality, 1880–1930* (London, 1985), esp. pp. 86–101; John Leech's cartoons for *Punch* in the 1850s and 1860s were always making fun of elderly spinsters, but the serious attack was W.R. Greg, 'Why are women redundant?', *National Review* 14 (1862) p. 436 quoted by Mary Poovey, *Uneven Developments. The Ideological Work of Gender in Mid Victorian England* (London, 1989), pp. 1–23.

Frederick Moon and which are now in the possession of my said niece Mary Moon and also the following articles of furniture now in the dwelling house at Leeds aforesaid wherein I now reside, namely my best Chintz Bed and window curtains, counterpain the same pattern, best white counterpain, old Wardrobe, Candle Screen and carpets in the best room'. The executors were also instructed to purchase an annuity of £100 a year on the lives of Mary and Frederick. Frederick must have been bankrupted and Hannah had intervened to purchase the family's furnishings. She now left them with furniture and £100 a year, about the minimum needed to secure a middle class standard of living. Each grant was protected from any further economic disaster. They were 'without the order, control, direction or intermeddling of the said Frederick Moon, or any other after taken husband, and notwithstanding her couverture', and perhaps more to the point 'without being subject or liable to the debts, contracts, or engagements of her said present or any future husband'. They were for her 'sole and separate use'. Everything was to be done in the name of the trustees and Mary's receipt alone was satisfactory evidence that they had discharged their obligations.

Family and possessions meant a lot to Hannah. In later codicils George Tinker got the family Bible, eight chairs, a chest of drawers and some bedding, whilst Mary had a 'middle sized silver teapot' added to her possessions. Just to show there was no ill will, husband Frederick got four volumes of *Voyages* and some silver tea tongs, which it is to be hoped his creditors did not lay their hands on.

Things

Women were 'things' people. Of the sixty-four female wills, 27 per cent were dominated by 'things' listed and allocated with care and detail. This was the case for only 15 per cent of the male wills. Wills full of 'things' were not otherwise different. The mean sworn value was £2159, slightly more than the £2059 for the categories people. The median was the same at £450. Nor was there much significant variation in terms of occupational status groups. The decision to nominate 'things' in a will was influenced by gender and individual preference. The difference was almost all accounted for by the widows amongst whom over a third were 'things' people. They allocated named items with care, often using them as part of their judgements and boundary marking.

Of the three very different views of the world offered in the wills, the 'categories' people were the cash economy capitalists who used the market to achieve their aims. The 'real estate' people, who had a key influence on the urban landscape, used their bundles of real property in the same

248 Men, women and property in England

way. The last group, the 'things' people, named specific items of property and allocated them to named individuals. In most of such wills, only a small part of an individual's possessions was being selected. The texture of such worlds was dominated by items carrying particular significance which affirmed and represented meanings from the past and from relationships with those named to receive them.

Elizabeth Craven was the widow of Joseph, a stone mason.[47] She died in February 1830 with a sworn value of under £300. Her will began with some very specific bequests.

Nephew, John Craven Ryley
Mahogany desk, or bureau, feather bed, flock mattrass, pier glass and small oak stand
Nephew, Thomas Ryley
Oak chest of drawers, eight days clock, two silver table spoons
Nephew, William Ryley
My silver pint, mahogany card table, oak dining table, round oak tea table, seven silver tea spoons, my silver sugar tongs
Elizabeth Hutton, wife of John Hutton of Leeds.
My mahogany elbow chair, my red and white china and the sum of £50 in money
John Mawson of Leeds, gentleman
My silver gill and cream jug
Elizabeth Killoony, my niece of Brides Alley, Dublin £30
John Rutledge, brother to the above Elizabeth £30
Sarah Craven, niece of my late husband £50

There was nothing primitive about this will. Elizabeth knew all about trust funds and the difficulties of minors. The residue was used to set up a fund for the three Ryley nephews to provided income until the youngest was 21 years old and then to be divided 'equally between them...share and share alike'. They also got real estate in Union Street, the heart of clubland, as tenants in common to ensure that they would act together.

Being a 'things' person had little to do with low socio-economic status. Despite her wealth, Mary Coldcall was a 'things' person. Margaret Keir, widow of Horsforth, niece got her light mahogany chairs and the round mahogany tea table as well as the blue and white tea service. This preference was maybe a recognition of companionship where the pair had sat around the table many times. Margaret shared the silver plate with another niece, Mary Cadman, who got the rest of the household goods. Six nieces were to divide up the wearing apparel, linen and quilts.

When men adopted the 'things' view of the world, they named a more limited number of items and did so for very specific reasons.

---

[47] Probate 21 May 1830.

Samuel Raistrick of Mabgate End, victualler, died in August 1830.[48]
He began his will,

'I give and bequeath to my dear wife Jane Raistrick, one bed and bedding, my
eight best chairs, one mahogany chest of drawers, one clock, one oak tea table, one
white table, one corner cupboard, my silver plate, linen and china and such other
articles and things as may be necessary to furnish her a house with'.

There were echoes here of an older concept of the widow's chamber.
The widow's comfort and share of the common property of marriage was
assured through material rather than monetary provision.

Other men left specific items as acknowledgement of relationships that
were important to them. George Austin, butcher, left Scott's *Commentary
on the Bible* to his son John as a sign of my affection for him.[49] Samuel
Gilpin, bricklayer, had six sons but began his will, 'I give and bequeath
unto my son James my piano forte and all other my musical instruments
whatsoever as his own for ever'.[50] It was only possible to guess at the
shared interests represented by this bequest.

These listings of items were nothing like the detailed inventories which
were presented in the probate records of the early eighteenth century.[51]
Inventories were often prepared during probate but few survived. Where
they did, they provided only a very general account of the estate and
showed the concern for categories which dominated the text of most wills.

The estate of Grace Ann Horfield who died in March 1831 was
brought for administration in April with a sworn value of £800.[52]
Attached was the schedule of her personal estate.

	£	s	d
Household goods and furniture	29	8	0
Plate, linen and china	4	2	6
Horses and harness	36	5	6
One pig	2	0	0
Money in the house	615	0	0
Wearing apparel	2	11	6
No real estate			
Total	689	7	6

[48] Probate 27 January 1831. Sworn value £200.
[49] Probate 9 February 1831. Sworn value £200.
[50] Probate 21 May 1830. Sworn value £100.
[51] L. Weatherill, *Consumer Behaviour and Material Culture in Britain, 1660–1760* (London, 1988).
[52] Probate 27 March 1831.

The estate of Margaret Whitehead, spinster, was more advanced in terms of female investment strategy but even more lacking in detail.[53]

	£	s	d
Household furniture	10	0	0
Due on a promissory note	1553	5	0
Due part of brother's personal estate	150	0	0

The inventory of Joseph Shaw, butcher, who died in November 1831 still remains in the ecclesiastical courts records at York.[54]

	£	s	d
Household goods and furniture, plate, linen, china etc	204	18	0
Live and dead stock and fixtures and utensils of trade	80	8	6
Book debts	550	0	0
Cash in the bank	19	18	0
Cash in the house	120	2	0
Arrears in rent	13	5	6
Total	988	12	0

These inventories demonstrated the importance of cash and of inter personal debt as well as the limited importance of banks, other institutionalised forms of asset holding and the taking of detailed inventories of possessions.

Such detailed inventories were often taken during the process of probate, and survived on rare occasions scattered amongst the legal papers of individuals and families. John Hebblethwaite was one of the leading merchants of Leeds at the end of the eighteenth century. His name was in the very selective listing of the 1797 directory. He had been amongst the first to mount a Whig challenge to the then Tory Anglican domination of Leeds public life. After his death, his executors ordered a detailed inventory of his property and household contents. This was completed on 6 June 1840 by Thomas Hardwick, one of several licensed appraisers in Leeds who were a key part of the probate process. The account of the dining room showed the detail of a full probate process and also the selectivity of those who listed property in their wills.

[53] Probate 27 Auust 1831. Sworn value £2000.
[54] Probate 31 December 1831. Sworn value £1000.

Dining Room. Brussels carpet, Brunswick hearth rug, steel fender, set of polished fire irons, stained easy chair and chinz cover, two settees, ten mahogany chairs, two foot stools, mahogany card table, two knife cases, two sets of scarlet maroon Windsor curtains with Japan and gilt cornice and curtain pins, mahogany oblong low table, druggett, three green venetian sun blinds, table cover, set Derbyshire spar chimney ornaments, small foot stool, white muslin curtains.[55]

This was brought to a conclusion by the recapitulation at the end.

	£	s	d
Household furniture and effects	202	4	0
Silver plate	182	16	6
Linen	17	9	6
China and glass	21	9	16
Books and pictures	18	12	0
Wearing apparel	10	4	6
Jewels and ornaments of the person	6	6	0
Wine and other liquors	138	12	6
Horse and carriage	20	0	0
Implements of husbandry	10	17	6
Total	628	17	6

The listings in the wills were about choice, significance and perception and not about a record of possessions. Extracting listed items from wills which did not entirely take refuge in the impersonal world of categories created a distinct picture. Counting items rather than wills, the largest group was 48 silver items. Silver was an important carrier not just of value but also of identity. John Bickerdike, gentleman, left 'unto my nephew John Bickerdike, my silver tankard marked with the letters JAB'.[56] Samuel Dickinson, surgeon, gave 'to my dear daughter Eleanor a silver tea pot and stand marked S L D'.[57] Elizabeth Garbutt, widow of pattern maker John Garbutt, gave the eldest son of her husband's brother 'my husband's silver' watch.[58] Elizabeth and others with the same type of will divided teaspoons, tablespoons, sugar tongs and cream jugs between

[55] DB 43/10. Inventory and valuation of the household effects and other personality of the late John Hebblethwaite, 6 June 1840.
[56] Probate 27 July 1830. Sworn value £5000.
[57] Probate 22 April 1830. Sworn value £450.
[58] Probate 26 August 1830. Sworn value £300.

Table 6.3 *Gender and 'things' in Leeds wills, 1830–34*

	Male	Female	Total	Male (%)	Female (%)
Total	202	64	266	75.94	24.06
Things	31	17	48	64.58	35.42
Books	22	5	27	81.48	18.52
Silver	13	11	24	54.17	45.83
Clocks	5	4	9	55.56	44.44
Watches	11	2	13	84.62	15.38

children and nephews and nieces. Other items such as watches, clocks and books, which might be thought to express personality and identity, appeared in fairly small numbers. The part played by men and women in the allocation of some of the key groups of 'things' was very different. Women were twice as likely to be handing out silver items and clocks than might be expected from their share in the total sample of will makers. They were under represented when it came to books and watches. Only two of the thirteen watches were in female wills and one of those was 'my husband's watch'.

Amongst the books there were five bibles and other named books, mostly religious in content. Mary Moxon left 'my set of valuable books called *Devotional Comments* to Samuel Moxon, the son of the late Samuel Moxon and also my Godson. Elizabeth Garbutt left Josephus *History of the Jews* and Woods *Dictionary* to her late husband's brother, but Fletcher's and Harvey's works went to the Ebeneezer Chapel library. John Hick, gentleman, gave three books *Looking unto Jesus*, *God's Sovereignty* and *Lyric Poems* to his son John, and my family bible, *Village Dialogues* (two vols), Harvey's *Works* (8 vols), and Booths *Reign of Grace* to his daughter Mary.[59]

After the silver items, the largest grouping consisted of beds and bedding. There were forty of these. Many wills specified that this was the best bed, or a feather bed. Frequently the beds came with hangings, one with a best quilt and another with a counterpane. After that there were fifteen tables, twelve groups of chairs and twelve chests of drawers. There were eight mirrors whilst only seven wills mentioned pictures. In seventeen cases the items were working tools such as looms, jennies or tenters, scaffolding poles, cranes and scales.

[59] Probate 17 April 1832. Sworn value £450.

What was surprising, given the importance attributed to possessions for the identity and status of the middle classes was the small number of wills which allocated specific items. Only about a fifth of the wills did so and, even in these, only a small and selected number of items were included in an action, which all other evidence indicates was about family and the affirmation of family identity. There were two potential explanations for this. Possessions, in as far as they were significant, were significant for the life time of the individual and the household. When that was finished the importance was gone. The next generation had acquired their own possessions. The possessions of the dead were, in most cases, a store of value which, as in the instructions of so many wills, were to be turned into cash and distributed, share and share alike, through the neutral and homogenising medium of the cash market economy.

Another explanation lies in the nature of the probate process, which involved the valuation of the possessions of the dead and the subsequent auction sale. It was at this point that the continuity of possession in the family was achieved. In a few wills children were given the option to purchase at valuation. This ensured fairness between children in the manner which the manuals advised for those who wanted to maintain family harmony. It also left choice to those who were inheriting. The whole process was one which valued individual choice, albeit disciplined by custom, practice and morality, but choice none the less.

The texts of early nineteenth century wills were an excellent source for the culture of property but a limited and specific source for the study of material culture. A small number of items were handed on with specificity and care. They tended to be items which had durability and portability. They were items which could be both a store of value and a store of meaning such as silverware, watches and books. Beds and bedding formed a second bulkier group. They represented both value and comfort.[60] The examination of the 'things' represented and mentioned in the wills demonstrated that most possessions had a temporal and life time significance which came to an end with the life of the owner. If any possessions were to be passed to another family member, this was a matter of choice for that member. The objects were to be filtered and valued through the homogeneity of cash price in the market as the appraiser's visit and auction did their work. For the middle classes, this was an age in which preference and fashion outweighed tradition when it came to possessions.

---

[60] S. Nenadic, 'Middle-rank consumers and domestic culture in Edinburgh and Glasgow 1720–1840', *Past and Present* 145 (Nov 1994), 122–56.

Trusts

So far women's access to property has been discussed and defined in a very specific way, which assumed the commonsense definition of a common law, capitalist, market-based society, namely that ownership entailed complete access to the benefits and disposal of all aspects of property, including use, enjoyment, the exclusion of others, the appropriation of income streams, and the ability to dispose, to sell, to use as collateral for loans or to invest in a business venture. Such an absolute concept of property dominated argument and debate from John Locke to John Stuart Mill.[61] It was legitimised through the notion of appropriation by labour and accumulation through trade and the cash economy. Imperfections were admitted according to the social and political views of the writer. For some it was the widespread and dangerous extent of poverty, for Mill it was the legal disabilities of women and the injustices of primogeniture. Few of the theorists noted that, in practice, property was rarely absolute.[62] Entail, mortgage, collective forms of property such as the corporation, the charity and tenants-in-common, dower, local custom and surviving feudal rights, as well as the urban disciplines of town government, all limited and divided control. The unbundling and limiting of property rights was the key to the trust, and the trust was the key to the property relationships of many women. Large numbers of women experienced property in the form of an income stream from a trust. This experience was characteristic of middle class women and was one which they shared with minors and a small number of males.

John Reffit was a cloth dresser in 1822 but had retired, 'gentleman', by 1829. He made his will on 21 April 1831 and died three weeks later. His instructions included many of the features of those establishing a trust. They were unusual only in that it was his daughter rather than a widow who was the major beneficiary. He began,

I dispose of my real and personal estate in the manner following...All my messuages or dwellinghouses, cottages, warehouses and other hereditaments situate at a place called Garland's Fold at the bottom of Marsh Lane in Leeds aforsaid and also at Hunslet...I give and devise unto my friends John Catlow of Leeds aforesaid pawnbroker and Thomas Hampshire of the same place Sheriffs

---

[61] J.S. Mill, *The Principles of Political Economy*, first published 1848. (London, 1970) D. Winch (ed.), pp. 349–68; J. Locke, *Two Treatises of Government*, first edition 1690 (Cambridge, 1960), edited with an introduction by Peter Laslett, pp. 327–44; C.B. MacPherson, *The Political Theory of Possessive Individualism. Hobbes to Locke* (Oxford, 1962), pp. 197–221.

[62] J. Brewer and S. Staves (eds.), *Early Modern Conceptions of Property* (London, 1996), esp. the introduction and essays by I. Shapiro, R. Gordon, D. Sugarman and R. Warrington.

Officer...Upon Trust that they my said Trustees...do and shall when and as soon as they or he shall think proper sell and absolutely dispose of the said messuages, cottages and other heriditaments either by public auction or by private contract and either together or in parcels for the most money that can be reasonably obtained for the same

He instructed regarding the 'monies to arise from the sale' that,

Upon Trust that they my said trustees...do and shall put and place one third part of the said monies at interest upon real or government security or securities and vary and transpose such securities from time to time, when and as they or he shall think proper and do and shall pay the interest and dividends to arise from the said one third part of the said monies unto such person or persons only as my daughter Mary by any writing or writings under her hand from time to time shall direct or appoint, notwithstanding any couverture she may be under; and in default of such direction...into the proper hands of my said daughter Mary, exclusive of any husband she may happen to marry[63]

The other thirds went to daughter Sarah Ann and son James, who was a minor. This was a careful and limited construction of property rights through a trust. It protected the two women from the authority which the law gave to husbands over their wives' property, but also placed major limits on the authority of the two daughters. When they died, their share was to go to their children in ways specified by John Reffitt. In some cases, the construction of a trust was implied by the instructions given to executors without the word being used in any formal sense. Henry Firth, the blacksmith in the weaving village of Wortley gave

unto my beloved wife Susanna Firth, all the rents of those houses with the blacksmith's shop and premises situate in Wortley, likewise the rent of my estate in Armley...to be applied for her sole support during her natural life.[64]

He then gave instructions on the disposal of that estate after his widow's death. Whether they were called trustees or not, the executors of both wills were left with considerable management tasks.

Of the 266 wills in the sample, 188 or 70 per cent established a trust of some kind. Most were established by men. Out of 202 male wills, 156 (78 per cent) established trusts, but so did 32 (50 per cent) of the women.

The assets involved in a trust varied. There were those like Michael Thackrey[65] and John Reffit who directed the assets of the trust to be placed 'on real security or on the government security'. Others like Henry

[63] Probate 21 November 1831. Sworn value under £2000.
[64] Probate 22 December 1831. Sworn value under £100.
[65] See Chapter Three.

Firth and John Rose[66] preferred the rents of real estate with its multiple meanings. There were a small number which used both forms of investment. There was a male preference for real property. Whilst 83 per cent of the trust makers were male, only 79 per cent of those who chose the 'at interest' form were male, but 87 per cent using the real property form were male.

There was little evidence to show that such trust capital was used to sustain male business capital, although it was often important in the transitional phase after a death. The preference was to move such capital as rapidly as possible from the high risk male business areas of the family property. Robert Jowitt used his mother's and sister's trust capital to sustain his business in the early years after his father's death, but his early property strategy was dominated by moving this capital out of his business. A number of the wills made specific and limited provision for trust capital to remain with a business in the awkward period of transition following a death. The assumption was that normal strategy moved such capital away from the family business. Such a strategy made sense from the point of view of the family as a whole, for it spread risk away from the high potential income but potential total loss area of the business and placed some in a carefully protected, specifically created legal personality, the trust. In as far as family strategy was about spreading risk, the trust was central to such a strategy.

In the 1820s and 1830s, trust assets were dominated by two major areas of national investment, which reflected some of the preferences of women who owned property in their own right. The first was the government funds which, since 1717, had been managed by the Bank of England. There was some evidence that the ownership of the funds overall was a South of England preference. Between 1807 and 1845, there were 3000 people who died in England with money in the funds, but only five came from the Lancashire cotton town of Stockport.[67] Of the 375 wills in the Leeds sample, only five appeared in the Bank of England registers of those who died with money in the funds.[68] The second area was real estate which was owned either directly or, in an unknown percentage of cases, was the subject of a mortgage.[69] The

---

[66] See Chapter Five.
[67] A.J. Owens, 'Small fortunes: property, inheritance and the middling sort in Stockport, 1800–57', PhD thesis, University of London (2002), p. 89; D. Green, 'Independent women, wealth and wills in nineteenth century London', in J. Stobart and A.J. Owens (eds.), *Urban Fortunes. Property and Inheritance in the Town, 1700–1900* (Aldershot, 2000), pp. 195–222.
[68] Private correspondence with Dr Alistair Owens now at Queen Mary Westfield College, University of London.
[69] R.J. Morris, 'The friars and paradise: an essay in the building history of Oxford, 1801–1861', *Oxoniensia* 36 (1971), pp. 241–5.

analysis of the Leeds Soke Rate books showed that, in the areas for which the books survived, there were thirty-seven women owners and forty-six owners who were executors or trustees.[70] A large part of the urban fabric of Britain was made possible through the finance and credit provided by a combination of the property cycle and the trust fund. Despite the opportunities of urban growth, there was still a great hunger for suitable assets for the trust funds and the later stages of the life cycle and, hence, the coming of railway shares was welcomed as a major opportunity. [71]

Estimates of the part played by the trust in the lives of women and minors and in certain areas of national investment were possible, producing an order of magnitude rather than a precise measure. Although sworn value was not and cannot be used as a true valuation of the property that was transmitted through inheritance in the Parish of Leeds in the early 1830s, it can be used as a rough indication of the proportions involved. The total upper limit of the sworn value of property transmitted in the 266 wills was £498, 685. Out of this, some 85 per cent was involved in wills where all or part of the property was transmitted first into a trust. Measuring real estate was even more problematic. This was done in terms of the minimum number of 'units' of property implied by the language of the will.[72] This calculation produced much the same result. Some 87 per cent of the units of property were involved in wills which established trusts.

This needs to be modified with an estimate of the proportion of an estate which was drawn into trust. In the majority of cases this can only be done through the language of the will and a series of heroic assumptions. If the language implied the trust took all the estate, then 100 per cent of the sworn value or units of property were assigned to the trust. If most of the property was assigned to the trust, then 80 per cent was assigned, if only a part, then 50 per cent and, if a minor residue was implied, 20 per cent was used. A calculation based on these assumptions suggests that 47 per cent of both the personal property and real estate which was brought into probate through a will during the period of the sample was placed initially in some form of trust.

Assuming that property was distributed evenly by age group across the adult population and that all property was owned by the probate population, then the proportion of Leeds property by value placed in trust each

[70] See previous chapter.
[71] S.A. Broadridge, 'The sources of railway share capital' in M.C. Reed (ed.), *Railways in the Victorian Economy. Studies in Finance and Economic Growth* (Newton Abbott, 1969).
[72] See Chapter Five.

258 Men, women and property in England

year was 1.75 per cent.[73] This was based upon an adult (20 years and above) death rate of 36 per thousand, which was derived from the Registrar-General's figures for the Leeds District in 1841.[74]

This proportion needs to be added to property accumulated in trust from previous years. The proportion would have been reduced by death. In this case the death rate of those over 50 years old was used, which proved to be 93 per thousand.[75] The proportion of property accrued from earlier years was also adjusted for population increase. The population of Leeds more than doubled between 1811 and 1841. This important adjustment took into account the fact that the population of earlier years was substantially lower than that of the 1830s. When this was done, the proportion of property in trust, both real and personal at any given time during the late 1820s and early 1830s, was around 15 per cent. A substantial amount of wealth was limited by restrictions to investment in passive forms of capital. By altering some of the assumptions, the proportion can be increased and reduced but it is the order of magnitude which matters rather than precise figures. An assumption that middle class adult death rate was lower than the overall population,[76] to say 30 per thousand, would produce a proportion of just over 12 per cent, but Chadwick in his report indicated that middle class adult death rate was very little different from that of the working classes.[77] It was the ability to keep children alive which differentiated the classes. The figure of around 15 per cent was a speculative estimate of the proportion of the wealth of Leeds people partitioned and directed to low risk investment.

The will makers who created trusts tended to be of higher economic status than those who did not. This was not surprising. Creating a trust had a cost. There was a significant management cost. This might have been explicit in terms of lawyers' fees or implicit in terms of demands made upon family members and friends who were trustees of the will. The terms of the trust also placed limits upon the potential earning power of the capital involved by restricting investment to low risk areas.

---

[73] This was 3.7 per cent of the 47 per cent of the probated property which it was estimated went into trust each year. The percentage of the adult population who died each year was 3.7.

[74] *Third Annual Report of the Registrar-General of Births, Deaths and Marriages in England* (London, 1841); Census of England and Wales, Parl*iamentary Papers* 1843, vol. 22; also Appendix to the Ninth Annual Report of the Registrar General of Birth Deaths and Marriages, *Parliamentary Papers* 1849, vol. 21.

[75] Same sources as previous footnote.

[76] This reduced the percentage of Leeds property coming through probate and into the 'trust' environment each year.

[77] E. Chadwick, *The Sanitary Condition of the Labouring Population of Great Britain*, 1842, edited with an introduction by M.W. Flinn, (Edinburgh, 1965), pp. 229–31.

Table 6.4 *Trusts and the sworn values of probate, Leeds 1830–34*

Trust	Mean	N	Median
None	871.15	78	200.00
At interest	3203.10	100	800.00
At interest and real	1400.00	21	600.00
Real property	1214.84	61	200.00
Household goods	1153.33	6	150.00
Total	1874.76	266	450.00

Note: These tables are all based upon the 1830–34 sample of wills from the Parish of Leeds.

Table 6.5 *Units of real property and trusts, Leeds 1830–34*

Trust	Mean	N	Median
None	1.00	78	.00
At interest	1.68	100	.00
At interest and real	2.62	21	2.00
Real property	6.44	61	3.00
Household	1.17	6	.00
Total	2.64	266	1.00

The measure of economic status in terms of real property, using the minimum number of units implied by the language of the will, was again only an indicator.

Not surprisingly, those who brought substantial amounts of real property to probate had a preference for trusts based upon real property, whilst those who wanted the trust money placed 'at interest' had higher sworn values for personal property.

The majority of those who benefited from these trusts were women. In some wills, the benefiting group had a mixed set of relationships with the will maker, often as a result of demographic loss and damage. Thus, income might go to daughters and grandchildren where one child had died, leaving children. The majority of the wills established trusts for individuals, most of whom were women, and for groups which were dominated by women.

In Table 6.6 categories overlapped. Thus, a trust providing for a widow and daughters was counted twice. Widows dominated but significant

Table 6.6 *Beneficiaries of trust as a percentage of total wills, Leeds 1830–34*

	N	%
Children	24	12.70
Daughters	21	11.11
Grandchildren	8	4.23
Nieces	17	8.99
Sisters	14	7.41
Wives	112	59.26
Total wills with trusts	189	

Table 6.7 *Gender of will maker and relationship to beneficiaries, Leeds 1830–34*

	Male	Female	Total
Children	9	3	12
Daughter	17	3	20
Grandchildren	1	4	5
Nephews	0	3	3
Niece	7	6	13
Other	4	6	10
Sisters	7	7	14
Total	45	32	77

numbers of other women, daughters, nieces and sisters, acquired these limited property rights, as did a number of minors.

The gender of the will maker had a considerable influence. By definition, men created all the trusts for wives, although one women created a trust for her husband and another for her co-resident business partner. If this group of men and all those who did not create a trust were excluded from the analysis, then men showed more concern for children and women were more involved with sisters, nieces and nephews than would be expected statistically.

Sole and separate use

In many wills, the income and property left to women was hedged around with a further condition. Daniel Brooke was not a wealthy man but made his will with some care.[78] He was a druggist operating in Lady Lane east of Briggate. He made his will in January 1832 and was dead in May leaving a widow and two children who seem to have been minors. He instructed his executors

To convert such part of my personal estate as shall not be in specie at the time of my decease into money and invest the whole of the said personal estate upon government or real security at interest and pay the interest and dividends thereof and also the rents and profits of my real estate unto or permit the same to be received by my Dear Wife Ann Brooke for and during the term of her natural life for her own Maintenance and the Maintenance and Education of my Son John and my Daughter Mary Ann Emmery or any child or children we may have, the same to be paid to my said wife by two equal half yearly payments in each year and the first payment to be made at the end of six months after my Decease, and the same to be for the sole and separate use of my said wife and not to be subject to the Debts, Controul or Intermeddling of any Husband she may marry and her receipts alone be sufficient discharge to my said trustees for the same.

With a sworn value of £200 and some real estate, the indications were that this would produce a useful but small income for Ann and her young family, but if she re-married that income flow would be protected from the misfortunes or misappropriation of her future husband. In fact, she decided to remain in the business and appeared in the 1834 Directory as Chemist and Druggist at 12 Lady Lane.

The same provision was often made for daughters. Henry Arnott, gentleman, was a substantial owner of cottage and house property in south Leeds.[79] He directed that the rents and profits of these were to go to his daughters for their natural life,

paid into the proper hands of my said daughter Mary Hindle and not into the hands of her said present or any future husband, but that the same shall be for her own sole and separate use and benefit, and that the receipts of my said daughter Mary Hindle alone, notwithstanding her present or any future couverture shall from time to time be sufficient discharge to my said trustees, it being my intention that the same shall be wholly independent of and freed and discharged from the debts control and engagements of her said present or any future husband.

Thus, both men and women not only set up trusts but also went to considerable trouble to defeat couverture.

Thus, some 32 per cent of men and 17 per cent of women took care to defeat couverture. The difference was mostly accounted for by the male provision for wives (11 per cent of male will makers), but men were also significantly more likely to leave property for the 'sole and separate use' of

---

[78] Probate 15 November 1832. Sworn value £200.
[79] Probate 6 May 1831. Sworn value £200.

Table 6.8 *Instructions reserving 'sole and separate' use, related to beneficiary and to gender, Leeds wills 1830–34*

Beneficiary	Will maker		Total
	Male	Female	
Daughter	30	5	35
Percentage of total	85.70	14.30	100
Percentage of gender	14.90	7.80	13.20
Niece	6	5	11
Percentage of total	54.50	45.50	100
Percentage of gender	3.00	7.80	4.10
Sisters	6	1	7
Percentage of total	85.70	14.30	100
Percentage of gender	3.00	1.60	2.60
Wife	23		23
Percentage of total	100.00		100
Percentage of gender	11.40		8.60
None	137	53	190
Percentage of total	72.10	27.90	100
Percentage of gender	67.80	82.80	71.40
Total	202	64	266
Percentage	75.90	24.10	100

their daughters. Women left property in this way to daughters and, above all, to nieces. Those doing so were mostly widows.

This was part of a larger process whereby a significant number of middle class women were given limited but protected and independent property rights. Of the 131 men in the sample who made a provision for a widow, only 17 per cent made an absolute gift of property. This group was, in general of lower economic status and either had no children or had adult children. The use of a trust to make limited property rights available to women was not restricted to the husband–wife relationship. The trust was used in 77 per cent of male wills and 50 per cent of female wills to transmit limited property rights, usually in the form of an income stream to widows, daughters, sisters and nieces. The provisions to defeat couverture were in 32 per cent of male wills and 17 per cent of female ones. There were five people who made an absolute gift of property for 'sole and separate use' but, for the most part, those who acted to defeat couverture also used trusts.

The 'sole and separate' group were, in general, of higher economic status than the rest of the sample. The sworn value had a mean of £3012 as against £1420 for those who did not use this provision. The median was £700 as against £300 and the real property indicator had a mean of

3.7 units against 2.2. The trust users overall had a sworn value with a mean of £2291 and a median of £450.

Thus, a significant number of middle class women were able to enter marriage with an independent and protected income. How did this come about in a generation which was consolidating and extending the subordination of women to men in terms of both ideology and practice? In one sense, the trust was a form of female subordination. In terms of life cycle strategies, the trust was the most potent element of 'life after death'. It transmitted and enforced the wishes of the dead, husbands, fathers and also aunts and mothers. But by transmitting wishes in this way the device of the trust compromised the subordination of many women in marriage. This was the result of a simple tension. All women had a father and many a previous husband. In these cases, the status, identity and responsibilities of one male came into conflict or potential conflict with those of another male, husband or future husband. The result of this was the creation of small but significant fragments of economic independence for women which survived marriage. One means of resolving this tension was the marriage contract but this was of little importance to the will makers in this middle class sample. The means they used was the trust, often with specific provision for sole and separate use in marriage. Although these provisions were less common in female wills, half the women who made wills acted to ensure that female beneficiaries gained this limited form of independence. Thus, significant numbers of middle class women gained an independent income stream from the carefully crafted legal personality of the trust. In some cases, women gained these fragments of independence as a result of the care and forethought of other women but, in the main, such independence was a result of the clash between one form of male power and another form of male power, between the identity, ambitions and responsibilities of the dead and those of the living which came to a focus on the fortunes of wives, widows, daughters, sisters and nieces.

How then did the trust work in practice? Trusts could operate for many years after the death which created them. They were a crucial and subtle part of the family and gender politics of middle class society. They did indeed represent life after death.

7   Life after death

The last chapter began as an enquiry into the specific relationships between women and property but ended as much more than that, for many of the property strategies used by and for women were, in practice, female preferences rather than limited to women. The use of 'things' to mark and affirm relationships and meanings, the aversion to real property, the importance of property as an income stream rather than absolute property and the use of trustees were all closely associated with women, but not specifically female in the sense that the loss of property rights in marriage or the claim to thirds and dower were female. Likewise, questions about the experience of women as they received trust based income was about more than women's experience and ability to make choices. The experience and ability to make choices within the trust relationship was only one aspect of the trust.

The importance of the limitations and protections of the trust for wealth holding has already been demonstrated. This chapter looks at the nature of the trust. This is about the economic history of 'life after death'. The chapter will show how the trust worked in practice. Many lasted for a considerable length of time as both legal and economic entities. In many cases, there was no distinct boundary between the tasks of executor and trustee. The role of executor involved the transfer of property under the will whilst that of trustee involved longer term management of that property for purposes and under contingencies outlined in the will. The workings and practice of the trust revealed many aspects of the nature and practice of family. This part of the enquiry deepens the understanding of middle class family in this period as a networked family with nuclear families and other forms of household embedded within it. The network can be identified, and was identified to its members by the practice of the gift. When successful, that practice sustained the family as a risk spreading network in an insecure world.

Nathan Rider's children

This part of the enquiry begins by following the affairs of Nathan Rider's children in the 1820s.

They were located in the Lupton, Rider, Wareham and Stocks network which originated in the mid-eighteenth century amongst a cluster of clothiers based around Mabgate to the north of Leeds centre.[1] Marriage, trade, religion and geography brought them together. They were members of the Independent Call Lane Chapel. They intermarried. By the 1820s, the cousinage links criss-crossed the network and naming practice made identity difficult. They married out, into the tradesmen, shopkeeper families of Briggate and the Headrow. Intermarriage consolidated capital and the trust-based network, but marriage out brought in new sources of capital, credit, contacts and skills. A strong network benefited from both. The central group called themselves clothiers but evidence shows that their interests crossed the functional boundaries of merchant, manufacturer and clothier. They were a Leeds-based network but by the late eighteenth century were increasingly dispersed geographically.

The first story was one of a minor and rather nasty little family row. Like many such incidents, no-one really had any interest or desire in its continuation but never found it easy to back off. Hence, this argument shed light upon many of the rules and structures which governed a key set of relationships. It also revealed the complexity and confusion which could engulf the boundary between family and business. There were a number of issues here, seniority, gender, status, economic fluctuations and bankruptcy, the meaning of real property, debt, life cycle strategies and geographical networks.

At one stage Mary Rider complained that she could not follow what was happening; the historian and the reader may well sympathise so it would be wise to begin with an outline of the main characters.

Nathan Rider was a clothier who had his dwelling, business and property in Mabgate. He wrote his will in 1811 and died in 1813, leaving a widow Hannah, who lived until 1826. They had eight children, who were listed by gender then age in all documents. They were
Jonathan
David
Joseph

[1] This account was based mainly upon the Lupton papers which were deposited in the business archives of the Brotherton Library University of Leeds and referred to by box number.

Sarah
Elizabeth
Mary
Hannah
Martha.

Martha died just before Nathan and hence falls out of the story. Nathan's will, like many others, made provision for his widow. She had the right to £40 a year and to their dwelling house and household contents 'provided she remain his widow'. The executors were William Lupton, merchant, cousin and fellow leading member of Call Lane chapel and David Metcalf, dyer.[2] The provisions of the will and their conduct of the estate took especial care to treat all children, male and female, with strict equality. They were to turn all real and personal property into money as opportunity arose and make suitable divisions between the children.

The density of relationships involved was increased when William Lupton took David Rider as partner in 1819. The articles of partnership indicate that David was the junior partner. He had been brought in to do the work whilst the older man took things easy. Terms were dictated by Lupton, 'whereas, the said William Lupton from his confidence in the industry and integrity of the said David Rider' agreed to take him into the business of cloth merchant for seven years.[3] The firm was to be William Lupton and Co. Lupton could dissolve with four months notice. He controlled all capital, profits and effects. Lupton agreed to 'bring into the said joint trade either in money or goods a sufficient capital to carry on the said trade', but 'David Rider shall diligently apply himself to the best of his skill and power in managing the said joint trade and that the said William Lupton shall be at liberty to give such attention and assistance only as may be agreeable to him'. Interest at 5 per cent was to be paid on Lupton's capital and on any capital that David Rider brought into the business. He was 'at liberty' to bring into capital any sum not exceeding a third of that employed by Lupton. Any profits remaining after costs went three parts to Lupton and a quarter to David Rider. Important in the light of later events, there was provision for arbitration 'to the determination of two indifferent persons'.[4] In addition, 'for the satisfaction of each party

---

[2] Box 131 of the Lupton papers concerned the affairs of Call Lane Chapel. The two men appeared in subscription lists, a call for a minister and lists of wardens between 1814 and 1823.

[3] Articles of a partnership between Messrs Lupton and Rider, cloth merchants, 1819, Business Archives Lupton 115.

[4] Articles, p. 7.

the said stock in trade and all buyings and sellings rects and payments and all accounts and transactions relating to the said Joint trade shall from time to time be duly and regularly entered in proper Books which shall be kept at the place where the Business shall be carried on and to which each party shall have access'.[5]

If things had gone well, David should have been able to build up his capital from profits and draw a modest sum for his own living expenses as Robert Jowitt had done, but this was not to be. Potentially, this was an excellent bargain in which David was able to enter the early stage of the adult life cycle releasing William Lupton to enjoy a quasi rentier stage.

The firm of William Lupton and Co became tangled with the estate of Nathan Rider. There were several elements in this and the complex of accounts, cash flows and balances are set out graphically from the point of view of Mary Rider (Fig. 7.1).

Property began in the estate of Nathan Rider. Here the executors turned it into cash which was then entered in the executors' account together, with any rents and interest from real estate and debts remaining in the estate. Once the partnership had been formed in 1819, this account was entered into the firm's books and each of the legatees (one of whom, David, was a partner) had their own account with the firm from which they could draw cloth but usually cash. In Mary's case, this money found its way to Thirsk where she lived with brother Joseph and sister Hannah, leaving behind a balance which was joined by the twice-yearly dividend on her share of the 3 per cent consols and, in 1826, a legacy from Mrs Hinchcliffe, another member of the network.

The major characters were all there. There was the dead head of household reaching out through his will and executors to care for his widow, but on his own terms. There were the brothers who followed in the business, Jonathan, of whom little is known, and David who used family connections for what he hoped was an advantageous partnership. Joseph moved out to extend the geographical network. He did not claim an occupational title but he talked of his clients and lending money out on security after the manner of many solicitors, but in early documents he was called a clothier. Sarah was the married sister and appeared in the documents as Mrs Linsley. Joseph Linsley was a clothier, also with an address in Mabgate. Mary and Hannah were the two unmarried sisters, important but often showing a helplessness beyond that which law imposed upon them.

Although two sons and his son-in-law stayed in the merchant clothier business, there is no evidence that Nathan Rider was disposing of his

---

[5] Articles, p. 3.

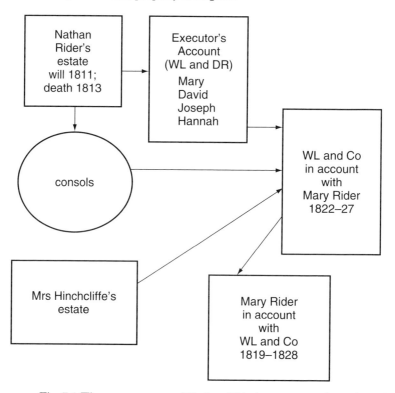

Fig. 7.1 The management of Nathan Rider's estate seen from the point
of view of Mary Rider, 1819–28.

Note: Statement of the affairs of the late Mr Nathan Rider of Leeds and
the manner in which the property left by him has been disposed of by his
executors, Lupton 126; Extracts from accounts of William Lupton and
Co with Mary Rider, Lupton 122; Messrs Lupton and Co in account with
Mary Rider, 1822–27, Lupton 122; Miss Mary Rider in account with
William Lupton and Co, 1819–26, Lupton 122. (Mary tended to see
both dividends and cash withdrawals as income.)

property in order to ensure the continuity of his business. His assets were
to be turned into money. His main objective was equity between his
children and a limited but respectable life style for his widow.

The accounts of Nathan Rider's estate showed that at the end of his life
he had disposed his property with judicious skill to suit his means, his
knowledge base and his strategic needs.[6] The consols were listed at face

---

[6] Summary account of the Executors of the late Mr Nathan Rider, 1813–27, Lupton 126.

Table 7.1 *Valuation of the estate of Nathan Rider, 1813*

	%	£
Real estate	43.55	2744
Consols	31.74	2000
Stock in trade	3.92	247
Debts	3.50	220
Money at interest	17.17	1082
Cash	0.13	8
Total	100.00	6302

value and divided between legatees on that basis. The real property was valued at sale price. Real property, urban cottages, houses and building land were important in his portfolio, but he sought for balance with loans and consols. These were easier to liquidate and transfer than real property. They helped in the early management of the executorship. By the time of this end of life cycle snapshot, the value of the business was relatively slight. Little importance was placed on the value of household contents, although the executors did take an inventory, which did not survive in the archive.

The executors managed this estate like a small business, albeit with the distinctive aims of supporting the widow, Hannah Rider, and liquidating it in as favourable a manner as possible. The rent income from the real estate was maintained at a fairly constant level and covered Mrs Rider's annual payment with ease. Sales were made as opportunity arose and formed the basis of payments to the legatees. The income from real estate not only paid Mrs Rider but provided for taxes on the property and some substantial repairs as the estate was prepared for sale (Figs. 7.2, 7.3).

The management of an estate of this kind did not involve a simple transfer of property. The trustees had obligations to Mrs Rider which lasted until her death in 1826. They were also empowered to sell 'such part of the Testators Real Estate as his said Trustees might think proper before his said Wife's Decease and for dividing the same...into eight equal shares', one for each of the eight children.[7] Thus, Lupton and Metcalf managed Nathan Rider's property over a 14-year period. The result of the progressive and protracted liquidation of the estate was an

---

[7] Terms of Nathan Rider's will recited in deed of 7 September 1826 for the sale of part of the real estate, Lupton 126.

270

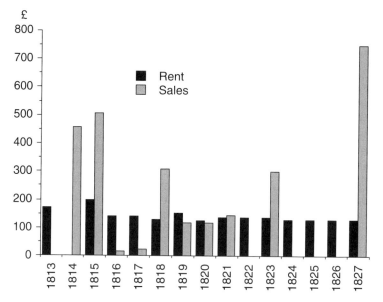

Fig. 7.2 Income from rent and sales from the real estate managed by
Nathan Rider's executors, 1813–27.

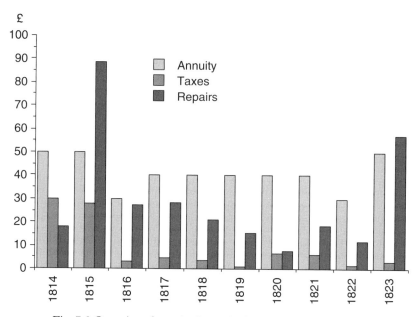

Fig. 7.3 Outgoings from the 'estate' of Nathan Rider, 1814–26.

uneven flow of cash to each of the surviving children. An excellent summary of the executors' accounts survives for the years 1814–23 but after that the historian must rely upon the confused and obviously incomplete scraps copied by the cousins from personal papers and the company books. Part of the dispute arose from the unclear and imperfect way in which David Rider had entered his drawings from the company into the partnership accounts. Although, in theory, each of the children was treated equally, the outcome of that equity differed according to gender and marital status. The unmarried daughters followed the most straightforward pattern and Mary's letters make it possible to trace income from the estate (Table 7.2). There were two flows involved here. The first was that from the estate to Mary's account with the firm, later joined by the twice-yearly payments of dividends from the consols and by Mrs Hinchcliffe's legacy to Mary. The second flow was Mary's drawings from that account.

The balances, though not precise, indicate that although there was enough missing to fuel the argument, the information does give a fairly complete picture of the flows into and out of Mary's account with William Lupton and Co, with the exception of some drawing from the account, notably in the early years and of the entry of interest which would have added small amounts to the income side. There was an early flow of income coming from the easily liquidated assets. After that there was little until the property boom of the early 1820s provided opportunities for the sale of real estate, and then the death of Mrs Rider released the trustees from their obligations. The consols were sold in 1827 and the cash sent directly to Mary at Thirsk.[8] The final sale of the real estate and the resulting distribution of cash was not included in these accounts.

The balances which were left with the firm were modest, between £300 and £700 at the most. Even doubling this to include Hannah's very similar deposit with Lupton and Co, there is no way in which it can be said that the unmarried sisters were essential to the capital of the firm. It looked as if the company was providing the sisters with substantial banking services. Subsequent events do suggest that the sisters' deposits may have been part of David Rider's stake in the firm, not in any legal sense but as an implicit signal of commitment. This modest holding may also have been implicit security for money advanced to the male members of the Rider clan, given that their relationships with the executors of Nathan Rider and with William Lupton and Co were very different from those of the sisters.

[8] Letter from Hannah and Mary Rider to William Lupton and David Metcalf, 18 September 1827, Lupton 138. The consols were sold for £591.

Table 7.2 *Mary Rider's account with William Lupton and Co, 1814–28 (All amounts in pounds decimal)*

	Income	Consols	Drawings	Balance
1814	204.73			
1815	73.91	8.81		
1816	45.86	8.81		
1817	10.00	8.81		
1818	60.00	8.81		
1819	25.00	8.81	15.00	317.889 (May)
1820	26.00	8.81	35.35	
1821	19.97	8.81	10.00	
1822	13.27	8.81	35.00	388.77 (Jan)
1823	142.12	8.81	35.00	
1824	18.00	8.81	58.00	
1825	110.00		60.00	
1826	17.90		40.00	
1827	68.68		25.00	297.21 (April); transferred to Joseph Rider's account
1828	0.00			262.56 (Oct); final receipt from Darnton[a]
Totals	835.44	88.1	313.35	
Total income	923.54			

The completeness of this account can be tested in a number of ways. The total recorded income, including the consols dividends was £923.54. Deducting the drawings listed in the accounts and letters, this left £610.19, which was just a little short of the total of the two final balances of April 1827 and October 1828, which was £559.8. As Mary's interest had not been added, some of the pre-1819 drawings were probably missing from the accounts. When the final balance was tested from the recorded balance of January 1822, then the balance calculated from the recorded income and drawings was £17 short at £532.17, suggesting that the interest due to Mary had to be added before the final settlement was made.

★ Income 1814–23 calculated from executors' accounts.[b]; consols transferred 1815, £295.11s.3d, the face value, was attributed to each sibling except Mrs Linsley

★ Income 1824–28 from Mary's letter and attached account, 23 Feb 1828.[c]

★ There was no consols dividend recorded after 1825, although the letters show that the stock was not sold by the executors until 1827.

★ 1827 was the year of Mrs Hinchcliffe's legacy.

★ The drawings 1819–27 were from Mary's February 1828 letter and confirmed by Joseph[d]; *Mary's earlier letter of 30 Sept 1827 had much the same figures.*[e]

Notes: [a] Receipt for money received from Darnton Lupton signed by Mary Rider, 3 Oct 1828. Lupton 122; [b] Lupton 126; [c] Lupton 122; [d] Letter from Joseph Rider, 2 July 1828, Lupton 122; [e] Lupton 122.

Table 7.3 *Joseph Rider's account with William Lupton and Co,
1814–28 (All amounts in pounds decimal)*

	Income	Consols	Drawings	Balance
1814	204.73			
1815	73.91	8.81		
1816	45.86	8.81		
1817	10	8.81		
1818	60	8.81		
1819	25	8.81	21.2	139.55
1820	26	8.81	75	132.25
1821	19.97	212.45	283.02	92.73
1822	13.27		151.53	34.11
1823	142.12		*	-125.51
1824	18		*	*
1825	110		*	*
1826	35		*	*
1827	68.68		35	-585.36
1828	0			

Note: For 1814–23 the information came from the Executors' account, Lupton
126; for 1824–27 from Joseph Rider's account with William Lupton and Co,
1814–28, Lupton 122. Mrs Hinchcliff's legacy was included in the 1827 total.

Amongst the male members of the clan only Joseph's accounts can be
deduced with anything like completeness (Table 7.3).

The information was very incomplete but, with a total recorded income
of £1117.85 and a final recorded deficit of £585.36, Joseph had taken
£1703.21 from the account. The income flow was very like Mary's as it
should have been under the terms of the will. There was one exception. In
1821, he turned his consols into cash and this entered his income stream.
Incomplete evidence for his drawings from the firm show that in the early
1820s, he began to withdraw capital from his account, which was in
deficit by 1823 and this deficit continued to rise. At the end it was at
least £585. This was very like half the sum which Mary transferred to
Joseph's account in 1828.[9] The assumption must be that the other half
came from Hannah.

What Joseph was doing with the cash was not clear but he used the
legacy as a source of capital not of income as Mary and Hannah did. He
also used his relationship with the firm of William Lupton and Co to

[9] Letter from Joseph Rider to Darnton Lupton, 4 January 1828, Lupton 148; 'You are
aware that my sisters have requested you to balance my account out of the money in your
hands belonging to them.'

further extend the cash flow initiated by the legacies. The accounts were balanced by the capital sums owned by the unmarried sisters. They had membership of Joseph's household but this was not a cost free exercise. In 1828, whether by the implicit rules of family mutuality or explicit pressure will never be known, the bill arrived.

Even less is known about the details of the relationships of the other male members to the estate, except that they must have had income flows much like Mary, Hannah and Joseph. What is known showed that the male relationship was about business capital and its insecurity.

In Joseph Linsley's case, this operated through his wife. He was listed as a merchant of Mabgate in the 1822 Directory. Between 1811 and 1813, he married Nathan's daughter, Sarah, and was given £200 which Nathan in a codicil directed should be regarded as part of his share of the estate. In 1819, Linsley was declared bankrupt, but David Rider seems to have advanced him money on the specific security of his share of the estate. Thus, David had first claim on the cash flow from his father's estate and the assignees under bankruptcy got nothing until 1825 when their rights were bought out for £250 by the trustees of the estate who acted with the consent of the others.[10] In August 1825, Linsley immediately settled his rights from the estate on his wife and children with David and Joseph as trustees. Characteristically, the family acted to regain control of the family money and to ensure a minimal standard of living for its members, notably the women and children threatened by the insecurity of trade in the 1820s.

Brother Jonathan was also bankrupt in the early 1820s. His share of the estate had been vested in the assignees but the rest of the family were trying to buy out those rights and, thus, regain control. By August 1826, nothing had been done.[11] This desire to buy out the rights of non-family members may have arisen from the manner in which real property was left to the legatees as tenants in common, thus ensuring that all had an interest in the fate of all during the period in which the estate was being turned into money and distributed.

David was the enigmatic figure here. The row had much to do with his conduct of the partnership and his relationships with many of the others was clearly strained, but he avoided insolvency and the historian's gaze. At the end of the process the argument came down to who paid certain interest charges – i.e. paid for the use of Lupton and Co money by the Rider family. On 30 June 1828, David paid £5.1s.10d to Hannah Rider

[10] Statement of the affairs of the late Mr Nathan Rider, Lupton 126.
[11] Statement of the affairs of the late Mr Nathan Rider.

jointly with Darnton Lupton, now head of the firm after his father's death, and that seemed to settle what remained of the row.[12]

Several things emerge from this story. The first is the slow unwinding of the urban estates. These family republics were not simply transferred and broken up. In this case, 'the estate of Nathan Rider' lasted for fifteen years after his death. In part, this was driven by events of the family cycle, notably the coming of age of children and the death of his widow. The fifteen years were not a simple matter of collecting income and paying bills. Parts of the estate were sold as opportunity arose and this was determined by the fluctuations in the local property and building market. These trusts did not have the long term aims of the aristocratic dynastic settlement, nor did they have the long vision of the institutional trusts which were important in real estate development in many cities, notably in Scotland.[13] The family trusts were important in a small but significant part of the property market in towns and cities like Leeds. These properties were held with the medium-term aim of securing income under the terms of a trust rather than maximising revenue in the broader sense. These trusts were scattered across Leeds. They were often hidden from contemporary and historian by the fact that they were entered into documents under the name of the trustees. By the nature of the life cycle, they tended to be in areas of the town where the strategies of a generation were maturing. These trusts were part of a larger set of management structures which saw the accumulation, creation and management of urban real estate driven by the aims of family strategies. The landscape of Leeds was a product not only of old field boundaries, the cost/revenue expectations of the building cycle and the growing sensitivities of social class but also of the multiple meanings and aims of family strategies.[14]

The widowhood of William Lupton's Ann

Despite their evident authority the Lupton family was no more immune than others from the insecurities of demography and the market economy. In the 1820s, two widows were left with children to look after.

---

[12] Receipt signed by Hannah Rider, 30 June 1828. Lupton 146.
[13] R. Rodger, *The Transformation of Edinburgh. Land, Property and Trust in the Nineteenth Century* (Cambridge, 2001).
[14] M.W. Beresford, *East End, West End*, esp. pp. 5–22; J.P. Lewis, *Building Cycles and Britains Economic Growth* (London, 1969); R.G. Rodger, *Housing in Urban Britain, 1780–1914* (London, 1989); D. Ward, 'Environs and neighbours in the "two nations": residential differentiation in mid nineteenth century Leeds', *Journal of Historical Geography* 6 (1980), 133–62.

Middle class family strategy left them with the resources to cope. The strategies set in place by their dead husbands left two very different imprints upon the landscape of Leeds.

The 1820s was a difficult decade for the Lupton network. Its economic focus, the firm of William Lupton and Co, made little or no profit.[15] The fluctuations in the years after the end of the Napoleonic wars made trading conditions difficult and the decision to bring David Rider into partnership was a disaster, in part because of the latter's inexperience and in part because of William Lupton's attempt to withdraw from the day-to-day supervision of the business. The tensions surrounding the management of the estate of Nathan Rider were symptomatic of this insecurity. Economic insecurity was compounded by the deaths of two of the leading males in the network. Arthur died in Paris in 1824. He was the travelling member. He had made his will in New York and was reported to have shot himself in Paris whilst in the delirium of a high fever.[16] He left a widow and young children. Four years later in 1828, his elder brother William died, again leaving a widow with a young family. The eldest son, Darnton, was only 22 years old. The ability of the network to recover from such disasters was remarkable. By mid century the Luptons had gained an economic security which carried them into the twentieth century and Darnton was a leading public figure who was elected mayor of the borough in the mid-1840s. The records demonstrate two key elements in the ability of the network to recover, the multiple use and development of urban real estate and the relationship between widows, executorships and the trust. There was no standard pattern of action. The basis of strength was the flexibility and multiple meanings of these elements in the face of insecurity and risk.

The two widows, both called Ann, were left with much the same problem. They needed to maintain their standard of living and status and to establish their children in the upper ranks of the middle classes into which they had been born. Their social and material resources were much the same – membership of an active and extended family network, unspecified personal estate, much of it located in the intermittently illiquid assets of the family merchant business, and substantial and usefully located urban real estate.

This estate had originated in the successful mid-eighteenth century career of David Rider. He held substantial property in the Mabgate area

---

[15] R.G. Wilson, *Gentlemen Merchants. The Merchant Community of Leeds, 1700–1830* (Manchester, 1971), pp. 114–21.

[16] C.A. Lupton, *The Lupton Family of Leeds* (Leeds, 1965), p. 38; Last Will and Testament of Arthur Lupton, New York 5 November 1821, Lupton 126.

of Leeds and, in 1788, added another block of land between Wade Lane and the road going north from Briggate which came to be called North Street. In 1773, his only daughter, Olive, had married Arthur Lupton, neighbour, clothier and merchant. In his will, David Rider gave Arthur and Olive a 'natural life' interest in his landed estates which was then passed to David's grandsons.[17] The division had an element of eldest male preference which would have looked out of place in a later urban middle class generation. William took half whilst the other half was shared by the other two grandsons which meant that, when David died, William was left with 5/8ths and Arthur with 3/8ths. All this was held as tenants in common. This form of ownership was an excellent way to force family members to act together but cumbersome for the development of property in an active capitalist market which looked for clear title to assets in the market. In 1811, William and Arthur agreed a division of the property in which William took possession of the estates at what was then called Town End.[18]

The Town End property had several elements. There was the cloth dressing mill built by Arthur Lupton in 1788, a substantial house and warehouses on the north side of the property and a close of land stretching back to Wade Lane, which was used as a tenter garth for stretching and drying the cloth in the open air. It was the perfect location for the merchant clothier of the late eighteenth century, a period when successful upward social mobility lay in the finishing and merchanting end of the trade. The property lay between two old routeways going north from the old centre of Leeds. Its make up was typical of the small narrow fields enclosed from the cultivation strips which had been created north of the medieval borough.[19] In the eighteenth century this was the place for the leading merchants. The major mansions of the Denison family, the wealthiest of the Leeds merchant community in mid-century, were adjacent to the Lupton properties. By the 1820s, it was also a location under pressure from the urban expansion of Leeds.

William's widow, Ann, was left with a young family which included two boys on the edge of adulthood. The family had an active and insecure business as well as the real estate. Ann comes through the documents as a lady of considerable initiative and skill. In later life, she lived to be 81 years old, she was remembered for 'great aunts parties' in the house to which she retired in the proto suburb of Potternewton north of city

[17] Will of David Lupton, 4 November 1789. Lupton 128.
[18] Abstract of the Title of Mrs Lupton to premises at the North Town End in Leeds, 1830. Lupton 127.
[19] Beresford, *East End, West End*, pp. 18 and 35–61.

centre.[20] She was daughter of John Darnton, tobacconist on the Headrow. William clearly had faith in her abilities and made her sole executrix of his will. The gap in family strategies and finances left by William's premature death was to be filled by the active development of the urban estate which Ann now controlled. In doing this she demonstrated the manner in which such estates operated to sustain family status and opportunities as well as their location in the urban economy. The property changed its meaning from being a factor of production in the family business, a workplace and the location of living space and amenity to a source of capital, profit and rent as she adjusted to the changing patterns of demand for living space and of flows of capital looking for investment opportunity.

In 1831, she laid out Merrion Street, running along the side of the mill and extending across the old tenter field to Wade Lane.[21] The plots were intended for terraced houses with yards or small gardens at the rear. When Ann came to build on her own account the houses were costed at £200 each. They were to be respectable houses of modest status with provision for some more substantial plots to the north around the taste-fully named Belgrave Street with its carriage way and garden square. The first sales were to Richard Philips, maltster, who was adding to the property he owned immediately to the south. He bought eight lots in the south-west end of the street. Christopher Kemplay, the schoolmaster, was doing the same in the centre of the south side of the street. He had recently inherited property from his father.[22] The probate had been completed in May. Christopher's share of an estate, valued at 'under £16,000', no doubt helped with the purchase price of four lots for £250 and the potential building costs of £200 for each house. Kemplay's sons were due £1000 each as well as their share of the residue. They were to be tenants in common of father's land between Merrion St and St John's Church. In addition to the sales to Philips and Kemplay, Ann sold other lots to a grocer, a butcher, a coachman, another schoolmaster and a joiner. In the main, these reflected the life cycle investment ambitions of tradesmen and shopkeepers of a middle class status ranked just below that of the Luptons. By 1834, the street had eighteen entries in the directory and six in the poll book. These six all had home, and often

---

[20] C.A. Lupton, *The Lupton Family,* p. 44.
[21] This account was based upon a series of property sale deeds, abstracts of title and sale notices, together with many receipts and accounts from tradesmen contained in Lupton 127. The information has been supplemented with data from the Baines and Newsome *Directory* of 1834 and the 1832 and 1834 *Parliamentary Election Poll Books.*
[22] Will of Richard Kemplay, gentleman, probate 16 May 1831.

business, in the street and four were amongst the original purchasers. Others, like Joseph Battye, the joiner, purchased in order to build and sell on to people like George Jenkins, the attorney's clerk. The street also contained twelve non-voters, including two cloth dressers, a cloth drawer, two joiners, two shopkeepers and a warehouseman.

By February 1834, the strategy of breaking bulk and selling on to the lower status ranks of the middle classes, many of whom then joined the ranks of the owner–occupier–rentier, which suited those a little less ambitious than Ann, was a strategy which was beginning to get decreasing results.

Three new tactics were employed.[23] The two sons, now in their 20s, engaged in a spot of land assembly with their mother and purchased the land once belonging to John Cussons, which backed onto the northern 'strip' of the property which their mother controlled. This gave them the ability to lay out a new Belgrave Street but, more important, to accumulate land for sale to the trustees of the intended Belgrave Chapel. This added a substantial £1200 to the revenue stream, and a respectable chapel always added value to any urban estate development. Given that this was an Independent Congregational Chapel, it is difficult to believe that the Lupton connection with Call Lane was irrelevant to the deal. The family network made a more modest contribution through the purchase of a plot on the north side of Merrion St by the two Luccock spinsters, Elizabeth and Maria. They were part of the cousinage network which had recently been reinforced by the marriages of Ann's sons to two Luccock girls. It was a symptom of the Lupton's insecurity that the sons favoured marriages within the network, increasing its density, rather than marriages which extended it. The character of the purchasers of the plots changed. Purchasers were dominated by a bricklayer/builder, a joiner and builder, and a plasterer. In other words, the building trade moved in to purchase, build and sell on. In some cases, Ann eased this process by extending loans to people like John Briggs, bricklayer. Meanwhile, her sons were breaking bulk and selling on the ground they had laid out in Belgrave Street, a process which finished in 1847 with a sale to William Smith, a joiner, who was also on their mother's list of purchasers. In the dark economic days of 1840, Ann had actually employed William Smith to finish five houses in the street to ensure the continued momentum of the family estate. In the late 1830s, the exercise became as much a capital spreading operation as a capital acquiring one. Again, this would not have been uncomfortable for someone as aware of the need to spread risk as

[23] This section is again based upon the deeds and invoices in Lupton 127.

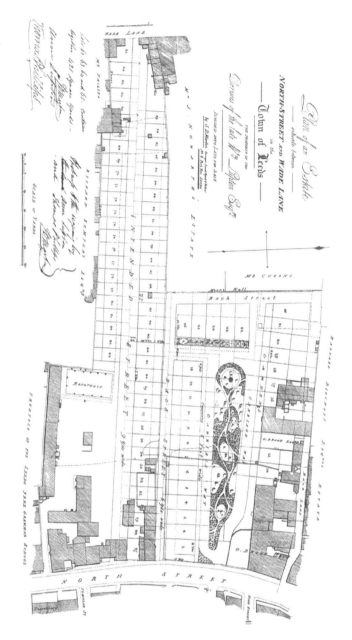

Fig. 7.4 Plan of an estate situated between North Street and Wade Lane in the Town of Leeds divided into Lots for Sale, c.1830.

Source: Lupton 127.

Table 7.4 *Revenue from the Merrion St estate related to the economic fluctuations of the Leeds economy, 1830–48.*

	Revenue	Expenditure	Indicators of peaks in economic activity		
1830	273			Profits	Textile capital
1831	1794			Profits	
1832	646				
1833				Profits	Textile capital
1834	461				
1835	1200				
1836	448		Malt Tax/Poor Law	Profits	Textile capital
1837	1962				
1838	1422				
1839	636		Malt Tax/Poor Law	Profits	
1840	350	329			
1841					
1842					
1843					
1844					
1845				Profits	
1846			Malt Tax		
1847	789				
1848					

Notes: Lupton 127 and Morris, *Class, Sect and Party*, pp. 80–3. Column 3 marks the peaks of the Malt Tax collection and the troughs in Poor Law spending, Column 4 the peaks in profits from the Jowitts and from Marshall's, the flax spinners, Column 5 the peaks in fixed capital investment in the West Riding wool textile industry; see W.G. Rimmer, *Marshalls of Leeds*, p. 317; D.T. Jenkins, *The West Riding Wool Textile Industry*, p. 156.

Ann must have been. By this time, the problem had been solved. The land bank accumulated by grandfather in law had done its work. The business was secure for another generation. Mother had moved out to Potternewton and the sons had time to take an active part in public life, with Darnton becoming mayor in 1845.

The estate produced a fluctuating income for Ann and her sons throughout the 1830s and 1840s. Ann's fluctuating income was related to those in the local economy as a whole with a lag of some twelve months.

Each set of peaks in profits, industrial capital investment or the indicators of income and wages drove the process forward. Conditions got more difficult and required more development initiative in the late 1830s and in the 1840s.

Meanwhile, the estate, like many others, had provided employment and income to a wide variety of professionals, service providers and tradesmen.[24] S.D. Martin was surveyor and land agent. Other services were provided by the inevitable lawyers such as Atkinson and Co and Robert Barr. William Smith, joiner and builder, appeared in several roles, as purchaser and as tradesman completing five houses for Ann. Others, like William Scott, were engaged in 'paving, draining and forming the road' in Belgrave Street. He had also excavated the cellars along the North Street frontage. Joseph Crampton had done the 'pavings and edgings' in Merrion Street. Costs like these were smartly passed onto the purchaser. There were minor roles for Thomas Inchbold, lithographer, John Heaton, printer, and Hernaman and Perring, printers, as well as the publishers of the two newspapers, *Leeds Mercury* and *Leeds Intelligencer*. The development of family estates like Town End/Merrion Street created a swirl of activity throughout the urban economy.

A few of the houses created by this process remained into the 1970s. The line of Ann's street had been wrecked by the extension of Briggate in the 1890s and the rebuilding of the central business district in the 1970s was completing the work, but there was enough left to show the substantial, if plain, nature of the housing with its broad windows and stone facings. The multiple ownership and intermittent nature of the building process left breaks in bonding and roof lines as an indication of the ownership patterns but Ann's layout and sale document had kept the houses roughly in the same status range (Figs. 7.5a and b).

When, in the late 1830s, Ann became anxious that the momentum of estate development should not slacken, she began to finance the building of houses directly. William Smith, joiner, was now employed as her builder rather than appearing in the record as purchaser. He agreed 'a house according to the accompanying plan to be built in Merrion St and finished in a most substantial and workmanlike manner for the sum of two hundred pounds'.[25] The plans showed a house with two bedrooms, a sitting room, kitchen and a privy in the yard, as well as a cellar for pantry and coal storage. A water cistern for 400 gallons fed a pump and sink in the kitchen. Given the often irregular nature of water supply in Leeds, that was a valuable feature (Figs. 7.6a, b and c).

The houses were 21 feet wide including a narrow 3'6" passageway leading from Merrion St to the back lane. They fitted neatly into the plot width on the original sale plan. One reason Ann began to finance building directly was her desire to maintain the land price of around 13 shillings per square yard for she had agreed with some purchasers that she

---

[24] The names come from the invoices in Lupton 127 supplemented by information in the 1834 *Directory*.
[25] Lupton 127, 26 June 1838.

Fig. 7.5a House in west end of Merrion Street, Leeds.

would refund them money if she allowed the price to drop in later sales. The only variant was in the lots which she carved out from the mill site on the valuable North Street frontage. These she sold to, amongst others, a grocer and a butcher for sums that varied from 25 shillings to 40 shillings per square yard.

By the time the large scale Ordnance Survey map was published in 1852, the bulk of the estate was full (Fig. 7.7). The outcome was apparent disorder and the mixture of residential property of varying quality, industrial building and workyards. Here was the mixture which health reformers, domestic ideologists and latter planners hated so much. It was a mixture which appeared in family estates as varied as those of John Rose and William Hey. It was a mixture which made sense in terms of the strategies of families like the Luptons as the same space took on different meanings under pressure from three different sorts of influence, generational development, the building cycle and the need to spread risk

Fig. 7.5b Lower eastern end of Merrion Street, Leeds.

as family situations changed. Ann Lupton's plans of the early 1830s imposed the partial discipline of the 21 foot plot size. By the end of the development, when the Luptons had moved away, that discipline slipped and the map showed that the last plots were filled with back to back housing, notably in Belgrave Street which the sons had sold in large blocks to developers, and in the plots south of Belgrave Chapel which had been taken by the Luccock spinsters. Family network might produce ready purchasers but it was not an effective discipline.

There were several processes at work here, the demands of the family property cycle, the need to recover from the damage done by premature death, the fluctuations of the Leeds economy and the expansion of urban Leeds northwards from the centre. The results included the securing of a key element of the Lupton family network and the development of a peri urban world of merchant mansions and finishing mills into a densely built mixed use, mixed status area of an industrial city.

The Black Horse and Schedule E

A few minutes' walk to the east of Merrion St was an area which became closely bound up with the fortunes of another Ann Lupton, but with very

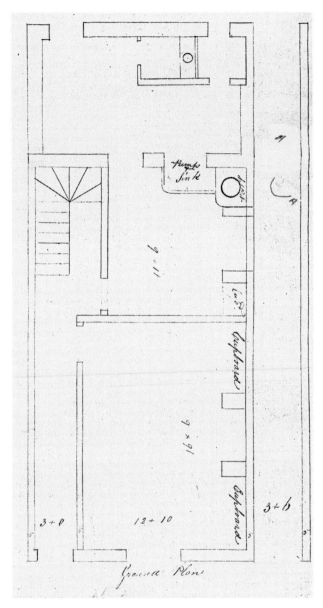

Fig. 7.6a Plan of a house to be built in Merrion Street, Leeds, 1838, ground floor.

Source: Lupton 127, 26 June 1838.

286

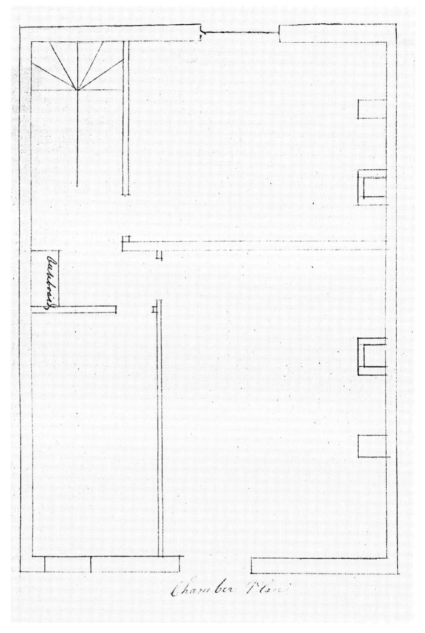

Fig. 7.6b Upper floor.

287

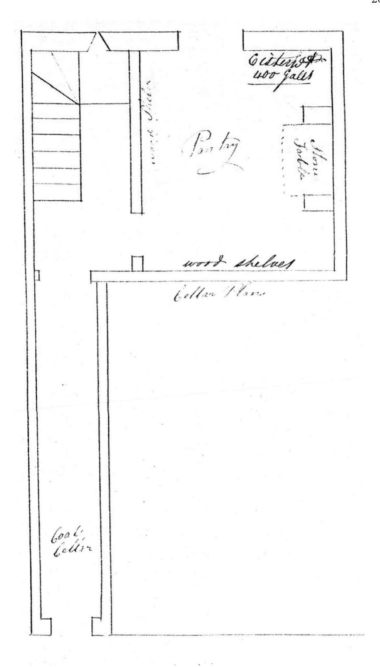

Fig. 7.6c Cellar plan.

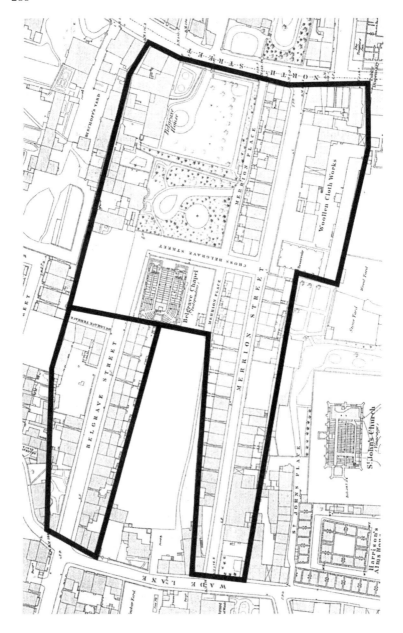

Fig. 7.7 Plot boundaries and outcomes of the Merrion Street estate as
shown on the Ordnance Survey large-scale town plan surveyed in 1847.

different consequences both for the widowed lady herself and for the landscape. Arthur's Ann faced the same sort of problems as William's Ann had done, but with variations in practice, strategy and resources, which had important consequences. In part, the more passive approach of Arthur's Ann was a result of the personal resources she brought to the situation. She was Arthur's second wife, his first having died after childbirth. Ann was the daughter of a gentleman farmer from Chesterfield and would not have access to the urban commercial wisdom of the daughter of an elite Briggate shopkeeper–tradesman like Ann Darnton. Ann faced a family strategy more damaged than anything William had left behind and did so with more slender resources. When Arthur killed himself in Paris, Ann was 40, with four young children still alive, daughters aged 12, 10 and 8 and a son aged 5. Moreover, she only had access to 3/8th of the Lupton–Rider estate. Grandfather's preference for the eldest male weakened one part of the network in exactly the sort of manner which the advocates of equitable inheritance warned about.

In part, the variation in outcome was a result of the choices made by Arthur whose will was dated New York, 5 November 1821.[26] In terms of practice his will was an odd mixture of minor gentry and middle class. Personal property was divided equally between his children but the real estate went to his eldest son, another Arthur, on condition that £1500 was paid to youngest son Benjamin when the latter was 21 years old. Ann was to have an income of £200 a year on condition she remained unmarried. That, at least, was characteristic of men who had minor children and perhaps a recognition that Ann was not practised in urban ways. The trustees were William Lupton and Thomas Cadman, tobacconist, who were allowed to make 'an adequate and liberal allowance for the education and maintenance of my children'. This was a will made in haste with a lack of advice and precision so that the trustees needed legal advice on a number of occasions.

In part, the different outcome was a result of the different nature of the area. Mabgate was rapidly becoming part of urban north Leeds and growing in density and complexity, but it still had many characteristics of 'rural formlessness'.[27] The folds and garths were filled with cottages serving the needs of the eighteenth century generations of clothiers with their houses, warehouses, finishing shops and mills. The land had the multiplicity and flexibility of meaning which suited the clothiers' ambitions and insecurities, store of value, security for credit, asset for the

[26] Lupton 126.
[27] W. Benjamin, *Reflections. Essays, Aphorisms, Autobiographical Writings*, P. Demetz (ed.) (New York, 1986), p. 125, writing about Moscow in the 1920s.

rentier income of old age, widowhood and minor children, and factor of production for the business, in this case space for the tenter ground of cloth finishing. It was a familiar list and not one which invited the urban discipline of street frontages, paving and drainage. The area was liable to flooding from the stream which attracted and served the clothiers. The ownership structure was mired in a web of trusteeships and assigneeships that were detached from the use value of the ground. To the east was the land laid out by Paley, whose ambitious property development plans had led him to bankruptcy and his assets into the hands of the assignees.[28] Adjacent to Arthur Lupton's Middle Fold was the Linsley land, which we know was tied into bankruptcy in the 1820s.[29] A little to the north was the estate of Nathan Rider, which had been slowly broken up by the trustees in the interests of the distant household in the rural market town of Thirsk. It was an area subject to the slow economic redundancy of the clothier and the move towards the merchant–finisher and eventually to the merchant selling direct from the warehouse. This was a move which William Lupton and his sons followed with some skill but which produced ill-resourced confusion in both the urban landscape and the family strategies of Mabgate.

The outcome was passive management. The estate was subjected to few developmental pressures. The rents were collected. There was a tenants' supper each year and a coronation tea drinking in 1839. This may have been a survival from an earlier generation of paternalistic management or perhaps Ann brought some rural assumptions into her peri-urban estate. By the 1830s, the estate was being managed by Nathaniel Sharpe, land agent. He charged 5 per cent of rents received and insured the property for £600 with the Leeds and Yorkshire Fire Office.[30] The surviving accounts show a modest and irregular flow of rent. The arrears would mount up before being collected in. Some of this was a reflection of the poverty and insecurity of many tenants. Part was wise paternalistic management. The largest allowance was to Widow Johnson in 1838 after the death of her husband Charles, landlord of the Old Buck Inn. By 1840, she had paid off the deficit and was taking her share of the rent suppers along with Thomas Flowitt of the Black Horse. Expenses were modest. Only in 1835 was there any suggestion in the

---

[28] M.W. Beresford, 'The making of a townscape: Richard Paley in the East End of Leeds, 1771–1800', in C.W. Chalklin and M.A. Haviden (eds.), *Rural Change and Urban Growth*, pp. 281–320.

[29] A Plan of a Detached Estate situate in Mabgate near Leeds, the Property of Mr Lupton, taken July 1802. Ms 442/80 Brotherton Library, Leeds University.

[30] The surviving receipt was for 1838–39. Lupton 128.

accounts of major spending on the estate. Apart from that year, Sharp was able to pay 'Mr Lupton' between £50 and £80 each year. This must have been Darnton, taking over the trusteeship after his father's death.[31] This was not enough for Ann's £200 a year, but then the net residue of grandfather Arthur Lupton's estate had been £19,001, so that the trustees would have had plenty of other assets to provide for the widow and the education of the young family.

Because the Mabgate estate was embedded in a complex set of accountable legal obligations, accounts were presented and receipts collected with some care as money passed from agent to trustees and trustees to widow and children. Enough of these receipts and accounts survive to show something of the irritations, attention to detail, tedium and bad temper which was part of extracting money from an urban estate of this kind. Management costs in terms of time and unpleasantness were high. Sharpe earned his 5 per cent and, in doing so, showed why many investors, especially women and those of high status looked for something a little less direct when it came to extracting a rentier income for old age or widowhood. The turnover of tenants was considerable, 30 per cent in five years. Pleasanter obligations, like paying Martha Johnson her £1.6s. for the rent supper were accompanied by the unremitting attention to repairs. These were ageing houses of indifferent quality. There was 6s. for repairing George Clark's door and door frame together with the wood nails and labour and the 4s. for Holliday's shutter and back window paid to Joseph Knowles in April 1839.[32] Knowles was a regular for payments for such work. A year later it was 'ceiling joist fixing, floor repairing and nails'.[33] Equally frequent was work such as 'To range and oven facings and fixing same in Cottage no.79' signed by Hannah Holliday for George Brooke. Then there was the constant flow of demands for local property taxes, Poor Rate, Soke Rate and Watch Rate.[34] Some issues were more contentious, such as the argument over the contribution to the subscription for a wooden bridge over the beck opposite the Black Horse.[35] Rent arrears were usually managed in a benign way but could become a matter

---

[31] Nathaniel Sharpe in account with the trustees of the late A. Lupton, 1835–40. Lupton 126, 127 and 128.

[32] Receipts signed by Nathanial Sharpe, 15 April 1839 and 13 April 1839. Lupton 126.

[33] Receipts from Nathaniel Sharpe, 21 April 1840. Lupton 128.

[34] This account was based upon Lupton 126, 127 and 128, which contained the accounts, receipts and letters concerned.

[35] Letter from Edward Lawson to John Hezmalhalch, 27 April 1836. Hezmalhalch was the millwright, whitesmith and licensed valuer who lived in Sheepscar Bridgehouse, 27 Millwright St. Edward Lawson was also a Mabgate machine maker, part of the firm of Samuel Lawson and Sons, engineers and machine makers, 34 Mabgate.

for open conflict. Benjamin Stead had been in the habit of leaving an arrears of £2.10s on his cottage. In 1838, things got nasty. Court summons were delivered to John and Martha Wilks,

Containing an information and complaint against you, for that you did on or about the nineteenth day of January instant fraudulently receive, convey away and carry off from and out of a certain tenement or dwelling house situate at Leeds in the said borough lately held by one Edward Stead now deceased as tenant thereof to the said Nathaniel Sharpe certain goods and chattels not exceeding the value of fifty pounds to prevent the same from being distrained for rent and arrears . . . [36]

Mrs Lupton, Arthur's Ann, lived in Grove Terrace, a modest and respectable street west of Wade Lane and Merrion St. In the 1834 *Directory*, the house was still in Arthur's name. She distanced herself from her urban estate in terms of social and geographical space. She was already distanced in legal terms by the trustees under her husband's will. They, in turn, distanced themselves in management terms by employing Sharpe.

Men like Nathanial Sharpe played an inconspicuous but crucial role in the demanding business of urban property management which tied family strategies to the urban built environment. Sharpe made this property management the basis of a very successful middle class accumulation. Perhaps, as a result of his experience in estates like those of Merrion Street and Mabgate, his own choice of assets had little place for real estate. When he died in 1868, his assets were dominated by railway and canal shares. His real estate consisted of four pews in Leeds Parish Church, two in Trinity Church, a patch of building land and, significantly, two houses in Merrion Street. His will, which gave a life interest to his sisters and then passed everything to a nephew in Whitby, directed that the real estate be sold but 'it being nevertheless my desire that my Railway Shares should not be sold unless deemed absolutely necessary'.[37] His trustees found in the 1870s that this produced an annual income of just under £500, which would have provided the basis of a comfortable middle class household. His mother had died in 1838. Her asset structure was dominated by £7031 in consols. She lived in Nile Street and Nathaniel nearby at the top of North Street. His father was a merchant who had died in 1807 and appointed Mr William Lupton as one of his trustees. Nathaniel chose his living space close to the rough and tumble of the multi-faced family estates of north Leeds. These he managed for

---

[36] Magistrates Court delivered to Martha Wilks, 22 January 1838.
[37] The papers of Nathaniel Sharpe are in the West Yorkshire Archives at Sheepscar, DB 37 and contain copies of his will, 1 April 1868, and the executors' accounts for himself and his mother.

others but for himself he chose a very different asset structure to that of his clients.

When the Ordnance Survey map of 1850 was published, Middle Fold, the Old Buck and the Black Horse looked much as they must have done in the late eighteenth century. The only sense of form was given by the

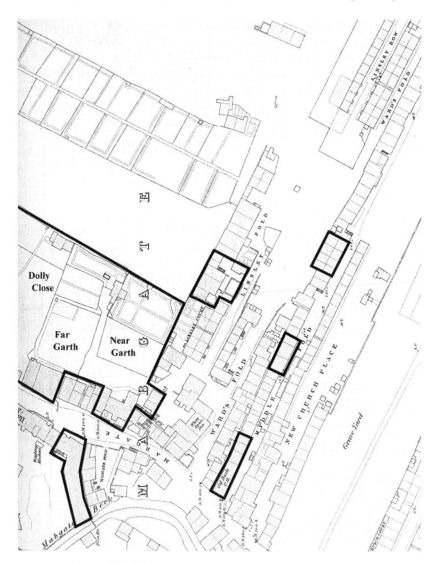

Fig. 7.8 The Mabgate estate of Mrs Arthur Lupton on the Ordnance Survey large-scale town plan surveyed in 1847.

shadow of the long narrow field, which long ago had resulted from the enclosure of cultivation strips and then been preserved by the needs of cloth finishing in the tenter garths of north Leeds. They stand in sharp contrast to the crowded and disciplined ranks of the bye law back-to-backs which surrounded the Mabgate area. In 1800, even in 1820, a family like the Luptons would have valued such an estate for its flexibility. It was a store of value, a basis of capital investment, of spreading risk and, for a family in need of credit in the difficult years between 1800 and 1830, a visible sign of their economic status. Management costs were not as onerous as they would later become. The family lived nearby and dealt in the harsh and direct world of hiring wage labour and bargaining with their suppliers. But, by the 1830s and 1840s, such houses were an embarrass-ment for a family network with aspirations to join and sustain its place amongst the liberal elite of Leeds public life, especially for someone like Darnton who, by the 1840s, was a prominent public figure. By the 1840s, these houses had already suffered the indignity of being classed in Schedule E of the 1842 Leeds Improvement Act. In 1842, Arthur's son, Arthur, had come of age and had recently married. He was listed as owner of the Old Buck, the twelve cottages of Middle Fold and the Black Horse, with its croft, yard, skittle ground, brewhouse, pig cote and garden. This meant they were potentially subject to compulsory purchase and demoli-tion in the five years following the Act. In fact, it was not until the public health acts of the 1890s that serious attempts were made to demolish the likes of Middle Fold. The 1842 Act was about imposing order on the urban fabric. It was concerned with road widening, draining, lighting and moving the frontages of buildings to a coherent building line.[38] The demolition of ill-built and unhealthy urban cottages was, in practice, only incidental to this aim. Significantly, the Act made specific provision for the structures of ownership which emerged from the family strategies described here. Provision was made to enable those under 'disabilities' to sell. This meant legal disabilities and included married women. The money from such sales could be lodged with trustees and laid out at interest for the party concerned. In other words, the trustee provisions of the characteristic male will with widows and children in mind, could be replicated. Even where there was no disability of this kind, the act recog-nised the life cycle function of such property ownership and allowed owners to sell in return for a perpetual annual rent charge paid from the Improvement Act rates.

---

[38] *Leeds Improvement Act*, 1842; M.J. Daunton, *House and Home in the Victorian City. Working Class Housing, 1850–1914* (London, 1983), esp. pp. 11–88.

Table 7.5 *Units of property from Schedules D and E, Leeds Improvement Act, 1842*

	Number	%
Male	604	65.65
Female	99	10.76
Trustees/executors	174	18.91
Charitable trustees	12	1.3
Institutions	31	3.37
Total	920	100

The Leeds Improvement Act of 1842 made a very modest contribution to the demolition of unhealthy property, although it did make some contribution to the widening of streets and imposed some discipline on new building. The Act also provided an insight into the ownership structure of several areas of Leeds, including the area around Leeds Bridge, the yards to the east of Briggate and behind Kirkgate and the Mabgate area. These were 'mature' urban areas, the result of several generations, both in terms of family and topographical influences. The list of property and property owners confirmed the influence of both women and trusteeships in urban property. The results were summarised in terms of numbers of units of property.

Compared with the ownership of the property bundles in the surviving Soke Rate books, the listing in the 1842 Improvement Act contained a slightly higher proportion of female owned properties (c.2 per cent more) and of properties owned by institutions (again 2 per cent more) but the major different was in the legal personalities (trustees, executors and assignees) who held 19 per cent of the scheduled properties compared with the 11.5 per cent in the more representative Soke Rate.

For Arthur's Ann and her family, the little estate did its job. The rents played a part in maintaining the widow within her own social status ranks. The children were educated and two of them married into the family of Charles Wicksteed, who became minister of Mill Hill Chapel.[39] Ann died in Sidmouth in 1848.[40] The history of Mabgate and Arthur's Ann shows the manner in which the trust could create very 'passive' capital by distancing its beneficiary from the process of decision making. This passivity helped create disorderly and undynamic elements in the urban fabric.

[39] W.L. Schroeder, *Mill Hill Chapel, Leeds, 1674–1924: Sketch of its History* (Hull, 1924); H.M. Wicksteed, *Charles Wicksteed, a Biography* (London, 1933); C. Wicksteed, *Lectures on the Memory of the Just, being a Series of Discourses on the Lives and Times of the Ministers of Mill Hill Chapel* (Leeds and London, 1849).
[40] C.A. Lupton, *The Lupton Family*, p. 39.

The rescue of Sarah Stocks

The trust funds played a key role in supporting widows and minor children. These funds also provided resources for daughters and for women in second marriages. The funds usually provided a little extra income and some fragments of independence in the subordinations of gender. If things went wrong, such funds played a key role in combating the damage done to the status, welfare and strategies of the middle class family by bankruptcy and economic misfortune. In such instances, the networked family acted most directly as an agency for risk spreading. The asymmetries of gender provided both vulnerability and a key resource in the practices involved in such risk spreading. If such practices were to be effective, then the male leaders of the network needed to accept very precise obligations, especially obligations to female members. This was central to the case of Sarah Stocks. The responses to her difficulties and dependence separated those who failed and those who accepted the responsibilities of male dominance.

The story began in 1794 with the death of Mrs Mary Wareham. She left her daughter, Sarah, £600 in trust. The trustees were Nathan Rider, Arthur Lupton, merchant of Leeds, and Thomas Wareham, wine merchant of Leeds.[41] They were selected from the 1790s generation of merchant–manufacturer–clothiers based around Mabgate and were a part of the cousinage network, which had its origins with the mid-eighteenth century Riders. In 1806, Sarah married John Stocks. His family network was based in Huddersfield and had links in Manchester. They themselves moved to London. Sometime in the early 1820s, John Stocks became bankrupt. To make matters worse, he had borrowed £250 from his wife's trust fund to finance a property deal in London. By a mixture of ill luck and incompetent management, his bankruptcy was declared whilst this money was in his books and before the mortgage deeds had been completed and lodged with Sarah's trustees. Thus, the money was lost. At the same time, Sarah found out that Uncle Wareham had, in 1817, sold her consols and invested the money in a mortgage which had been used to finance Wareham's own property deals in Leeds.[42] In November 1823, Sarah wrote to William Lupton,

Sir, I fear you will think me troublesome but since I wrote you have been under considerable anxiety respecting the money Uncle Wareham has in his possession I wish to acquaint you I knew nothing of Uncles remouving the money till all was

---

[41] Indenture dated 18 October 1817 between Thomas Wareham and William Lupton regarding the trust from the will of Mary Wareham. Lupton 124.
[42] The account of Sarah Stocks was based upon letters and deeds in Lupton 124.

settled when he wrote me 27 november 1817 saying I have sold out of the 3%s and got you a mortgage for 460 pounds at the same time informing me the mortgage deeds was placed with you which I was glad to hear he also said Mr Lupton and himself wished the Interest to accumulate to make up the Original Sum but that has been out of my power nor can I at present having many little debts I earnestly wish to discharge: should Mr S keep his situation as I trust he will I hope I may be enabled after a short time to do it – what I dislike is Uncle's not saying the mortgage was upon his own estate which leads me to fear it was done for his own benefit more than mine Uncle Rider was many times hurt and displeased with Uncle Wareham's conduct yet I have been unwilling to believe that he would act dishonourably if he has I think he ought in Justice to me and my children make up the sum the money would have made had it continued in the Funds till this time when by selling out it would have made up more than the Original sum situated as we are I feel it much I may be too warm but I cannot but notice Uncle's charging the postage of every letter since 1817 – I think it mean though it may be right . . . I really am ashamed to give you so much trouble but I hope you will excuse it knowing how uncomfortably I am placed I must not say any thing about it to Mr Stocks now[43]

The 'trust' which the working of the networked family required was gone. Sarah understood enough to know that with falling rates of interest the sale value of her stock would have increased since 1817. She was a little unfair as it is likely that the move from consols would have increased the annual income on her money from around £20 a year to around £30 a year, which the higher rates of a mortgage would have brought. It was the sense that she had been tricked and that Wareham had acted for his own benefit rather than that of the trust which did the damage.

William Lupton, who by now had taken his father's responsibilities in this matter, moved in as the peacemaker and adviser. He wrote to Mrs Stocks,

Since I was in London I have seen Mr Stocks's father and brother who live at Huddersfield, they seem ready to assist Mr Stocks in every reasonable way if he will exert himself, but I do not think they require too much when they wish for active energetic exertions from both of you and with Mr Stocks principles it would surely be most agreeable to him to receive nothing but the result of his own efforts, which would be by far the most independent mode of supporting his family. Will you excuse my stating that I think it would be of incalculable advantage to your daughter if your Husband's friends could be prevailed upon to take her to live with them in the country – the benefit to her health would no doubt be great and I should think it would be highly satisfactory to you as her mother to have her placed in a situation where she would be more comfortable than it is in your power to make her[44]

---

[43] Sarah Stocks, London to William Lupton, 12 November 1823. Lupton 124.
[44] William Lupton to Sarah Stocks, 4 November 1823. Lupton 124.

The network was buzzing, but the principles of individuality were being enforced along with the sense of obligation. Lupton himself, who had the balance of the trust fund on the firm's account books, was also sending small sums to Mrs Stocks to help with the household expenses. He arranged for her to be given a small residual left with her husband's assignees in bankruptcy and rescued her watch which had found its way into the hands of the London solicitor acting for her husband's creditors. At the same time, William Lupton was in close contact with another member of the network, Jo Rider at Thirsk, who found a mortgage for £500 of Mrs Stocks's money.

Meanwhile, Sarah's distress, distrust and helplessness grew,

I write in consequence of Mr Stocks having been out of a situation nearly three months being obliged to leave Mr Dickinson on account of illness. My daughter likewise has been much indisposed so that the little money I had by me is now spent which compels me to beg the favour of you to send me five pounds as soon as convenient this I ask reluctantly and I think nothing would have obliged me to have done it but the fear of my children wanting bread – Mr Stocks is now better and has now advertised in *The Times* for a situation but I much fear he will not succeed if not he must leave London which I doubt not would add much to the comfort of his family. . . . Uncle Wareham is incapable of acting or thinking therefore if you would have the goodness to influence him as you think best[45]

The sense of bitterness was very great, although Wareham was by now an old man.

On 23 August she asked Lupton for £5 and added, 'I had been at Mr Robinsons solicitor for Mr Stocks bankruptcy. I waited upon him again this morning . . .'. Robinson looked at papers and agreed that there was a balance of £32 in the hands of Mr Hedges but needed 'permission and sanction' from Uncle Wareham to release this. Robinson was reluctant to call another meeting as this would entail extra expense which would take half the remaining funds. She asked Lupton to ask Wareham to write to Hedges.

Uncle may perhaps recollect Mr Hedges having my watch in his possession as a security for £16 10 shillings . . . I shall be glad as a little money could never be more useful to us than now I fear you will think me very troublesome but I thought Uncle Wareham unable to attend to it without your advice.[46]

By October she was planning to leave London. She wrote to Wareham as she still needed his signature to release the money and her watch. The furniture was coming by canal to Manchester and the family by steam packet to Hull and Selby. That they had furniture to send suggests that

[45] Sarah Stocks to William Lupton, 12 August 1824. Lupton 124.
[46] Sarah Stocks to William Lupton, 23 August 1824. Lupton 124.

'household contents' were, directly or via a trust, in Sarah's name adding slender protection for the family. She added 'I am labouring under great anxiety of mind so much so that I can scarcely write . . . with best regards to Aunt Lizzy, Mary and all the family'. Sarah was in deep trouble and returning to her home base.[47]

Stocks himself made little direct contribution to this rescue but his one surviving letter shows a man on the edge of breakdown. The letter was full of anger and despair. The rambling argument leaves the reader wondering if John Stocks's 'illness' was depression or alcohol. Despite the incoherent grammar, the letter shows an instinctive sense of how the networked family worked. He was aware of the function of reputation and that his sole remaining influence with his brothers was the threat to their reputation, both economic and moral, of allowing one part of their family network to fall into destitution.

John Stocks, 53 Watling St, London to Lupton:

Yesterday my wife write Mr Wareham, which I should feel much obliged, by your enquiring into its contents, altho I did not read it, I understand it stated our present deplorable condition, and applications we have made to my father, and brothers, say William at Huddersfield, Sam and been at Manchester, all of whom are in very respectable circumstances especially Sam, and £100 a year to them, would only be as a drop in a bucket of water, and which they did agree would be paid to us, until I could get into a situation, they have once one it, and Sam, says now, I see if we allow you £100 per year, you will never look out for a situation, but to convince you; you shall look out for one, we will not give you any more money, so I can not, if you go to gaol, or to the bottom of the sea, I do not care what becomes of you – This very great professor of Methodism, I fear his heart is become rather callous, but he has got the good things of this world, which covers or overlooks many little blunders from the precepts of Christianity, this mighty brother of mine, told my father, in my presence, to his face, he being the third son, with such an air of presumption, that he was very sorry, that ever I was born, but I have some small reason to regret that I have been made the dupe of this my said bro Sam for he was the entire ruin of me in this world. I simply permitted him to draw bills upon me in Town to the amount of many thousands of pounds, which first broke my back, pig upon bacon was the order of the day, until he got completely round, which terminated in my total ruin, and for this brotherly kindness I get such abuse as the following at Manchester he said to me get out of my house immediately, never let me see your face again, I wish the coach may turn over with you, an break your neck. You ought long since to have gone to new Southwark bridge, and then thrown yourself over but above all things, if you had the spirit of a man, you would long ago have acted in the same manner as Lord Londonderry did for you are become a disgrace to us as a family, and many other equally disgraceful sayings to me, that was repugnant to my wounded feelings,

---

[47] Sarah Stocks to William Lupton, 17 October 1824. Lupton 124.

and generally low and depress in spirits – we are now in debt about a £100 for rent, meal, bread, drink, and necessaries, and we have no means ourselves to discharge the same . . . but the fact is this, I have been so low spirited and so much afflicted by the reverse of Fortune, that I am half the year, and not fit for a situation, nearly like a child in comparison, but my kind brother recommend the Tread Mill to me to cure all my diseases, the above I declare before my God and you sir, to be correct, and you can make use of it, in any way, you may best approve . . . John Stocks.[48]

Just as Uncle Wareham had lost trust, John Stocks had lost all the authority that went with the male family role. As matters settled down in October, Sarah wrote to Lupton from Huddersfield,

Your favour of the 26 Sept I duly received and thought it more prudent under all circumstances not to mention it to Mr Stocks – I have also to acknowledge the receipts of ten pounds which be received from Cousin David Rider feeling greatly obliged to you for the trouble you take. I remain. Dear Sir yours respectfully Sarah Stocks.[49]

Between 1823 and 1825, Lupton had extracted Sarah's money from the Wareham mortgage. First he placed it on the books of William Lupton and Co and then transferred it to a mortgage on agricultural property near Thirsk, which Jo Rider had negotiated for him. Sarah was now settled with a modest income, helped by a legacy of £68, her share as one of the many second cousins of Mrs Hinchcliffe. By 1825, the Stockses were also providing a small allowance to help keep the damaged household within the middle classes.

The rescue of Sarah Stocks involved two sorts of process. In part, it was a matter of hard legal and financial logic. Accounts were requested and legal opinions were sought before any action was sanctioned. In part, it was a matter of trust and the gift economy of the networked family. William Lupton, or rather the firm of William Lupton and Co, supplied banking services. Jo Rider, in his turn, supplied legal services and detailed knowledge of the agricultural land and mortgage market. Throughout, reputation was crucial.

Obligation, reputation and the need for the unencumbered control of property all worked together and the networked family was the basis upon which action was taken and to which action was referred.

Networked families

These accounts, of Nathan Rider's children, the Lupton widows and Sarah Stocks, all, in different ways, make visible to the historian the

---

[48] John Stocks to William Lupton, 18 July 1823. Lupton 124.
[49] Sarah Stocks to William Lupton, 24 October 1826. Lupton 124.

workings and processes of the networked family. The Lupton–
Rider–Wareham–Stocks network was a Leeds network but, by the 1820s,
it had acquired a familiar geographical shape. There were members
in Huddersfield – a simple extension based upon the network's dominant
economic interest, in this case wool and woollen cloth. There were
members in Leeds and London. In this case, the metropolitan–provincial
link was not a successful one. There was an important branch in Thirsk,
which provided a link to the very different environment of the county
agricultural market town. There was also an overseas branch, which did
not feature directly in the case studies. John Luccock, one of William
Lupton's many cousins, spent time in New Orleans and Rio attempting to
extend the network's commercial range and opportunities.

This variety strengthened the network for it spread risk. For all her
troubles, the London failure of Sarah Stocks was compensated for by the
strength of the Leeds–Huddersfield–Manchester links. The Thirsk link
gave William Lupton knowledgeable access to the agricultural economy,
which was crucial in a middle class urban society with a hunger for reliable
rentier income earning assets. The detailed local knowledge, which Jo
Rider had, was vital to Lupton as he placed money. When he placed
Mrs Stocks's money in 1824, he noted that he had 'no security but the
confidence that I feel that you will take full care to see that everything
was safe . . .'[50] For all their minor rows, William Lupton and Jo Rider
trusted each other, or rather they knew each other and knew exactly how
far they might trust each other. Accounts were exchanged at intervals and
the failure to keep adequate accounts was one cause of their disagree-
ments. The relationship was valuable to both of them and, despite the
disputes, Jo took care to repair relationships with a gift. He asked Lupton
to accept a gift of books on account of our gratitude 'for the assiduous
attention paid to our interests, during the long period for which our
Family affairs remained under your judicious direction', and Lupton
acknowledged this gift of nine volumes of Walter Scott's work.[51] The
exchange of gifts was vital in making and sustaining the network. The
network was important enough to Joseph for him to make sure that
he repaired with this symbolic gift any damage caused by the bad temper.
The real exchange was in services rather than material goods. In this case,
the exchange of services involved William providing banking services,
credit, and introductions to business whilst Joseph provided legal services, advice and links to the agricultural mortgage market. The gift was

[50] William Lupton to Joseph Rider, 27 October 1824. Lupton 124.
[51] Joseph Rider, Thirsk to William Lupton, 10 October 1827; William Lupton to Rider,
undated draft. Lupton 122.

carefully controlled. The argument over the accounts showed that rights and claims were enforced with some precision as an aspect of the trust which the network required for its smooth working.

Reputation and trust were vital to the working of the network. This was why the dispute with David Rider was so important. All the indications were that David was incompetent rather than dishonest, had tried to cover his mistakes and then that William Lupton had assumed that the accounts he held for the Thirsk Riders would, at least for a time, cover the losses incurred by David.

> Your brother has shown me your letter of Saturday written with an impression quite different from what is my view of the case. In the conversation you allude to the amount of the returns of last year were stated, upon which any calculation of profit was grounded – it is the continuance of not getting this profit, together with making purchases on speculation, that is when we have no orders for the goods that form the grounds of dissatisfaction.

It was too much trouble to find what had happened since Darnton became a partner but, as far as William could see, no profits had been made. David could provide no proof that profits had been made and the balance of the accounts showed trade to be in debt.

> As to the proposal that has been hinted at, it may be needful to state what it was – Your brother is in debt to the concern £1895 3 10 exclusive of interest, to which will be to add about £750 belonging to two of your sisters which although entered to his account I consider myself to be responsible for – The trade is in as much deficient as would I apprehend take all his share of the value of your father's estates to make up his proportion of the loss and the proposal mentioned to me was to add £500 to all these sums for the sake of quietness.[52]

Reputation mattered to both of them and Lupton said he would go to arbitration 'but for the unpleasantness of exposing such affairs even to confidential friends'.[53] The same sentiments were expressed as they managed the outcome of Jonathan's bankruptcy,

> certainly take the earliest opportunity of suggesting to the other parties interested the purchase of Jonathan's share. I fully agree with you on the expediency of keeping it in the Family.[54]

The loss of reputation for John Stocks was not really the matter of his bankruptcy, for that was an experience shared and feared by many in the network, but the belief that he was failing to make an effort. This was what

---

[52] Undated letter from Darnton Lupton to Joseph Rider. c.1827–28. Lupton 122.
[53] Darnton Lupton to Joseph Rider. c.1827–28.
[54] Joseph Rider to William Lupton, 13 November 1824. Lupton 124.

made Uncle Wareham so awkward. In September 1824, he told Sarah, '...I do not understand the question, but am convinced that it is from Mr Stocks own active personal exertions that permanent good can alone be expected'.[55] Both John and Sarah talked of his illness. Be it drink or depression, nothing was said. Quite different was the treatment for Jonathan. He was subjected to plenty of advice but care was taken to buy him out from the assignees and secure both his status and that of the network. The near disaster of Sarah Stocks was linked to the destruction of trust between her and Uncle Wareham and, ultimately, between her and her husband for she was taking care that John Stocks did not know about the small sums which Lupton was sending to her. Her rescue depended upon her trust for William Lupton and, through him, Jo Rider.

There were many features of the networked family as a risk-spreading institution but a crucial one was the subordinate status of women. This status was secured by the legal personality, or lack of it, of married women and by the exclusion of women from active economic positions, especially major positions in commerce and the professions. Often this subordination was enforced by simple ignorance. Mary Rider made occasional contributions to the dispute but confessed she found the accounts incomprehensible and told Lupton,

As I before requested, you may settle my Brother Joe's account out of mine and pay me the balance. I have not paid any attention to the interest, not knowing how to calculate it.[56]

This was important, for accounts had iconic status in the argument and the inability of the sisters to fully understand what was happening ensured their subordination. Ignorance played an even more important part in Sarah Stocks's misfortunes. Uncle Wareham kept her ignorant of his manipulations of her money, whilst her husband was equally limited in the information he gave his wife.

These processes created a legal, social, economic and moral personality which was not only limited but also 'protected'. The main feature of this was the trust, established by a variety of means, but mainly through wills and testaments. The legal trust provided the women concerned, and the nuclear families and households of which they were members, with a protected income flow. The £20–£30 a year income which Sarah had from her mother's trust was little more than an unskilled casual labourer might expect in the market economy, but in her personal and family crisis

---

[55] Thomas Wareham to Mrs Stocks at Mr Beetons, St Anthony's Church Yard, Watling St, 4 September 1824. Lupton 124.
[56] Letter Mary Rider to William Lupton, 23 February 1828. Lupton 122.

it was the difference between destitution and survival. This subordinate and protected status showed in a variety of ways. Such status entailed specific types of respect and protection from the active males of the network. Jo Rider exploited such assumptions as he directed his anger at William Lupton,

I am now writing for my sisters not for myself. You must be aware how painful it must be to me to prolong a correspondence on this subject with yourself whom, till the late schism between you and my brother, I had always been accustomed to consider as most remarkably willing to meet and remove difficulties, where any existed – It is needless for me to say . . . that late events have changed that favourable opinion, I cannot but see that you raise objections for the sole purpose of annoyance, and I put it to yourself, whether such conduct towards two Females, who have placed implicit confidence in you, be becoming in a man whose character ought to be of some value to him – In this view of the subject I will say no more – I beg to leave it to the workings of your own conscience. You say that you have paid my sister's money to my brother David – Now, if that were so, you know that it was without their sanction or knowledge and your having misapplied the money would not make you less responsible . . . you have always treated these accounts as kept with your firm . . . it was a specific object of agreement made by yourself and your son Darnton, in my presence that the sum, which was to be paid to my brother on leaving the partnership was to be exclusive of the sums due by you to my sisters for which your firm was still to continue liable[57]

The care which both took of Sarah Stocks suggested that reputation, both within the network and of the network, depended upon the ability to sustain the network's dependent women at a minimal standard. In a sense, this was what many of the widowhood provisions of the wills were doing. The widows' limited rights were usually the first call upon an estate.

In all this a key figure emerged. The networked family was dominated by a number of 'patrons'. These were always adult males. Their position was defined by practice and by the status accorded them by others. William Lupton was just such a patron for the Lupton–Rider–Wareham–Stocks network. The qualities required were economic status, leisure, the trust of others in the network and an ability to negotiate and follow legal and economic practice. In the maelstrom of opportunity, risk and insecurity, which economy, society and demography provided for the British middle classes, the patron was in demand as executor, as trustee, as provider of banking services and provider of positions in commerce across a network built over three to four generations. Joseph Henry Oates and William Hey II held the same sort of place

---

[57] Joseph Rider to William Lupton, 29 February 1828. Lupton 122.

in their networks.[58] The patron's advice and approval were sought on many topics. He was expected to help with a wide variety of problems. The existence, effectiveness and authority of the 'patron' could have an important influence on the fortunes and ability to sustain risk of many members of the network. William Lupton's relationships with Nathan Rider's children showed how varied the activities of a 'patron' could be. In 1819, he had taken David Rider as a partner because he was sure of his 'integrity', a decision which proved a disaster. In 1822, he advanced £200 to Joseph Rider to help him develop his business as a solicitor in Thirsk.[59] This decision appeared to have worked well. Nathan's trust fund was the security for the advance.

A sum of £200 or thereabouts would for various reasons I am persuaded be of great advantage to me in business and I have already frequently felt the inconvenience of not having a fund of that kind to resort to. If it could be advanced whether through the medium of yourself or by my brother or sisters, it might be secured by a transfer of my share of the residuary property under my father's will. My practice is increasing, and I doubt not but it will eventually fully answer my expectations, but I think the sum I have mentioned would greatly assist me.

Patrons like Lupton appeared everywhere in family and community matters. He was prominent in the affairs of Call Lane Chapel. He was executor for the family and for the Briggate shopkeeper elite into which he had married.[60] He even acted for one Thomas Eagle, who had been committed to the Asylum at York, as well as for the property and affairs of his cousinage network.[61] There were advantages in addition to the obvious status. The flows of family capital in and out of the firm of William Lupton and Co were often a matter of the provision of banking services, but Lupton was not averse to retaining these flows in the business at times of seasonal difficulty. In 1824, discussing Mrs Stocks's money with Jo Rider, he wrote

Having lately been making extensive purchases, it would be more convenient not to pay it for a few weeks to come, but besides that is it not unusual before the money is paid to have the writings all ready ?[62]

[58] The patron had many of the qualities but also a geographical spread wider than that of the 'community broker' identified for mid-eighteenth century Colchester, S.D'Cruze, 'The middling sort in 18th century Colchester: independence, social relations and the community broker', in J. Barry and C. Brooks (eds.), *The Middling Sort of People: Culture, Society and Politics in England, 1550–1800* (London, 1994), pp. 181–207.
[59] Joseph Rider to William Lupton, 6 January 1822. Lupton 122.
[60] Executors' papers for Thomas Brunton, grocer of Briggate. Lupton 121.
[61] Papers relating to the estate of Thomas Eagle. Lupton 122.
[62] William Lupton to Joseph Rider, 27 October 1824. Lupton 124.

In return for services provided, Lupton gained a small amount of extra capital for trade, but he took care to justify the delay on grounds of legal practice rather than his own financial needs. The status and access to occasional bits of finance could be hard earned. There was Jo Rider's bad temper and the pleading of John and Sarah Stocks. Usually the cost was the tedious and meticulous attention to the detail required by other people's affairs. Take, for example, the matter of being executor for Mrs Elizabeth Hinchliffe of Leeds. This lady was embedded somewhere in the cousinage network. When she died she had no children alive but had buried two husbands. This left property to be 'turned into cash' and used to provide legacies for a vast range of second cousins, including Nathan Rider's children. The residue was then divided between a slightly different selection of second cousins. That was an excellent way of reminding everybody of how extensive the network was and how import- ant William Lupton was in that network, but it involved filling in Legacy Duty forms for each legacy and another round of taxation forms for the residue payments. In addition, there were letters finding out which cousin was still alive and, if not, who was entitled to their share. All this before the question arose of Mrs Hinchliffe's right to dispose of property, which had been part of the property within her first marriage, a serious matter because somebody wanted the silver watch.[63]

At times, being the patron of the network was a matter of being a point of reference for those in need of advice. It was to William Lupton that the troubled John Luccock wrote about the problems of being a family man far from home. Amongst the details of trade and bills of exchange to which he had committed the partnership was a sense in which commer- cial trust and matters of family were bound together.

You consider my letters it seems as a common property. I am glad if they afford entertainment but they are written with so little care and so frequently touch upon confidential circumstances that some discretion should be used in communicat- ing their contents and besides everyone will not view them with the partial eye that my friends do. To my children I have been generally anxious to impress some useful lessons applicable to their condition and circumstances in life with the hope that they would read them, not only on the day when they are received but in some future year when they can more fully appreciate the feelings of a fathers heart and may recollect with pleasure that they are possessed of a father who above all things was anxious that they should be qualified to fill their stations well and to enjoy as much of felicity as human nature can.[64]

---

[63] Executors' Papers for Mrs Elizabeth Hinchliffe, 1826. Lupton 123.
[64] John Luccock to William Lupton, New Orleans, 18 January 1823. Lupton 123.

William was on call across the network. Authority and responsibility were evenly balanced.

The story of Mrs Jane Hey

The family and property strategies of William Hey II were amongst the most successful and robust of the Leeds middle classes. He had inherited and developed the business of apothecary and surgeon from his father. He had inherited, developed and extended his share of his father's real estate. Five children had reached adulthood. At least two sons had entered the business, presenting William II with the prospect of a pleasant 'retirement'. His daughter had married John Atkinson, son of a leading Briggate shopkeeper–tradesman and leading Tory Anglican solicitor. William II's impact on the urban landscape of Leeds still survives where he burrowed his way out from the front-of-street Briggate property he had inherited and made his contribution to the first 'west end' of Leeds in the form of the elegant mansions of Albion Place and the high status shops of Commercial Street. This success was marred and threatened by the premature death of his son, John. It was not clear what went wrong but, by the end of 1837, John was dead, leaving the plans for the business in disarray and leaving a widow, Jane, with six children.

William II moved to repair the damage. He returned to share the business with William III, his surviving son, and took care to ensure the welfare and support of his dead son's family. Evidence of the immediate form of support does not survive but, in 1844 when William II died, his will indicated the resources and strategy available for the support of Jane and her family. By his will dated 2 February 1841, he directed that

I give and devise my estate situate on the north side of Commercial Street in Leeds aforesaid consisting of five several dwelling houses and shops with the appurtenances unto my said son William and my son in law John Atkinson of Leeds aforesaid Solicitor . . . to the use of my daughter in law Jane, the widow of my late son John and her assignees during her widowhood . . .

After that, the property was for the benefit of his six grandchildren, John, Frances, William, Janet, Charles Edward and Caroline Emily as tenants in common.[65] In addition to this, William II set aside £1000 for Jane and her family, as well as her share of the residue. The sworn value of the estate was 'under £30,000' which, given that William, then in the later stages of the life cycle, was unlikely to have large debts, meant that Jane's trust was likely to have received around £5000 from her fifth.

[65] Will of William Hey, died 2 February 1841. DB 75/2.

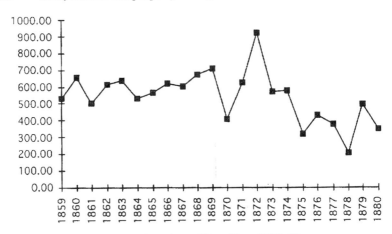

Fig. 7.9 Summary of receipts of Jane Hey, 1859–80.

The relationship between Jane and John Atkinson produced a series of letters that reflected the voice of the widow whose property consisted of that very specific and limited form, the rights to an income stream under a trust. They revealed the mixture of dependency and agency which was entailed in the trust. The letters reflected concern and deference but a determination to sustain the welfare and progression of her own family. She was acutely aware of her own status both in terms of rights and obligations. What emerged was a relationship of assertive subordination. The letters went first to John Atkinson and then to John William, his son, who took over the task of managing the trust when his father died in 1855. The letters began in the late 1840s and usually had three parts. There were thanks for money received, questions about the management of the trust and chatter about the family.[66]

No formal accounts survive but the information in the letters was enough to reconstruct Jane's income flow in the 1860s and 1870s. She received a mildly fluctuating income of around £500 which declined in the late 1870s. This, with care, was quite enough to sustain a middle class household and set the children on their way in the world.

The letters showed Jane Hey totally embedded in the family into which she had married. There was no mention of parents, brothers or sisters. She was part of the Hey family and the trust was a key

[66] This account was based upon letters and receipts in the Atkinson and Hey family papers, deposited with the West Yorkshire Archive Service, Sheepscar, Leeds, especially DB 75/14, DB 75/16 and DB 75/17.

mechanism to achieve this. There was an undercurrent of anxiety and vulnerability which revolved around the appropriate actions to sustain her status in the network. John Atkinson and then John William were often reference points. There was the matter of family funerals in the 1840s in which the distress of recent widowhood was very evident.

I ought to have written to you before to acknowledge the rct of £55 – but as you gave it to me in the presence of many witnesses you will not have been very uneasy. I wish we could have seen a little more of you – but not having been asked to go to the funeral of course I could not. It seems Samuel had got a notion that because I did not go to Isabella's funeral abt 12 yrs ago and because I had then said that ladies did not go to funerals at WCastle I would never go to one, and that I was not even to be asked whether I would or not – consequently the subject was never mentioned to me. I never was more astonished in my life when they told me yesterday. I was very much disappointed not to be present. A great deal more must have been made of my declining Richard's request than I ever intended. The only reason for not going (Wh however I did not mention thinking that it would be divined) Was that my own great sorrow was then too recent for me to bear to go to St Paul's Church on such an occasion – I felt I should break down and I don't like either for myself or others to do so in public. I mention these things because I know it was thought odd that I was not present. I should quite have enjoyed it. The service is so sublime and edifying and I should never have thought of not going when the ladies of the family went[67]

Even towards the end of her life, when she had completed the difficult task of bringing up her family, she was still checking the dos and don'ts of her position with John William,

but in all these matters I don't understand that I ought to have an opinion but only be guided by Uncle Hey and yourself by whom the money is held in trust for myself and children under their grandfather's will at least this is always as I have understood the matter as explained to me by your father.[68]

Despite the shaky grammar and the deference, Jane had not omitted to give an opinion. Throughout this correspondence, which continued into the 1880s, there was always the powerful presence of the dead.

I feel very much averse to do anything not quite in accordance with a will . . . I am surprised that Uncle Hey did not know that Debenture Stock was not an investment that could properly be made seeing that I hold some at present.[69]

[67] Jane Hey to 'Dear John' (Atkinson), 24 April 1852 Barrowash. DB 75/16.
[68] Jane to John William Atkinson, 22 October 1872. DB 75/17.
[69] 'My dear John Wm from your very affectionate aunt Jane Hey, Ockbrook', 20 April 1870. DB 75/14.

Jane had settled at Barrowash on the railway line between Derby and Nottingham. She was just south of the village of Ockbrook, where the parson was 'Uncle Hey', who became one of her trustees on the death of John Atkinson in 1855. This was a difficult parish dominated by its Moravian settlement. Samuel Hey does not seem to have been in good health but found replacement and help difficult as the parish needed people of some quality. In 1852, two other family members had been considered and rejected.

Robt would not have done for Ockbrook. the people have not the slightest attachment to the Church and unless the preacher is attractive (which Robt certainly is not) they won't go. The congregation would soon have consisted merely of the respectable inhabitants and their servants which was pretty much the case before Mr Hey had curates and having been accustomed to very interesting preaching of late they would feel the difference the more.[70]

Despite the evidence of potential family patronage, the Heys were a family who took their religion seriously. A branch of them had settled in the area and another household was established in the area living at nearby Sawley on the Trent near Long Eaton.

Jane Hey's anxieties were many as she constructed her status as a widow in the Hey family and planned the strategies to undertake her obligations. There was her own probity and creditworthiness. As financial pressures grew, she worried about being overdrawn at the Bank and insisted on paying her bills when they were due. In 1866, she wrote

I fear my tenants must have lost all their money by the Bank failures they are so long in paying their rents. I shall be very thankful to receive them for, as tradesmen say 'I have many heavy payments to make' at the beginning of the half year and I have nothing to pay them with – Uncle Sam says the only safe wy of banking now is to be on the wrong side of your bankers book. no doubt it is so but I am old fashioned enough not to like it.[71]

In part, this anxiety and the deference that went with it were a weapon with which she belaboured poor John William who, by now, was doing most of the work. Above all Jane Hey was concerned about family and that meant her children. In 1858, she told John William,

It is my duty you know to look after my children's property and when people are much engaged in their own business I am sure it is no wonder that other people's affairs slip thro. The said money would have been quite lost to them if I had not remembered it.[72]

[70] Jane Hey to 'Dear John', 24 April 1852, Barrowash. DB 75/16.
[71] Jane to JW, 22 February 1866. DB 17/17.
[72] Jane to JW, 25 February 1858. DB 75/17.

During the period of these letters, her children moved in various ways through their teens and twenties. This was a family amassing human capital and, hence, needing support during the vital period when professional men gained education and experience. The Hey network produced clergymen and medical men in large numbers. William was attending medical college in London. In 1850, Jane asked John Atkinson for advice,

had a letter from Mr Cunningham of Kings Coll: the other day in which he seems rather to advise me to enter Willie 'Perpetual' as it is called to every class, payment fee which is £107.2s instead of £96.12 for Coll & Hospital Fees – I shall be much obliged if you will tell me which is best . . . I suppose it is generally considered the best plan for the Students to reside in the College though I hear Edwrd did not find the situation to agree with him.[73]

The matter troubled her all winter and in April she wrote,

Dear John
  As I wrote on Sunday to acknowledge the rct of your letter I could not mention a matter abs which I wish to know how you will think it best for me to proceed. The fact is I am fairly aground for this quarter and I want to know whether it will be best for me to overdraw my account at the Bank in the hope that I shall be righted next half year, which will probably be the case, or whether it would be better to dispose of my Leeds Water Works shares – Samuel advocates the former – It is a thing I dont much like, but as I have never done it before, I should not have much hesitation about it – The entrance fees etc of Kings College are the things that have hampered me and also the circumstances of my having received less from the shops and from Railways.[74]

She was allowed, under the will, to ask her trustees to draw on the capital for her children's education but to do so would have reduced future income and the evidence of the letters showed that sustaining her children in the status ranks to which the Heys were accustomed was not easy. Jane's sons John and Charles William went into the church but their progress became entangled with plans for marriage.

Charlie and his Ellen have just left us this morning – She is a very nice ladylike girl and sings beautifully – I am very pleased with her in every way.[75]

But matters were not as simple as that.

Charlies 'alarming sacrifice' is not to take place for some time. Dr Ch** made them promise not to marry for 18 months and then of course it will depend on

[73] Jane Hey to 'Dear John', 18 September 1850. DB 75/16.
[74] Jane to John Atkinson, 16 April 1851 Barrowash. DB 75/16.
[75] Jane to JW, 30 October 1861. DB 75/17.

circumstances whether they do or not. I think he has been a fortunate man. We like Ellen very much. You would admire her voice and singing.[76]

Matters were equally delicate for John.

John's engagement was kept secret for some time because Miss Metcalfe's mother did not like it to be called an engagement till he got a living. However as she was allowed to come here with the acknowledged character of an engaged person we don't of course consider it a secret now. We all like and admire her very much.[77]

In both cases, the pressure for delayed marriage came from parents. When the weddings did take place, they provided yet more pressure on Jane's finances.

I do find an error in yr acct which turns the tables in my favour. You have omitted to enter £100 E I Coupons... I am selfish enough to rejoice in the mistake for Weddings under the most favourable circumstances are very expensive affairs, and two within a year is rather heavy work.[78]

The demands on her income were fairly hectic during this period.

I have had a letter from John this morning asking for money and as I have none to give him I must come upon you. Will you be so good as to send me the East I Coupons. I have also the Debenture Coupons £8.16 I did not receive last 1/2 yr. I fear you find it difficult to get Uncle Heys signature but may I suggest the post as a medium of communication and if he would send the coupons direct to Uncle Sam for his signature it would save time of course I should direct the rcpt to you.[79]

My children are all crying 'give, give' and I have nothing to give them – I have only received £149 from you this yr and the Railway Coupons/Indian have not been recd by me – I think the interest of the money Gt Uncle Hey has in his hands and also Bicker's qrs rent are due sometime in the beginning of this month.[80]

These were difficult years but Jane's strategy was clear; she wanted to establish her children.

Do you think you can let me have the E I Coupons before the 25th? I am anxious to help Charlie as much as I can to pay his bill for furnishing and an instalment is due on that day... He is so hard worked with the Cathedral and his Church and Parish – John I think has got a very nice thing but unfortunately it is not a permanency.[81]

Given her ambitions and sense of obligation to her children and the task she had inherited on her husband's death, Jane Hey lived very close to the

[76] Jane to JW, 6 November 1861. DB 75/17.
[77] Jane to JW ,15 July 1863. DB 75/17.
[78] Jane to JW, 13 October 1864, Barrowash. DB 75/17.
[79] Jane to JW, 3 March 1863, Barrowash. DB 75/17.
[80] Jane to JW, 1 April 1862, Barrowash. DB 75/17.
[81] Jane to JW, 11 March 1865, Barrowash. DB 75/17.

edge of her income. Her problems indicated the limits of the trust form. It was true that the capital could be drawn upon for the education of her children, but she could not begin to move that capital into the high risk, high income potential areas which required entrepreneurial inputs. All she could do was to ensure that the rents and dividends arrived on time and question the year-to-year management of her trust in the assertive and deferential manner which fitted her status. John William was given an especially difficult time in the 1860s.

Property had many meanings for Jane Hey. Accounts and receipts were especially important to her. In 1847, she worried that she did not have a written acknowledgement of money in the hands of Uncle Hey. As financial pressures mounted on her in the 1850s and 1860s, she made more frequent demands for a statement of accounts from John William. 'I am not able today to compare particularly our accounts but I have no doubt I shall find all correct. If I do not I will let you know'.[82]

There was always a courteous delight when she found an error and John William was informed of the matter in no uncertain terms.[83] As in so many cases, these accounts had a powerful and iconic status in regulating relationships between family members. For people like Jane they were not simply a matter of recording and validating obligations and rights but also a means of maintaining control at times of financial pressure. As family financial pressure grew, she was keenly aware of her bank account. 'I don't like to draw my banker dry', she told John William in May 1861. There was evidence that record keeping was quite casual in a family in which mutual trust was high, but Jane's concern had a practical side. She wanted a record of money she had left in Uncle Hey's hands and explained,

the only reason that Samuel mentioned for having it invested was that human life is so uncertain and that if Uncle Hey were to die, which heavens forbid and there was no acknowledgement of his having the money in his hands there might be some difficulty about it[84]

Jane was also enmeshed in a world of coupons, debenture and share certificates. Again, she was anxious that these should always be in the right hands. These documents, their signs and symbols, mediated between her and the world which produced her wealth. The Empire was a matter of East India Railway Debenture Stock, whilst nearer home the London and North Western and Great Eastern produced other and equally crucial flows of income.

[82] Jane to JW, 6 November 1861. DB 75/17.
[83] Jane to JW, 13 October 1864, Barrowash. DB 75/17.
[84] Jane to JW, 25 February 1858. DB 75/17.

In Jane's letters there was a sense of property as gendered knowledge of which she was on the edge. It was good gender politics to plead ignorance of property and this she did.

I shall be quite satisfied with any arrangements you and Uncle Hey make abt the Indian debentures and am only too thankful to have my business matters settled for me as I am shamefully ignorant abt debentures stock etc etc.[85]

A year later she was asking,

if anything has been done abt raising the Rents of the shops. I suppose the tenants will require some notice perhaps before Xmas. I don't understand these things but of course you do.[86]

This was all very well but Jane was anything but ignorant and personal politics demanded that she be well informed. She knew about bank failures and property management. The letters show that she discussed investment and loans and the quality of the latest railway share issues.

I am sorry to trouble you but I cant help feeling anxious abt the Llynn and Ogmore – Why dont they pay the int? I feel the more anxious as I have been told that the Welsh Railways generally are bad investments. What does Uncle Hey think of it?[87]

As the pressure on family finances grew, she knew exactly when to expect payment from the various investments of the trust. 'I have not received the Manchester and Sheffield coupons this year. They used to be sent in January and July. Uncle Sam has been out of sorts lately'.[88]

When it came to the details of property management regarding the Commercial Street shops, the Atkinsons mediated between her and the immediacy of negotiating with tenants and arranging repairs, but she was well informed. There was a question about rents in the late 1840s and she knew about evidence in bank books and William Hey's account books, which showed that rents had been raised after improvements.

What a plague them tenants is! I am truly sorry you have been to so much trouble on my account and greatly obliged by all you have done . . . I am sure I ought to be thankful that on the whole my money matters have been so flourishing and neither be surprised nor cast down when any little loss occurs but I do feel annoyed that you should be so much bothered and not the less so because you do all for me with such good will – I don't know whether this is a good time of year for letting shops

[85] Jane to JW, 14 December 1870. DB 75/17.
[86] Jane to JW, 17 November 1871. DB 75/17.
[87] Jane to JW, 6 August 1872, Ockbrook. DB 75/17.
[88] Jane to JW, 16 Aug 1862, Barrowash. DB 75/17.

but as I hear trade is reviving everywhere I hope you may not have much trouble in procuring a satisfactory tenant[89]

She knew the qualities of the various tenants.

Carry has just discovered that Uncle Hey says Bickers wants a lease. I don't see any objection as he is such a good tenant. What do you and Uncle Hey think? Your decision will satisfy me.[90]

I quite agree with you and Uncle Hey as to the advisability of letting Mr Hopkinson make the alterations in the premises he wishes – A good tenant is not to be despised.[91]

Jane never voted in an election, but her sense of property and family linked the two in her mind. When the sale of the Commercial Street shops was suggested, she was cautious and had the interests and status of her male children in mind.

With respect to Hopkinson's buying the property, I trust entirely to your and Uncle Sam's judgement who has now I suppose succeeded to the trust. John may have a wish to keep the property as by having it, I suppose both he and Charlie would have a vote for Leeds when they succeed to it upon my death . . . We have still a little snow upon the ground.[92]

There was a tense relationship between Jane Hey's ambitions and her income, with its rigidities and uneven flows. At the same time, she was often prepared to soften the edges of the hard and precise contract implied in the accounts in order to sustain the family network. There was the question of Uncle Sam Hey's interest in 1850. Uncle Samuel seemed to have borrowed money from the family trust [at a good market rate of interest], and then suffered a reduction of income when the dividends on his railway shares fell. Jane's response was immediate.

Of course you are aware that the last named gentleman is in great pecuniary difficulties and so I told him I would only receive the same interest for my money that he does – I believe he gets 3 or 3½P.Ct (I forget which) and pays me 5%. He would not agree to this but I think he might be brought to it if you and Wm do not disapprove. I suppose if the money had been invested in any other way the rate of interest would have decreased and therefore it seems scarcely right that I should not bear some share in the deficiency . . . he might pay me less till things look up again if ever . . . Samuel is in good spirits and retrenching in earnest. James has had notice to leave and the Horse and Phaeton are to be sold . . . I have recd Aunt Hudson's legacy and the rent of the warehouse.[93]

---

[89] 'Dear John', 13 June 1850, Barrowash. DB 75/16.
[90] Jane to JW, 3 November 1863 Barrowash. DB 75/17.
[91] Jane to JW, 20 June 1865, Barrowash. DB 75/17.
[92] Jane to JW, 12 February 1876, Ockbrook. DB 75/17.
[93] Jane Hey to 'Dear John', 13 March 1850. DB 75/16.

John Atkinson and William Hey must have decided on a more modest reduction, for Jane wrote a few days later that she had shown their letter to Samuel

> He says he is perfectly satisfied with the decision. It is not quite so much in his favour as I expected but as you and William think it right and give such good reasons for your opinion I have nothing to do but to agree . . .[94]

Samuel was in some need of assistance. He wrote to John Atkinson the following day,

> my chief trouble is, that I don't know where this reducing will end. If I were satisfied on solid grounds that we are at the worst, my tail would rise an inch or two at once – It has not been below the horizontal all thro' – because the moment I saw the reduction of the dividend, I determined on the reduction of the establishment. I sent an advertizement to the Wednesday's paper and by the following Monday morning, phaeton, cart, horse, harness, saddle, in short every scrap of articles connected with the stable were sold and money received.
> You must bear in mind that besides Jane's loan Richard holds a mortgage of £1200 at 4½% on my Sutton Farm. There ought to be a little reduction of interest there I think . . . I shall want another share selling to make me straight, my calculation being quite thrown out.[95]

Here the economy of the gift was very much in evidence from a woman who had experienced the family network's 'rescue' from the disaster of widowhood.

Property was a matter of share coupons and dividends, of shops and tenants in Commercial Street and relationships with trustees and family. It was also a matter of capacities. It was a means to an end. The trust produced the income which sustained the status and welfare of children and household. 'I pay my rents on the day', she wrote at one point when asking where her money was. She could protect the vulnerable. There was Charlie with his weak chest and the trips to Ilkley and Scarborough instead of Leeds which did not agree with him. Property gave her the capacity to sustain them in their education and early marriage. As she wrote to John Atkinson early on 'I often think dear John, how thankful we ought to be, that so far, our children are so promising'.[96] This property placed her for ever in the family into which she had married and in which she had been widowed. The network had safeguarded her through the trust with property in a very specific form. She managed this relationship with commitment and skill. Her assertive deference was appropriate and

[94] Jane Hey to 'Dear John', 2 April (assume 1850), Barrowash. DB 75/16.
[95] Samuel Hey to 'Dear John', 3 April 1850, Sawley. DB 75/16.
[96] Jane Hey to 'My dear John', Barrowash, 28 December 1846. DB 75/17.

gave her an agency that was as effective as it was limited. She had a sense of obligation and of subordination but with very clear claims and rights.

The letters of Jane Hey were a record of 'life after death' working with success. There was none of the crisis and anger as there was in the Rider and Stocks letters. The practices of the trust worked as they should to counter the damage done by premature death to family strategies. Jane remained, for the most part, self-directed. There was no evidence of threat or discipline. The boundaries of her actions were self-imposed. She was prisoner of her conscience and consciousness. Within that, her agency was complete. She operated within a set of rules to which all parties in her network of relationships referred. Some of these were the 'rational' rules of expert knowledge, of law, of medicine, of financial and property management. Others were the normative rules of the paternalist bargain. She fulfilled her allotted roles. She made demands upon the system. In this case, the system was able to supply the means and the support which enabled her to maintain the status of one element of the family and to place her children in middle class status positions. Like many males, she did not seek to reproduce father's occupation amongst her sons. The continuity of 'and son' was only one choice. She was able to use a wide range of resources, ability, inclination, capital – in this case human capital, and contacts to secure the results she wanted and her family expected.

The letters contained the day-to-day voice of a woman embedded in a family and network in which religion and religious identity were central, yet there was hardly a mention of a religious sentiment over more than 30 years of correspondence with two men, two family members who shared the same religious identity. The nearest she came to religion was the occasional mention of the work tasks of a village parson, the energy required to conduct the sacrament, deliver a sermon and catechise the children. Jane was sustained not by faith but by her family and social relationships and her own driving determination. She experienced gender as class and class as property. There was property in the direct sense of the Commercial Street shops with their rents, their repairs and the tenants. There was property in an indirect sense in the symbol system of shares, debentures and coupons, which delivered to the symbol system of bank account entries, which in turn delivered legitimate claims to the resources she required. Both these required the mediation of the male agents of the trust. In Jane's case, the system worked as it should to supply her with agency, material support, legal protection and limitations. The trust was a key element of the family as a risk spreading agency.

8   Networks and place

It is time to listen to two old ladies talking. Their words were written down in the 1890s by an uncle of Miss V.E. Oates of Geslingthorpe Hall in Essex who deposited them in the then Leeds City archives in 1946, assuring the archivist, 'my uncle was most accurate in all he said and wrote'. The memories focused on the years between 1820 and the 1870s. This was a record of chatter. It was about being a young woman in the Leeds of the middle classes. This was oral history by proxy with the voices of the two women talking of the best houses, intimate friends, gay parties and recording the alternations of enthusiasm and dismissal with which they judged the attractions of both sexes. The chatter began with Leeds but rapidly spread beyond the borough.

The argument of this book has proceeded in terms of property, of income, of trust and rents and dividends. The analysis has involved notions of status and network. These ladies recorded the way in which the processes and strategies involved were experienced and remembered by two keen-eyed participants once the account books had been put away, the advice manuals closed and the deeds lodged in the lawyer's office. The ladies showed a close knowledge of the Oates and Luptons. They knew of the Hey and Jowitt families but were not involved directly in those networks. One of the ladies had close links with Mill Hill Chapel and they had some links with the Call Lane congregation. This chatter, as it was recorded, was full of judgements of wealth and status and of personal qualities and relationships. They were full of a sense of place and a selective projection of family as genealogy. They provided an ideal source for mapping the meaning of network for these middle class families.

The two ladies were Miss Wainhouse and Mrs Buckle.[1] Miss Wainhouse was the daughter of Edward Wainhouse, merchant, who

---

[1] The reminiscences were written on a series of unnumbered manuscript sheets deposited with the West Yorkshire Archive Service at Sheepscar as C A Remin Oates. The account in this chapter was based upon those papers supplemented by material from the 1834 *Directory*, the 1832 and 1834 *Parliamentary Poll Book* and the database constructed for R.J. Morris, *Class, Sect and Party*.

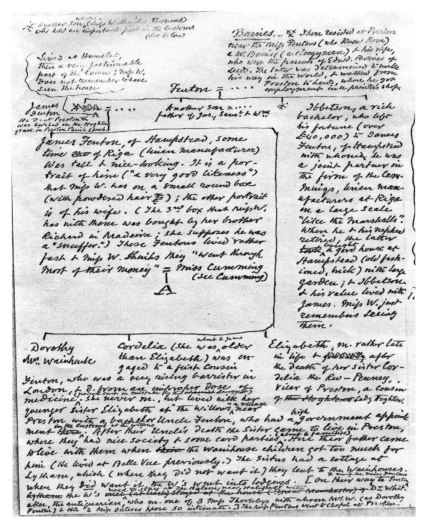

Fig. 8.1. Extract from the reminiscences of Miss Wainhouse.

lived at Belle Vue, built, or at least insured, for the first time in 1791–92, a rather isolated house in the growing west end of Leeds.[2] He was a fairly unremarkable member of the Leeds elite. He subscribed to the funds for the relief of the poor in 1829 and 1832 and he voted Tory for Michael Thomas Sadler in 1832 and for Beckett the banker in 1834. The

[2] M.W. Beresford, *East End, West End*, p. 309.

memories inhabited a world somewhere between the elite Unitarian Chapel of Mill Hill and the Parish Church on Kirkgate. Like the Oates, the Wainhouse family was part of the Mill Hill congregation. Like the Luptons, they were clothiers who became merchants. They owned land and property and were active in trade, imperialism and the professions throughout the nineteenth century. Mrs Buckle died around 1900 aged 93 and, despite outliving all her friends and indeed all her own children, she clearly enjoyed the privilege of the very old, namely judgemental reminiscence without fear of contradiction. She was born Mary Eastland into a minor branch of a Lincolnshire landed family with links to the Tennysons and Hildyards. She was orphaned as a very young child and, at the age of ten, came to live with her aunt, Mrs Rawsthorne, in Leeds. Here she celebrated the victory of the Battle of Waterloo, wore mourning for Princess Charlotte and married Francis Buckle, another unremarkable member of the merchant community of Leeds who had originated in Wensleydale. In the 1830s, his house, and probably his business, were in Wade Lane just west of Mrs Lupton's Merrion St estate.

The quality of their sense of network and family and place was at its best in Miss Wainhouse's account of the Fenton network, for her father had married into that network and his daughter's knowledge involved both detail and depth. There were several dimensions here. The first was family and its multiple relationships. Then there was the geography of the story. There was the structure of occupations and other claims upon income and property. Finally, there was an enthusiastic, often brutal, discourse of judgement drawing boundaries and assessing individuals. What mattered to the ladies was the relentless flow of detail, relationships and judgement which was family and society.

It is no good trying to give dates with any precision. This script has all the warnings of a good oral history transcript. The Fentons came from near Preston in Lancashire. They had links with a clergyman called Baines, father of Edward Baines the Leeds newspaper editor. This implied a mid-eighteenth century origin for the story. Some names are numbered for ease of reference.[3]

The Preston Fentons had four children.

---

[3] The next section has been written in a manner which attempts to reproduce the mixture of chatter and genealogy by which the two ladies provided us with access to the middle class families of Leeds in the first 70 years or so of the nineteenth century. One sheet of manuscript has been reproduced to indicate the way in which their questioner in the 1890s mediated this material. (Fig. 8.3)

James I   lived at Hunslet in the parish of Leeds but was buried in the 'Hogton' grave in Preston parish church.

Uncle Fenton   [it is Miss W who is talking] was founder of the Leeds Fentons who were Unitarians, unlike the rest who were 'church' people.

'another son'   held an important post in the Customs.

Ibbetson,   'a rich bachelor'.

It seems to be the next generation which set the social world for Miss W and where the geographies and judgements of her memories were most vital.

James I   had four children.

James II   was a linen manufacturer in Riga and settled in Hampstead. He was 'tall and nice looking'. These, the Fentons of Hampstead, 'lived rather fast' and 'Miss W thinks they went through most of their money'. James II married Miss Cumming.

Dorothy   married Edward Wainhouse from Halifax who settled in Leeds and was Miss W's mother.

Cordelia   was engaged to a first cousin, 'a rising barrister' in London who died 'from an improper dose of medicine'. She never married and went to live with bachelor Uncle Fenton [he who had the high government appointment] near Preston. 'After their uncle's death, the sisters (younger sister Elizabeth joined her) went to live in Preston, where they had 'nice society and some card parties (about six families)'. Here their father came to live with them when the Wainhouse children got too much for him. (He had lived at Belle Vue previously.) The sisters had a cottage at Lytham, which (when they did not want it), they lent to the Wainhouses . . .

Elizabeth   'married rather late in life after the death of her sister Cordelia. The Rev Penney, Vicar of Preston, a cousin of Lady Hogton'.

Now James II (Hampstead Fentons) married Miss Cumming and their children are worth attention as part of the network, its boundaries and exchanges.

Ibbetson   was the eldest son, carefully named after bachelor uncle. This strategy of nominal identity paid off as Uncle Ibbetson left his fortune of £40,000 to the Hampstead Fentons. Ibbetson himself was not such a good bet, however. He went into business with brother John. 'They were not successful. After he gave up business he lived in lodgings for a time in Boulogne; then settled in Brussels. He disappointed his family and married some one rather beneath him, but she was a good wife . . .'. Business failure and a socially unacceptable marriage placed Ibbetson on the boundaries of the group. Miss W retained a vague and imprecise knowledge of the Fentons of Brussels into the 1890s.

James III   'was a traveller for the Riga firm in which his father was a partner. He always dined and spent a day at St Anne's [the house in Burley was occupied by William Wilks, merchant, in 1834] whenever he came to Leeds, which he used to do on business. Mrs Grace took a great fancy to him and used to talk with him a great deal on these visits. He and his sister Dorothy were tall and gawky'.

John   'educated at Cambridge, took orders and preached a few times, but never had a living. Afterwards he joined his bro. Ibbetson in business and married a lady who was unfaithful to him. They did not live long together. He lived alone, half the year at Boulogne and half the year at Brighton'.

Margaret   'very pretty, was taken much into society by the Cummingses. She married Edward Bayley, who succeeded his brother Daniel as consul at St Petersburg'. Their son held 'a very high appointment in India'.

Janet   'Intimate friend of Lady Hunter and stayed with them when Sir Claudius Hunter was Lord Mayor of London'.

Dorothy   When Margaret died in St Petersburg she went there to look after the family.

Mary   'who probably may have lived alone at Hampstead at this time - she was the plainest of the family'.

The **Cumming** family required a brief explanation. The brothers John and Patrick were 'large linen manufacturers in Riga' and the family was based in London. John 'married a lady of high family. Miss W remembers being taken by Mrs James (II) Fenton to see her dressed for court. They had a very nice place near Barnet . . .' Their sister was Mrs James Fenton.

It is time to return to 'Uncle Fenton', founder of the Leeds Fentons. He had three sons.

James IV   eldest son, a bachelor who lived in lodgings. He was in great request at parties, as he was a pleasant man and a great talker; was a great deal at the Fentons of Hampstead (always a welcome guest there) and was very intimate with Mr John Marshall, who would always have him at his parties. He was constantly with Mr Marshall and a frequent visitor at the Wainhouses'.

Samuel second son. He lived in a good semi-detached house at Little Woodhouse, behind the house built by Frederick Oates (Belmont; another of the detached villas west of Leeds, now part of the University) and was in partnership with his brother James as a linen merchant. These Fentons took up with the Sadlers (two brothers Benjamin and Michael) who had an excellent draper's shop in Briggate, a few doors above Commercial Street (Miss W remembers seeing Benjamin serve in the shop and she thinks Michael did also). They took them into partnership. After Samuel's death (he died early) Benjamin Sadler married his widow and the younger brother Michael married his daughter. The Sadlers were High Church people and took the Fentons – this branch of them – away from Mill Hill Chapel. Michael Sadler entered public life, made many speeches and finally entered Parliament. When he made his speeches he always had Samuel Fenton in the background near at hand, sometimes behind a pillar to prompt him; could not get on without him; with him was very fluent.

William youngest son, 'in business in Leeds. He married someone quite beneath him and was cut by the family, so Miss W knew nothing about him. She had children. She thinks several'.

Finally, **Samuel**'s children. He married Miss Graeme. Their children were:

Samuel Graeme Fenton, eldest son. 'He conducted a branch of the linen business in Belfast for many years. Afterwards he retired and took up his residence at the Lakes, near Ullswater, but he did not long enjoy the latter'.

George second and youngest son in the army, died in India – an intense grief to his sister Harriet who was deeply attached to him.

Ann married Michael Sadler.

Harriet died unmarried.

There were several other bits of the network. There were the 'glass-house Fentons', another Leeds branch probably related to James I and named after their business. There were also the Wainhouses and the Sadlers.

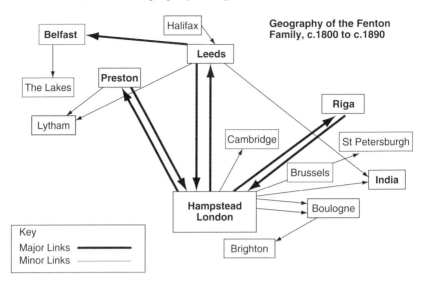

Fig. 8.2 The geography of the Fenton network.

The network had many aspects. The first was its geography. The Fenton network moved from Leeds to London to Riga and Belfast. Their neighbours in the pews of Mill Hill Chapel were the Oates. The family papers included not only the letters but also a list of deaths, births and marriages. These had been collected to form a family genealogy. Genealogy was important to these families, a sign both of the search for status and the need to assert identity against geographical dispersion. The outcome linked Leeds, London, Manchester, Jamaica and Seville and, in its structure, had a great deal in common not only with Fenton geography but also with other networks that can be mapped from the Leeds data (Fig. 8.3). Jane Hey's letters and the interactions of the Lupton–Rider–Stocks network provided two other maps. All had several features in common.

The most important dimension was the metropolitan one. It was rare for a network not to have a London link. England was an intensely metropolitan country. The great age of urban industrial growth, of Liverpool, Manchester, Birmingham and Leeds had resulted in London changing from being 12 times the size of its nearest rival to being five and a half times the second city.[4] Dominance was modified but never

[4] J. Langton and R.J. Morris (eds.), *Atlas of Industrializing Britain* (London, 1986) pp. 164–79.

Oates Family geography
   1780–1860

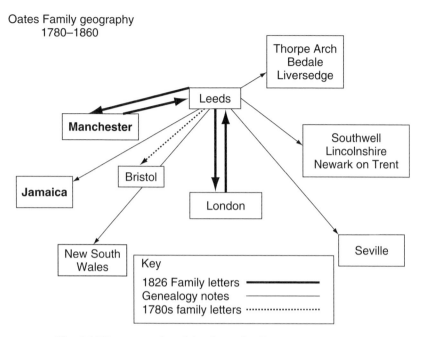

Fig. 8.3 The geography of the Oates family.

challenged. There were many reasons why this should be so. London remained the major finance centre. A family member in London was always an asset. In the financial crisis of 1825–26, Edward Oates, training as a lawyer, had been called into play to present some commercial bills for acceptance on behalf of his brother. This not only saved a few days which were vital in a liquidity crisis but also placed the matter in the hands of a family member who could be trusted to act with urgency, for Edward's income partly depended on the firm.[5] London was also a cultural and educational centre for the family. Miss Wainhouse started her schooling in Leeds but was then sent to a school at Campion Hill, Camberwell for two years. Here she was joined by the two Miss Bischoffs and Harriet Fenton and later by Margaret Oates. They spent the holidays at Hampstead. This served to consolidate the Leeds elite. The Fenton and Oates girls spend a great deal of time together at Low Hall back in Leeds. The schooling and visits to London also informed the girls about the London links and prepared them to sustain those links. At Hampstead

---

[5] See Chapter One.

she watched Margaret, daughter of the Hampstead Fentons. She remembered Edward Bayley, 'a very nice man, coming to Hampstead to pay his addresses'. There was also a cousinage link here from the Lancashire connection. James Fenton's brother-in-law, John Cumming, 'married a lady of very high family' and Miss W remembers being taken by Mrs James Fenton to see her 'dressed for court'. The Cummings also gave 'a very grand dinner party' every year, and Miss W travelled to London with the Marshalls to introduce them to the Cummings.[6] London provided the social stage which consolidated the family links of Fentons and Cummings as well as the elite identities of London Cummings and Leeds Marshalls. London was the place of medical college for the Hey family. It was also the place of contact for government employment, for employment in the many trusts, charities and corporations of the city. It was a great trading centre. John and Patrick Cumming were both major linen manufacturers in Riga. It was a place of economic failure for John Stocks. 'Blood' Atkinson, of the silk spinning Atkinsons went there and died 'in rather low water'. There was little sense of a north–south divide in these networks.[7] There was certainly a provincial–metropolitan relationship, which might bring disaster as it did for the Stockses, success as for the Fentons or simply anxiety as it did for the Oates.

The second dimension was trade. Leeds, Riga and Belfast were linked by flax. The Fenton–Cumming network moved around the Baltic and North Sea as the location of manufacturing, markets and raw material changed, always keeping a branch and contacts in London. Geography was not simply a matter of an international trading network but was sustained and extended by family and social links. There was gossip back in Leeds about the masked ball at St Petersburg at which Dorothy Fenton, she of Hampstead who was 'tall and gawky', who danced with Hamer Stansfeld of Leeds and 'attracted a great deal of attention, as she stood head and shoulders taller than he did'. Such gossip reinforced a sense of self and family that spread beyond Leeds and beyond the strict confines of trade for this event saw an overlap of the commercial and the

[6] The Marshalls were one of the wealthiest families in Leeds and, like the Fentons, members of Mill Hill Chapel. W.G. Rimmer, *Marshalls of Leeds*.

[7] The assertion of a north–south divide in economy and culture needs to be replaced by a sense of a provincial–metropolitan divide in terms of wealth and a metropolitan relationship in terms of culture. W.D. Rubinstein, 'The Victorian middle classes: wealth, occupation and geography', *Economic History Review* 30 (November 1977), 602–23; W.D. Rubinstein, 'Wealth, elites and the class structure of modern Britain', *Past and Present* 76 (August 1977), 99–126; Mrs Gaskell's novel *North and South* needs to be read in light of the manner in which family relationships link two aspects of provincial culture. Jane Hey would not have seen this as a division.

government service elements of the network. Then there was brother James, a partner in the Riga firm who always took time for his social contacts when he visited Leeds. Each network had dominant and associated interests. The Oates were wool and sugar. The Heys were medicine and the church. The Lupton–Riders were wool and woollen cloth. Even the choice of Thirsk as an outpost was not an accident as it was on the edge of a major hand loom weaving area centred on nearby Northallerton.[8] The overall distribution of the Leeds based networks reflected trade and industry. There were many links with Lancashire but few with the metal areas of Sheffield and the north east of England.

Empire was increasingly important. Sugar linked Bristol and Jamaica whilst the cheaper cloths of Yorkshire provided trade goods for Bristol merchants to export to the plantations. The Oates family spread along this network.[9] Empire had many meanings within these networks. Racial and cultural pride may well have been part of it, but India was the place where brother George had died and an uncle had 'a high appointment'. In other networks it might be different. For Mrs Jane Hey, struggling after her husband's death to maintain an elite bourgeois upbringing for her children, India was the place which provided dividends on the railway shares which would enable her to pay her son's university fees. Jane may not have appreciated it but the 5 per cent on the Indian Railway shares was a dividend underwritten by the Imperial Government.[10] They were much more secure than those Welsh railway shares that caused her so much worry. This India stock had a higher rate of return than government stock. Blood sacrifice and the anxieties of family strategies played a quiet part in the legitimation of imperial authority.

Lastly, came a group of smaller towns which gained a complex identity in the networks as retirement boroughs and places for health and recovery.[11] They were often crucial in urban–rural links. Thirsk was the place for the unmarried Rider sisters with their small but independent trust income. It was also the centre from which Joseph Rider found agricultural mortgages for Leeds money which was seeking rentier assets and land which

[8] Reports of the Assistant Hand-loom Weavers Commissioners, Part Two, *Parliamentary Papers*, 1840, vol. XXIII.

[9] K. Morgan, *Bristol and the Atlantic Trade in the 18th century* (Cambridge, 1993), pp. 90–106 and 184–218.

[10] W.J. MacPherson, Investment in Indian railways, 1845–1875, *Economic History Review*, 8, 2 (1955–56) 177–86; Captain Edward Davidson, R.E., *The railways of India: with an account of their rise, progress, and construction. Written with the aid of the records of the India Office* (London, 1868).

[11] R.J. Morris, 'The middle class and the British towns and cities of the Industrial Revolution, 1780–1870', in D. Fraser and A. Sutcliffe (eds.), *The Pursuit of Urban History*, pp. 286–30.

provided a store of value and an investment. Ockbrook and Sawley were small places. They were the part of the Hey network which Jane chose for bringing up her children on £500 a year. Not only did she have the support of the parsons in the family, but there were health reasons. The town of Ilkley and the nearby village of Ben Rhydding became especially important for Leeds people as health resorts. According to Mrs Buckle, there were not shops 'in the early days' and 'everything you wanted you had to bring with you from Leeds'. Even so the girls always liked to meet the coach from Ilkley to see who was getting off. The place was noted for its social prestige and for its mineral spring on the edge of Rombald's Moor and, by the 1840s, was gathering a collection of boarding houses, hotels and hydropathics as well as houses for those who were able to 'retire' there. Ilkley was important to Jane Hey for the visits which sustained her links with the family. She spent July there in 1850 and in 1874 she wrote 'After which we propose going to Ilkley – We hope to get refreshed and strengthened there for the heat has made me in particular very weakly and the shock of poor Miss Robert's death has shaken me a good deal – . Arthington is our last destination'.[12] From the start of her letters, she regarded Leeds with grave suspicion. In 1847 she refused to send her son John for a visit. 'I am anxious to keep him in the country as long as I can . . . as Leeds never agrees with him'.[13] Given the premature death of her husband, she had every right to be cautious of Leeds. Visiting brought Jane to Ilkley and the other 'health places' which became increasingly important to the middle classes. First they were places to visit and then places to live in away from the coughs and colds and chest complaints of Leeds.

The retirement location had always been an aspect of middle class life cycle strategy. As the parliamentary boundary commission surveyed those small country towns which had parliamentary seats under the old franchise, they noted that in many of them, as at Thirsk, there were rows of houses for those who had retired from the manufacturing towns.[14] The Lake District featured in the Fenton story as the final destination for a successful life cycle strategy. There were Torquay and Sidmouth on the south coast of England where Harriett Gott and Ann Lupton, Arthur's widow, finished their days. These locations drew together fragments of many middle class networks. Brighton and Boulogne were filling with families and single people who were living on the coupon clipping rentier

[12] Jane Hey to J.W. Atkinson, 28 July 1874, from Ockbrook. DB 75/18.
[13] Jane Hey to John Atkinson, 18 January 1847. DB 75/16.
[14] Parliamentary Boundary Commission, Reports, *Parliamentary Papers* 1831–32, vols. XXXVII–XXXIX.

income of joint stock companies or the remittances from legal firms which collected property income in distant towns. Retirement places were not always a matter of successful life cycle strategy but also shelters in times of failure. Boulogne provided such shelter for the weaker elements of the Fenton network, who had suffered marriage break up and failure in business. They would have met plenty of Leeds networked people. Thomas Bischoff, one of the Bischoff brothers who did not do well in business, was a frequent visitor. Bell Fenton of the Glasshouse Fentons went to live there with Miss Strickland. Joe Teale, the surgeon was less ambitious; 'his health failed and he went to live in Leyburn'.[15]

A strong network had a geographical shape which took in all or most of these types of location for this gave members a wide variety of options in terms of those opportunities which would help make best use of the variety of talents, qualities and inclinations of family members. Such variety and spread also gave them a variety of opportunities to cope with problems presented by health, demography and the economy.

The concept of network, both for the historian and the participants, can and could become amorphous and imprecise. There was no legal or bureaucratic definition like a census household, the table of kindred and affinities in the Anglican Book of Common Prayer[16] or the table of inheritance in Blackstone's account of the laws of England.[17] The network was amorphous because its existence needed to be constantly confirmed and reaffirmed by actions. To be a member of such networks was to have serious claims and hence membership was subject to serious scrutiny as Miss W indicated,

His (talking of her father) parents lived at Halifax but Mr W always declared that he had no relations there of that name. A Miss Wainhouse with a brother, a major in India came from Halifax to Belle Vue to claim relationship, but Mrs W said she did not establish the relationship and she was never heard of again.

The boundaries of the network were set in various ways. Two of the Fentons were marginalised because they failed to choose appropriate marriage partners. Ibbetson of the Hampstead Fentons disappointed in both business and marriage whilst William, the youngest son of 'Uncle Fenton', was even worse. He 'married someone quite beneath him and was cut by the family'. Whatever his fault, there was a William Fenton who was coal owner and merchant with property on the river near Leeds Bridge in the 1830s.

[15] This was a small market town in the North Riding of Yorkshire.
[16] C. Neill and J.M. Willoughby, *The Tutorial Prayer Book* (London, 1912), pp. 574–5.
[17] Sir W. Blackstone, *Commentaries*, vol. I, pp. 204–40.

In a very imprecise manner, gender and marriage provided another boundary to the mental map of family. The population of Miss W's memory comprised thirteen men and eight women, an unlikely ratio. The gender ratio of the 1851 population was 104 women to every 100 men, and likely to be higher for the adult population. The marriage fate of two of the men was not given. Of the remainder, 50 per cent of the women and 27 per cent of the men were never married. This was in a population in which some 9–12 per cent were 'never married'.[18] It would take an addition of five women to make up the gender ratio. If it were assumed that these five were married, then the female never married ratio would be 31 per cent. Populations like the Fenton network had a low propensity to marry, and no wonder given the sanctions against those who made the wrong choice. These numbers argue that those who married were more likely to drop from the mental map of family, and that women who married were more likely than men to drop from the network. The network took good care of its unmarried for they provided care and companionship, especially the women. The unmarried, both men and women, when they made their wills, also redistributed their fortune back into the network.

Whatever formed the boundary of family, illegitimacy did not. There was Mr Banks, 'a great man, lived Hunslet way with his sister, Miss B. He also had a natural daughter who lived with him and who married when they went to live near Doncaster. This was his only fault. He was in business'. Then there were Mr and Mrs Prest who 'lived in Woodhouse Lane (near the Totties); with them lived a natural daughter of Mr Prest's and a niece of Mrs Prest's'. All this proved no barrier to social visiting. Mr Wainhouse danced with Mrs Prest, and the Marshalls, Wilsons and other elite families visited them when they moved into the country. In the relatively small population of men who made wills in the 1830–32 sample, there were three examples of men who included illegitimate children in their family. There was James Mann, who not only allocated real estate in Holbeck and Wortley to the four children of his marriage but also real estate in Halifax Parish to 'my natural children' by the late Sarah Speight.[19] George Green, the pawnbroker, made provision for Elizabeth Bowker, 'my reputed daughter'[20] and Joseph Bottomley, yeoman, left the residue of his personal estate to Martha Green, single-woman, and the rents from his real estate for the benefit of Esther

---

[18] E.A. Wrigley and R.S. Scholfield, *The Population History of England*, p. 260; M. Anderson, 'The emergence of the modern life cycle in Britain', *Social History* 10 (1985), 69–87.

[19] Probate 16 February 1830. Sworn value under £1000.

[20] Probate 23 May 1831. Sworn value under £100.

Green, 'my natural daughter'. She was required to pay the interest on the mortgage of £650 and would take full possession of the estate when she was 21 years old. This estate amounted to ten dwelling houses on Wellington Terrace just off the Kirkstall Road, occupied by Bottomley and others.[21] The illegitimate had an inferior status to the legitimate but they were not excluded. Mary Horner, the Holbeck publican, left small amounts to the two illegitimate children of 'John Horner'.[22] Finally there was a sad and instructive correspondence tucked away in the papers of John Atkinson, solicitor, he who had the initial care of Jane Hey's trust. It was an account of life on the very margins of a middle class family network. In July 1816, John Atkinson, by then well established in his Leeds career received a very troubling letter from the firm of Clitherow and Sellwood of Horncastle, a small market town at the foot of the Lincolnshire Wolds.[23]

We are sorry to have to inform you that your Nephew Thomas Atkinson after conducting himself in the most exemplary manner in our service so much as to gain our entire confidence has suddenly absconded and we fear after embezzling money to a very great amount . . . to the amount of £500 and upwards. From the manner of his getting away, we did not suspect him of some days, and from conversation that has fallen from him at different times with the other clerks we think his object is to get to New South Wales. We have sent in pursuit of him and shall in course take all possible pains to discover his retreat.

It is supposed that he has taken a young woman with him, his wife and four children he has left in this place. He has mentioned lately some little property that he expected to receive in Yorkshire . . . When we have examined his accounts from time to time he was always so very correct, that we have been lulled into security[24]

Pinned to the back of this letter were several others. The evidence was silent until 5 May 1829 when Elizabeth Atkinson wrote from 686 Bowling Lane, Bradford,

I address these few lines to your honours and I hope that you will take into consideration as I have been left with four children now, near fourteen years, with them and I have never troubled anyone, but I am obliged at present for I am in great distress and unless you can do something for my children I shall be forced to go where they belong at this time my youngest son is now lying on his death bed and is not expected to recover again . . . If you will remember them with anything

---

[21] Probate 28 November 1832. Sworn value under £100.
[22] Probate 15 November 1832. Sworn value under £1000.
[23] These quotations were from a series of letters contained in DB 5/73 in the Leeds Division of the West Yorkshire Archives Service at Sheepscar.
[24] Letter to Mr Atkinson, 27 July 1816, DB 5/73.

I shall be very thankful to you let it be what it will as they have no father to provide for them and for want of work I am not able. [25]

John Atkinson wrote back directly and received a reply from Abraham Barraclough, also of 686 Bowling Lane,

I want nothing for me or her. Its for the children. I will provide for her. And had I not provided for both her and children she would have been obliged to gone were she belong I have done as much for them as if they had been my own for both her and children have been out of work for eighteen weeks and run into great debt and I have had that to pay and likewise her son John Atkinson . . . I was at the expense of putting him prentice and buying clothes suitable for his business and if your honour will remember them with anything I will be very thankful . . . and for Mr Thomas Atkinson, her former husband she as not hear from him this last thirteen years and ten months. There was a gentleman from Horncastle about two years since and told her to make herself content and think no more about him for she would never see him again. [26]

In 1830 and 1831 other letters followed asking for more 'consideration'. There was an increasing but subdued sense of threat and desperation in the letters as family health and the Bradford economy presented them with crisis after crisis. Abraham, in his rough prose, was clear where his obligations lay,

the doctor wants his bill settling and its not in my power at present as I have clothing to provide for them suitable for maurning [young John had died] and there is three children still remaing, which I am not oblige to provid for them, a gain it would be hard to see them turned out of doors and no one to look after them . . . neither do I wish to wrong them one farthing and I hope your honour will be pleased to remember them with something at this present time for I know that I have paid fifty pounds for them one way or another since I married their mother[27]

It was not clear if the threat to send the children where they 'belong' was a reference to family or to Poor Law settlement but it would have been an action which revived the old scandal to the detriment of the John Atkinson network. None the less, the requests of Elizabeth and Abraham were targeted with great precision. They were for the children and related to sickness, to the consequences of unemployment (economic failure) and to the costs of setting the children up in the world. Talking of Thomas's daughter Ann, Abraham told John Atkinson,

[25] Letter from Elizabeth Atkinson to Mr John Atkinson, attorney, 5 May 1829, DB 5/73.
[26] Letter from Abraham Barraclough to John Atkinson, 9 May 1829. DB 5/73.
[27] Letter from Abraham Barraclough to John Atkinson, 4 February 1830. DB 5/73.

there will be a place could she obtain it the person wants four guineas and her work
for twelve months to learn both Straw Bonnet and dress Maker[28]

This was a very different world from that of Jane Hey with her worries
over Charlie's chest, the falling dividend income of Uncle Sam and the
need to pay medical college fees for William, but the occasions which
legitimated claims on the network were the same, children's sickness,
economic failure and the need to provide children with a means of earning
their living. The prose style was very different but the strategy of assertive
deference was recognisably the same. Elizabeth Barraclough was at the
very edge of the network. Her life was very different from that of Jane Hey,
but her brief link with the Atkinson network provided a small safety net in
the uncertain economy of Bradford.

An unsuitable marriage was more likely to exclude than an unsuitable
conception. In the examples unsuitable was defined in terms of class and
status. It was also defined in terms of religion. Miss W disliked the
marriage between Benjamin Sadler and Sam Fenton's widow; 'Her
marriage with Benjamin Sadler was quite unsuitable, as he was a high
churchman. After her marriage she came no more to Mill Hill Chapel'.
In matters of class and status, the boundaries could be quite porous but
the entry fee was almost always property. James Kitson, the son of a
publican and a letter carrier's daughter, made his way into the elite of
Leeds society through business success and participation in the culture
of the Mechanics Institutions.[29] Property was not always gained
with the very public legitimacy of business success. There was the case
of Mr Bingley, a stone mason who came unexpectedly into a large
fortune which was obtained for him by Mr Upton, who knew that
he was entitled to it. Mr B was 'quiet in society and passed muster
very well'.[30]

One boundary, more clearly defined than others, was between the
middle classes and the gentry. Miss Wainhouse recalled the instructive
case of the Ikin family. Members of the family were variously merchants
and solicitors.

The Ikins lived here first [Park Place] and gave large routs which Mrs Wainhouse
attended, then they went to Headingley, where they only kept dinner company
[perhaps there was one ball which Miss W attended]. Then Mr Ikin (rather
unexpectedly) had a fortune left him and they went to live at Leaventhorpe

---

[28] Letter Abraham Barraclough to John Atkinson, 8 November 1831. DB 5/73.
[29] R.J. Morris, 'The rise of James Kitson, trades union and mechanics institution, Leeds
      1826–1851', *Publications of the Thoresby Society* 15 (1972), 179–200.
[30] This was from Mrs Buckle.

amongst the country gentry. After this Miss W called once on them but it was too far to go on calling . . .

The Ikens succeeded the Bischoffs at Headingley. The Wainhouses were intimate with them and Miss W has stayed with them at Headingley and when the Ikens left (they went into the country near Fryston and became too grand for their Leeds acquaintances)

The Becketts and the Marshalls were wealthy middle class elite families who were making their way into the gentry. Miss W knew exactly what upward social mobility looked and felt like. They were 'proud'. 'The Marshalls were all proud. They thought they were very rich people and so they were'. John Bischoff she met at parties. He 'was not proud like the other Bischoffs'. Despite her origins in the Lincolnshire gentry, Mrs Buckle recorded no contact with them in terms of visits and parties.

The porosity and imprecision of the family as network was closely linked to the need for activity which constantly renewed and reaffirmed. Our old ladies' chatter provided a litany of the processes which glued such networks together. There were card parties, gay parties, balls, dinners, walks and above all just 'visits'. Miss W recalled the case of the Hainsworth household,

Mrs Wainhouse and James Fenton also joined their whist evenings, got up for the entertainment of Mr H who was paralysed and very bad tempered. After his Death Mrs H was very gay and gave many parties. Miss Wainhouse spent a very gay winter visiting her aunts the Misses Fenton at Preston.

Walks were part of the process which bound the Oates and the Fentons together. They went

with the two Miss Thoresbys . . . one of whom afterwards married Dr Whitaker who were very intimate with Miss Fenton and the Oates. They used to be fond of walking along the river side from Leeds to Kirkstall Abbey . . . and were escorted by Mr Thoresby brother to the Miss Ts. They would start in the afternoon and spend the rest of the day at Kirkstall taking refreshments with them.

Mrs Buckle recorded the same walk in the company of Miss Teale. There was a minor industry providing refreshments on these walks. Mrs Buckle went to gardens at North Hall and remembers 'cracknells with gooseberry jam on it – a great treat'.[31] For Jane Hey visiting was crucial. Visits gave a structure to her life, provided her with the information she needed and the opportunity to ensure that the males who guarded her trust took necessary action. The mobility brought by modest wealth was vital to her

---

[31] These were a crisp, hollowed out form of biscuit.

independence. In the 1820s Mary Oates made frequent journeys to Manchester to visit her sister who had married brother Joseph's partner in trade. In the process she brought news and simply reinforced the family links between the two partners.

All were well aware of the implicit bargain of the gift economy. The network was bound together by the exchange of resources and services. In many cases this was a simple matter of companionship and care. Unmarried women were crucial in this respect and often travelled very large distances like Dorothy who went to St Petersburg to care for children after her sister died, or the story of Old Wilson whose sister came to live with him when his wife died. These exchanges often countered economic and demographic disaster or were used simply to counter the unevenness of experience. The experience of Mrs Buckle and the aunt with whom she came to stay in Leeds demonstrated this. Miss Eastland, the aunt, was one of twelve children and went to Leeds to live with Mrs Dawson who was childless. On her death Miss Eastland got only £5000 of the £40,000 left by Mrs Dawson, but this was enough to enable her to buy a house in East Parade for £500. She then married Rawsthorne who went into business in Lancashire and 'lost all he had'. On his death, Mrs Rawsthorne, who had protected half her money through a marriage settlement, returned to Leeds and established herself in Park Row with three servants and her niece. In both generations the bargain involved the exchange of children from one household stressed by overcrowding or premature death to the household of the unmarried, the childless or the widowed. Mrs Creed was the widow of a Major Creed and 'having no children she brought up George Vincent, eldest son of Captain Vincent'. Vincent's wife had died shortly after giving birth. The bargain could take many forms. There was the lonely widow and the merry widow. The case of Mrs H who entertained her bad tempered husband with card parties had already been mentioned. Miss W's judgemental memory was even more precise than usual.

Mrs H did her duty to her husband 'duly and truly' during his long illness (he had to be wheeled in a chair from one room to another) and never took so much as a cup of tea out of her own house for 17 years. After his death she became a gay widow and kept a great deal of company, giving large parties. She was very lively and I think dressy.

She was less sure of the story of Mrs Frank Wormald, the honeymoon widow

She was a Miss Gott and m. a man much her senior, who died at Matlock on the honeymoon, six weeks after the marriage

Wormald was a partner of the Gotts,

an old bachelor who married late in life a Miss Gott and much to the annoyance of his nephews settled £2000 a year on her for life, which she survived him to enjoy for 40 years ... There was much talk and gossip about it at the time.

She married again to a Mr Allen and went to live in Scotland, returning to Leeds after her second widowhood, still with her £2000 a year before going to live with her sister in Torquay.

The gift exchange often involved considerable amounts of property as when Ibbetson, the rich bachelor left his fortune of over £40,000 to the Hampstead Fentons. It was almost universal for unmarried members of the network to direct resources back into the network. In other cases it was shelter which was on offer. This might be the cottage at Lytham for holidays or more serious assistance such as the aunts who took in children on the death of a parent. The notion of exchange was implicit in these relationships. It was a gift exchange and not a legal bargain which might be enforced in the courts. The only sanction was reputation. When Miss Eastland was left only £5000 out of £40,000 by Mrs Dawson it was thought 'shabby'. The sanction of a threat to reputation was implicit in the arguments of the Lupton–Rider letters and in the incoherent threats which John Stocks visited upon the Lupton–Wareham family and his own brothers. Perhaps Mrs Dawson had misunderstood the 'rules' of the gift exchange when she accepted Miss Eastland's companionship or simply did not care what people thought after her death. For the living, reputation was important in an age when trust and credit were an important part of both business and family economics.

Reputation was built upon many things. Behaviour towards family members and others was important as was the prompt payment of bills. Jane Hey was always worried about this. Her wisdom was illustrated by the story of Miner and Scurr, a drapers shop in Briggate, 'where all the best people went'. Mrs Buckle and her aunt were in the shop

pricing some article of drapery when Mrs Thomson Lee came in and also priced it. The shopkeeper told Mrs Lee a much higher price than he had told the others, and being asked (after Mrs Lee had left the shop) why he did this, he replied that if Mrs Rawsthorne bought the article he knew he would get his money within a reasonable time, but that if Mrs Thomson Lee bought it, he would have to wait three years for his money – and he therefore could not let her have it so cheap as his other customers.

Other comments of Mrs Buckle confirmed this

Thomson Lee, a son without occupation, was a good deal with the officers at the barracks ... They [he married a Miss Greenwood] were always living beyond their means and stories were rife as to the shifts that they were put to.

Given the uncertainties of demography and the economy, few knew when the potential of the gift economy might be required or be activated by death, desertion, a credit crisis or business failure. The exchange between an overcrowded household and an empty household, as in the examples of Mrs Buckle and her aunt, or the acceptance of a nephew for apprenticeship and training, especially by the childless, events evident in many of the wills were a little more considered. Many of the 'servants' in the census records, have been identified as family members,[32] and probably originated in this process as did the favoured nieces and sometimes nephews who provided companionship to widowed and spinster aunts. The activities of the network were most visible in the care of widows, the care of minor children, the practice of equity to children, a practice justified by the part it played in sustaining family unity. Beyond that was the potential of the reserve army of siblings, cousins, nephews and nieces.

To be a member of a network was a non-trivial asset. The benefits were not simply the major ones of benefiting from a trust, as Jane Hey benefited, but the myriad details of support, sociability, information and introduction. Beyond that was the potential of 'the inheritance'. Deeply embedded in the middle class sense of self was not just the rational calculation and moral legitimacy of hard work and ability, as in the rise of James Kitson, but also the demographic lottery of the 'fortune' left by the unmarried and childless members of the network, as in the cases of Mr Bingley the stonemason, the Ikens and the Hampstead Fentons. To be a member of a family network of property owners was to hold a card in the lottery of the cousinage of the childless and the unmarried. This was not a simple matter of gambling. Care was needed to stay in the game. It was a game of skill and chance promoted by the processes of visiting, companionship and mutual identity. This last could be promoted by the strategies of name identity as in the Fenton case. Amongst the fears and fantasies of the middle classes, was the long lost uncle, or rather news of his death turning up with 'the inheritance'. This indeterminacy was partly a result of poor communication and the variation in size of the nuclear family. It also made sustaining the network a most important activity. Most uncles and aunts were not long lost but the result of frequent visiting.

The network was more than that. Those participating were well aware of the damage which could be done to hope and welfare by demography and the economy. The elements of the network continually fragmented, broke and reformed as they responded to damage. The chatter of Miss W

---

[32] E. Higgs, 'Domestic servants and households in Victorian England', *Social History* 8 (1983), 203–10.

and Mrs Buckle was deeply structured by the vagaries of demographics and the economy and the wreckage and reforming of life cycle ambitions and strategies that resulted. Mrs Buckle had suffered from the early death of her father and went to Leeds to stay with her aunt. There was the equivocal account of 'the honeymoon widow' and the sad tales of Mary Ann Oates who was engaged to be married three times and each time her lover died before the wedding. These cases were the talk of Leeds but equally important for their impact on the consciousness and sense of self for the middle classes was the quiet grief of Cordelia Fenton. She

was engaged to a first cousin Fenton, who was a rising barrister in London and d. from an improper dose of medicine (poison sent in mistake by the druggist). She never m. but lived with her younger sister Elizabeth at 'the Willows' a village near Preston.

The continual possibility of the premature death of husbands was central to the middle class attitudes to property, saving and ownership. The hazards of trade were equally important. There were the 'proud' Becketts who moved into the gentry, but also the two brothers who did not do well in trade and were 'in poor circumstances'. Mr Carr 'became unfortunate in business and had to sell St Ann's and Mrs B believes that after that, they lived entirely in South Parade'.

The network was a means of assessing individuals and their qualities, hence the ladies' memories were full of judgement. There were codes of sexuality and status that are now only partly legible. There was Miss Rimmington who was labelled without comment as 'a large masculine woman' but, in the main, sexuality was about marriageability and rarely about the details which concern late twentieth century curiosity. For young women, to be 'pretty' was an asset and to be 'plain' was a hazard. There was admiration for the family with 'three daughters all very good looking women who married well' and regret for Ann , '…a very pretty girl but her aunts [who brought her up] made her very old maidish'. As women grew older, they were 'handsome' like Mrs Coupland when she wore velvet or Mrs Frederick Oates 'who had a fine nose, bigger than her daughter Mary Ann'. These individual judgements were as much about sociability as about sexual attractiveness and enthusiasms. Mrs Grace 'was very agreeable and humorous and a great acquisition at card parties'.

Men were assessed with equal directness. The Colemans' son was 'a great beau at dances'. Judgement for men was often about trustworthiness and many had warning notices posted on them. Frederick Oates was 'good looking but affected'. The two Wormald sons were 'very fast and would dance and sit up all night'. 'Fast' was the warning note for the

Hampstead Fentons. There was 'Old Noddy Hudson of the Kings Mills popularly known as "the soak"'. Women also attracted caution; 'Mrs Wormald was a sprightly lady (quite a lady) and very fond of a flirtation with Mr Wainhouse (she was a great flirt)'. Marriageability, sociability and trustworthiness were the main elements of these often detailed judgements.

Status assessment had two dimensions. The reference was mostly to material wealth and associated patterns of behaviour. Old Wilson of Buckram House was 'a working man'. The father of the three Miss Oates was a 'Great Basha'. Status judgements also located people in terms of the sophistication of their behaviour and this was done in terms of provincial–metropolitan and urban–rural patterns. A brother of George Vincent married the daughter of the landlord of the hotel at Thorpe Arch and was 'rather rough and provincial'. Miss Brooke was 'fine woman . . . very Yorkshire . . . off of her own gooseberry bushes'. Both these were of established middle class economic status, but judgement placed them a little apart from Miss W and Mrs B.

How stands the sense of place?

Does this emphasis on network and a far flung family geography mean that the urban focus of many studies of the middle classes of England has been misguided, that the emphasis on Leeds, Manchester, Birmingham, Colchester, Black Country towns and the rest was simply an artefact of research design or certain features of political discourse? Should this focus disappear or at least be marginalised and replaced by networks of property, business, religion and family and by the flows of profits, people, gifts and information in a world of dances in St Petersburg, schools in London and deaths in Jamaica? Was it such matters that gave meaning to the discourse of status, class and family?

A second look at the mental map of Miss W gives some clues as to the way forward for the argument. Places were given meaning by people and the relationships between people. There was a recurrent phrase in her memories. Many of her memories end with individuals or families leaving Leeds. Thus

to return to Mr Coleman he had two sons who used to go to the dances. One especially, the eldest Robert John was a great beau, in the style of the Becketts. But the family left Leeds and Miss W doesn't know what became of them.

Hamer and Eliza went later to reside in Lancashire. The cause of this was that Eliza had an intimate female friend living there.

This pattern appeared in her account of Leeds families. For the families of which she was a part – Fenton and Oates, her memories followed them to London and beyond but many other families were only known as far as the boundaries of Leeds. Judgements were made. The 'wife who flirted' was noted. Often the ladies followed them one move but then their knowledge stopped. For the Ridsdale and Teale families, they were located in 'the neighbourhood of Leeds'. They were followed to Leyburn, Scarborough and Bath but then lost sight of.

Those who were not family were located firmly in the landscape of Leeds. The older generation was traced to the Hunslet Road area south of the river before it became surrounded by industry and warehouses, but most were located in Park Square and Little Woodhouse, the 'west end' which was developed between 1780 and 1850. At times the sense of place was reinforced by little sketches.

In phrase after phrase the status of families and individuals was located in the house.

On the left hand side approaching Park Row stood a large brick mansion, occupied by Mr Calverley (who took the name of Blaydes on account of some property he received) and was a partner in Beckett's Bank, where the Town Hall now stands. It stood in good grounds with a high wall all around and a carriage entrance on the right hand. Mr Blaydes' was a fine old brick mansion (very old) occupied by Mr Coleman (Miss W says he was a man of property and thinks he was without occupation). This house had its principal rooms and windows into South Parade and Park Row and had railings in front on those sides, but the entrance was from Park Lane. There was a carriage entrance and there was a small piece of ground on this side with Lilac trees.

There were excellent houses in Park Place occupied by very good family rooms on each side of the door...At the other end of South Parade was a fine brick house occupied by Mr Pearson...At the opposite corner of Park Row...stood two fine very old and black brick houses occupied respectively by Mr Gott and Mr Wormald...They were very good houses and were approached by a carriage drive...The Coleman's house at the end of South Parade was a very good one. It was a detached house with a brick wall around it; trees planted all round inside

And so they went on, the place, the fine brick, the lilac tree, good grounds, the family rooms and the carriage drive, each with the name of person and family attached.

There are a number of ways in which this tension between place and network can be explored. First, it is important to affirm the powerful self-referential nature of nineteenth century urban culture. The growing associational culture of nineteenth century civil society was firmly identified with the urban place.[33] Even when an association was part of a

---

[33] See Chapter Two, pp. 61–2.

national network the components, the auxiliaries, were firmly identified with the urban place.[34] Many political structures were identified with the urban place, such as the constituencies of many members of parliament, notably those linked to the new seats of the 1832 Reform Act. The new representative municipal corporations were constructed to give unity of identity to key urban places.[35] The new Poor Law unions were, wherever possible, gathered around an urban centre. Much knowledge was, and many knowledge based solutions were, not only spatial but also urban place based. Maps, surveys, the units of many of the new state statistical accumulations were predominately urban units. The most important of the new science based, industrial technology based services were delivered to urban places, notably gas, piped water, trams and electricity. The power of the identity and self-referential nature of the town was not total. There were still many regional units such as the Methodist Circuits and the county MPs. There were many metropolitan agencies like the banks, many publishing houses and the railway companies.

The urban was also the basis of collective political action. For a class of people who had little power as individuals, the massing of population and interests made the urban place ideal for middle class political action.[36] The urban middle classes amassed key items of collective capital, roads, lighting, bridges etc.[37] They formed associations to negotiate with the dominant national political alliances which dominated the state. The Anti-Corn Law League was the most spectacular of such collective actions but by no means the only one. In an urban location, the middle classes sought the prestige of a royal visit, a town hall or a park. The power and status claims of the municipal were their achievements.[38]

The town was the place of meetings, elections, service delivery and shelter as well as card parties, neighbours and 'the best houses'. Even the components of the family networks were labelled by Miss W in terms of their urban place, the Leeds Fentons, the Hampstead Fentons, the Brussels Fentons, each with their own membership and characteristics. This firm sense of place was in tension with a wide variety of flows which crossed and challenged the integrity of the urban place. There were flows

---

[34] Morris, *Class, Sect and Party*; J. Money, *Experience and Identity. Birmingham and the West Midlands, 1760–1800* (Manchester, 1977).

[35] Morris, 'The middle class and the British towns and cities of the Industrial Revolution'.

[36] D. Fraser, *Urban Politics in Victorian England. The Structure of Politics in Victorian Cities* (Leicester, 1976).

[37] J. Smail, *The Origins of Middle Class Culture. Halifax, Yorkshire, 1660–1780* (Cornell, 1994).

[38] S. Gunn, *The Public Culture of the Victorian Middle Class. Ritual and Authority in the English Industrial City, 1840–1914* (Manchester, 2000).

of people, letters, culture and knowledge. Visitors, gifts, news, property, books and newspapers were created and located in larger worlds.

The balance between place and flows with a wider spatial reference was influenced by several features. There were a number of changes which reinforced, extended and strengthened the networked aspects of middle class life and family. The most dramatic was in transport and communication. Although the slowness and discomfort of coach travel on the albeit improved roads of the early nineteenth century did not stop the likes of Mary Oates, they were a deterrent to movement. By the 1840s, the railways had made major changes.[39] It was no accident that Jane Hey chose Barrowash for her residence as this was the railway station for Ockbrook parish. By the 1860s, the railway brought her to family in Leeds and Ilkley.

Movement was not only a matter of people but also of information and cultural products. By the 1830s, an increasing portion of the population shared a body of knowledge that went beyond the common heritage of Bible and Prayer Book. The middle classes shared an increasing number of London newspapers as the steam press, the improved roads and then the railway increased circulations. Even those who read local newspapers, as many did, shared information copied from the London papers. Novels, periodicals, the 'useful knowledge' of advice manuals, pamphlets and magazines increased in quantity and commonality.[40] When the Fentons from Preston and Leeds met at the dinner table in Hampstead, they would share not only family news but a common base of newspaper news, poetry and novel reading. Many leisure products drew the imaginations and consciousness of the town beyond its specific boundaries. The theatre and the circus were not just entertainment but an education in the world beyond the specific place. London, Africa and India came to Leeds and were shared with the other towns on the route. Quasi leisure products, many of them promoted by the increasing number of voluntary societies, had the same quality of creating national middle class audiences who shared common experience. The visit of the officers of the 'national society' or the evening listening and looking when the converted African or the freed slave 'performed' were part of a process which not only extended middle class consciousness but increased the common elements of that consciousness.[41]

[39] W. Schivelbusch, *The Railway Journey. The Industrialization of Time and Space in the 19th century* (New York, 1986); M. Robbins, *The Railway Age* (London, 1962), pp. 43–56.

[40] R.D. Altick, *The English Common Reader. A Social History of the Mass Reading Public, 1800–1900* (Chicago, 1957).

[41] C. Hall, *Civilizing Subjects. Metropole and Colony in the English Imagination, 1830–1867* (Cambridge, 2002), pp. 290–336.

Despite such changes many of the basic structural features of the middle class situation held them to the urban place. The middle classes in this study were those who controlled capital, property and professional knowledge but shared that characteristic of the nineteenth century middle classes. As a group they were enormously powerful but as individuals weak and vulnerable. The urban location of many of these structures and cultural features related specifically to middle class situations, situations of profit seeking and privilege defending, locations for the strategies of business and family. The ownership structure of property was especially attuned to the urban place. The bulk of industrial units of production were controlled by resident owner-managers.[42] The urban elite was the local capital owning elite and their professional allies. There were powerful reasons why that capital, commercial, industrial and real estate should be spatially limited.

Urban real estate and housing was in the hands of a resident owner-occupier-rentier class. Such property provided direct income and investment to serve the business and family strategies of local resident decision takers.[43] The urban place, growing in size and complexity, also provided increasing opportunities and incentives for collective capital and key positive externalities, cloth halls, subscription libraries, paving and lighting, parks and town halls.

The key element here was trust, and trust was closely linked to knowledge. The management and accounting practices of the first half of the century were primitive. The only effective form of management was direct supervision. Management was recruited from family.[44] This was a strategy which provided knowledge of those recruited and ensured that those involved had a direct interest in the long term accumulation of capital and sustained income of the business. Investment in property was local. This was the only way in which the investor could expect adequate knowledge of the expected costs and income streams. Risk minimisation in an insecure world required the spatial proximity of residence and ownership.

There were ways of extending property ownership beyond the spatially bounded and these were related to family. Jane Hey had married into the Hey family. When she was widowed she was able to move to rural

[42] *The Making of a Ruling Class*, Benwell Community Project, final report series no.6, (Newcastle upon Tyne, 1976).
[43] M.J. Daunton, *House and Home in the Victorian City* (London, 1983), pp. 91–178; C. Bedale, 'Property relations and housing policy: Oldham in the late 19th and early 20th centuries', in J. Melling (ed.), *Housing, Social Policy and the State* (London, 1980).
[44] D. Crozier, 'Kinship and occupational succession', *Sociological Review* ns 13 (1965), 15–43.

Derbyshire to bring up her children because she was provided with a rentier trust income which included not only a national and international portfolio of shares but also commercial and residential property in Leeds. She could do this in part because of the proximity of one of her trustees, Uncle Samuel, and she could visit, harass and check on him to her heart's content. She was also able to act in this way because the management of her property was under the care of her cousin, John Atkinson solicitor. Not only was he known to her and those who established the trust for her, but his actions were under the scrutiny of an active, letter writing, visiting family network. Under such circumstances the modern discipline of the accountant and auditor was hardly needed. The row if he had done anything wrong would have caused him more damage than anything an audit could have done. The bad temper of the Lupton–Rider correspondence was only an indication of the penalties for anyone who slipped up under the eye of an active and strong family network.

On rare occasions the religious network might act as a channel of reliable information. As these networks were bound together by marriage alliances, this tended to be a version of the family as regulation and creator of trust relationships. In August 1845, Robert Jowitt, woolstapler and member of the Society of Friends, wrote to Edward Smith in Leicester,

It has occurred to us, that perhaps thou might be able to give us some information... respecting the house of Alfred Burgess and Co of Leicester. We have done some business with them for about a year and a half... [Burgess had asked for an extension of credit, £4000–£5000 for 3–4 months] ... and therefore take the liberty of asking the favour of thy candid opinion on the subject, which of course shall be treated quite confidentially. Canst thou also inform us whether Alfred's brothers are in partnership in the spinning concern and whether he has any other partners.[45]

There were signs that the balance of power between the urban location and the wider networks and flows moved against the urban in the second part of the century. The structuring of markets and social relations in 1900 did not provide the self evident urban focus which they had done in the first half of the century.

The life cycle strategies of the middle classes always involved the search for low risk, low management rentier assets to provide income for old age and for widows and children in the event of premature death. In the first half of the century these assets tended to be local and specific, real

---

[45] Robert Jowitt to Edward Smith, 14 August 1845. Jowitt Business Archives 32. Brotherton Library, University of Leeds.

property, mortgages and the occasional joint stock utility and infrastructure company. The only other alternative was government stock.
In mid-century the spatial restrictions tended to ease.

This was evident from a comparison of two lists of assets drawn up by
Robert Jowitt, merchant and Quaker. The first was from 1843 when he
was contemplating withdrawal from active business in favour of his son
and spending more time on the charitable activities of Leeds and the
Society of Friends, both important leisure activities.

A major balance on General Account with RJ and sons
Six Shares in Leeds Gas Company
Five Shares in Leeds South Market
Thirty Shares in Leeds and Yorkshire Insurance Company
Two Shares in Leeds New Bath Company
Six Shares in Leeds Victorian Bridge Company
Four Shares in Leeds Zoological Gardens
One Share in Leeds Library
Various Shares in York and North Midland Railway
Various shares in North Midland Railway Company
Twenty Shares in Newcastle and Darlington Railway Company
Two personal loans

By 1859, he had withdrawn from business and his income sources had a
very different geographical pattern.

Eastern Union Railway
Hull and Selby Railway
Pennsylvania Central Railway
Leeds and Yorkshire Railway
Rent from a warehouse in Leeds
Stockton and Darlington Railway Preference Shares
London and North Western Railway
North Eastern Railway
Hull and Holderness Railway
Midland Railway
Leeds Gas Company
Michigan Central Railway
Ohio and Pittsburg Railway
New Haven Railway

The geography of this move was significant. Through the London stock-
brokers, Foster and Braithwaite, Robert Jowitt had moved into a world
capital market free of the family network and free of location, although
the choice of stockbroker may well have been influenced by family and

religious network. His strategy was very different from his father in the 1790s and 1800s who had concentrated upon personal loans (often family), mortgages (all regional), and canal shares, again regional.

At the same time government stock became less attractive as rates of interest declined and a mild inflation took hold of monetary regimes. Life insurance began to be a normal part of choice of savings strategies and asset structures. This spread risk and took ownership away from the local.

In the second half of the century, empire offered increasing prospects of employment, identity and income for families like the Fentons. Professional and salaried employment increased with a focus on metropolitan government and finance as well as an increasing number of companies with national networks, notably the railways and banks. The increasing number of professional jobs with local authorities were only partially detached from the local but these were generating their own networks as evidenced by journals and associations. Individuals' careers and ambitions had been liberated, to a limited degree, from the local.

There was a tension between place and network. Miss W, Jane Hey and their fellow family members were able to experience and gain from that tension to the full for they were members of a strong and active network. They were able to maximise their choice of experience and opportunity and draw down varied means of support and rescue in times of trouble. Mrs Buckle came from a more fractured family experience and built a less active and extended network. Her voice was much more a Leeds voice. The possibilities and strengths of networks supplemented and did not eliminate the sense of place with its opportunities for detailed knowledge, closeness of supervision and massing of resources for everything from an evening playing cards to political campaigns and the building of chapels and town halls.

9   The economic history of the British middle class, 1816–70

> Some pains have been necessary to present the figures in such a form as
> may be least likely to lead to erroneous inferences, but all those who are
> in the habit of using statistics must be aware of the danger of relying
> upon them without an intimate acquaintance with the sources from
> which they are derived.[1]

So far, this account of the practices and processes which linked property to
the families and individuals of the middle classes has proceeded in terms of
the experience of individuals embedded in a variety of family networks.
This has been set against the general increase in the availability of material
wealth, goods and services over the period, but that increase was uneven
both in terms of time and of geographical, social and sectoral distribution.
Greater precision is required, especially as the need to sustain material
standards and social status in an environment of insecurity and risk has
played a key part in explanation. All these factors depended upon the
changing abilities of the economy to deliver access to material wealth.

Little attempt has been made to trace the course of the overall economic welfare of the middle classes in a period in which their political and
cultural assertiveness was evident in a variety of forms. The nature and
timing of this assertion may be disputed amongst historians, but all agree
that it was a key feature of British social development. The relationship
between the assertions and claims of the 'middle classes' and economic
structural change has been presented in a variety of ways, but little
attempt has been made to trace the changing levels of economic welfare
of whatever group has been identified as the 'middle classes'. Judgements,
if made at all, have tended to be cautious, leaving the field to the impressionistic claims made by contemporaries.

Judgements about the changing economic well-being of the property
owning 'middle classes', can be made from the published figures of the
revenue collected from probate and legacy duty in England and Wales and

---

[1] *Tenth Report of the Commissioners of the Inland Revenue*, Parliamentary Papers, 1866,
vol. XXVI, p. 131.

in Scotland. This duty was collected on a reasonably consistent basis from 1816 onwards. Probate duties had been first imposed in 1694 and a graduated scale was introduced in 1779. In 1815, this scale was extended and remained substantially unchanged until 1880. The amount was collected on an irregularly graduated scale. The duty was between 1 and 2 per cent of the sworn value of the estate. The percentage was at its highest for modest estates in the tax bands with upper limits in the £1000–£3000 range for sworn value. The taxes on administrations were a third higher than those on probated wills.[2] These figures were in no sense a direct measure of wealth but rather an indicator which, through the processes of probate and the life time accumulation of wealth, was related to the overall levels of wealth. In as far as the ability to accumulate and defend the value of wealth forming assets was an aspect of economic well-being, it also reflected the broader economic welfare of the property owning middle classes.

The probate, as has been shown, was levied on the gross value of personal estate. Given that rebates were made on the final settlement of account, variations in levels of debt should have had little effect, but the exclusion of real estate was important. In some senses, the exclusion of agricultural land, mainly identified with the aristocracy and gentry was helpful, as this simply reduced the 'noise' from an indicator being used for a study of the middle classes. The exclusion of urban freehold real estate was more serious as urban freehold property was a crucial asset for a large portion of the middle classes. To some extent, changing levels of urban real estate were reflected in the probate totals because much of such real estate was financed by mortgage loans, which appeared in the accumulations of personal property taxed under probate. Its impact would also be limited by the tendency in many towns for housing and land to be held under leasehold tenure, which would appear as personal property. Freehold real estate was also a component of industrial and commercial capital but, again, much of this would have appeared in partnership accounts, which would be taxed as personal property.

The raw figures of both probate and legacy duty show relentless, if uneven, levels of increase throughout the period. This was a reflection of rising population rather than being a summary of countless individual and family experiences. Figure 9.1 shows the per capita figures for Britain (England and Wales and Scotland).[3] Ireland is excluded as the basis of

---

[2] S. Buxton, *Finance and Politics. An Historical Study, 1793–1885*, 2 vols. (London, 1885) vol. II, p. 292.

[3] The population figures are derived from B.R. Mitchell and P. Deane, *Abstract of British Historical Statistics* (Cambridge, 1962), p. 8.

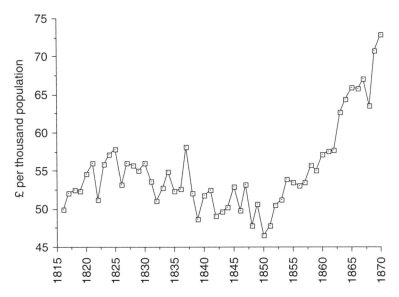

Fig. 9.1 Probate duty per capita in Britain, 1816–70.

collection and the general direction of economic change was very different from the other countries. This use of the total population of Britain to obtain the per capita figure, which is to be used as an indicator of middle class wealth, implies that the proportion of the population which might claim or be attributed middle class status remained constant over the period. Given that very little work has been done on the changing proportions of the 'middle classes' in the British population, this must be the best 'guess' available.

This graph measures the ability of the property owning classes to accumulate property and defend the value of that property and measures this in current prices. Two conclusions emerge. The graph shows the same substantial short run variations evident in other indicators of middle class economic fortune such as the incomes of men like Jowitt and Hey and the bankruptcies of the less fortunate. Secondly, the period divided into three. The years between 1816 and 1825 saw a substantial increase with only one pause in 1822. The early 1820s were a great decade in which to accumulate property. It was a period in which the falling rate of interest brought rising prices for the owners of government bonds.[4]

[4] G. Clark, 'Debt, deficits and crowding out: England, 1727–1840', *European Review of Economic History* 5, 3 (2001) 403–36.

Resources released by the end of the long war with France were being brought into production. This period was brought to an end by the economic crisis of 1826 which played a central part in the Oates correspondence. This disturbing crisis destroyed value, not just in South American Stock but also as a result of falling commodity prices and the resulting bad debts, liquidity problems and marking down of goods in the warehouses. Despite fluctuations and spectacular increases in the value of property in years such as 1837, there followed a long and irregular decline in the values indicated by the probate duty collection. This was brought to an end in 1850, after which values rose at an irregular but increasing rate. By this measure the decades of middle class assertion, the decades of the campaigns for the reforms of parliament and the abolition of the Corn Laws were decades when the ability to accumulate property was compromised and diminished. Middle class assertion was a matter of insecurity and not confidence.

If the assumption that the middle class share of the population remained constant is relaxed, this does not alter the verdict. If the middle class share of the population increased, then the decline of individual shares of wealth accumulation would be greater. If individual middle class shares rose, then this could only have happened if the portion of the population with middle class status fell, which in itself would have caused a major increase in the insecurities of class.

Such a judgement depended upon a measure made in current prices. Experience post-1920 has created a vivid awareness of the potential of sustained and irregular price inflation to destroy value and, hence, requires an examination of the series in terms of some form of constant price. Before this is done it is worth asking if the historical actors in this study, when they assessed their economic welfare as executors, testators and legatees, would have thought in this way. Contemporaries were vividly aware of price change. There were good years and bad years, usually related to the harvest but increasingly to foreign trade crises, but these were seen as short term. Many would reflect upon the value of their property in terms of the gold standard pound which they expected to be constant over the long term, rather than looking over their shoulder at the price of bread and cotton goods.

For those whose behaviour and sense of economic well-being was influenced by price trends as well as short term fluctuations, the historian has a variety of ways of assessing their mood and response. Two well-established price series make it possible to present the per capita probate duty in terms of constant prices. The series created by Rousseaux in 1938 relied upon wholesale prices and the unit prices of imports and, hence, took little account of changes in internal distribution costs. These were

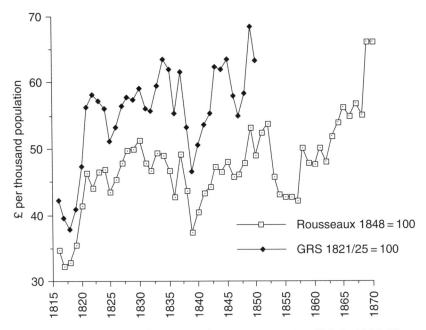

Fig. 9.2 Probate duty per capita at constant prices, Britain 1816–70.

especially important in the 1840s as inter city railways and the growth of early forms of multiple and department store styles of retailing began to make an impact.[5] It is, however, the only series which covers the whole period under review. The series generated by Gayer, Rostow and Schwartz contained a wider range of prices but the weighting of the series placed substantial emphasis on bread grains which played a major part in working class diet. Wheat and oats together made up 32 per cent of the index.[6]

This way of looking at the information from the probate duty totals again showed the importance of short run fluctuations, as well as the importance of the prosperity of the early 1820s. After that the picture was different from that presented through current prices. In the late 1820s and early 1830s, there was a period of stagnation. The 'real' value of middle class property accumulations was sustained by price falls, but this was followed by major losses in the late 1830s. This was followed by 'real'

[5] G. Crossick and S. Jaumain (eds.), *Cathedrals of Consumption. The European Department Store, 1850–1939* (Aldershot, 1999).
[6] These two series are available in Mitchell and Deane, *British Historical Statistics*, pp. 470–2.

gains in the 1840s. In other words, the middle class sense of economic well-being was boosted by price falls. Those who were aware of this factor may have been influenced in their views of free trade and the attempts of trades unions to increase or defend the labour cost element of goods and services. The 1850s were very different. Any apparent gain in terms of current prices was eliminated by rising prices. The Crimean War period stands out as a trough in 'real' values. Middle class consciousness was divided with some attacking civil service and aristocratic mismanagement whilst others supported the increased projection of national power in foreign affairs.

Like all price series, the two used above were an attempt to summarise a huge variety of prices and experiences. Each had strengths and weaknesses. More recently, three new series have become available for the central part of this period and suggest some modification of the judgements already made. The three new series were devised to reflect the experiences of three very different groups in society and were based upon the different spending patterns of those groups. In Feinstein's index for working class expenditure, food was given a 62 per cent weighting and within the food element, bread, flour and oatmeal were weighted 55 per cent. Rent was allocated a 14 per cent weighting. Boot, in his study of clerical incomes, devised two series for the middle classes. One assumed an annual income of £250, allocating 39 per cent to food, only 16 per cent of which was bread, flour and oatmeal, and 6.4 per cent to servants. Those who were attributed an income of £750 were allocated a weighting of 27 per cent for food, of which 11 per cent was bread, flour and oatmeal, whilst servants were weighted 10 per cent the cost of horses 3 per cent. Rent was 12 per cent in both cases.[7] These last two series were more important to the experience of the property accumulators who paid probate duty (Fig. 9.3).

The account rendered through the use of the three new series again shows the importance of short-run fluctuations and the gains of the early 1820s, although these gains are brought to an end much more rapidly by rising prices. The losses of 1826 were followed by recovery and fluctuations around a stagnating trend. The disaster of 1839–40 was even more evident, followed by recovery. There was a declining trend in the 1840s, especially for the £250 and £750 a year people. The experience summarised in this way can be presented in five-year periods (Table 9.1).

[7] H. Boot, 'Real incomes of the British middle class, 1760–1850: the experience of clerks at the East India Company', *Economic History Review* 52, 4, (November, 1999), 638–68.

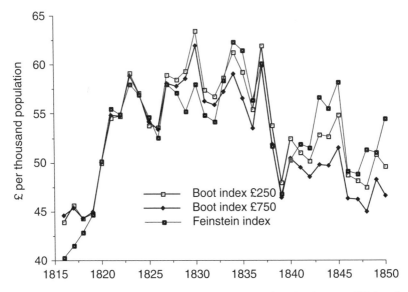

Fig. 9.3 Probate duty per capita in Britain deflated by Boot and Feinstein index, 1815–50.

The major gains of the early 1820s were followed by stagnation and minor gains in the late 1820s. The early 1830s marked a slight improvement whilst the late 1830s showed the losses. The results for the 1840s were mixed but the more appropriate series of Boot and Feinstein both showed losses in the ability to accumulate and sustain the value of property. Whatever set of results is preferred, the period which followed 1826 was one which could only have intensified the middle class need to follow strategies which would counter, contain and minimise risk and insecurity.

Now this was a period of modest if irregular gains in Gross National Product. If this did not show up in terms of middle class assets, where did it go? There are several possibilities.[8] The first must be that the probate duty figures as presented by the Stamp Office and revenue authorities were inconsistent and misleading, an artefact of the tax-gathering system that did not reflect any economic reality. All the evidence suggests that

---

[8] P. Deane, 'New estimates of Gross National Product for the United Kingdom, 1830–1914', *Review of Income and Wealth* 14 (1968), 95–112; N.F.R. Crafts, *British Economic Growth during the Industrial Revolution* (Oxford, 1985), p. 45; C. Feinstein, 'Pessimism perpetuated: real wages and the standard of living in Britain during and after the Industrial Revolution', *Journal of Economic History* 58, 3 (September, 1998), 625–58.

Table 9.1 *Probate duty paid per capita in Britain, 1816–70*

Date	Current prices	Rousseaux index (1848 prices)	GRS (1821–25 prices)	Boot £250 (1820–24 prices)	Boot £750 (1820–24 prices)	Feinstein (1820–24 prices)
1816–19	51.68	33.84	40.05	44.66	44.82	42.34
1820–24	55.00	45.06	55.04	55.14	55.12	55.10
1825–29	55.61	47.36	55.26	56.84	56.41	55.55
1830–34	53.66	48.88	58.85	59.52	58.09	57.54
1835–39	52.74	43.97	55.73	55.69	53.63	55.28
1840–44	50.65	44.38	56.76	51.83	49.58	53.17
1845–49	50.88	48.24	60.68	49.99	47.46	51.69
1850–54	50.01	48.84				
1855–59	54.19	45.18				
1860–64	59.92	50.35				
1865–69	66.62	57.88				
Percentage change in the current and real value of probate duty paid per capita in Britain between five-year periods, 1816–70.						
1816–19 to 1820–24	6.41	33.16	37.43	23.47	22.99	30.14
1820–24 to 1825–29	1.11	5.10	0.38	3.10	2.33	0.81
1825–29 to 1830–34	−3.50	3.20	6.50	4.70	2.97	3.59
1830–34 to 1835–39	−1.71	−10.03	−5.31	−6.44	−7.67	−3.92
1835–39 to 1840–44	−3.96	0.92	1.85	−6.93	−7.55	−3.82
1840–44 to 1845–49	0.44	8.70	6.91	−3.54	−4.29	−2.79
1845–49 to 1850–54	−1.71	1.24				
1850–54 to 1855–59	8.36	−7.49				
1855–59 to 1860–64	10.56	11.45				
1860–64 to 1865–69	11.19	14.95				

this was not so. Indeed, there is evidence that the efficiency and effectiveness of collection improved in the late 1820s after a parliamentary enquiry.[9] This, others things being equal, should have biased the figures in favour of middle class gains during the following years. Nor is there

[9] *Thirteenth Report of the Commissioners of Inquiry into the Collection and management of the Revenue...Board of Stamps, London.* Parliamentary Papers. 1826, vol. X; also *Fourteenth Report.*

evidence that the middle classes became better tax dodgers. There is no discussion of tax evasion in the contemporary literature and advice manuals. Indeed, the practice of pulling *inter vivos* loans to children back into 'hotch-potch' in order to serve the needs of equity between children suggests that testators went in the opposite direction and increased the property liable to probate duty. In the later reports, the Revenue was confident of its ability to collect probate duty in a consistent way.

The payment of the probate duty (we may include in that term the Administration duty) is necessarily the first step taken by the executor, as, without it, he cannot deal with the property of his testator, and our main security for the collection of the duty, as in the case of all stamp duties, consists in the invalidity which attaches to acts done without the authority of a duly stamped document. In this sense the Probate duty is popularly said to 'collect itself'[10]

There were only two important changes in probate duty in this period. Until 1860, all estates over £1,000,000 were charged £15,000. After 1860, a graduated rate of £1500 for every additional £100,000 was introduced for the very few estates above that amount. The 1860 report noted that, since 1815, only twelve stamps at the upper rate had been issued, although four of these had been issued since 1855. In 1864, wills and administrations valued at less than £100 were exempt. This involved the large number of estates which paid the ten shillings duty on probate or £1 on administrations. In 1848, when the Inland Revenue published a table of the distribution of stamps sold at the various levels on the scale, there were 3989 ten shilling people and 1745 £1 people. They were 22 per cent of the total number of probates and administrations stamped but only 0.4 per cent of the revenue of that year.[11] The impact of this change in the total revenue would have been trivial.

The missing real estate might account for the 'lost' assets. There are two useful indicators of the changing levels of building in this period. The first was the number of bricks charged with duty in England and Wales. The second was the quantities of crown and German sheet glass retained for home consumption in Great Britain (Fig. 9.4).[12] The figures suggest

[10] *Ninth Report of the Commissioners of the Inland Revenue*, Parliamentary Papers. 1866, vol. XXVI, p. 19.

[11] *A Return of the Number of Probates and Letters of Administration Stamped under each Grade of Duty in the Year 1848*, Parliamentary Papers. 1849, vol. XXX.

[12] B.R. Mitchell and P. Deane, *British Historical Statistics*, p. 235 derived from H.A. Shannon, 'Bricks – a trade index, 1785–1849', *Economica* 12 (1934), 300; A.K. Cairncross and B. Weber, 'Fluctuations in building in Great Britain, 1785–1849', *Economic History Review* 9 (1956); the glass series was taken from G.R. Porter, *Progress of the Nation*, (London, 1847), p. 257 and derived ultimately from revenue figures in Parliamentary Papers.

Table 9.2 *Gross domestic fixed capital formation in dwellings, 1811–60*

£m per annum decade average at 1851–60 prices				
1811–20	1821–30	1831–40	1841–50	1851–60
5.82	8.9	10.3	7.6	10.25

that resources, including the savings of the middle class, were directed towards the enhancement of real estate values through building construction, and that this would have increased the sense of prosperity in the early 1820s, but would also have compensated for the losses indicated by the probate figures of the 1830s. The 1840s remained a difficult period for the middle classes, although, once the figures were adjusted for population increase, the gains of the 1830s did not look so comfortable. Using these figures in this way assumes that the materials indicated were used for the urban house building which was such an important part of middle class assets. Many of the bricks would contribute to the works associated with the railway building of the late 1830s. The use of these figures also assumes that the balance between brick and stone remained constant. Feinstein's estimates of gross domestic fixed capital formation in Great Britain at constant prices give some support to the notion that the 1830s saw the accumulation of real property in house construction. His estimates involve the use of population figures as well as the brick index and were as in Table 9.2.[13]

These indicators are useful but they were not a measure of the degree to which the middle classes were able to defend the value of the resources they placed into enhancing the value of urban real estate. They also fail to give a measure of the degree to which externalities, such as population increases, local economic expansion and contraction as well as the influence of railway building enhanced and reduced urban real estate values.

Recent work on the income flows and stocks of capital value involved in dwellings (houses and shops) have not been in agreement but, whichever version is examined, it is impossible to see that middle class real estate, missing from the probate tax, as adequate compensation for the decline in the ability of the middle classes to accumulate assets and sustain their value. Clark used information from the various enquiries into the holding and renting of real estate by charities in England and Wales. From this he was able to estimate the rents and total income from rents derived

[13] C. Feinstein, 'Capital formation in Great Britain', in P. Mathias and M.M. Postan (eds.), *The Cambridge Economic History of Europe*, vol. VII (Cambridge, 1978).

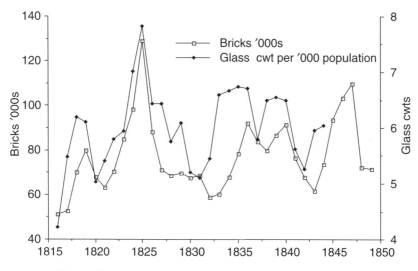

Fig. 9.4 Bricks and glass per capita, Britain, 1816–50.

from houses and shops in this period. The decadal average of income from house rents per capita of the population showed that the uneven rise of that income since the 1790s faltered in the 1830s and 1840s making it unlikely that real estate would be seen as compensation for the decline in the per capita value of the personal estate indicated by the probate taxes (Figs. 9.3, 9.4).

The rent index constructed by Clark from the charity properties showed the same faltering in the late 1830s and the 1840s. The index constructed by Feinstein, which placed greater reliance on the income tax returns, was more optimistic about this period because they recorded only slender gains at the start of the century. Either the 1803–14 tax returns were greatly under-assessed or the charity-owned properties were managed in very specific ways, for example by having more flexible leases able to respond to short-term market pressures.

The full account of net capital stock at the end of each decade prepared by Feinstein, showed, again, a faltering in the per capita accumulation of houses in the 1840s.[14] On these figures housing was unlikely to compensate for the decline in personal property. His calculations for total net fixed capital stock do provide questions for the results from the probate

[14] C. Feinstein and S. Pollard (eds.), *Studies in Capital Formation in the United Kingdom, 1750–1920* (Oxford, 1988), pp. 441 and 452.

Table 9.3 *Estimated rental income from land and farms, housing and shops, England and Wales, 1770–1869 (all at 1860–69 prices)*

Date	Population (millions)	Land and farms (£m)	Houses and shops etc (£m)	Land per capita (£m)	Houses per capita (£m)
1770–79	7.0	23.2	9.1	3.31	1.30
1780–89	7.6	23.0	8.4	3.03	1.11
1790–99	8.3	28.2	12.0	3.40	1.45
1800–09	9.2	39.0	17.5	4.24	1.90
1810–19	10.4	49.8	24.8	4.79	2.38
1820–29	12.1	43.5	29.4	3.60	2.43
1830–39	14.0	41.3	33.0	2.95	2.36
1840–49	16.7	42.3	37.0	2.53	2.22
1850–59	18.8	41.9	43.4	2.23	2.31
1860–69	21.1	46.3	60.2	2.19	2.85

Source: G. Clark, Shelter from the Storm: Housing and the Industrial Revolution, 1550–1909, *Journal of Economic History*, 62 (June 2002) 501, 505 and 506.

Table 9.4 *Index of rent income constructed by Clark and by Feinstein, England and Wales, 1780–1889. (Rent index 1860–69=100)*

Date	Clark outside London rent index	Clark geometric mean	Feinstein
1780–89	44	45	40
1790–99	48	50	43
1800–04	66	68	48
1805–09	79	80	51
1810–14	96	92	59
1815–19	88	85	59
1820–24	88	88	54
1825–29	90	91	53
1830–34	95	91	60
1835–39	90	89	70
1840–49	89	86	78
1850–59	90	90	85
1860–69	100	100	100
1870–79	107	110	115
1880–89	109	118	123

figures. The results from the railway building and associated investment showed very clearly. These did not show in the probate figures. There were two possibilities. The national income accounting may well underestimate the depreciation and writing down of asset values required as a

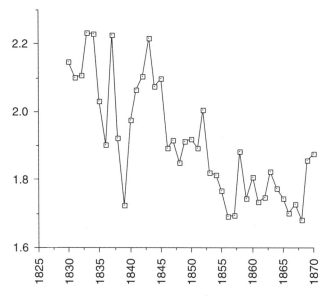

Fig. 9.5 Ratio of probate duty to GNP, United Kingdom, 1830–70.

result of the decline in the value of railway shares. More likely the movement of value between various types of assets as a result of the way in which rail building was financed was also a means of moving asset value between generations, so that the older generation who held passive assets like the rail shares and debentures lost to those who held more active assets such as the loan stock and trade credits for work done. The gains of this generation would have their impact on probate in the 1860s.

The probate series reflected the accumulation of property and the ability to defend its value. It was not an indicator of income. Thus, some of the 'missing' value could result from a shift in the propensity to save and, hence, the balance between savings and consumption. There were indications that this was the case. If the probate duty totals as indicators of asset accumulation are matched with Dean's 1968 estimates of national income, then setting aside the year-on-year fluctuations, the ratio between GNP and probate duty changed some time in the early 1840s. This showed more clearly if five-year averages were used.

The same sort of conclusions emerge when the annual average probate figures are compared with the total investment and Gross Domestic Product figures generated by Feinstein (Table 9.5).

The indications were that the prosperity and release from war of the early 1820s moved the middle classes into new levels of consumption.

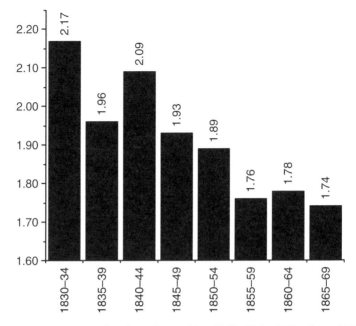

Fig. 9.6 Ratio of probate duty paid to GNP, United Kingdom, 1830–70 (five-year periods).

Table 9.5 *Ratio of probate duty paid to GDP and total investment, Great Britain 1811–60*

	Total investment (£m per annum)	GDP (£m per annum)	Probate (£)	Ratio £000s probate to £m total investment	Ratio £000s probate to £m GDP
1811–20	27.5	200.0	709,529	25.80	3.55
1821–30	40.0	275.0	842,663	21.07	3.06
1831–40	46.5	365.0	913,574	19.65	2.50
1841–50	61.0	450.0	983,116	16.12	2.18
1851–60	81.5	595.0	1,262,978	15.50	2.12

Source: Feinstein, *Cambridge Economic History of Europe*, p. 91.

Note: Crafts's suggestion of lower rates of economic growth than those implied by the Feinstein GNP figures only applies to the period up to 1831. Even if his figure of 1.97 per cent growth per annum is used for the whole period, it would reduce rather than eliminate the shift in the ratio. Note that as the argument is based upon ratios, the total figures are used. Using per capita figures would make no difference to such ratios. See *British Economic Growth During the Industrial Revolution*, p. 45.

This was compromised by the poor performance of the economy in the late 1820s and the late 1830s and early 1840s. Instead of reducing consumption to sustain asset accumulation, the middle classes sustained consumption. The behaviour of individuals like Jowitt suggested that this was the manner in which the middle classes responded to short term variations in income, and all variations would appear short term as year-on-year decisions were taken. This behaviour moved the savings schedule into a different relationship with income.

Such movements of behaviour were hard to measure. Much of the evidence was anecdotal and impressionistic, such as Porter's account of the content of middle class houses.

In nothing is the improvement here mentioned more apparent than in the condition of the dwellings of the middle classes. As one instance, it is not necessary to go back much beyond half a century to arrive at the time when prosperous shop-keepers in the leading thoroughfares of London were without that now necessary article of furniture, a carpet, in their ordinary sitting-rooms: luxury in this particular seldom went further with them than a well-scoured floor strewn with sand, and the furniture of the apartments was by no means inconsistent with this primitive, and, as we should now say, comfortless state of things. In the same houses we now see, not carpets merely, but many articles of furniture which were formerly in use only among the nobility and gentry: the walls are covered with paintings or engravings, and the apartments contain evidences that some among the inmates cultivate one or more of those elegant accomplishments which tend so delightfully to refine the minds of individuals, and to sweeten the intercourse of families.[15]

The pictures of eighteenth and nineteenth century interiors do show a move from scrubbed boards and empty areas of carpeting to houses stuffed full of 'things'. Although this form of consumption would have resulted in the accumulation of assets, these assets were likely to see heavy levels of depreciation as wear and tear and fashion took their toll. There are indications that the consumption of services and goods such as servants and education, clothing and furniture did increase in this period but the literature directs attention to the 1860s rather than the 1840s. The cultural history of consumption has tended to leave the 1830s and 1840s as a dark age. The department store, the mass manufacture and import of pianos and the spread of male fashion clothing have all been identified with the 1850s and 1860s.[16] The limited evidence on servants is especially opaque as the figures from the 1841 census were collected on a basis which makes comparison with 1831 and 1851 impossible. There was a steady increase

[15] G.R. Porter, *Progress of the Nation*, p. 522.
[16] C. Ehrlich, *The Piano. A History* (London, 1976); C. Breward, *The Hidden Consumer. Masculinities, Fashion and City Life, 1860–1914* (Manchester, 1999).

in the portion of the labour force described as servants but this cannot be located with any precision within the period under discussion.[17]

Some of the shift in the consumption function, especially in the late 1830s and the 1840s was a result of an increase in 'involuntary consumption'. Although the portion of national product directed to investment was sustained at around 10 per cent between 1780 and 1860 and might have increased a little in the 1830s and 1840s, evidence suggests that the middle classes found it hard to sustain the asset value of the claims which represented such capital accumulation in their portfolios. The middle classes were hungry for rentier assets to sustain them in the later stages of the property cycle. From 1820 onwards they were faced with two uncomfortable developments. The supply of government stock was reduced as was the return to capital on that stock. At the same time, high status members of the middle classes were increasingly reluctant to engage directly in the business of owning and managing urban real estate. More and more turned to equities in the form of shares of joint stock companies. In the 1820s, there were a scattering of insurance companies, public utilities like gas and water and the canal companies but the totals were small. The late 1830s and the 1840s brought huge numbers of railway shares which were eagerly purchased by the rentier asset seekers. These were men and a few women, people like Robert Jowitt and Jane Hey's trustees, who subscribed, paid successive calls on their shares and retained them for the planned income of old age and widowhood. They were not speculators. They failed to sustain the value of their assets for a number of reasons. The 1830s saw men like Jowitt move away from assets which were local or at least closely linked to their family networks, and which they could evaluate on the basis of personal knowledge and experience. By the 1840s, Jowitt and his like were dealing in a national and international market. Their knowledge was mediated by a newspaper and investment press, by specialist sharebrokers and by the published information of the railway companies and their accountants. Although there were groups of specialist sharebrokers in places like Manchester and Edinburgh in the 1820s, there was no organised stock exchange outside London to create a 'market'. Shares might be traded privately or auctioned with little knowledge of the prices gained from recent sales. Even as provincial stock exchanges began to organise, the knowledge which informed the market was imperfect and often misleading. There was no systematic and uniform standard for published railway company accounts until the legislation of

---

[17] T.M. McBride, *The Domestic Revolution* (London, 1976) p. 36.

1868. In the 1840s, current running costs were often attributed to the capital account, to enable companies to declare 'profits', pay higher dividends and push up share prices. When this failed or was found out, capital costs were pushed to current account and profits, and dividends and prices fell. Even when estimates of costs and revenue were honestly made and published for shareholders they were often misleading. Cost overruns were frequent as the activity linked to rail construction pushed up the price of land, labour and materials. This forced the companies to raise loan capital or pay contractors in shares, thus lowering the value of the initial equity.[18] There was little conception of depreciation. This immature and inefficient capital market had a considerable ability to 'consume' the value of even the best shares held by the most careful investor. In their hunger for rentier assets to requite the needs of the later periods of the life cycle, the middle classes raised their investment horizons from the local to the national to the international. The inefficiency of the institutionalised capital market, together with poor and misleading information flows, together with their own inexperience and lack of knowledge led to a systematic loss of asset value.

The Inland Revenue was aware of the link between the revenue from probate duty and the changes in the prices of shares and other assets over the previous twelve months. In 1860, they noted 'the rapid increase of the value of personal estate acquired by the expansion of trade and enterprise in modern times...'[19] Like many stamp duties, probate was affected by the general level of prosperity. In years of difficulty, there was a tendency to delay payment and 'far more important in its effect upon receipts is the depreciation in the value of stocks and shares and other investments of capital'.[20] The legacy duties were not such an accurate reflection as they were influenced by contingencies which had been established many years previously, notably the many legacies which were payable when the life or widowhood interests in a trust fund were brought to an end by death or marriage.

---

[18] M.C. Reed (ed.), *Railways in the Victorian Economy. Studies in Finance and Economic Growth* (Newton Abbott, 1969), especially articles by Pollins and Reed; R.C. Michie, *Money, Mania and Markets* (Edinburgh, 1981); D.M. Evans, *The Commercial Crisis, 1847–1848* (London, 2nd edn. 1849, reprinted 1969), pp. 123–6 attributes the substantial fall in railway share prices in September 1848 to the realisation of such cost over-runs.

[19] *Fourth Report of the Inland Revenue*, Parliamentary Papers, 1860, vol. XXIII, p. 17.

[20] *Eleventh Annual Report of the Inland Revenue*, Parliamentary Papers, 1867, vol. XXI, p. 18.

The 1830s and 1840s were a period which saw major difficulties for those who sought to accumulate rentier assets and sustain and defend their value into the later stages of the life cycle. This could only increase the anxiety and insecurity which were already key aspects of middle class experience and property strategies. The acuteness and creation of middle class consciousness was a product of anxiety rather than confidence. This anxiety was only increased by the cumulative year-on-year decisions which shifted middle class preferences towards higher levels of consumption. These years of anxiety stood in sharp contrast to the decades 1816–25 and the 1860s which had been marked by the successful accumulation of those rentier assets which were marked by the changing levels of probate duty totals.

Appendix

The appendix reviews two sets of figures which lack the consistency of the 1816–70 probate duty series and then compares that series with the income tax take following its reintroduction in the 1840s. These results confirm the conclusions derived from the probate duty figures.

Legacy duty, 1816–70

The legacy duty showed the same general pattern of outcomes despite the warning from the Stamp Office and Inland Revenue reports that the take from this duty was less closely related to year-on-year changes in prosperity. When set against probate duty, the returns to the legacy tax did show greater year-on-year levels of variation but followed the same general trend (Fig. 9.7).

Probate duty and Income Tax, 1840–70

When the probate duty per head was compared with the income tax take per penny of standard rate, there was a general level of compatibility, with the exception of the financial crisis year of 1867.[21] Property values were much more vulnerable than earned income to financial crisis. There was a break in continuity of the income tax series in 1853–54 when a higher rate of tax was introduced for incomes over £150 per year (Fig. 9.8).

---

[21] The simple correlation coefficient r^2 was 0.88.

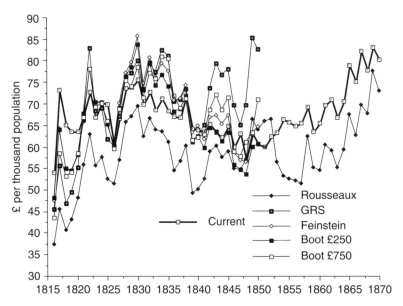

Fig. 9.7 Legacy duty per capita at current and constant prices, Britain, 1816–70.

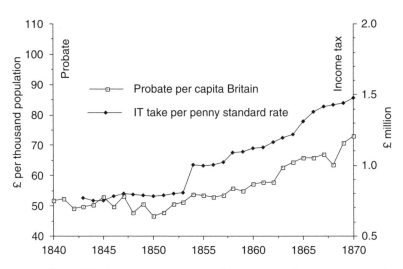

Fig. 9.8 Probate duty per capita and income tax take per penny standard rate, Britain, 1840–70.

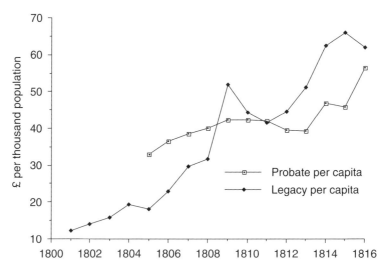

Fig. 9.9 Legacy and probate duty per capita in England and Wales, 1801–16.

Legacy and Probate duty, 1801–16

The figures pre-1816 do not have the same consistency as the 1816–70 figures but, when presented as duty paid per thousand of the population, they do suggest that the experience of the successful accumulation of property and defence of its value was one which predated 1816 and was compromised only by the economic crisis of 1812.

10   Conclusion and epilogue

The relationships of men, women and property and the strategies of families and individuals have been explored through the fragmented, partial and distorting lenses of account books, letters, property deeds and, above all, the text of wills.

The first outcome was the identification of a cast of characters which went well beyond that of the law books, advice manuals, poetry and sermons which created the ideal of domesticity, relentlessly directing attention to man, wife and children. Many case studies did place the married man concerned for wife and children at the centre of decision taking, but he was accompanied by unmarried brothers and unmarried sisters. Beyond them were uncles and aunts, siblings, nephews and nieces, whose roles changed according to their status as married or unmarried, childless or having children still alive. Beyond them were the shadowy figures of the dead – dead children who were left orphaned or single-parent grandchildren, dead husbands who left widows and minor children.

The text of a will was a highly specialised way of looking at an individual's relationships and strategies, but it was one of the few occasions on which a large number of individuals could be interrogated in a reasonably consistent way. Only 40 per cent of the will-makers in the Leeds sample found themselves in the situation of the male head of household with wife and children, the responsible decision-taker. Diversity of situation and potential decision-taking strategies were key features of the property holding classes.

Central to all the stories in this study was insecurity. The middle classes, the property holders, were an immensely privileged group in a society of great inequality, but those privileges were continually compromised by insecurity and potential insecurity. Such insecurities were both demographic and economic. No planning was secure against premature death. Those who had achieved the ideal of husband, wife and children and had emerged from the slaughter of infant mortality and the hazards of childbirth feared the destruction of their marriage through the premature death of a spouse as much an early twenty-first century couple might be concerned about separation and divorce. They knew that at least one of those children who had survived the treacherous first year of life was likely to die before their parents. The chatter of Miss Wainhouse and Mrs Buckle was full of hopes wrecked by death. The honeymoon widow was discussed along with the young lady whose fiancée died between marriage and engagement. Indeed, both the ladies, whose memories were scribbled down in the 1890s, had lives structured by the early death of parents. For others, like Joseph Henry Oates and his wife, insecurity was not the ultimate disaster of death but a slow wearing away of energy through illness and injury.

The second insecurity was economic. There were many examples of insolvency bringing an end to business and professional practice. Sometimes this was a matter of poor planning and irresponsibility. Miss Wainhouse and Mrs Buckle knew how to identify such people, especially when they were asking shopkeepers for credit. But the Birmingham banker, Thomas Attwood, knew that for many it was a matter of bad debts unpaid and the catastrophic fall in stock prices during a slump. Most would avoid insolvency but all would know that they faced substantial falls in personal income as an inevitable part of even a well-managed business life. Good strategy took this into account. This was what prudence and foresight meant in the moral discourse of the period. Those who were fortunate had set consumption levels well below their normal income so that in a bad year they simply had to delay savings plans.

A third dimension should perhaps be distinguished from the economic, namely a social dimension, the threat to reputation. At one level, this was involved with credit and trust and was an aspect of economic resources. Jane Hey's concern to pay bills on a regular basis was characteristic as was Mrs Buckle's scorn for those who did not. Reputation often operated in a more indirect way. The ability to sustain a minimum living standard for women was vital as was the matter of care for children who fell within family responsibility. It was perhaps for this reason, that the wills and the gossip recorded muted approval for the care of illegitimate children but families brought severe sanctions on those whose marriages did not meet with approval.

In many cases, disaster brought temporary delays and sometimes substantial changes to plans. Losses in the late 1830s meant that Robert Jowitt had to delay his plans for a busy retirement involved with the philanthropic activities of Leeds and the Quaker connection. For William Hey II, his son's sudden death in 1837 meant that he had to return to an active involvement in the medical practice he had hoped to pass on to his two sons. It was Jane Hey who represented one of the major concerns of an insecure world. As men made and remade their wills, the prospect of premature death leaving a widow with minor children was central to their strategies. Jane and the two Ann Luptons were amongst many whose husbands had been caught early by death.

Gender was not the only dimension to the strategies of the property holders of Leeds. Age and generation were equally significant. Whilst these dimensions influenced ambitions and ideals, it was economic status and resources which set the limits to possibility. Responses were also influenced by knowledge, personality and the cultural, social and economic resources offered by occupational and business networks. Strategies were constructed within and influenced by three very different ways of viewing property. The 'cash economy capitalist' brought everything together in the market-based valuation of money. Others were 'urban peasants' whose strategies and ambitions were based upon bundles of real property. Finally, there were 'things' people who endowed specific objects with social and personal meaning before bequeathing them to specific people. The strategies of the property-holding middle classes were influenced by available resources, by the situations of age, gender, generation, marital status and children but, above all, these strategies were structured by the potential for disaster in an insecure world. Death and insolvency, debilitating illness and injury, sharp declines in income and resources were ever present.

It was the property cycle which drew these features together. The property cycle was related to the life cycle ambitions of the individual and the family. The property cycle interacted with the year-on-year changes of trade and investment cycles in the wider economy but, in detail, it was related to the life cycle stages of the individual. It was as pervasive for the property owner as the poverty cycle for the wage earner. The property cycle was about capital and assets. It was about access to capital. It was about the accumulation of capital. It was about the defence of the value of that capital. The property cycle began with the accumulation of entrepreneurial capital, often in conditions of heavy indebtedness. Entrepreneurial capital was high risk, high potential gain and high in management costs. Once the balance of debt and credit had been made positive, the individual turned to the transformation of assets in rentier capital with the key qualities of low risk, lower income and low management input. Within this pattern of life cycle capital acquisition and accumulation, the difference in perspective of the merchant, the manufacturer, the tradesman, the shopkeeper and even the professional were much reduced. In the entrepreneurial phase, there were differences in the qualitative nature of capital between the manufacturer with major fixed capital needs, the merchant with account books dominated by the mobile capital of stock in the warehouse and debts owed, and the professional man with a human capital amassed through early, low, and often negative income years of education, apprenticeship and training. Even at this stage, all faced the insecurity of changing markets, fluctuating values and vulnerable reputations in matters of product, service and credit. All these owners of capital knew that their comfort, status and success as they grew older depended upon the accumulation of rentier assets. The range was the same for all of them, houses, mortgages, loans on personal security, government stock and joint stock company shares. The differences in choice depended upon variations in the knowledge base associated with the different types of capital. The tradesman, builder and shopkeeper preferred the local, especially the mortgage and cottage property. The elite merchant, manufacturer or professional man with access to national and international family networks, with their knowledge flows, was confident in a wider range of choices. If social class was about property, then there was little to divide the class fractions of merchant, manufacturer, professional, tradesman and shopkeeper. The property cycle was predominantly though not exclusively a male matter. Women, especially the spinsters and some of the widows, had access in an attenuated form. Most wives had only an indirect participation. Everyone involved feared the insecurities which threatened their welfare, ambitions, privileges and strategies.

In the first sixty or seventy years of the nineteenth century, the family, especially the networked family, was the only effective agency through which the individual decision taker could spread risk. It was the networked family which rescued Mrs Buckle after the premature death of her parents and Mrs Stocks after the financial failure of her husband. The networked family was defined by practice. Relationships and membership were claimed, acknowledged and affirmed by a 'gift' network of visits, loans, services and was most visible in the process of probate and inheritance itself. Within this network, the individual decision-maker had a repertoire of strategies available and might choose to operate at the level of nuclear, stem or extended family, with the sub-elements of cousinage and sibling alliances, according to circumstances. The wider and stronger the network, the more the options available, the greater the damage which could be sustained without breakdown, and the greater the ability to sustain and respond to the risks of demography, illness and the economy. Variety was a key quality which brought strength. The network was strengthened by geographical spread, especially where this involved a link with the metropolis, as in the case of the Oateses and the Fentons. It was strengthened when merchant and professional positions were brought together, as in the case of the Luptons. Urban–rural links also expanded the options. Male and female, married and unmarried, childless and those with children all provided qualitatively different positions within the network. This variety was a key aspect of risk spreading.

The status of the family network as the sole, effective agency for spreading risk was not to change until late in the nineteenth century. For the bulk of the century, institutional risk spreading was insecure and underdeveloped. Life insurance was imperfect and little used except as a means of securing a loan. Pension was a word associated with specific and corrupt payments from government to its supporters. The concept of the career and salary scale, especially one based upon merit and achievement, was unknown until the arrival of the large-scale banks and railway companies of the last third of the nineteenth century and the expansion of employment in local government and the civil service. The limited liability joint stock company was not available to small businesses and, in any case, little used outside the railway industry. The concept of the private limited liability company to protect the 'family' from commercial risk was an end of century innovation. The knowledge flows available in national and international stock markets were imperfect and rightly mistrusted. Even after reforms like the Railway Act of 1868, there were many disasters to deter the middle class investor, such as the collapse of the Glasgow banks in 1857 and 1878.

The text of the wills revealed a number of the dominant strategies. Even in death, the first move was to secure reputation. All debts and expenses were to be paid. Next, where appropriate, the widow was provided for and special care taken of any minor children. Then followed the dominant strategy of treating all surviving children with studied equity. They might have to wait for a part of their 'fortune' until the death or remarriage of the widow, but the striving for equity was central to the meaning of family and property for the middle and artisan classes who made their wills. Gifts and support given *inter vivos* were called back into hotch-potch. Inequalities of earlier support were evened out. Discrimination on the grounds of conduct was rare. The advice manuals and legal textbooks saw this equality as a means of avoiding family disputes, but there were further structural consequences hinted at by Adam Smith's analysis of partible inheritance. Dividing an inheritance was in itself a means of spreading risk. Amongst the Stocks and the Luptons, the failure of one brother or brother-in-law, still left the others to care for wives and children, or to reposition property, debts and nephews in ways which sustained the reputation overall of the family group. Dividing the inheritance had the further effect of making it very unlikely that any one individual could retire from active business

immediately on inheriting and still sustain the levels of welfare and consumption set by parents. Partible inheritance ensured the reproduction of
an active profit-seeking middle class.

The wills showed the manner in which different levels of the family
repertoire of strategies might operate. The nuclear family of wife and
children was always first preference, but beyond that was the reserve army
of cousins, siblings, nephews and nieces. This group might inherit where
there were no children. They might provide continuity for a business.
They might provide help in times of crisis or simply provide flows of
information and the support of visits and sociability. Even those who were
apparently secure in their nuclear family and developing property cycle
knew that if their plans were disrupted by disaster and difficulty, then the
most likely source of support lay in the reserve army. This was the
networked family. Kin were a resource who were valued and cultivated
by an active 'gift' economy. Even those who never called upon the network knew that the potential for support which lay in the network was an
asset of considerable worth.

The instructions of the will were also part of a process which created a
variety of trusts, which were central to the family as an agency of risk
management and to the gendering of the equity with which children were
treated. Sometimes the trusts were created in a formal way with trustees
named and potential investment assets specified. In other cases, the terms
of the will made clear that the executors were expected to manage the
estate for a considerable number of years under terms laid out in the will.
Trusts were created to provide income for widows and to provide income
for daughters and for the support of minor children. In part, this was an
aspect of the process by which women were taken out of active participation in the economy. It was also a way of protecting daughters and widows
from fortune-hunters and from the insolvency of any future husband they
might have. Throughout the eighteenth century, the lawyers and the
Courts of Equity had become more skilled in protecting this income
stream. The trust was also a way of ensuring a partible and, usually
male, dynastic continuity. The end point of most trusts was the equitable
division of resources between children or between appropriate members
of the reserve army.

The use of trusts, together with the needs of the rentier phase of the
property cycle, created a great hunger for low risk, low management
capital assets. Government stock, assets related to the urban infrastructure, to canals, turnpikes and agricultural improvement were all sought
after. For most investors and trust managers this created a focus on the
local and the regional. This changed in the 1830s and 1840s when
the opportunities offered by railway stocks drew many investors into the

national and then international market for railway stock. Jane Hey's portfolio was typical. An initial element was a row of shops in Leeds but by the 1850s this was joined by East India Railway stock. Her 'property cycle' was directed towards the human capital of her sons. This depended upon knowledge and decisions taken in the property markets of Leeds as well as on the fortunes of the British Empire. Both relied on the agency and probity of first a brother-in-law and then a nephew. The local and regional phase had a number of specific effects related to the property 'interests' of the urban middle classes. The inequalities of urban society, combined with the needs of the family property cycle in the face of insecurity, created characteristic forms within the urban landscape. The mixture of workshop, with substantial, front of the street and poorer back of the street housing was a reflection of changing family needs. These properties were at once working capital, rentier income assets and inheritance for the varied needs of sons and daughters. The mixture of function reflected this. On a slightly broader basis, the search for mortgage assets drew the urban middle classes into agricultural mortgages. For people like John Jowitt in the early part of the century it would have been hard to see a division between the interests of urban and rural capital. It was only through the availability of national and international assets through the railway share market and substantial urban property assets in the growing towns that the urban middle classes were able to contemplate the politics of Corn Law repeal, which separated them from the rural interest. By the late nineteenth century, the increasing diversity and geographical range of assets meant that a growing portion of the middle classes found that their rentier interests were divorced from the local. That portion tended to be the elite of merchants, manufacturers and professional men whose knowledge flows gave them confident access to wider capital markets. This division of interest between urban elite and the rest of the middle classes began to show in different attitudes to the politics of urban property. By the 1890s, the property in Mabgate had changed its meaning from being the income which ensured that Ann Lupton, Arthur's widow, remained in the middle classes, to being a slum property and a legitimate target for some of the first clearances of such property in Leeds. In terms of material income and dependence, the upper status ranges of the middle classes were increasingly free of locality.

The trust, with its heavily gendered nature, and the structure of the property cycle, added depth and strength to the meaning of the networked family and to the repertoire of strategies available to the individual decision maker. The nuclear family with children was the preferred option, as the advice manuals predicted, but these nuclear family units were part of a larger system which provided a huge reserve and gave meanings to the other characters in the system. The unmarried woman, limited by law and practice in terms of access to the profit seeking economy, was banker, rescue agency, and conveyor of information to the network. The childless couple, or even the widowed or spinster aunt, was a reserve who might take in orphaned children, or perhaps exchange lodging for the companionship of nieces who came to live with her. The wives and daughters with their trust income not only brought a little independence into the finances of many women, married and unmarried, but provided a defendable reserve of income in the event of a husband's death, desertion or bankruptcy. Small but significant amounts of capital were placed in trust, associated with female members of the network and isolated from commercial claims. Above all, the family was a means of transmitting and defending status. The actual and potential inheritance of a business was only one means of doing this. Status was transmitted by education, contacts, usually from within the family network, and by credit. Choices were made according to individual qualities and the changing demands of the market for the profit-seeking talents of the middle classes. The varied gift exchange of visits, services and inheritance was one means of sustaining the network and its credibility.

The networked family was able to operate in this way because it was a network of privileged knowledge and, hence, important in the building and generating of trust. Given the imperfections of other systems of commercial knowledge, such as the stock exchange, management accountability and information on creditworthiness, the family network of knowledge was vital. This did not mean that all members of the network were trusted. It did mean that the network knew who could be trusted and who could not. Hence, the transaction costs associated with credit could all be reduced within the family network. Choices about which son or nephew to bring into management could be made with more accuracy.

Female difference was a key part of the variety available within a family network. The unmarried woman was an active agent in the strength of many networks. The widow and the spinster were crucial to the risk-spreading strategies. A network which contained and sustained a number of such women was stronger than one which did not. They visited, tended the sick, made loans, rescued the economically unfortunate and were the low-risk investors who sustained parts of the network when male high-risk entrepreneurship failed. A family network which had a number of female-based trusts, money in trust for minors who had lost their father, a number of independent females, individuals spread across a variety of economic income earning and asset-holding positions, and spread across a variety of geographical locations was a network which was stronger and better able to counter the shocks of demography and the economy than networks which lacked those features. In the same way, networks which kept in contact with each other and sustained the basis of knowledge and trust were stronger. Now many of these features were costly. Travel and visiting took time and money. The management of trusts required skill, time and sometimes professional assistance. It involved the opportunity cost of foregoing the potentially higher entrepreneurial income. It involved the opportunity cost of excluding women from the cash income earning economy. Hence, the higher the initial economic status of a group, the more likely it was to sustain a widespread network with all these strengthening features. In turn, the superior knowledge, easier credit and greater variety of options made it more likely that the network would remain high status. This was a self-sustaining and self-reproducing set of processes.

For the middle classes, the dominant structuring feature of the relationships of family and property was not gender but risk management. Gender subordination and difference was a resource within the strategies of risk management. It was an opportunity inherited and sanctioned by many generations of practice. Women were indeed a 'hidden investment' but not primarily in the male-led business. The case studies, like that of the Jowitt family, do contain examples of female trust capital being used to sustain male business capital but this was a temporary strategy. Such capital was moved as rapidly as was possible away from the business and invested in a variety of more stable rentier assets. The separation of male and female capital was a major imperative in family strategies as was only to be expected if the gendering of capital was an aspect of risk management.

The specific legal and social personalities of women were risk management assets in the strategies of the nuclear and networked family. It was the qualitative difference of the female situation in relation to property which made them such a major resource in the face of hazard. This gender subordination was restructured and recultured in the face of new opportunities of wealth and hazard but, in doing so, a number of powerful contradictions were embedded in the system which will be explored at the end of this section.

Several things not on the agenda of the networked middle class family were important. There was no sense of a division between north and south. The Fenton and Oates networks were as active in their links to London and Bristol as they were in links to Lancashire and Belfast. The evidence provided by the geographical distribution of asset-holding patterns were an illusion created by two features. The first was the geography of economic opportunity. The coalfield economic growth areas were primarily in the North and Midlands of England. The second was the location of London in Southern England. England was and is an intensely metropolitan country. The networked families of Leeds recognised this by sustaining links to metropolitan elements of the network. This was a matter of centre–periphery in a highly centralised metropolitan country not a matter of northern and southern socio-economic provinces.

There was no evidence of the privileging of eldest sons and little of privilege to sons. Equity was gendered but remained central. There was also little sense in which the family house had any value other than its asset value. After the death of the head of household most family homes were sold and the proceeds divided between the children. In some cases, the sons were offered first choice of purchase at valuation. In many cases, the house was used to provide accommodation for the widow, but despite the central part of domesticity in middle class ideology, home was an ideal and not a specific item of real estate. There was nothing resembling the attachment of family and estate amongst the aristocracy and many of the gentry. Indeed, the insubstantial and non-specific inter-generational practice of 'home', like the lack of interest in primogeniture, was a feature of practice which distinguished the middle classes from the aristocracy. Linked to this was the low interest in specific possessions. The bulk of family possessions were expected to be sold. As with the case of the attitude to the family house, this implied a respect for individual choice operating within the market economy.

Many of the features identified in this enquiry were not new in the first half of the nineteenth century. Some can be identified by the later years of the seventeenth century, closely associated with the increase in commercial activity and the dominance of the common law courts in England. The processes and relationships of the first half of the nineteenth century would be better described as a system reaching maturity rather than as one which displayed prominent features of novelty. That maturity was linked to increases in material wealth, to sustained increases in population, increased rates of urbanisation and uneven changes in economic structure. It was also linked to the rapid increase in rentier assets created first by agricultural and urban expansion and then by the building of the railway network.

Such an analysis gives an unduly static account of the relationships of men, women and property during the eighteenth century. At the very least, the systems of gendered equity, widowhood life interests and net-worked families must have become available to a wider range of people as population and prosperity grew. Other directions of change can only be deduced from other studies of inheritance and family practice. Using these to place the current study in the context of long run change was problematic. There were variations in sources and in legal and administrative systems. The methodologies of the studies varied as did regional, social and economic circumstances. There is enough to make some estimates of the broad directions of change, and of the typicality of the Leeds sample as a representative of the years between 1800 and 1850.

Earle's study of the London middle classes between 1660 and 1730 provided an initial point of comparison.[1] His sample, originating in the records of the Court of Orphans and records of the London trades and companies, by its nature excluded the childless and most professional groups. There were many features in common with the Leeds people of 1800–50. The dominant concerns were the payment of debts and expenses, the care for a widow and ensuring that children inherited, but there was evidence of a change of emphasis. For the bulk of this period London still operated under customary law but this allowed considerable freedom to the testators. Of personal property, a third went to the widow, a third to the children and a third was the 'dead's part', in other words could be freely disposed of. The end result was an equitable division between children. Real estate was different. Around 40 per cent of those who made a will directed their real property to the eldest son. Overall, only 64 per cent of the wills directed an equitable division between children. In the Leeds sample, 85 per cent of the wills instructed an equitable division and only 10 per cent gave any preference to sons, 7.5 per cent of them to eldest sons. A second point of comparison made it possible to estimate the changing agency of widows. The London study makes no mention of the use of 'trusts' although many of the widows clearly had a life interest, especially in real property. The most measurable contrast was in the proportion of widows who were appointed as executors. Of those who died leaving a widow, 21 per cent appointed the widow as sole executor and 58 per cent as a joint executor. In the Leeds sample, 11 per cent appointed their widow as sole executor and 23 per cent as a joint executor. Using Leeds 1830–34 and London 1660–1730 as markers, there was a move to reduce the active participation of widows in the inheritance process and to affirm and strengthen the equity with which children were treated.

Other available studies confirm the general directions of change. Erickson's survey of a variety of studies made of seventeenth century communities showed that between 60 and 80 per cent of men with widows appointed their widows as sole executors. If joint executorships were included as well, then the figures rose to a range of 77 to 96

---

[1] P. Earle, *The Making of the English Middle Class. Business, Society and Family Life in London, 1660–1730* (London, 1989), pp. 315–23, 392 esp. footnotes 27–29, and pp. 394–408.

per cent.[2] Ascott's study of 1450 Liverpool wills probated between 1660 and 1760 found that, of the 874 men with widows, 30 per cent were named as sole executors and 44 per cent as joint executors.[3] Berg's study of Sheffield and Birmingham in the eighteenth century had an emphasis on women's active participation in the economy. It involved female wills and the wills of male metal workers. Of the total number of executors appointed, around 30 per cent were female.[4] The comparable Leeds figure for 1830–34 was 24 per cent.

These figures have deliberately not been tabulated as they were generated by studies with different methodologies, research aims and sources but the general orders of magnitude and the direction of change were consistent. If being appointed an executor is taken as an indication of women's agency in the economy, then that agency was in decline from the seventeenth to the eighteenth century and reached a low point in the first half of the nineteenth century. The term agency rather than power is used here as the terms of the wills and the directions and trusts involved limited the decision-taking ability of executors throughout the period.

The Liverpool study provided another measure of the degree to which urban property owners insisted on equity between their children. A detailed examination of the wills of the 1700s and 1740s showed that, as in London, testators thought differently about real and personal property. In matters of personal property, 20 per cent of men favoured their eldest son in both decades, but the proportion which directed an equal division between all children rose from 17 to 38 per cent. With real estate, the proportion who favoured their eldest sons in some way fell from 48 to 40 per cent, whilst the proportion whose directions indicated a desire for equity rose from 19 to 50 per cent.[5] The different source base and methodology, and the small numbers in each sample, meant that comparisons could not be made with precision, but the broad comparison with the Leeds figures indicated that during the eighteenth century the drive towards treating all children with equity in matters of inheritance became increasingly dominant. This is especially so when it is considered that the Leeds 10 per cent favouring sons and eldest sons was often made up of those who made quite trivial marks of preference, whilst the earlier figures included groups of eldest sons who gained all the real estate.[6]

[2] A L. Erickson, *Women and Property in Early Modern England* (London, 1993), p. 158.
[3] D.E. Ascott, 'Wealth and community in Liverpool, 1650–1750', PhD thesis, University of Liverpool (1996), p. 331.
[4] M. Berg, 'Women's property and the Industrial Revolution', *Journal of Interdisciplinary History* (1993), 235–50.
[5] Ascott, 'Wealth and community in Liverpool', pp. 355–6.
[6] In Liverpool, this was 24 per cent in the 1700s and 29 per cent in the 1740s.

Two studies located in the first half of the nineteenth century provided a test of typicality of the Leeds wills. Davidoff and Hall looked at 622 wills, dated between 1780 and 1855, from Birmingham, Edgbaston, an elite suburb of Birmingham and from Witham in rural Essex.[7] Twenty-eight per cent of the executors were wives, comparable with the Leeds figure of 24 per cent. There was 'some evidence of partible inheritance' in 79 per cent of cases, again close to the 85 per cent of Leeds. Owen's study of Stockport between 1800 and 1857 also had much in common with Leeds, but key differences suggested cultural influences on the strategy and management of inheritance in different socio-economic contexts. Stockport was dominated by cotton manufacturing firms, the bulk of which employed less than 200 people. Partible inheritance was again dominant. It was employed in some form by 70 per cent of men with children, but in appointing executors these men were very different from Leeds and Birmingham. Eighty-four per cent of them included their wives amongst their executors. There were other indicators of a different emphasis in terms of property relationships. Seventy per cent of the will makers of Stockport owned some cottage property, as did 55 per cent of the female will makers.[8] The comparable figures in Leeds were 53 per cent overall and 38 per cent for women. In Berg's study of Birmingham and Sheffield, 47 per cent of the women held some real property.[9] In general, women preferred male executors. Lane showed that in the market town of Ashby (1750–1835) executors for women were 68 per cent male whilst in nearby stocking-weaving Hinckley the figure was 77 per cent. The Hinckley women were more likely to own real estate. Thirty-eight per cent of the female will makers did so as against 24 per cent in Ashby.[10] London was distinctive. Some 34 per cent of probated wills were female rather than the 18–24 per cent in comparable studies.[11]

The three studies showed the importance of trust based strategies for managing inheritance, although proportions varied. In Leeds, 70 per cent of the wills contained some form of trust based strategy. The figure was 83 per cent for men with widows, whilst in Stockport only 59 per cent of the

[7] L. Davidoff and C. Hall, *Family Fortunes. Men and Women of the English Middle Class, 1780–1850* (London, 1987), pp. 205–12 and 462.

[8] A.J. Owen, 'Small fortunes: property, inheritance and the middling sort in stockport, 1800–57', PhD thesis, University of London (2000), pp. 93, 170, 191 and 205.

[9] Berg, 'Women's property and the industrial revolution', 241.

[10] P. Lane, 'Women, property and inheritance: wealth creation and income generation in small English towns, 1750–1835', in J. Stobart and A. Owens (eds.), *Urban Fortunes. Property and Inheritance in the Town, 1700–1900*, (Aldershot, 2000), pp. 172–94.

[11] D. Green, 'Independent women, wealth and wills in nineteenth-century London', in Stobart and Owens, *Urban Fortunes*, 195–222.

wills were trust based and in Davidoff and Hall's study trusts were identified with only a third of the cases.[12]

Despite the imperfections of these comparisons, the results have enough in common to identify general directions of long term change. The system emerged from the dominance of common law over customary law. By the early eighteenth century, common law and the associated legislation allowed almost total freedom to the English will maker. This was a dominance tempered by the interventions of the Courts of Equity. The Ecclesiastical Courts, despite their responsibility for probate, had an almost totally subordinate position. There were four dimensions of change over the eighteenth century.

There was a reduction in the direct agency of women in matters of property as indicated by their declining participation in executorships. Secondly, there was a drive towards the almost total use of partible inheritance for all types of property. This was recognised as an assertion of middle class identity and needs against the primogeniture of the gentry and aristocracy. Within the English common law tradition, primogeniture was a matter of the cultural and dynastic ambitions of a social class and had little to do with any structural imperatives of land owning. In the eighteenth century, the thirteen colonies of North America and, in the nineteenth century, amongst the growing European population of New Zealand, equity between children emerged as the dominant imperative for will makers at all levels of economic status.[13] Indeed, the broad trends identified in eighteenth century England were also evident in the colonial and post-colonial societies of the thirteen colonies and newly independent United States which had adopted and developed English common law traditions.[14] Thirdly, there was a move away from treating real and personal property in fundamentally different ways. The holding and bequeathing of one or the other were simply different strategies for achieving family and life cycle aims. Lastly, the experience of the first part of the nineteenth century reflected the increasing importance of trusts for managing inheritance and family strategies. The use of trusts in this context had been perfected over the eighteenth century. The studies differ on the overall importance of trusts. They also differ on the

---

[12] Davidoff and Hall, *Family Fortunes,* p. 209; it is not clear why the difference should be so great. It may be that the Birmingham and Witham studies had much stricter criteria for the inclusion of a will in the trust based category.

[13] J. McAloon, *No Idle Rich. The Wealthy in Canterbury and Otago, 1840–1914* (Otago, 2002).

[14] C. Shammas, M. Salmon and M. Dahlin, *Inheritance in America from Colonial Times to the Oresent* (Rutgers University Press, 1987); T.L. Ditz, *Property and Kinship. Inheritance in Early Connecticut, 1750–1820* (Princeton, 1986), esp. pp. 157 et seq.

implication of such trusts. Davidoff and Hall regarded them as one aspect of female subordination within the middle class family, whilst Berg saw the protected female income stream of the trust as an aspect of the limited but important economic opportunity and independence available to women.[15]

These were important changes and were to have important consequences and meanings but, in some senses, the continuities were more important than such changes in practice and emphasis. Inheritance was still about family. Charitable bequests were rare and the spectacular ones gained disproportionate attention. Gifts to 'friends' were also rare and usually minor. Family was about care for a widow and minor children, and then about the division of property to surviving children. Failing the existence of widow and children, property was directed towards siblings, nieces, nephews and other blood relatives.

Studies of late twentieth century practice again revealed more continuity than difference. Will making was about the nuclear family and blood relatives. The differences in emphasis serve to highlight some features of the situation and practice of the 1830s. The main change in emphasis has been towards an increasing emphasis on the conjugal relationship. Few will makers in the late twentieth century in Britain or the USA would have left a spouse or partner with a third of an estate. Spouses usually inherited the whole of an estate either for life or with the assumption that they would bequeath that estate in accordance with shared wishes. In part, this reflected the central importance of the owner-occupied house amongst middle class inheritable assets. To divide an estate into 'thirds' would usually force a disruptive change in location and a substantial reduction in welfare on a surviving partner. The other major middle class asset, pension rights, also reflected the conjugal emphasis. Such rights die with the holder, except for limited widowhood benefits. Nineteenth century railway shares were inherited by children and others. Twentieth century pension rights were not. The twentieth century also saw the growth of legislation which placed limits on the freedom of the will maker, such as that which gave both spouses 'rights' in the marital home. Since 1985, tax law has privileged transfers to a surviving spouse over those to children and others by making such a transfer tax free.[16]

Some of the changes in emphasis were a response to demographic change. Under the demographic regimes of the first 80 years of the nineteenth century, individuals might expect to inherit from parents

[15] Davidoff and Hall, *Family Fortunes*, p. 209; Berg, 'Women's property and the Industrial Revolution, 241.
[16] J. Finch et al., *Wills, Inheritance and Families* (Oxford, 1996), pp. 20–2 and 39–48.

sometime in their late 30s and early 40s.[17] In other words, at just the point at which they might move into the rentier asset accumulating stage of the life cycle. In the late twentieth century, most individuals would expect to inherit in their early 60s, when such a phase was normally near completion. This has led to the increase in 'generation hopping'. In many cases bequests are made directly to grandchildren, who are often in their 30s. This has the practical long term effect of avoiding one episode of inheritance tax but also results in a more individual recognition of grandchildren. In eighteenth and nineteenth century practice, grandchildren inherited *per stirpes*, in other words they got an equal share of their dead parents' share. They were substitutes for dead parents. In the late twentieth century, grandchildren tend to inherit equally across the group. Overall, the late twentieth century reflected remarkable continuity, with changes in emphasis in response to changing demographic and institutional conditions.

The practice of the Leeds will makers of the 1830s was part of a system which had reached maturity as a result of a long development which can be traced back to at least the late seventeenth century and the collapse of customary law. From the perspective of gender subordination, there were many contradictions. There was a reduction in the active economic agency of women. The decline in the widow as executor was one indicator of this. It is impossible to measure if there was less use of women to provide business continuity. There was probably less use of marriage settlements but more use of 'trusts' which gave women a particular, if circumscribed, economic independence. The perfection of the trust involved both greater restrictions on women's use of their 'property' but also greater protection of the independence and income stream which remained. The ideological privileging of married women, wife and mother ran alongside the importance of the 'spinster' to the strength of any network: the Betsy Trotwood syndrome. These contradictions were more than analytical ones. They appeared with increasing intensity in the practice of the nineteenth century. By the 1840s, the middle classes had almost perfected gender subordination in both law and ideology but even in that decade, when the frontier of legitimate respectable female activity was probably at its most restrictive, there were pressures which would, within a generation, create the first cracks in a gender subordination which had been reproduced and developed over many centuries.

---

[17] J. Finch et al., *Wills, Inheritance and Families*, pp. 5–7; M. Anderson, 'The emergence of the modern life cycle in Britain', *Social History* 10 (1985), 69–87.

In the 1820s, the system of gendered equity in a networked family of nuclear preference was tested in an environment of unprecedented material resources. The family networks faced new levels of wealth accumulation, goods and services, investment decisions and consumer ambitions. In the 1830s and 1840s, railway shareholding offered a qualitatively different investment opportunity to the safety of government stock and the local nature of mortgages, house property and personal loans. The institutional structures and knowledge flows required were of a very different kind. These were the decades when rising populations, especially rising urban populations, provided increasing investment opportunity in urban housing and infrastructure. Paradoxically, the increase in passive rentier investment opportunities increased the independence of women within the restrictions of the trust. These were the decades when a mildly ageing population increased the proportion who were seeking rentier assets.[18] They were decades of increasing consumption and, within the ideology of separate spheres, women were the agents and managers of consumption within the family. More consumption also provided more agency to women.

The ideology of separate spheres was not new, but between 1820 and the 1850s more and more people could afford to implement such an ideology. It was intrinsically expensive to withdraw adult women from the active income earning cash economy and to equip them with servants and the material capital of the domestic base. The opportunity cost of separate spheres can be seen by comparing the fate of the two Lupton widows. William's Ann was trusted with the direct management of the property. She ended her life as a much loved and respected old lady with her two sons well-established in the elite of Leeds. The old property was the base for a respectable terrace of middle class housing. When the going had got tough she had taken a direct part in the development of the estate. Arthur's Ann had been left with no agency and ended her days in Sidmouth drawing income from one of the major slum properties of Leeds. The use of the trust was itself an expense. Trusts involved professional management fees or, at the very least, the opportunity cost of time and energy provided by leading males in the network. As wealth and income grew, more could afford the 'luxuries' of separate spheres and protected female income flows. This was a system that was being perfected and extended to a wider range of middle status people and families.

[18] E.A. Wrigley and R.S. Scholfield, *The Population History of England, 1541–1871: A Reconstruction* (Cambridge, 1989 (first edn. 1981)), p. 529.

As the system of separate spheres, male coverture and gender subordination was refined and perfected in law, ideology and practice in the 1830s
and 1840s, the stresses and contradictions were already beginning to
show. The 'Act to Amend the Law relating to the Property of Married
Women', 33 and 34 Victoria c. 93, which gained the royal assent in
August 1870, did not bring major changes in the property rights of
married women, but it was important as the first break in a near-perfect
system of legal and ideological dominance. It was also important for a
bitter and passionate debate which revealed and explored the importance
of gender difference in the networked family and the powerful destabilis-
ing nature of the contradictions within that system. This was part of a
wider debate on the boundaries and redefinition of citizenship and civil
rights which involved class, gender, race and Empire.[19]

The Act itself was short, only twenty clauses, but not as simple as it
might have been. Basically, it gave married women the right to their own
earnings from employment, from trade 'carried on separate from her
husband', and from 'the exercise of literary, artistic or scientific skill'.
Such earnings were to be considered 'to be property held and settled for
her separate use, independent of any husband to whom she may be
married'. In particular, her property was protected if it was held in the
form of savings bank deposits, government stock and joint stock company
shares, or friendly and provident society holdings. She was to have sole
use of freehold and personal property left to her in wills. She was to be
able to sue for property and wages in her own name. On the basis of her
separate property, she could be sued for debts incurred before marriage.
It was a messy and incomplete solution to the problems which the Act was
trying to solve. It had to be changed in 1874 and again in 1880. But it was
the first break in a male-dominated system of property law which had
been consolidated over 300 years.[20] The Act bore all the scars of the
process by which it was created. It is suggested here that the process was
the exploitation of weaknesses in the dominant value system rather than a
direct challenge to that system. This chapter is not so much concerned
with the inadequacies of the Act as with the social and political pressures
which created the Act, and to the manner in which these were related to
the processes and practices of the middle class use of property within the
networked family.

---

[19] C. Hall, K. McClelland and J. Rendall, *Defining the Victorian Nation. Class, Race, Gender and the Reform Act of 1867* (Cambridge, 2000).
[20] E. Reiss, *The Rights and Duties of Englishwomen* (London, 1934); R.H. Gravenson and F.R. Crane (eds.), *A Century of Family Law* (London, 1957).

A bill to amend the law on married women's property was first presented to Parliament in 1857 as a result of a petition organised the year before by a committee of women formed by Barbara Leigh Smith. The petition gained the support of a wide variety of women active in literary and intellectual life, ranging from Mrs Gaskell to Jane Loudon and Mary Howitt, thus ensuring public attention for the petition.[21] The bill was lost amidst the excitement of the general election of that year, diversions caused by the successful Divorce Reform Act, and the coherent opposition of those who saw a change in the law as a threat to the security of property and to the family. In April 1868 another bill was introduced, was amended and failed, but this time it was referred to a parliamentary Select Committee. As a result of this committee's work, the bill reappeared in February 1869. Twelve months later it was reintroduced and passed through to the House of Lords where further heavy amendments were made. These were accepted by the Commons and the bill became law. This progress enables us to compare the changed conditions and tactics of success with those of failure thirteen years earlier.

The evidence before the Select Committee identified the major pressures for change, or at least those pressures which were to be effective before the House of Commons.[22] The case had been carefully prepared by two pressure groups, the National Association for the Promotion of Social Science (NAPSS) and the Law Amendment Society (LAS). The NAPSS represented the organised origins of British sociology. It was founded in 1857 as a major pressure group and agency for the formation of public opinion. It always had a place for drink related papers at the annual congress.[23] The LAS was a liberal organisation dedicated to the rationalisation of the complex confusions and contradictions of the British legal system. The case was presented by two barristers, John Westlake and G.W. Hastings, who were, respectively, committee member and honorary secretary of the NAPSS. Hastings had been involved in the efforts of

---

[21] L. Holcombe, *Wives and Property: Reform of the Married Women's Property Law in 19th century England* (Toronto, 1983), pp. 57–8; M.L. Shanley, *Feminism, Marriage and the Law in Victorian England, 1850–1895* (London, 1989), pp. 2–78; O. Anderson, 'Class, gender and Liberalism in Parliament, 1868–1882: the case of the Married Women's Property Acts', *Historical Journal*, 46,1 (2003), 59–87.

[22] *Select Committee on the Married Women's Property Bill*, Parliamentary Papers, 1867–68, vol. VII.

[23] P. Abrams, *The Origins of British Sociology, 1834–1914* (Chicago, 1968); L. Goldman, *Science Reform and Politics in Victorian Britain: the Social Science Association, 1857–1886* (Cambridge, 2002), pp. 47–51 and 113–27, and 'The Social Science Association, 1857–1886: a context for mid-Victorian Liberalism', *English Historical Review*, 101 (January, 1986), 95–134. Both Hastings and Westlake were on the organising committee.

1856–57 when he was secretary of the LAS. The 1870 Act was a well organised case of 'pressure from without'.[24] The supporting cast of witnesses included a London police magistrate, other QCs, the Revd. Septimus Hansard, Rector of Bethnal Green, the chairman of the Rochdale Equitable Pioneer Co-operative Society, several experts on law in the United States, where some states already had provision for married women to own property,[25] and A. J Mundella. When asked why Nottingham had not petitioned for the bill, the latter replied disarmingly, 'It is not much known in the country; not generally. We are not so thoroughly posted up in these social questions as people in Manchester'.[26]

The debate which led to the 1870 Act fell into two phases. In 1868, the introduction and first reading of the Bill was followed by the Select Committee. This was a period of confident assertion by the reformers and strident almost panicky opposition. The Bill was a radical one needed, said the preamble, because 'the law of property and contract with respect to Married Women is unjust in principle'.[27] By the time the Bill was reintroduced in 1869, the opposition had identified the concessions required, marginalised the reformers and, to the dismay and anger of the women's movement, were on course to produce the Act of 1870 designed, said Lord Penzance on the Bill's introduction in the House of Lords, to settle a few 'grievances'.[28]

The debates of 1868 in the Select Committee and the House of Commons were male debates. It was an analysis of the family economy and values developed over three or four generations by the likes of Joseph Henry Oates, Robert Jowitt and Jane Hey. It was a debate which took place in terms of the dominant value systems of the ruling and middle classes. In this forum the challenges of Barbara Leigh Smith and others were muted. Westlake during his evidence disarmingly claimed that a married woman having property did not affect 'the authority of the husband over the wife'.[29] The reformers and their opponents conducted

---

[24] P. Hollis (ed.), *Pressure from without in Early Victorian England* (London, 1974).

[25] N. Basch, 'Invisible women. The legal fiction of marital unity in nineteenth-century America', *Feminist Studies*, 5 (1979) 346–66.

[26] Select Committee on Married Women's Property Bill, *Parliamentary Papers*, 1867–8, Q 1570.

[27] A Bill to Amend the Law with respect to the Property of Married Women, *Parliamentary Papers*, House of Commons, 1867–68, vol. III, 375.

[28] Second Reading of the Married Women's Property Bill, House of Lords, 30 July 1869, *Hansard*, cols., 979–82; Holcombe, *Wives and Property*, pp. 166–85; Slanley, *Feminism, Marriage and the Law*, p. 76.

[29] Select Committee on Married Women's Property Bill, Q.338; B. Griffin, 'Class, gender and liberalism in Parliament, 1868–1882: the case of the Married Women's Property Acts, *Historical Journal*, 46,1 (2003), 59–87.

the debate in terms of the values and assumptions of a male parliament, their lawyers and their property owning, rate paying male constituents. Herein lay the importance of this debate for understanding the systems and processes of gender, family and property explored in the case studies of this history.

The most important witness was John Westlake. His evidence was backed up and elaborated by other witnesses but it remains a crucial document of English gender relationships, certainly middle class gender relationships. Its general tone was cold and forensic. Only at rare moments does it allow a view of the deeply held commitment, anger, fear, and a sometimes implied and scarce concealed violence, behind the arguments and relationships which he explored. The documents of the Lupton, Hey and Jowitt families showed a system working, facing problems and usually solving them according to mutually understood aims and values. The lawyer who had practised for 14 years at the Chancery Bar dealt with things when they went wrong. He was also deeply involved in that fertile and productive triangle of the utilitarian liberalism of the Law Reform Society, the informed elite feminism of Langham Place and the self-aware values of the educated upper middle class. Law books and leading cases form an odd window on the values and social relationships of any society. They form and were informed by the values and practices of the society in which they were embedded, but at the same time were driven by their own logic of consistency, argument, evidence and precedent. Conflict and the breakdown of relationships, which led to the court room and the lawyers chambers, forced the learned judges to specify the values and arguments by which they made decisions. Nowhere was this more in evidence than in the Courts of Chancery with the ever present tension between the internal logic of precedent and legal argument and the demands of a changing property owning society. Westlake himself noted that cases which came to court were those which involved 'difference and dispute' and not a fair reflection of 'what has happened'. These were not random samples. This was the morbid pathology of the relationships of property, gender and family. The disputes showed both where the contradictions lay in practice and also forced those involved to spell out the values and principles upon which the system operated. This was the basis of Westlake's evidence.

The mid-nineteenth century English legal system was fragmented. There were four separate jurisdictions, common law, equity, ecclesiastical and maritime law as well as a scattering of survivors from local customary laws. From the late seventeenth century onwards, common law and equity had become increasingly dominant.[30] It was the differences between these two which created both opportunity and disquiet for the property owning classes. Under common law, the position of a married woman was governed by the theory of coverture. In the familiar phrases of Blackstone and the nineteenth century legal textbooks, 'The very being and legal existence of the woman is by the common law suspended during the marriage, or at least is incorporated and consolidated into that of the husband, under whose wing, protection and cover she performs everything'.[31] As the Select Committee reported, 'The wife is incapable of contracting, and of suing and being sued'. Personal and real estate were treated differently. Westlake explained, 'With regard to personal property by common law, marriage operates as an absolute gift...As regards real estate, the husband is entitled to the receipt of the rents and profits during the continuance of the marriage'.[32] There were a number of modifications to this. Paraphernalia was '...a very small exception indeed; it only amounts to this, that she may keep jewellery or little things that the husband allows her to have for herself. She may keep them, in the administration of his estate after his death, as against her husband's legatees, but not as against his creditors, except her necessary wearing apparel'.[33] Westlake admitted that he had never known this have any importance. There may have been some symbolic importance linking a married woman's status with clothing and jewellery. A second area involved what were called 'chose in action'. Negotiable instruments like a Bill of Exchange or bank notes were indeed a 'gift' to the husband, but other assets needed some action to 'reduce them into possession', such as debts owing, promissory notes, rent arrears and legacies. These were assets which in theory still belonged to the wife until the husband had taken action. This was important if the husband was to die insolvent for such assets could not be touched by creditors.[34] As regards real estate, 'the husband cannot sell it without her consent, and after his death it survives to her or her heirs, but pending their joint lives the husband can

[30] W.S. Holdsworth, *A History of English Law*, 4 vols., (London, 1931 (first published 1903), vol. I, pp. 133, 186–7, 213–30 and 459–66; W.R. Cornish and G. de L. Clark, *Law and Society in England, 1750–1950* (London, 1989), pp. 11 and 23–32.
[31] J.E. Bright. *A Treatise on the Law of Husband and Wife as Respects Property, Partly Founded upon Roper's Treatise, and Comprising Jacob's Notes and Additions thereto* (London, 1849), p. 1.
[32] Select Committee on Married Women's Property Bill, Q.7 and 11.
[33] Select Committee on MWP Bill, Q.20
[34] Bright, *A Treatise on the Law of Husband and Wife*, pp. 34–40.

deal with the income as he pleases, and dispose of his interest without her consent and without making provision for her'.[35] To the opponents of change, this was a major protection for a married woman, but it was a right modified by the so called 'courtesy of England' under which, once a child had been born to the marriage, the husband became in effect not just tenant for the duration of the marriage but tenant for the rest of his life, before the estate passed to the children.[36]

Again, in theory, the common law protected a married woman's interests through dower. Westlake explained,

The ancient law of dower was this, that if the husband died leaving the wife surviving, she was entitled to the enjoyment for her life of one-third part, to be set out by metes and bounds, of all the real estate which he had been seised of at any time during the continuance of the marriage.[37]

This sounded important but the lawyers of the eighteenth century had long ago found the means of barring dower in conveyances. This had been done in some of the Leeds wills, but it should be noted that the widows were always offered property which was at least as valuable as their rights to dower might have been. Dower might have had a deterrent effect against any men who might have been tempted to reduce their widow's share below the half to a third many gained. But this was increasingly irrelevant after the passing of the Dower Act of 1833; for

by the Dower Act, passed in 1833, the dower of the wife is placed at the absolute mercy and pleasure of her husband; he can defeat it by an alienation of the estate, he can defeat it by his will; and it is only now reserved to her in case of his dying intestate and having made no contrary alienation.[38]

Meanwhile as the Select Committee reported,

The Courts of Equity have, on the other hand, been occupied from a very early period in elaborating a system under which the wife may, by ante-nuptial arrangement, escape from the severity of the common law. They began by recognising the separate existence of the wife, inventing a process by which, through the medium of trustees, a separate property could be secured to the wife free from the control of her husband; in respect of this separate property they subsequently recognised that she could enjoy all the incidents of property, could contract, and be made liable on her contracts, and indirectly sue and be sued in Equity.[39]

[35] Select Committee on MWP Bill, Report p. 1.
[36] Select Committee on MWP Bill, Q.11–14.
[37] Select Committee on MWP Bill, Q.25.
[38] Select Committee on MWP Bill, Q. 25.
[39] Select Committee on MWP Bill, Report p. 2.

The use of trustees to secure the property of married women was initially adopted by the Courts of Equity when property had been placed with the Court either for care or because of legal dispute. The Courts acted upon the often quoted principle that those who seek equity must do equity. This practice was extended over the eighteenth century to a growing number of situations.

This was the system of trustees which was increasingly used by the will makers to secure property for widows and daughters. By the end of the century married women could apply to the court to ask for a 'separate estate' to be created to protect property acquired during marriage, such as an inheritance. In the late eighteenth century, the system was developed in two ways. First the husband was recognised as a legitimate trustee. At one level this increased the husband's power, but it also enabled the wife as a beneficiary to the trust to take action against her husband in Equity. Most important was the perfection of the system by which a wife was prevented from anticipating her income from the trust. This meant that the income could only be paid upon her receipt 'from time to time as it arises'. In other words, claims were only valid for debts incurred after the income became due. This had a double effect. It was a defence against 'the persuasion of her husband to part with the estate' and 'the restraint upon anticipation serves a useful purpose in preserving some income which the family may live upon in case of the husband's bankruptcy . . .'[40] Hence it was used, Westlake claimed, the most where a husband was in trade. Although he steered the discussion of separate estate with restraint upon anticipation towards issues of trade and debt, Westlake did admit that such provisions had a major impact on the power balance within marriage and was, in his liberal utilitarian view, the basis of a major improvement in the quality of decision taking within marriage and in the resulting family welfare.

I consider a separate estate, even without the restraint upon anticipation, to put the women in a very independent position as to her husband. If the husband is in trade, she is liable no doubt to be persuaded by him to embark her separate property in his trade, and she very often gives way to that persuasion, and I am far from saying that in a great number of cases it is not the best thing for the family, and quite right that she should do so. But with regard to the relative position of the husband and wife, I can state that from a great abundance of cases in my personal experience, that the possession of a separate estate does really give the wife a very independent position, and causes her to be more consulted in matters which concern the management of the household and the education and putting out in

[40] Select Committee on MWP Bill, Q. 84.

life of the children, and gives her in the family a position of real importance corresponding to that separate estate.[41]

There was a double argument here. He recognised that the variety of legal personalities provided by women was a crucial aspect of the defence against insecurity. He also saw this as part of the power balance within the family. To the liberal this was not simply a power battle but also an addition to family resources in the matter of decision taking, another aspect of risk spreading.

The political and legal debate showed considerable variation in practice. Some husbands claimed they had nothing to do with payments from separate estates, others waited eagerly for each payment. The influence of the separate estates created by the trust depended in part on the wording of the trust but also upon the characters and power balance within each marriage. The separate estate could mitigate but never eliminate the potential brutality of the male domination of marriage.

Once they had outlined the existing structure of law, Westlake and his allies began their attack by outlining the contradictions and inconsistencies which such a structure implied. They did this not just in terms of injustice to women but principally in terms of values dominant amongst the property owning classes who elected their parliament. They argued in terms of the rights of property, in terms of commercial morality, honesty in matters of contract and credit, in terms of the protection of women, the welfare of families and children and the responsible conduct of class relationships.

Even within the operation of common law property was treated in inconsistent ways. If a wife's property was freehold then she had the right to be consulted over its disposal, but if that property was leasehold, then the husband could dispose of it as he wished, although 'if he does not dispose of it during his life it reverts to the wife surviving him'.[42] In other words, it remained 'a chose in action'. Thus, in places like Leeds where the bulk of property was freehold, a wife had limited protection but in leasehold towns like Sheffield or parts of London there was none. Even Equity behaved in odd ways. The judges had allowed wives equity to property coming to them after marriage but often reserved half to her use and half to the husband or his creditors.

The most serious inconsistencies involved debt and credit. The problem was this. There were many thousands of women in England who had an income stream from their 'separate estate'. The sensible tradesman

---

[41] Select Committee on MWP Bill, Q. 84.
[42] Select Committee on MWP Bill, Report p. 1.

would be very happy to grant them credit in the usual way and expect the bills to be paid each year or each quarter, and most women like Jane Hey would be anxious to pay on time, not least to maintain their reputation but, as Westlake explained, 'she can dispose of her separate estate as if she were femme sole, but that is limited by the principle that she has no power to contract except with reference to her separate estate; I mean no general power of contract . . . [he spoke of] . . . debts which she has contracted with tradesmen for goods supplied'. The debt had to be contracted with specific reference to the separate estate. It was assumed that debts involving writing such as bonds, bills and notes did refer to the separate estate, but oral commands, in other words the bulk of debts with tradesmen, did not. Even then 'a failure of justice arises from the uncertainty as to how much proof the court will be satisfied with'. In any case, action to recover such debts needed to be taken against the separate estate and hence involved a suit in Chancery which was more expensive than the normal remedies of the common law. Even so the remedy was 'imperfect'. The result was immorality and temptation for married women.

by giving married women the power of holding property to their separate use, in the way that they have done, while unable to accompany the power with a fuller measure of the responsibility for contracts and obligations which property ought to carry with it, it is very questionable whether courts of equity have not, to a serious extent, lowered the standards of honour and morality, with regard to pecuniary matters among married women. We see them resorting to shifts to avoid contracts being made good . . . with a frequency which, in my opinion, speaks very ill for the moral effect upon married women of the present condition of things by which they are allowed in Chancery the benefits without the responsibilities of property.[43]

Capitalism does not like a situation in which debts cannot be collected and contracts enforced and Westlake knew this.

As the debate unfolded Westlake, his fellow lawyer Hastings and their allies revealed a strong sub agenda, a line of argument which took them to the heart of the way in which the middle and upper classes thought about themselves and about their relationship with the working classes. Their Bill in its radical 1868 form was designed amongst other things to empower working class women and by doing so serve the moral and family welfare of the working classes. The angel in the house was already a key figure in middle class ideals of domesticity and the angel of the slums was emerging as a part of the middle classes view of 'the slums'.[44]

---

[43] Select Committee on MWP Bill, Q. 74–9.
[44] A. Wakeman, *The Autobiography of a Charwoman* (London, 1900, 2nd edition) and the evangelical sentimental novels of Silas K. Hocking provided perfect examples of the angel of the slums.

The essential goodness of women, in which the middle classes believed with great passion, was seen as an agency for the reduction of poverty, drunkenness and violence.[45] Empowering working class women would enable them to assert and promote the values of work, education and savings. The NAPSS had always had a powerful anti-drink strand and the promotion of women's property rights was an aspect of this.[46] In a more general way the middle classes had, since the 1790s, seen the reformation of working class behaviour as part of their own class assertion and identity in civil society. A long cast of characters was produced to support this. The Rev Septimus Hansard, Rector of Bethnal Green, believed a change in the law to give women the right to their own earnings 'would tend to raise the social position of women ... and anything that would raise the social position of women among the working classes would practically raise that class themselves'.[47] 'Among the working classes, the humbler classes of artizans and mechanics, the women represent the great virtue of providence ... [with property rights, she would] ... save more money for the family than she does now'. He talked of the 'temptations' of the husband and the 'interest' of the wife. His analysis was as much a matter of situation as it was a matter of the innate nature of men and women. The wife was 'practically the great educator of the working classes'. With regard to savings banks 'it would be so exceedingly exceptional that the women would put it by for any other purpose than for her own family and for her husband' hence could not lead to anything but 'domestic happiness'. He warned his audience, 'among the working classes the woman occupies a far more important position even than she does in our own class ... all the home influence is hers'[48] He was followed by John Smith Mansfield who confirmed what was a standard 'story' of the debate, that of the drunken and brutal husband who appropriated the earnings of the hard working wife devoted to family interests. In many cases this was compounded by the accounts of husbands who deserted their wives only

---

[45] W.E. Houghton, *The Victorian Frame of Mind* (Yale, 1957), pp. 341–52; J. Tosh, *A Man's Place. Masculinity and the Middle-Class Home in Victorian England* (Yale University Press, 1999), pp. 46–51; the 'angel' image of women may have been a male fantasy but it was a powerful one, C. Christ, 'Victorian masculinity and the angel in the house', in M. Vicinus (ed.), *A Widening Sphere. Changing Roles of Victorian Women* (Indiana, 1977), pp. 146–62; M.J. Peterson, 'No angels in the house: the Victorian myth and the Paget women', *American Historical Review*, 89, 3 (June 1984), 677–708; P. Branca, *Silent Sisterhood. Middle Class Women in the Victorian Home*, (London, 1974); M. Girouard, *The Return to Camelot. Chivalry and the English Gentleman*, (Yale, 1981).

[46] *Transactions of the National Association for the Promotion of Social Science Conference on Temperance Legislation* (London, 1886); B.H. Harrison, *Drink and the Victorians The Temperance Question in England, 1815–1872* (London, 1971), p. 237.

[47] Select Committee on MWP Bill, Q. 1193.

[48] Select Committee on MWP Bill, Q. 1193–8.

to return and seize hard won earnings from taking in washing or keeping a small shop. The magistrates were unable to stop this because the common law gave the returnees every right to their wives' property and earnings.[49] The President of the Rochdale Equitable Pioneer Co-operative Society completed this line of argument with an account of the many women who held money in the Society, and the refusal of the officers and committeemen of the Society to allow husbands to draw that money. At the same time they were afraid that a legal challenge might force them to pay out to husbands. The Directors of the Society, he said, were 'altogether working men . . . I have never known a case where they have declined to protect a woman; they have done their utmost to protect married women from having their money squandered by improvident husbands'.[50] Such evidence and argument appealed both to the male protecting role regarding women and to the self-appointed role of the middle classes as guides and guardians of the lower classes. This was a powerful argument but in the short term was to prove a fatal weakness for the reformers. This argument was appropriated by the opponents of fundamental reform. It was the topic which dominated the 1869 debates. The House of Lords redesigned the Bill so that it did little more than protect the earnings of working class women and the savings they might place in Savings Banks and Co-operative Societies. To the anger and dismay of the ladies waiting in Manchester and in the Kensington and Langham Place groups, their opponents, by making a minimal concession to solve a 'grievance', had once more avoided serious change.

The dominant arguments produced by Westlake and Hastings depended upon a series of legal cases which they believed exposed the contradictions and inconsistencies of the existing system. These were cases which drew upon key features of the social system and values which informed the relationships of men, women and property and, by doing so, provided not only a part of the process which led to legal change but exposed the morbid pathology of those relationships. The law courts provided an arena in which the exploration of the breakdown and failure of a set of social relationships forced participants to provide an account of the way in which that system 'ought' to be working.

Jane Gallagher was an unlikely character in the list of those who have fought for the rights of women, yet in her own way her activities were as disturbing to the structures and practices of male domination as the forceful arguments and petitions of Langham Place and the Manchester Committee. In 1849, she became a customer of John Burton and William

---

[49] Select Committee on MWP Bill, Q. 1212–65.
[50] Select Committee on MWP Bill, Q. 1283–7.

Watson furniture dealers in Liverpool. They made enquiries and found that she was a married woman who had for some years lived apart from her husband who resided in Manchester and to whom she paid a small allowance. Assuming that she had separate property, they were happy to supply her with goods and a substantial amount of credit. Between 1856 and 1858, she paid £284.10s. towards her account and then refused to pay the rest amounting to £372.2s.6$^{1}/_{2}$d. At this point Burton and Watson became insolvent and assigned all their property, including Mrs Gallagher's debt, to Johnson, the plaintiff, on behalf of the creditors.[51] Meanwhile, Mr Gallagher was dead and the assignees in bankruptcy brought an action against his executor who was Jane, only to find that Mr and Mrs Gallagher had executed a deed of separation in June 1856 which involved, amongst other things, placing all her property, especially the assets of her business as a wine merchant in Liverpool, in trust for her sole use 'notwithstanding her coverture'. The deed also included an agreement to live apart and a covenant by William Seabrook Chalkley, the trustee, to indemnify Gallagher against his wife's debts. In 1859, by another smart manoeuvre, Jane sold the contents of her house to Chalkley and bought them back for £1390 which just happened to be the size of a debt she owed him.[52] Not surprisingly the owners of the Burton and Watson debt thought that was the fraudulent preference of one creditor over others and they headed for the courts. Meanwhile Chalkley had become bankrupt and Jane had been processed under the Act for the Relief of Insolvent Debtors. Out came the law books, Roper on *Husband and Wife* and Sugden on *Powers*, appeal followed decision, and the learned judges eventually decided 'there is no separate estate which can be reached to answer the demand'. The case law upon which equity depended indicated 'that the bonds, bills of exchange and promissory notes of married women are payable out of their separate estates', but 'that in order to bind the separate estate by a general engagement, it should appear that the engagement was made with reference to and upon the faith or credit of that estate'.[53] Legal doctrine and practice meant that it was the separate estate which had to be liable: 'Her person cannot be made liable either at law or in equity'. The court thought it was obvious that she had intended to pay the original debt from her separate

[51] The firm of Burton and Watson, cabinetmakers and upholsters were recorded in *Gore's Liverpool Directories*, 1849, 1855 and 1857 but had disappeared by 1859. [Information from Paul Laxton of Liverpool].

[52] *Gore's Liverpool Directory*, 1855 records Chalkley as Secretary to the Liverpool Tradesman's Loan Society and an agent for the Royal Insurance Company.

[53] Johnson v. Gallagher, *English Law Reports*, vol. XLV, p. 969. The case was heard 12 and 19 February and 15 March 1861.

estate but found no way of attaching the debt. The final despairing comments of Lord Justice Knight Bruce in the Court of Appeal of Chancery summed up the mess created by the contradictions of gender: '... no reliance can be placed on what this woman has stated' and finally 'I am much impressed with the great difficulty of the case'.

The next story came from the case of Harrison v. Grady which was decided in November 1865. At issue was the sum of £64 claimed by Mr Harrison a surgeon for attendance on Mrs Grady. His problems were caused by the chaotic relationship of the Gradys. In 1856, they lived apart under articles of separation. The wife had a separate estate yielding about £108 a year. This was received by Mr Grady who 'allowed' her £40 a year. At this time, the surgeon's bills were paid by Grady on his wife's written instructions, as she put it 'out of any funds of mine in your hands'. Then, in January 1857, the couple were reconciled and began to live together. In 1861, 'a fresh breach occurred' but they now lived in separate rooms in the same house. Some bills were paid and others remained unpaid. It was not clear if Grady was paying from the separate estate or not. In September 1864, Grady 'sold all his furniture and went to live in lodgings'. His wife also took lodgings. Harrison was left chasing his unpaid bills. After a period of great uncertainty Harrison eventually got his money, but the problems were many. Ironically, the period when she had been turned out into lodgings was easiest. A wife who had been turned out of doors was entitled to pledge her husband's credit for necessities and medical care was clearly a necessity. He could only rebut this if he could show that his wife was provided with an allowance to cover such bills, and £40 was not enough. The years 1862–64 were the problem. A husband's responsibility for his wife's debts was linked to cohabitation, but was living apart in the same house cohabitation? Even if it was, the wife only acted as her husband's agent, but her husband's responsibility ended if 'the goods ordered are altogether unsuited to her husband's station in life', but it was 'the right of the husband to fix the style in which his wife shall live'. Harrison only got his money because the judges decided that the disputed evidence of a conversation between Harrison and the Gradys sanctioned the medical attendance at issue.[54]

There were several issues here. The first was the confusion caused to the tradesmen concerned by the existence of the separate estate. The second was the universal one of credit. This was not a cash society. Goods and services were supplied on credit and bills were expected to be paid every quarter, sometimes annually. The insecurity and risk involved in

---

[54] Harrison v. Grady, Court of Common Pleas, *The Jurist* (24 February 1866), 140.

this practice was increased by the ever present risk of bankruptcy in an economy where trade and prices experienced severe fluctuation.

These and other cases often involved a private deed of separation. These had evolved in the late seventeenth century and employed the trust to negotiate the property issues involved for the women concerned. They were still legally married. The creation of such deeds did not involve the judicial processes of the Ecclesiastical and, after 1857, the Divorce Courts.[55] The cases refer to deeds of separation which must have been signed and witnessed like other legal contracts and documents, lodged in lawyer's offices and deed boxes, only to appear in a court when matters like the payment of bills were under dispute. The increasing frequency with which such instruments appeared in the leading cases suggested that such forms of legal separation rather than divorce were the established means of resolving marital disputes, especially when such disputes were based upon personal incompatibility.[56] The existence of income from 'separate estate' must have made it easier for women to negotiate ways out of unsatisfactory marriages.

The leading cases spelt out the social assumptions behind the decisions. The husband's responsibility was clearly linked to cohabitation. The wife was seen as an agent, much in the way that a manager might be the agent of the owner of a business. Her authority was linked to two things, the concept of necessities and the concept of goods and services suitable to the husband's 'station and degree'. The case of Jolly v. Reeves explained these concepts.

Messrs Jolly were hosiers and linen drapers in Bath who had, during 1860 and 1861, supplied drapery and millinery goods to Mrs Rees and her two daughters. Rees was a gentleman of 'small fortune' residing at Killymanellugh House, some two and a half miles from Llanelly railway station in Carmarthenshire with his wife, two daughters, and four sons. His wife had an income of £65 a year from her separate estate and an allowance of £50 a year from her husband. In 1862, Messrs Jolly came looking for their money. Rees refused to pay and the matter came to the Spring Assizes in Bristol and then to the Appeal Court in February 1864. As with many of these cases which often turned on the detail of circumstances, the jury trial found in favour of the tradesman but the Appeal Court reversed the judgement, more interested in protecting the authority of the male head of household than in the general interests of

---

[55] O. Anderson, 'State, civil society and separation in Victorian marriage', *Past and Present* 163 (May 1999), 161–201.

[56] L. Stone, *Road to Divorce. A History of the Making and Breaking of Marriage in England* (Oxford, 1995), pp. 149–69.

commercial justice. In the initial trial Rees was not helped by the fact that he failed to pay the agreed £50 allowance with any regularity, but his own account is worth quoting in full for it outlines the central place which disputes over the control of household consumption had in household gender politics.

Before 1851, I had reason to be dissatisfied with the expenditure of my wife. In that year, I had communication with her as to her future course. She had an income of £65 of her own settled to her separate use, which I never interfered with. On that occasion I distinctly told her not to pledge my credit, and that, if she wanted anything necessary, if she would come to me, I would either give her the money, or give her an order on tradesmen whom I would select. After that I gave orders to the Llanelly tradesmen for goods required for the house. I afterwards furnished my wife with money for the purpose of supplying what was wanted for the children. In 1861, I gave her a cheque for £50, entirely for drapery for the children. I supplied her with money for what I considered necessary and proper, to the extent to which my income enabled me, and more. I entirely supplied my sons. I supplied my wife with money at the rate of £50 a year since 1851. I had no knowledge of the claim of Messrs Jolly till I received a letter from them in 1862. I had not known of the goods being supplied by them. The goods were not sent to Llanelly with my knowledge: parcels directed to me are always directed to my house . . . I never saw invoices before my wife's death [January 1863]. I never exercised any control over her private income.[57]

The claim that Rees was responsible for his wife's debt depended upon the obligations of cohabitation, the notion of necessities suited to the known social position of the family and the principle of agency. As one of the attorneys argued, '. . . during cohabitation, a wife has implied authority as an agent of her husband to pledge his credit for necessaries suitable to her station'. As they dug around in previous cases, they found that,

If a husband makes no allowance to his wife he gives her a general credit . . . for which he will ultimately be liable . . . But, if he supplies her with sufficient allowance for the purpose of paying for these necessary supplies, and the tradesman with whom she deals has notice of it, and afterwards trusts her, he does so at his own peril, and will only be entitled to recover by proving that in fact the allowance was not regularly paid.

The failure to make regular payments was a weakness in Rees's defence and that was enough for the jury. On appeal, the judges turned their attention to the nature of the position of a wife as her husband's agent. It was claimed, '. . . a wife is the general agent of her husband with reference to such matters as are usually under the control of the wife . . . the agency of the wife cannot be got rid of so long as cohabitation continues'. They

---

[57] Jolly and another v. Rees, 1 February 1864, *English Law Reports*, vol. CXLIII, p. 931.

likened this to one partner in a business acting on behalf of the others, and to 'the case of warranty on the sale of a horse, given by the servant of a dealer'. This authority, it was claimed, 'may be expressed or implied, or arising from conduct'. In other words, the private arrangement between husband and wife did not count unless it was known to the tradesmen, who was entitled to make inferences from the general pattern of behaviour of the household. However, the majority opinion of the court sustained the husband's authority and showed just how limited was a wife's discretion in matters of household consumption. 'The husband sustains the liability for all debts: he should therefore have the power to regulate the expenditure for which he is to be responsible, by his own discretion, and according to his own means'. The social theory on which this was based attributed the earning of income solely to the husband and a subordinate and limited responsibility for consumption to the wife as agent. She was 'within certain limits his domestic manager'.[58]

A wife's discretion was very limited. If a wife left her husband without his consent, then she had no authority, but if he turned her away, say by going to live with another woman, 'she has the authority of necessity to pledge his credit for necessaries supplied to her'. Even in this case he could limit her authority by showing that he paid a 'sufficient' allowance. In the case of Johnston v. Sumner, the Sumners had parted by mutual consent and poor Johnston, a milliner in London, tried to recover the sum of £160 for dresses and millinery supplied to Mrs Sumner. He was told, in a familiar phrase, that although authority could 'be express, or implied, or arising from conduct... the burthen of proof is on the person who has trusted the wife'. He did not get his money.[59] Five years earlier Mr Reneaux was seeking £30 owed to his wife, a milliner, on account of dresses supplied to Mrs Teakle, but Teakle showed that he had no knowledge of his wife having these dresses. She always wore them when he was out. He showed that she did not need them, having been supplied by other milliners and anyway they 'were of an expensive description'. Again, the jury had awarded the debt to the supplier, but hopes were to be dashed in the Appeal Court.[60] Mrs Teakle had been a nuisance to a number of tradesmen. The previous day Mr Reid sought to recover money owing 'for certain musical publications'. Teakle was forced to outline his personal budget. He had £350 a year, paid £65 for his house and allowed his wife £30 a year. She claimed 'a certain quantity of music was a necessity for a person in her station of life', but Teakle showed that

[58] Jolly v. Rees, 937.
[59] Johnson v. Sumner, 7 May 1858, *English Law Reports*, vol. CLVII, p. 469.
[60] Reneaux v. Teakle, 23 April 1853, *English Law Reports*, vol. CLV, p. 525.

he did not know of the music concerned and had earlier sent Reid a note saying 'he would not be answerable for any debt contracted by a person calling herself Mrs Teakle'. [61]

There were endless minor variations to the subterfuge involved when trust had broken down between husband and wife over matters of household consumption and the tradesmen were left in a legal no person's land of uncertainty. Two cases from the 1820s involved tradesmen seeking payment from Mr Benedict, a lawyer who was a special pleader. Mrs Benedict had been a busy lady. Montague, a working jeweller had supplied her with jewellery to a value of £83 and received only £34 on account. Seaton wanted payment for kid gloves, ribands, muslins, lace, silks and silk stockings 'thirteen pair of which, of a very expensive description were charged for as having been delivered on one day'. First Benedict showed that none of this was a necessity in terms of his station in life. He lived in a ready furnished house in Guildford Street. The furniture was not new and some was very shabby. He had no man servant. His wife had brought a 'fortune' of less than £4000 to their marriage in 1817 and she was allowed £60 a year and had had plenty of jewellery at the time of their marriage. Next he showed that he had no knowledge of the articles concerned being delivered and so could not have given 'assent'. He left his house at ten every morning and returned at five. The goods at issue had always been delivered to the house in the middle of the day. He had seen his wife wearing the gloves and some of the silk stockings and was willing to pay for these. Although cohabitation was demonstrated, the authority implied was rebutted because 'these articles were not necessary for the wife of a person in his degree', and he had no knowledge of the goods being acquired and, hence, there could be no implied authority. As in other cases, the progress of this dispute through the courts reflected important status divisions within the middle classes. The juries supported the claims of the tradesmen. The judges in appeal looked after the authority of the husband. Indeed, in this case, they treated the tradesmen involved with considerable contempt. Montague was told

There were some things which it might and must always be presumed the wife had authority to buy, such as provisions for the daily use of the family over which she presided.

But, the court was asked

---

[61] Reid v. Teakle, 2 May 1858, *English Law Reports*, vol. CXXXVIII, p. 1346.

Is it then to be presumed, that a husband working hard for the maintenance of himself and his family, keeping no man-servant, and living in a house badly furnished, would authorize his wife to lay out, in the course of six weeks, half of her yearly income in trinkets? If the tradesman in this case had exercised a sound judgement, he must have perceived that this money would have been much better laid out in furniture for the house, than in decking the plaintiff's wife with useless ornaments, which would so ill correspond with the furniture of the house ... there was gross negligence on the part of the plaintiff if he ever intended to make the husband responsible. If a tradesman is about to trust a married women for what are not necessities, and to an extent beyond what her station in life requires, he ought in common prudence to enquire of the husband if she has his consent. ... Where a tradesman takes no pains to ascertain whether the necessity exists or not, he supplies the articles at his own peril.[62]

The counter point of jury and Appeal Court was again important. In a jury trial, the mainly middle class jury, possibly with sympathies to the tradesmen, tended to give maximum authority to the theoretical power which the doctrine of necessities gave to women.[63] The leading cases quoted in the legal textbooks had been sieved through the arguments of the Appeal Courts and the judges who were drawn from a higher status social elite, possibly with sympathies to the minor gentry whose credit was being pledged by their wives and claimed by the tradesmen.

The logic and precedents of these cases was traced back through a series of cases running from the late seventeenth to the early part of the nineteenth century. There were cases in which purchasers had failed to secure annuities which they believed were secured on a 'separate estate'. Most were about personal and household consumption in an uncertain commercial world. Many of the early cases tended to be gentry in dispute with London tradesmen. Manby v. Scott (1663) was often quoted. Dame Scott had left her husband and he had refused her offer to return. The unfortunate tradesman had failed to collect his debts. As the judge said at the time,

the wife is but a servant, who without assent, precedent and subsequent, cannot charge the master, but because the property of the wives ... is in the husband, it is but reasonable that the husband should allow his wife necessaries.[64]

[62] Montague v. Benedict, 26 January 1825, *English Law Reports*, vol. CVII, pp. 867–9; Seaton v. Benedict, 11 June 1828, *English Law Reports*, vol. CXXX, pp. 969–71.

[63] M. Finn, 'Women, consumption and coverture in England, c.1760–1860', *Historical Journal*, 39, 3 (1996), 703–22.

[64] Manby v. Scott, *English Law Reports*, vol. LXXXIII, p. 816.

But that was not enough to enable Manby to collect his money. The lessons from this case were quoted with relish in the disputes of the 1850s and 1860s.

If the husband shall be bound by this contract, many inconveniences must ensue. The husband will be accounted the common enemy; and the mercer and the gallant will unite with the wife . . . Wives will be their own carvers, and like hawks will fly abroad and find their own prey. It shall be left to the pleasure of a London jury to dress my wife as they think proper.[65]

It was a characteristic of the development of gender relationships that a pattern of relationships and practices developing within the gentry and urban elites, mainly in and around London, then spread to the middling and middle classes.[66] In some cases the practices were modified in specifically middle class ways as with the inheritance practices of gendered equity. In other cases these practices took on new meanings in the middle ranks. 'Separate spheres' had a very different meaning within the gentry and urban elites to the meaning and implications within the business, workshop and professional offices of Leeds and Birmingham. The gentry was a class which gained its identity and meaning from elegant leisure, conspicuous consumption and collecting rents, sometimes directly and sometimes in the form of political influence. For the middle classes, as cases like the Benedicts indicated, class involved men who left the house to work each day and women who managed the household under their direction. The details of the late seventeenth and eighteenth century case law derived from a gentry and aristocratic led legal system, and often involved gentry, or rather gentlewomen, in dispute with professional and tradesmen classes over matters of debt and financial obligations.

This exploration of the legal landscape cast a very sharp light upon the asymmetrical bargain of gender inequality. In theory, the wife offered subordination and the 'gift' of her property during coverture and, in return, the husband undertook the obligation to care for her, including responsibility for her debts. This responsibility centred upon cohabitation, the concept of necessities for the chosen 'station in life' and of agency. The legal cases showed just how limited and contingent this responsibility could be. In practice, the husband had a very wide

---

[65] Quoted in Jolly v. Rees, p. 935.
[66] See the literature and evidence reviewed in the second edition of L. Davidoff and C. Hall, *Family Fortunes* (London 2002), xiii–xlix; A. Vickery, 'Golden age to separate spheres? A review of the categories and chronology of English women's history', *Historical Journal*, 36, 2 (1993), 383–414; A. Vickery, *The Gentleman's Daughter. Women's Lives in Georgian England* (Yale, 1998); N. Tadmor, *Family and Friends in Eighteenth-Century England* (Cambridge, 2001).

discretion and could redefine, almost at will, the meaning of necessities and station in life for his household. This male acceptance of major responsibility in return for subordination and privilege was much debated in other areas of law as a justification for male dominance but, in practice, was found to be very limited. It was true that husbands were responsible for the costs of wife and children who required help from the Poor Law, but this was only a charge after his family had become paupers and implied no obligation to prevent them falling into poverty. For the middle classes, the law relentlessly returned to the Appeal Courts to defend the husband's authority and, in doing so, still left massive areas of uncertainty for a tradesman to weave a way through when supplying goods and services. When Isabella Beeton chose the title for the first edition of *The Book of Household Management* in 1868, she chose with some precision, for the middle class wives she addressed were indeed managers with all the responsibility and dependent agency of the manager of a factory to the capitalist owner. The 1850s were a decade of increasing consumption, and household consumption was women's business. Hence, the worries of those who believed in contract and the honest payment of debts intensified and spread to more and more individuals and areas of society.

In this context the strategy of the anti-reformers emerged in the parliamentary debates and in the questions put to Westlake and Hastings in the Select Committee. Women, they believed, were clearly in need of 'protection'. The means of demonstrating this were a series of stories, told as 'moral fables' and all based upon experience. These stories provided a potent and disturbing mixture of brutality and sexual threat from other males, together with alcoholic drink and brief periods of female independence. During the Select Committee hearing, Powell asked Westlake

a question of considerable delicacy . . . you mentioned a case where someone succeeded in debauching a woman; I wish to ask whether you think that it would be conducive to the happiness of married life if a woman, perhaps a good woman, but still possessed of personal attractions, was to go out into the world and be negotiating in shares or in other affairs of life with agents and people of various classes, who might not be notorious of their high notions of what was right.[67]

It was a potential and, for the immediate future, a fatal weakness of the reformers that they allowed themselves to be led into this area of discourse. They often presented their case in terms of the need to protect

---

[67] Select Committee on MWP Bill, Q. 249.

women for they knew that such a presentation would appeal to many undecided MPs and voters. Westlake told the story of

> a case in which he was counsel for a widow who had property to the amount of some hundreds a year left her by her husband who was a tradesman. A travelling pedlar came in her way and succeeding in intoxicating her and inducing her to marry him.[68]

The antis were all too ready to protect women and saw the limited bills of 1869 and 1870 in just that light. Even Lopes, a leading anti, admitted the need to deal with 'the spoilation of the savings of the women of the humbler classes by dissolute and idle husbands'.[69] Women were presented as victims who needed protection from male evil and their own weaknesses. Powell felt that the use of separate estate with restraint on anticipation indicated 'a certain weakness on the part of women against which it is desirable that society should guard them'.[70] In parliament, Lopes claimed the bill would be no protection to women because '... it could not be doubted that women were more liable to be imposed upon than men'.[71] Everyone was easier with the notion that it was working class women who needed protection from the violence of working class men. As the Rev Septimus Hansard told the Select Committee, 'amongst the very lowest stratum of our population [there is amongst men] a very great deal of brutality and disregard for the marriage tie'.[72] Although the gentlemen of the Select Committee were more at ease talking about working class violence, the diversion of the debate away from rights and justice towards protection took place in the context of a growing knowledge of brutality and violence within middle class marriage. The extensive reporting of cases under the Divorce Act of 1857 created a very public knowledge of middle class male violence to the considerable shock of those men who were keeping their part of the bargain of protection.[73]

Women also appeared in the debates as predators who needed protection from themselves just as husbands needed protection from them. The sexual predators of the sixteenth and seventeenth centuries were replaced by the credit and consumer predators ready to pledge the property of the

---

[68] Select Committee on MWP Bill, Q. 130.
[69] House of Commons, 14 April 1869.
[70] Select Committee on MWP Bill, Q. 112.
[71] House of Commons, 10 June 1868, Second Reading.
[72] Select Committee on MWP Bill, Q. 1193.
[73] A.J. Hammerton, *Cruelty and Companionship. Conflict in Nineteenth-century Married Life* (London, 1992; A. Horstman, *Victorian Divorce* (London, 1985); G. Savage, 'Erotic stories and public decency: newspaper reporting of divorce proceedings in England', *Historical Journal* 41, 2 (1998), 511–28.

devoted male.[74] Memories of Mrs Benedict, Mrs Teakle and Mrs Rees haunted the debates. Westlake and Hastings were subjected to a torrent of 'what ifs'. Mr Goldney asked, 'Supposing a woman drank and dressed very extravagantly?'[75] 'Marriage settlements', Mr Lopes told the Commons, 'were not sanctioned by the law in order to protect the wife against the husband, but to protect her against her own improvidence'.[76]

The second area of argument centred around the need to protect the authority of the male husband which the anti-reformers believed crucial to domestic order and happiness. Lopes claimed that the Bill would 'introduce discomfort, ill feeling and distrust where hitherto harmony and concord had prevailed . . . The married women of England' he felt 'would prefer that spirit of mutual confidence, which was the great element of happiness in marriage'.[77] The bill '. . . would go far to impair the confidence that ought to exist between husband and wife, and which was the mainspring of domestic happiness'.[78] The sense of moral threat felt by the opponents of reform was evident in the questioning of Westlake and Hastings in the select committee. Westlake was constantly accused by Ayrton of wanting to make marriage into 'a contract to concubinage'.[79] Amongst the 'what ifs' of the debate was the image of the wife arrested for debt.

suppose there was an extravagant wife, to whom the husband was nevertheless fondly attached. She might be arrested for debts perhaps at the dinner table, and the husband would either have to pay them or allow her to go to prison.[80]

or the working class version outlined by Karslake.

If this bill passed, a hardworking journeyman, whose employment took him from home, might find on his return, that his wife was in gaol instead of taking care of his family.[81]

There was little sense or logic in this as the reformers pointed out, but the passion with which these points was made was a reminder of the degree to which the middle classes had built their security, their risk management in an insecure world, upon the male-led networked family. These arguments were a reminder of the degree to which female difference,

---

[74] R.B. Shoemaker, *Gender in English Society, 1650–1850* (London, 1998), pp. 15–43; A.J. Fletcher, *Gender, Sex and Subordination in England, 1500–1800* (Yale, 1995), pp. 3–82.
[75] Select Committee on MWP Bill, Q. 742.
[76] House of Commons, 14 April 1869.
[77] House of Commons, 10 June 1868, Second Reading.
[78] House of Commons 14 April 1869.
[79] Select Committee on MWP Bill, Q. 202.
[80] Lopes, House of Commons 10 June 1868, Second Reading.
[81] House of Commons 10 June 1868, Second Reading.

especially legal difference, was a part of family risk management strategy. There was a sense of panic that reform would destroy a structure of relationships which had served the welfare of many families. At one point Hastings claimed that the radical 1868 version of the bill would not affect 'the authority of the husband over his wife'.[82] He was an accomplished pressure group operator. It was not clear if he really believed this or simply did not want to confront too many prejudices at once.

The inequality of the domestic order was legitimated by the anti-reformers' sense of the gender bargain which Lopes set out at some length. On marriage, personal property passed to the husband together with an effective life tenancy of any real estate. In return,

> the wife upon marriage obtained perfect impunity. Her husband became liable for her antenuptial debts; he was bound to support her children by a prior marriage; he was liable in the event of any action brought against his wife for civil tort, and any property purchased or acquired by him was subject, in case there was no will, to her thirds or dower. Thus there was nothing unequal or harsh in the law, which was consistent with the whole relations between husband and wife. It was founded on the principle that in return for the confidence of the wife, the husband gave her protection and support; that he was most competent to deal with any property belonging to either; that there must be one head of the family, and that he was the proper head. That principle of law had worked well for centuries, and there was no reason why it should be altered.[83]

As the Attorney-General said later in the debate,

> It is true that the wife gives up a certain amount of interest in her property to her husband, but what does she get in return? Perfect immunity from the debts contracted by herself. A wife may order goods for which her husband must pay.

It was part of the reformers' case that this bargain had broken down. Dower could be set aside with ease. The increasing importance of personal property in a commercial society meant that women's interest in real estate during coverture was less relevant. The development of case law meant that male obligation in matters of credit and the Poor Law was often trivial.

The gender bargain then was seen to be unravelling but the argument also revealed two very different views of the legitimate pattern of social authority. The first was hierarchical. Inequality was justified by the acceptance of obligation by the dominant. This sense of hierarchy dominated accounts of social and political authority in the eighteenth

---

[82] Select Committee on MWP Bill, Q. 339.
[83] House of Commons, 10 June 1868, Second Reading.

century.[84] It was embedded in the racial theory which took missionaries to Africa and Jamaica.[85] It drove the understanding of class relationships which led to the creation of a wide range of philanthropic and educational organisations directed by the middle classes for the working classes.[86] It was central to the way in which most men thought about and justified gender relationships. Indeed, many of the reformers spoke as if they were simply repairing the damage done in recent years to the gender bargain by the abolition of dower and the increasing importance of personal property.

Against this emerged a sense of the infinite worth of the self-directed individual which had informed radical theory and produced its most potent expression in Mill's *On Liberty*, published in 1859. *The Subjection of Women*, published in 1869, and deeply influenced by Harriett Taylor, who became Mill's wife after her first husband's death, and by Helen, his step-daughter, was a work which applied these ideas in a more specific manner to gender[87] Authority was based upon decisions taken by self-directing well-informed individuals who had heard and taken into account each other's arguments and interests. In general, the reformers argued in terms of hierarchy but there were two occasions when they broke cover and revealed some of the social theory from which they derived legitimacy. J S Mill spoke at length in the 1868 debate,

A large portion of the inhabitants of this country are now in the anomalous position of having imposed on them, without their having done anything to deserve it, what we inflict as a penalty on the worst criminals. Like felons they are incapable of holding property. And the class of women who are in that position are married women, whom we profess a desire to surround with marks of honour and dignity. It seems to be the opinion of those who oppose the measure that it is impossible for society to exist on a harmonius footing between two persons unless one of them has absolute power over the other. This may have been the case in savage times, but we have advanced beyond the savage state; and I believe it is not found that civilized men and women cannot live with their brothers or with their sisters except on such terms, or that business cannot be successfully carried on unless one partner has the absolute mastery over the other.

---

[84] H.T. Dickinson, *Liberty and Property. Political Ideology in Eighteenth-Century Britain* (London, 1977).

[85] C. Hall, *Civilizing Subjects. Metropole and Colony in the English Imagination, 1830–1867* (Cambridge, 2002).

[86] R.J. Morris, *Class, Sect and Party. The Making of the British Middle Class: Leeds, 1820–50* (Manchester, 1990).

[87] J.S. Mill, *Autobiography* (London, 1873), p. 265. The Oxford University Press cheap edition of 1912 grouped *The Subjection* with *On Liberty* and *Representative Government* with an introduction by Millicent Garrett Fawcett who saw the three works very much as part of a political whole. Stefan Collini editing for Cambridge in 1989 also gathered *The Subjection* with *On Liberty* and then added *Chapters on Socialism* and an introduction looking back to 1970s and 1980s feminism, p. xviii.

The family offers a type and a school of the relation of superiors and inferiors, exemplified in parents and children, but it should also offer a type and a school of the relationship of equality exemplified in husband and wife. I am not insensible to the evils which husbands suffer from bad and unprincipled wives. Happily the sufferings of slavery extend to the slave master as well as to the slave ... it is only by doing justice to people that we can hope to prevent their enroaching upon the rights of others. Would the hon. member for Colchester accept for himself exclusion from all rights of property, on condition that someone else should pay his debts, and make atonement for his wrongs? ... (he agreed) if the rights of husband and wife are to be equal, their obligations ought also to be equal.[88]

This sort of argument was dismissed by Karslake with all the patronising sneers of the practical man, the experienced lawyer, for the intellectual,

in spite of that hon. Member's great ability and research, he had treated the matter as regarded husband and wife in a philosophical rather than a practical spirit ... he did not think the hon gentleman appreciated sufficiently the difference between a man and a woman in this country ... he did not mean to disparage the writings of the hon. Gentleman for they all knew that one of the greatest of philosophers had written the most fanciful and even the most irrational things with regard to women.[89]

Westlake, goaded by the rather sneering depreciation of his ideas as an amoral contract for concubinage during questions from Ayrton, put aside his judicious lawyer mode for a moment and delivered some basic liberal utilitarian theory to justify extending a wife's independence within marriage,

The children, and in fact the husband and wife themselves, will then obtain the advantage of whatever wisdom and judgement may be found upon either side; the husband and wife being in a position which is obviously more independent than that in which the present law puts them, each of them will have an opportunity of making his or her wisdom and judgement in the management of family prevail and be respected in that proportion in which it ought to be respected; whereas now it often happens that the family entirely loses the benefit of what wisdom and judgement the wife may have, because she is not in a position in which she can make it felt against the arbitrary authority of the husband.

Others like Jacob Bright saw matters in terms of a gospel of work, a sort of moral labour theory of property which John Locke would have recognised. For him, labour was the strongest title to property and 'to his mind property created or earned by a woman was still more sacred ... Nature had put barriers in the way of her earning her own subsistence, and the

---

[88] House of Commons, 10 June 1868, Second Reading; given the polished prose, this was probably the result of the corrected 'proofs' of his speech supplied by Mill to the editors of *Hansard*; Olive Anderson, 'Hansard's Hazards: an illustration from recent interpretations of Married Women's Property Law and the 1857 Divorce Act, *English Historical Review* (1997), 1202–15.

[89] House of Commons, 10 June 1868, Second Reading.

law instead of assisting her weakness, denied her the commonest protection'.[90] This was his response to the Manchester petition for the Bill. But it was the legitimating bargain of hierarchy that was embedded in the family experience of William Lupton, Robert Jowitt and William Hey. They were males of authority who felt they had earned such authority through their trusteeships, loans, apprenticeships and care for the females of the family in difficulty.

Both the reformers and the antis drew upon a legitimating sense of history. There were two accounts of the importance of history available. In the first, society moved from a 'savage' condition to one of 'civilization'. This view was embodied in Mill's statement. Reform was part of that. Hobhouse justified developments in the Courts of Equity as an aspect of historical progress: the judges were 'were constantly introducing principles which were more suitable to the advanced state of society in which the judges who introduced the principles were living'. They introduced 'a civilized code of law'.[91] In the second, social and legal arrangements were justified as products of the sustained organic historical development after the manner of Edmund Burke's attack on the French Revolution.[92] Beresford Hope combined his sense of Englishness with his sense of the legitimating role of history,

Married life in England was in a more pure and satisfactory condition ... [than either Europe or USA; this must be due to the laws] ... an admirable instance of practical national common sense ... old fashioned people like himself were not ashamed to declare that it was written in nature and in Scripture that the husband was and ought to be lord of his household.[93]

As Mr Raikes advocated the limited reforms of 1869, he reassured everybody. He admitted that some thought the Bill was part of 'the general enfranchisement of women ... if that were so then the Bill aimed at destroying the mutual relations that existed between men and women from time immemorial. ... He did not think that the time had arrived when the country would be willing to see them (women) placed upon a position of entire equality with men. The prospects of women would not be improved by their descending from the high position they now occupied in civilized life, and becoming the antagonists of men, and by their

---

[90] House of Commons, 10 June 1868, Second Reading.
[91] Select Committee on MWP Bill, Q653–4.
[92] E. Burke, *Reflections on the Revolution in France*, (New York, 1955. Original publication 1790).
[93] House of Commons, 14 April 1869.

roughing it through life'.[94] Opponents still held this fantasy position despite all the evidence they had heard.

Under this second view of history, the present was legitimated by the past and reform must be a series of minor adjustments to restore and adapt existing structures and practices. At times the reformers appealed to this sense of history. Hastings claimed that ancient law was favourable to women and 'In the middle ages when our common law took its origin, the amount of personal property was comparatively small; the property of the law making class was land, and the law was framed to meet the case of real property ... she had her dower out of every acre'.[95] The reformers often presented themselves as simply making a few adjustments in light of historical change and thus getting back to the principles of the system legitimated by history. Mr Headlam was a supportive MP. Talking of the older systems of law he said

When that law sprang up personal property scarcely existed. There were no railway shares for instance. It was therefore not unreasonable that a husband, on becoming liable for his wife's debts, should take possession of her effects.[96]

The literature of debate outwith parliament demonstrated that this was not a simple matter of progress and regression. There were those on both sides of the battle to extend or restrict the power and agency of women who saw their version of change as 'progress' towards civilisation. Ruskin was no less sure than John Stuart Mill that his views marked moral and material progress for women. When he delivered the lectures in Manchester in December 1864, which were published as *Sesame and the Lilies,* he drew an enticing image of 'difference'. He spoke of 'she and her Lord' and the 'helpmate of man'. He warned that 'there never was a time when wilder words were spoken' and extolled 'the wisdom and virtue of a women ... infallibly faithful and wise counsellors ... incorruptibly just and pure examples ...'.[97] This was quite different from Mill's *Subjection* which began '... the legal subordination of one sex to the other – is wrong in itself and now one of the chief hindrances to human improvement,' and concluded with the claim that the 'dull and hopeless life to which women are condemned ... leaves the species less rich ... in all that makes life

[94] House of Commons, 21 July 1869.
[95] Select Committee on MWP Bill, Q 331.
[96] House of Commons, 10 June 1868.
[97] J.M. Lloyd, 'Raising lilies: Ruskin and women', *Journal of British Studies* 34, 3 (July 1995) 325–50.

valuable to the individual human being'.[98] The outcomes of this debate were neither inevitable nor linear. Indeed, despite the relentless logic of the evidence before the 1868 committee and the breezy confidence of the reformers in the preceding debate, 1868 was a brief moment and the tide of 'injustice' was to roll back for another 10 years. John Stuart Mill's text of that year may resonate with the dominant views of the late twentieth century, but it was by no means a dominant strand in the debates of the 1860s and the following decades. Mill's own elegant contribution to the parliamentary debate was ignored by other reformers and treated with dismissive contempt by opponents.

This was the age of Carlyle and Ruskin. Ruskin's view might look like therapy for a failed marriage, but he was a popular lecturer who drew full audiences in venues from Oxford to Bradford and Manchester.[99] Unlike Mill's *The Subjection*, *Sesame and the Lilies* was rarely out of print. His views can be condemned for their restrictiveness, but he advocated education for women in ways that were welcomed by many in the women's movement, and which echoed the views of Anne Jameson, who had inspired many of those in the Langham Place group. The notion of educating women for their moral and domestic roles was one basis from which the women's movement sought to extend the legitimate public role of women.[100] John Ruskin, with a failed marriage and an unrequited love for a girl nearly forty years younger than himself, was a likeable man to whom the gender culture of the mid-nineteenth century had done no favours at all. He certainly had none of the patriarchal dominance which structured Carlyle's marriage.[101]

---

[98] *Sesame and the Lilies* was reprinted many times with a variety of cheap and popular editions. It was much used as a school prize. Tim Hilton, *John Ruskin* (Yale, 2002, original editions *John Ruskin. The Early Years*, 1985 and *John Ruskin. The Later Years*, 2000), pp. 373 and 376. My copy published by George Allen in 1886 was given as a 'class prize' to Ethel Morris [no known relation] of Form III upper of Higher Tranmere College for Girls in 1888. The quotations are from pp. 114–15 of that edition. My copy of *The Subjection* came from Longmans, Green and Co of London, New York, Bombay and Calcutta in 1909, edited with an introduction by Stanton Coit, PhD, claiming that the work had been out of print 'for many years'. I have found no evidence that it was ever given as a school prize. The British Library has two editions for 1869 and then no more until a 1906 copy of the Coit edition.

[99] M. Hardman, *Ruskin and Bradford* (Manchester, 1986). *Sesame and the Lilies* was published in 1865 and had reached the 13th edition by 1898. Some 160,000 copies had been sold by 1905, Hilton, *Ruskin*, p. 373.

[100] D. Birch and F. O'Gorman (eds.), *Ruskin and Gender* (Basingstoke, 2002), especially the essays by O'Gorman, 'Manliness and the history of Ruskin in love', and L.H. Peterson, 'The feminist origins of "Of Queen's Gardens"'. This contrasts with an earlier view, K. Millet, *Sexual Politics* (New York, 1970).

[101] G.A. Cate (ed.), *The Correspondence of Thomas Carlyle and John Ruskin* (Stanford, 1982), pp. 1–58; R. Ashton, *Thomas and Jane Carlyle. Portrait of a marriage* (London, 2002).

In 1868 Carlyle was emerging from the renewal of a bitter debate with liberal thinkers like Mill over the African populations of Jamaica and the other Caribbean islands. This had been re-ignited by the disputes surrounding Governor Eyre's harsh response to the Morant Bay disorders of 1865.[102] It is worth repeating the swipe at his opponents in the Morant Bay debates, which Mill was unable to resist.

I am not insensible to the evils which husbands suffer from bad and unprincipled wives. Happily the sufferings of slavery extend to the slave master as well as to the slave.

He sensed quite clearly that the same sort of patterns of thought that influenced changing views of the emancipated slaves were also blocking changes in views on women's civil rights. The structure of the debates over slavery and marriage, of race and gender had much in common. The claims derived from rights and individuality were countered by claims of natural and scientific 'difference'. It was no accident that many of the men and women involved in claims for female rights and emancipation gained inspiration from the anti-slavery campaigns.[103]

Carlyle was a crabbit wee man whose literary career was nearing its end. He had an intoxicating, if at times incomprehensible, way with words, no time for Mill's sense of individual liberty, and a marriage in which both parties seemed to make each other blissfully unhappy.[104] Carlyle's authoritarian concern for the welfare of humanity led him to scornful condemnation of anyone or any social group which did not match up to his gospel of work and morality.[105]

The cosy textuality of domesticity held sway. This was the decade of the first edition of Mrs Beeton and the great poems of Tennyson. *The*

---

[102] C. Hall, *White Male and Middle Class* (Cambridge, 1992). The terms of the dispute were set by earlier writing. [Thomas Carlyle], Occasional discourse on the Negro Question, *Fraser's Magazine* XL (December 1849) 670–9; J.S. Mill, 'The Negro Question', *Fraser's Magazine*, XLI (January 1850) 25–31; Carlyle then extended and republished his text with the more aggressively racist title, Thomas Carlyle, *Occasional discourse on the Nigger Question* (London, 1853); in 1859, Anthony Trollope joined in with a mildly 'entertaining' account of Jamaica which effectively fixed the stereotype of the black population as lazy and intellectually inferior, I.G. Jones, 'Trollope, Carlyle and Mill on the Negro', *Journal of Negro History* 52, 3 (July 1967), 185–99.

[103] L. Billington and R. Billington, 'A burning zeal for righteousness. Women in the British Anti Slavery Movement, 1820–1860', in J. Rendall (ed.), *Equal or Different. Women's Politics, 1800–1914*, (Oxford, 1987), pp. 82–111.

[104] There was a mixture of sympathy and criticism in two very different accounts. I. Campbell, *Thomas Carlyle* (Edinburgh, 1974) and E. Sitwell, 'Jane Welsh Carlyle, 1801–1866', in *English Women* [sic], (London, 1942).

[105] G.A. Cate, *The Correspondence of Thomas Carlyle and John Ruskin*.

Princess gave a voice to both sides. The old king gave a clear voice to difference.

> Man for the field and woman for the hearth:
> Man for the sword and for the needle she:
> Man with the head and woman with the heart:
> Man to command and woman to obey:
> All else confusion.

This was the argument from subordination and order that the anti-reformers of the parliamentary debate would have been happy to quote, but Tennyson also revealed the brutality in the same voice.

> Man is the hunter; woman is his game:
> We hunt them for the beauty of their skins;
> They love us for it and we ride them down.
> Wheedling and siding with them
> ... Thus I won
> Your mother, a good mother, a good wife.[106]

That might have raised a chuckle in the gentlemen's club, but Tennyson was nothing if not resident poet to the middle classes and gave another voice to Princess Ida, who sounded like the well brought up daughter who clothed assertive argument in graceful ladylike poetry.

> She rose upon a wind of prophecy
> Dilating on the future; everywhere
> Two heads in council, two beside the hearth,
> Two in the tangled business of the world,
> Two in the liberal offices of life,
> ... Poets, whose thoughts enrich the blood of the world.[107]

These were thoughts which inspired and were quoted by Bessie Parks, Barbara Leigh Smith and others in the women's movements of the 1850s and beyond. They were sentiments which had echoes in the arguments of the reformers of the 1860s.[108]

Beyond all this, worried tradesmen were looking for their money, deserted wives lived with the fear that their earnings and savings might be stripped away from them by returnee husbands, the logic of high birth rate, high death rate demography made a mockery of deeply cherished

---

[106] The two quotations are from *The Princess; a Medley*, Book V. *The Princess* was first published in 1847 and had reached the 17th edition by 1868.

[107] *The Princess*, Book II.

[108] P. Hirsch, *Barbara Leigh Smith Bodichon. Feminist, Artist and Rebel* (London, 1998), pp. 34, 44–5, 243.

plans and the market forces of the trade cycle tempted and dumped the most diligent into bankruptcy.

In 1868, the reformers attacked in terms of a series of dominant values the centrality of family welfare, the rights and obligations of property and the need for certainty in collecting debts, together with the middle class mission to 'reform' working class behaviour especially in the defence of working class women from brutal husbands. But the reformers were drawn into an increasingly narrow debate around the protection of working class women and their opponents seized the chance to make minimalist concessions. The cracks in the fabric of male domination were papered over in the amended Bill of 1870 and there the matter rested for a decade.

The theory behind the 1869 Bill was clear. Women from wealthy families were provided for by the system of settlements and separate estate with restraint upon anticipation, although it was agreed by both sides that this system was designed to defend family property against the misfortunes and lack of wisdom of both husbands and wives. There was a problem regarding working class wives. There were claims that the Divorce Act of 1857 had provided for this, but most agreed that the internal politics and potential brutality of working class marriage meant that this was not the case, so the Act of 1870 would be passed to provide for what Lord Penzance called this 'grievance'.

Those who had listened to the debate would know that this left out the bulk of the middle classes. The reformers were tempted by the 'not us' view of the problem.[109] The reformers had pointed out that settlement was unsuited to those of small fortunes. Hobhouse warned that the system of 'settlements and trusteeships is a costly one'. The issue was one of opportunity cost as well as direct cost. It was simply unwise for many middle class families to place their capital in such an inflexible situation.

I do not think they (settlements) are very suitable to people of small means, because people of small means constantly require the expenditure of their capital; it is very much more often beneficial to the family, the husband and wife and children and all, to spend the capital where there are small means, than where there is a large fortune to fall back upon; freedom is in fact more necessary when you have a small property, than where you have a large one.[110]

In the debate Shaw Lefevre admitted, 'The system of settlements and trusteeships was quite inapplicable to persons of small means, on account

---

[109] Griffin, 'Class, gender and liberalism'.
[110] Select Committee on MWP Bill, Q. 673.

of the difficulties and expenses attending it'.[111] The following year Russell Gurney suggested that small properties were those under £300 or £200.[112]

The reformers were skilfully edged away from any prospect of interfering with middle class arrangements. This was the disputed ground. There was to be little protection for or from the likes of Jane Gallagher. For the moment, male authority was to remain its contradictory self, but those contradictions and weaknesses remained.

There were many changes needed before the male-led networked family with its embedded nuclear families, its widows and spinsters, its reliance on the differentiated legal personalities and economic capacities of men and women could be allowed to die. The next decades were to bring some of these. Effective life insurance was a product of the late nineteenth century. The growth of banks, railway companies, the Civil Service and local authority employment brought the career and the pension fund within reach of many.[113] The spread of female education created the basis for ideological, social and political assertion at all levels. By the 1890s, the growing use of the Private Joint Stock Company provided an alternative legal basis for the gendered equity of the networked family.[114] That said, it would take many generations for the male-led networked family to unwind its powerful cultural and structural dominance. The debates and the enquiry of 1868 exposed many key weaknesses in the structure and practices of the male-led networked family with its gendered equity as a means of securing the welfare of the middle class family against economic, demographic and social insecurity.

The outcome of the 1870 Act demonstrated just how robust was the existing male-led structure and practice. The system constructed in the years between the late eighteenth and the mid-nineteenth century was one of great strength. Its cultural authority was formidable. All who took part in the debates of 1868 and 1869 had deep experience of the value of the existing system in sustaining family welfare in the face of risk and uncertainty. These legal structures had been elaborated and employed in a wide range of family situations. The economic logic of the property

---

[111] House of Commons, 10 June 1868.
[112] House of Commons, 14 April 1869.
[113] John Westergaard and Henrietta Resler, *Class in Capitalist Society. A Study of Contemporary Britain* (London, 1975), pp. 87–92, 108–17; Harold Perkin, *The Rise of Professional Society. England since 1880* (London, 1989); Les Hannah, *Inventing Retirement* (Cambridge, 1986), pp. 5–14; Les Hannah, *The Rise of the Corporate Economy* (London, 1976), 8–26.
[114] Robin Mackie, 'Family ownership and business survival: Kirkcaldy, 1870–1970', *Business History* 43 (July 2001) 1–32.

cycle, of gendered equity, of separate spheres, independent female difference and male patrons all interacting within the networked family had
provided a flexible resource. It would be several generations before substantial modification was to come about.

Bibliography

Manuscript sources

West Yorkshire Archive Service, Leeds

Oates Papers Letter to 'My dear nieces' 1788. Oates acc. 1258.
A ledger containing accounts and prices of cloth together with a list of births deaths and marriages of the Oates family, 1782–1859. Oates acc. 1131
Letters from Joseph Henry Oates to his brother Edward, 1821–34. Oates O/R
Reminiscences of Miss Wainhouse and Mrs Buckle, Oates, remin.

Dibb–Lupton Papers John Atkinson Rent Account Book, 1810–15, DB 5/54.
Trust accounts of the executors of John Atkinson, who died 2 December 1833, DB 5/61.
Executors Papers of Thomas Atkinson, 1807. DB 5/71.
Letters to John Atkinson regarding his nephew, 1816–13. DB 5/73.
Professional papers of John Atkinson, DB 5/84.
Will and probate related papers of Nathaniel Sharpe, 1807–68. DB 37.
Inventory and valuation of the household effects of the late John Hebblethwaite, 1840. DB 43/10.
Affidavit showing the number and ages of William Hey I's children, 1828. DB 75/1.
Will of William Hey senior, 1818. Will of William Hey II, 1844 and of William Hey III, 1871 DB 75/2.
Deeds concerning the Albion Street/Commercial Street Properties, DB 75/5.
Deeds regarding sale of land in Albion Street area, 1840–60. DB 75/6.
Details of property sales in Albion Place area, 1844. DB 75/6.
Stock certificates, letters from Samuel Hey of Sawley and others, concerning the estate of William Hey III. DB 75/7.

Letters from Jane Hey and others, probate and legacy duty forms and others papers regarding estate of William Hey II, 1844–74. DB 75/14.

Letters from Jane Hey to John Atkinson, 1847–51, together with a number of receipts. DB 75/16.

Letters from Jane Hey to John and John William Atkinson together with receipts, 1855–80. DB 75/17.

Further letters from Jane Hey to John William Atkinson, 1873–75. DB 75/18.

Account Books and papers of William Hey II regarding income and expenses of his real estate. DB 75/19.

William Hey Personal Account Book, 1827–42. DB 75/20.

William Hey Personal Account Book, 1837–43. DB 75/21.

Brotherton Library, University of Leeds

Jowitt Papers   Robert Jowitt, Private Ledger, 1803–45, BAJ 2.

Robert Jowitt, Private Ledger, 1854–62, BAJ 3.

Robert Jowitt's Cash Book, BAJ 1805–28, BAJ 4.

John Jowitt and Sons, Private Ledger A, 1806–31, BAJ 10.

Robert Jowitt and Sons, Private Ledger, B 1831–44, BAJ 17.

Robert Jowitt and Sons, Private Ledger C, 1845–60, BAJ 18.

John Jowitt, Junior, Private Ledger, 1832, BAJ 23.

John Jowitt, Junior, Private Ledger, October 1848, BAJ 24.

Letters to John Jowitt, clothier, at Churwell near Leeds, 1775–76. BAJ 30.

Robert Jowitt, letter copy book, Mar 1844 to Apr 1846, BAJ 32.

John Jowitt, Junior, ledger, 1775–1815, BAJ 38 and 39.

Lupton Papers   Articles of partnership between William Lupton and Thomas Rider, 1819. Lupton 115.

Letters between William Lupton, Darnton Lupton and Joseph Rider and his sisters, 1827–28. Lupton 122.

Accounts and papers of the executors of Mrs Elizabeth Hinchcliffe, 1826–27. Lupton 123.

Letters of John Luccock to William Lupton, 1822–27, Lupton 123.

Correspondence of William Lupton with Sarah Stock, John Stocks and Joseph Rider, 1823–25. Lupton 124.

Wills of the Rider Family, 1757–1813. Lupton 126.

Executorship papers of estate of Nathan Rider, 1813–23. Lupton 126.

Mabgate property and executorship papers of Arthur Lupton. Lupton 126.

Merrion Street deeds and receipts and papers of Ann Lupton. Lupton 127.

Account Book of Executors of Arthur Lupton, 1831–40. Lupton 127.

Accounts of the Mabgate Property managed by Nathaniel Sharpe, 1833–37. Lupton 127.

Receipts and accounts from the Mabgate estate of executors of Arthur Lupton, 1838–40. Lupton 128.

Borthwick Institute, University of York

Wills and administrations from the Court of Ainstey and the Prerogative Court of York, 1830–34.

Parliamentary Papers

Thirteenth report of the Commissioners of Inquiry into the Collection and Management of the Revenue . . . Board of Stamps (1826), vol. X.

First Report by the Commissioners Appointed to Inquire into the Law of England Respecting Real Property (1829), vol. X.

Stamp Duty received in the year 1829 (1830), vol. XXV.

Inquiry into the Practice and Jurisdiction of the Ecclesiastical Courts of England and Wales (1831), vol. XXIV.

Parliamentary Boundary Commission Reports (1831–32), vols. XXXVII–XXXIX.

Secret Committee on the Bank of England Charter (1832), vol. VI.

Fourth Report by the Commissioners Appointed to Inquire into the Law of England Respecting Real Property, House of Lords (1833), vol. XXII.

Factory Enquiry Commission, Supplementary Report, Part 2 (1834), vol. XIX.

Reports from Assistant Hand Loom Weaving Commissioners (1840), vol. XXIII.

Third Annual Report of the Registrar-General of Births, Deaths and Marriages in England (1841), vol. VI.

Census of England and Wales, 1841, (1843), vol. XXII.

Appendix to the Ninth Annual Report of the Registrar General of Birth Deaths and Marriages (1849), vol. XXI.

A Return of the Number of Probates and Letters of Administration Stamped under each Grade of Duty in the Year 1848 (1849), vol. XXX.

Census of Great Britain, 1851 (1852–53), vol. LXXXVIII.

Fourth report of the Inland Revenue (1860), vol. XXIII.

Ninth report of the Commissioners of the Inland Revenue (1866), ol. XXVI.

Tenth Report of the Commissioners of the Inland Revenue (1866), vol. XXVI.

Select Committee on Married Women's Property Bill (1867–68), vol. VII.

Eleventh Annual Report of the Inland Revenue (1867), vol. XXI.

A Bill to Amend the Law with Respect to the Property of Married Women (1867–68), vol. III.

Royal Commission on the Distribution of Income and Wealth, Chaired by Lord Diamond. Report no. 1, Initial Report on the Standing Reference, Cmnd. 6171 (HMSO: London, 1975).

Department of Trade and Industry, DTI – the Department for Enterprise Presented to Parliament, January 1988, Cmnd. 278 (HMSO: London, 1987–88), vol. LIV.

Law Reports

'Harrison v. Grady, Court of Common Pleas', *The Jurist* (24 February 1866), 140.

'Johnson v. Gallagher', *English Law Reports*, vol. XLV, 969.

'Johnson v. Sumner, 7 May 1858', *English Law Reports*, vol. CLVII, 469.

'Jolly and Another v. Rees, 1 February 1864', *English Law Reports*, vol. CXLIII, 931.

'Manby v. Scott', *English Law Reports*, vol. LXXXIII, 816.

'Montague v. Benedict, 26 January 1825', *English Law Reports*, vol. CVII, 867–9.

'Reid v. Teakle, 2 May 1858', *English Law Reports*, vol. CXXXVIII, 1346.

'Reneaux v. Teakle, 23 April 1853', *English Law Reports*, vol. CLV, 525.

'Seaton v. Benedict, 11 June 1828', *English Law Reports*, vol. CXXX, 969–71.

Directories and Poll Books

Edward Baines, *History, Directory and Gazetteer of the County of York, vol. I, West Riding* (Leeds, 1822).

William Parson, *General and Commercial Directory of the Borough of Leeds* (Leeds, 1826).

The General and Commercial Directory of the Borough of Leeds (Baines and Newsome: Leeds, 1834).
Poll Book of the Leeds Borough Election, 1834 (Leeds, 1834).
Poll Book of the Parliamentary Election for the Borough of Leeds (Leeds, 1832).

Newspapers

Leeds Mercury, 1829–51.
Leeds Times, 1837–39.

Maps

Jefferys T., *A Plan of Leeds, 1770* (London, 1772).
Giles, Netlam and Francis, *Plan of the Town of Leeds and its Environs, 1815* (Leeds, 1815).

Bibliography

Benwell Community Project, *The Making of a Ruling Class, Two Centuries of Capital Development on Tyneside*, Final Report Series 6 (Benwell, 1978).
Caste in the Evangelical World (London, 1886).
'Considerations in the Law of Entail, London 1823', *Edinburgh Review* **40** (1824), 350–75.
Evangelical Alliance, *Report of the proceedings of the conference held at Freemasons Hall, London, 19 August to 2 September 1846* (London, 1847).
Evangelical Review (April 1811), 230.
Leeds Improvement Act (1842).
'List of scientific societies and field clubs', *Nature* **8**, (23 October 1873).
'On equity in wills', *Christian Observer* (September 1814), 564–6.
'On the duty and mode of making a will', *Christian Observer* (July 1811), 423.
'On the moral construction of wills', *Christian Observer* (April 1811), 226.
Annual Reports of the Leeds Guardian Society (Leeds, 1831–51).
'The limits of testamentary bequests', *Eclectic Review*, New Series 4 (1852), 191.
Transactions of the National Association for the Promotion of Social Science Conference on Temperance Legislation (London, 1886).
Abrams, P., *The Origins of British Sociology, 1834–1914* (Chicago, 1968).
Addis, J.P., *The Crawshay Dynasty. A Study of Industrial Organization and Development, 1765–1867* (Cardiff, 1957).
Alborn, T.L., *Conceiving Companies. Joint Stock Politics in Victorian England* (London, 1998).
Allott, W., 'Leeds Quaker Meeting', *Publications of the Thoresby Society* **50** (1965).
Altick, R.D., *The English Common Reader. A Social History of the Mass Reading Public, 1800–1900* (Chicago, 1957).

Anderson, B., *Imagined Communities, Reflections on the Origin and Spread of Nationalism* (London, 1983).

Anderson, M. 'The emergence of the modern life cycle in Britain', *Social History* **10** (1985), 69–87.

Anderson, M., *Family Structure in Nineteenth Century Lancashire* (Cambridge, 1971).

Anderson, M., 'The social implications of demographic change', in F.M.L. Thompson (ed.), *The Cambridge Social History of Britain, 1750–1950, vol. II* (Cambridge, 1990), pp. 1–70.

Anderson, M., 'The social position of spinsters in mid-Victorian Britain', *Journal of Family History* **9**, 4 (Winter 1984), 377–93.

Anderson, O., 'Class, gender and Liberalism in Parliament, 1868–1882: the case of the Married Women's Property Acts', *Historical Journal* **46**, 1 (2003), 59–87.

Anderson, O., 'Hansard's Hazards: an illustration from recent interpretations of Married Women's Property law and the 1857 Divorce Act', *English Historical Review* (1997), 1202–15.

Anderson, O., 'State, civil society and separation in Victorian marriage', *Past and Present* **163** (May 1999), 161–201.

Anderson, P. 'Origins of the present crisis', *New Left Review* **23** (Jan–Feb, 1964), 26–53.

Anderson, R.D., *Education and Opportunity in Victorian Scotland* (Oxford, 1983).

Arensberg, C. and S.T. Kimball, *Family and Community in Ireland* (Harvard, 1940).

Ashton, R., *Thomas and Jane Carlyle. Portrait of a Marriage* (London, 2002).

Atkinson, A.B., 'On the measurement of inequality', in A.B. Atkinson (ed.), *Wealth, Income and Inequality* (London, 1973).

Atkinson, A.B., *The Economics of Inequality* (Oxford, 1975).

Attwood, T., *The Remedy or Thoughts on the Present Distress* (London, 1819).

Baker, R. *Report of the Leeds Board of Health* (Leeds, 1833).

Baker, R., 'Report upon the condition of the town of Leeds and of its inhabitants, by a Statistical Committee of the Town Council, October 1839', *Journal of the Statistical Society of London* **2** (1839), 397–424.

Baker, R., *On the State and Condition of the Town of Leeds in the West Riding of the County of York* (Leeds, 1842), reprinted in the local reports on *The Sanitary Condition of the Labouring Population Directed to be made by the Poor Law Commissioners*, no. 23 (London, 1842), pp. 348–407.

Barnes, D.G., *A History of the English Corn Laws from 1660–1846* (London, 1930).

Basch, N., 'Invisible women: the legal fiction of marital unity in nineteenth-century America', *Feminist Studies* **5** (1979), 346–66.

Bedale, C., 'Property relations and housing policy: Oldham in the late nineteenth and early twentieth centuries', in J. Melling (ed.), *Housing, Social Policy and the State* (London, 1980), pp. 37–72.

Beeton, I., *The Book of Household Management* (London, 1861).

Benjamin, W., *Reflections. Essays, Aphorisms, Autobiographical Writings*, P. Demetz (ed.) (New York, 1986).

Beresford, M.W., 'Prosperity Street and others: an essay in visible urban history', in M.W. Beresford and G.R.J. Jones (eds.), *Leeds and its Region* (Leeds, 1967), pp. 186–99.

Beresford, M.W., 'The making of a townscape: Richard Paley in the East End of Leeds, 1771–1803', in C.W. Chalklin and M.A. Havinden (eds.), *Rural Change and Urban growth, 1500–1800*, (London, 1974), pp. 281–320.

Beresford, M.W., 'East End, West End. The face of Leeds during urbanization, 1684–1842', *Publications of the Thoresby Society*, 60 and 61, nos. 131 and 132, (1988).

Berg, M., 'The first women economic historians', *Economic History Review* **45**, 2 (May 1992).

Berg, M., 'Small producer capitalism in 18th century England', *Business History* **35** (1993), 17–39.

Berg, M., 'Women's consumption and the industrial classes of 18th century England', *Journal of Social History* (Winter 1996), 415–34.

Berg, M., 'Women's property and the Industrial Revolution', *Journal of Interdisciplinary History* **24** (1993), 233–50.

Berman, M., *Social Change and Scientific Organization. The Royal Institution, 1799–1844* (London, 1978).

Billington, L. and R. Billington, 'A burning zeal for righteousness: women in the British anti-slavery movement, 1820–1860' in Jane Rendall (ed.), *Equal or Different. Women's Politics, 1800–1914* (Oxford 1987), pp. 82–111.

Birch, D. and F. O'Gorman (eds.), *Ruskin and Gender* (Basingstoke, 2002).

Blackstone, Sir W., *Commentaries on the Law of England*, 18th edition with the last corrections of the author and copious notes by Thomas Lee, Esq. 4 vols. (London, 1829).

Bonsor, K.J. and H. Nichols, 'Printed maps and plans of Leeds, 1711–1900', *Publications of the Thoresby Society* **47**, 106 (Leeds, 1960).

Boot, H., 'Real incomes of the British middle class, 1760–1850: the experience of clerks at the East India Company', *Economic History Review* **52**, 4, (November, 1999), 638–68.

Borsay, P., *The English Urban Renaissance. Culture and Society in the Provincial Town, 1660–1770* (Oxford 1989).

Bowdler, J., *Reform or Ruin, Take your Choice, in which the Conduct of the King, the Parliament, the Opposition, the Nobility and Gentry, the Bishops and Clergy, etc., is Considered, and that Reform Pointed Out which alone can Save the Country* (London, 1797).

Branca, P., *Silent Sisterhood. Middle Class Women in the Victorian Home*, (London, 1974).

Breward, C. *The Hidden Consumer. Masculinities, Fashion and City Life, 1860–1914* (Manchester, 1999).

Brewer, J. *The Pleasures of the Imagination. English Culture in the Eighteenth Century* (London, 1997).

Brewer, J. and R. Porter (eds.), *Consumption and the World of Goods* (London, 1993).

Brewer, J. and S. Staves (eds.), *Early Modern Conceptions of Property* (London, 1996).

Briggs, A., 'Thomas Attwood and the economic background of the Birmingham Political Union', *Cambridge Historical Journal* **9** (1948), 190–216.

Briggs, A., *The Age of Improvement* (London, 1959).

Briggs, A., 'The language of 'Class' in early nineteenth-century England', in A. Briggs and J. Saville (eds.), *Essays in Labour History* (London, 1960), pp. 43–73.

Briggs, A. *Victorian Things* (London, 1988).

Bright, J.E., *A Treatise on the Law of Husband and Wife as Respects Property, partly Founded upon Roper's Treatise, and Comprising Jacob's Notes and Additions thereto* (London, 1849).

Broadridge, S.A., 'The sources of railway share capital', in M.C. Reed (ed.), *Railways in the Victorian Economy. Studies in Finance and Economic Growth* (Newton Abbott, 1969).

Brown, F.K., *Fathers of the Victorians: the Age of Wilberforce* (Cambridge, 1961).

Burke, E., *Reflections on the Revolution in France* (New York, 1955), original publication 1790.

Buxton, S., *Finance and Politics. An Historical Study, 1793–1885*, 2 vols. (London, 1885).

Cain, P.J. and A.G. Hopkins, 'Gentlemanly capitalism and British expansion overseas: I. The old colonial system, 1688–1850', *Economic History Review* **39**, 4 (1986), 501–25.

Cain, P.J. and A.G. Hopkins, 'Gentlemanly capitalism and British expansion overseas: II. New imperialism, 1850–1945, *Economic History Review* **40**, 1 (1987), 1–26.

Cairncross, A.K. and B. Weber, 'Fluctuations in building in Great Britain, 1785–1849', *Economic History Review* **9** (1956).

Calhoun, C. (ed.), *Habermas and the Public Sphere* (MIT, 1994).

Campbell, I., *Thomas Carlyle* (Edinburgh, 1974).

Cannadine, D., 'Victorian cities: how different?', *Social History* **4** (1977), 457–82.

Cannadine, D. *Lords and Landlords. The Aristocracy and the Towns, 1774–1967* (Leicester, 1980).

Cannadine, D., *Class in Britain* (Yale, 1998).

Carlyle, T., 'The Corn Law rhymes', *Edinburgh Review* (July 1832), 338–61.

Carlyle, T., 'Occasional discourse on the negro question', *Fraser's Magazine* **40** (December 1849), 670–9.

Carlyle, T., *Occasional Discourse on the Nigger Question* (London, 1853).

Cate, G.A. (ed.), *The Correspondence of Thomas Carlyle and John Ruskin* (Stanford, 1982).

Chadwick, E., *Report on the Sanitary Condition of the Labouring Population of Great Britain, 1842*, M.W. Flinn (ed.), (Edinburgh, 1965).

Chaytor, M., 'Household and kinship: Ryton in the late 16th and early 17th centuries', *History Workshop* **10** (Autumn 1980), 25–60.

Christ, C., 'Victorian masculinity and the angel in the house', in M. Vicinus (ed.), *A Widening Sphere. Changing Roles of Victorian Women* (Indiana, 1977).

Christie, J.T., *Concise Precedents of Wills with an Introduction and Practical Notes* (London, 1849), 14–15.

Clapham, J.H., *The Bank of England. A History*, 2 vols. Vol. II, 1797–1914. (Cambridge, 1944).

Clark, G., 'Debt, deficits and crowding out: England, 1727–1840', *European Review of Economic History* 5, 3 (2001) 403–36.

Clark G., 'Shelter from the storm: housing and the industrial revolution, 1550–1909', *Journal of Economic History* 62 (June 2002).

Clark, P. *British Clubs and Societies, 1580–1800* (Oxford 2000).

Cole, G.D.H. *A Short History of the British Working Class Movement*, 3 vols. (London, 1925).

Cole, G.D.H. and R. Postgate, *The Common People, 1746–1946* (London, 1938).

Colley, L., *Britons: Forging the Nation, 1770–1837* (Yale, 1992).

Colls, R., *The Pitmen of the Northern Coalfield. Work, Culture and Protest, 1790–1850* (Manchester, 1987).

Corfield, P.J. (ed.), *Language, History and Class* (Oxford, 1991).

Corfield, P.J., 'Class by name and number in eighteenth century Britain', *History* 72 (1987), 38–61.

Cornish, W.R. and G. de L. Clark, *Law and Society in England, 1750–1950* (London, 1989).

Cory, I.P., A Practical Treatise on accounts, mercantile, partnership, solicitors, private. 2nd edn., (London, 1839).

Cowman, K., 'The Battle of the Boulevards: class, gender and the purpose of public space in later Victorian Liverpool', in S. Gunn and R.J. Morris (eds.), *Identities in Space. Contested Terrains in the Western City since 1850* (Aldershot, 2001).

Cox, J., *Wills, Inventories and Death Duties* (London: The Public Record Office, 1988).

Crafts, N.F.R., *British Economic Growth during the Industrial Revolution* (Oxford, 1985).

Crafts, N.F.R. and C.K. Harley, 'Output growth and the British Industrial Revolution: a restatement of the Crafts–Harley view', *Economic History Review* 45, 4 (1992), 703–30.

Crafts, N.F.R., S.J. Leybourne and T.C. Mills, 'Trends and cycles in the British Industrial Revolution, 1700–1913', *Journal of the Royal Statistical Society* Ser. A, 152 (1989), 43–60.

Craik, G.L., *The Pursuit of Knowledge under Difficulties*, 2 vols. (London, 1833).

Crompton, R. *Class and Stratification. An Introduction to Current Debates* (Cambridge, 1993).

Cross, C., 'Wills as evidence of popular piety in the Reformation period. Leeds and Hull, 1540–1640', in D. Loades (ed.), *The End of Strife* (Edinburgh, 1984), 40–50.

Crossick, G. *An Artisan Elite in Victorian Society. Kentish London 1840–1800* (London, 1978).

Crossick, G. and S. Jaumain (eds.), *Cathedrals of Consumption. The European Department Store, 1850–1939* (Aldershot, 1999).

Crozier, D., 'Kinship and occupational succession', *Sociological Review* ns 13 (1965), 15–43.

D'Cruze, S., 'The middling sort in 18th century Colchester. Independence, social relations and the community broker', in J. Barry and C.Brooks (eds.), *The Middling Sort of People: Culture, Society and Politics in England, 1550–1800* (London, 1994), pp. 181–207.

Dahrendorf, R., *On Britain* (University of Chicago for the BBC, 1982).

Daunton, M.J., *House and Home in the Victorian City. Working Class Housing, 1850–1914* (London, 1983).

Daunton, M.J., *Progress and Poverty. An Economic and Social History of Britain, 1700–1850* (Oxford, 1995).

Daunton, M., ' "Gentlemanly Capitalism" and British industry, 1820–1914', *Past and Present* **122** (Feb 1989), 119–58.

Davidoff, L., M. Doolittle, J. Fink and C. Holden, *The Family Story. Blood, Contract and Intimacy, 1830–1960* (London, 1999).

Davidoff, L. and C. Hall, 'The architecture of public and private life. English middle class society in a provincial town, 1780–1850', in D. Fraser and A. Sutcliffe (eds.), *The Pursuit of Urban History* (London, 1983), pp. 327–45.

Davidoff, L. and C. Hall, *Family Fortunes. Men and Women of the English Middle Class, 1780–1850* (London, 1987 and 2nd edn. 2002).

Davidson, Captain E., (R.E.), *The Railways of India: with an Account of their Rise, Progress, and Construction. Written with the Aid of the Records of the India Office* (London, 1868).

Dawson, F.G., *The First Latin American Debt Crisis. The City of London and the 1822–25 Loan Bubble* (Yale, 1990).

Deane, P., 'New estimates of Gross National Product for the United Kingdom, 1830–1914', *Review of Income and Wealth* **14** (1968), 95–112.

Dennis, R., *English Industrial Cities in the Nineteenth Century* (Cambridge, 1984).

Dickens, C., *David Copperfield* (London, 1849–50).

Dickinson, H.T., *Liberty and Property. Political Ideology in Eighteenth-Century Britain* (London, 1977).

Digby, A., *Making a Medical Living. Doctors and Patients in the English Market for Medicine, 1720–1911* (Cambridge, 1994).

Ditz, T.L., *Property and Kinship. Inheritance in Early Connecticut, 1750–1820* (Princeton, 1986).

Duman, D., *The Judicial Bench in England, 1727–1875* (London, 1982).

Dwyer, J. *Virtuous Discourse. Sensibility and Community in Late Eighteenth Century Scotland* (Edinburgh 1987).

Earle, P., *The Making of the English Middle Class. Business, Society and Family Life in London, 1660–1730* (London, 1989).

Ehrlich, C., *The Piano. A History* (London, 1976).

Eliot, G., *Middlemarch* (London 1871–72, Penguin Library Edition, London 1965).

Elliott, Ebenezer (Corn Law Rhymer), *Centenary Commemoration* (Sheffield City Libraries: Sheffield, 1949).

Elliott, E., *Chambers Papers for the People*, no. 8, (Edinburgh, 1850).

Elliott, Sir W., 'Presidential Address', *Transactions of the Botanical Society of Edinburgh*, **10** (November, 1870).

English, B., *The Great Landowners of East Yorkshire, 1530–1910* (London, 1990).

English, B. and J. Saville, *Strict Settlement. A Guide for Historians* (University of Hull. Occasional Papers in Economic and Social History, no. 10 (Hull, 1983).

Erickson, A.L. *Women and Property in Early Modern England* (London, 1993).

Evans, D.M., *The Commercial Crisis, 1847–1848* (London, 2nd edn. of 1849, reprinted 1969).

Feinstein, C. 'Capital formation in Great Britain', in P. Mathias and M.M. Postan (eds.), *The Cambridge Economic History of Europe*, vol. VII. (Cambridge, 1978).

Feinstein, C., 'The rise and fall of the Williamson Curve', *Journal of Economic History* **48** (1988), 699–729.

Feinstein, C., 'Pessimism perpetuated: real wages and the standard of living in Britain during and after the Industrial Revolution', *Journal of Economic History* **58**, 3 (September, 1998), 625–58.

Feinstein, C. and S. Pollard (eds.), *Studies in Capital Formation in the United Kingdom, 1750–1920* (Oxford, 1988).

Ferguson, A., *An Essay on the History of Civil Society*, F. Oz-Salzberger (ed.) (Cambridge, 1995).

Field, J., 'Wealth, styles of life and social tone amongst Portsmouth's middle class, 1800–75', in R.J. Morris (ed.), *Class, Power and Social Structure* (Leicester, 1986), pp. 67–106.

Finch, J. et al., *Wills, Inheritance and Families* (Oxford, 1996).

Finn, M., 'Women, consumption and coverture in England, c. 1760–1860', *Historical Journal* **39**, 3 (1996), 703–22.

Fletcher, A.J., *Gender, Sex and Subordination in England, 1500–1800* (Yale, 1995).

Foster, B.F., *The Origin and Progress of Book Keeping* (London, 1852).

Foster, J., *Class Struggle and the Industrial Revolution. Early Industrial Capitalism in Three English Towns* (London 1974).

Foster, W.D., 'Finances of a Victorian GP', *Proceedings of the Royal Society of Medicine* **66** (January 1973).

Fraser, D., 'The politics of Leeds water', *Publications of the Thoresby Society* **53**, 1 (1970), 50–70.

Fraser, D., *Urban Politics in Victorian England. The Structure of Politics in Victorian Cities* (Leicester, 1976).

Freeman, S., *Isabella and Sam. The Story of Mrs Beeton* (London, 1977).

French, H.R., 'The search for the 'Middle Sort of People' in England, 1600–1800', *Historical Journal* **43**, 1 (2000), 277–93.

Gadian, D., 'Class formation and class action in north west industrial towns, 1830–50', in R. J. Morris (ed.), *Class, Power and Social Structure*, pp. 23–66.

Garrard, J. *Leadership and Power in Victorian Industrial Towns, 1830–80* (Manchester, 1983).

Gatrell, V.A.C., 'Incorporation and the pursuit of liberal hegemony in Manchester, 1790–1839', in D. Fraser (ed.), *Municipal Reform and the Industrial City* (Leicester, 1982), pp. 15–60.

Geertz, C., 'Religion as a cultural system', in M. Banton (ed.), *Anthropological Approaches to the Study of Religion* (London, 1966).

Gellner, E., *Conditions of Liberty. Civil Society and its Rivals* (London, 1994).

Gerth, H.H. and C. Wright Mills (eds.), *From Max Weber. Essays in Sociology* (London, 1948).

Girouard, M., *The Return to Camelot. Chivalry and the English Gentleman*, (Yale, 1981).

Gleadle, K. and S. Richardson (eds.) *Women in British politics, 1760–1860: the Power of the Petticoat* (London, 2000).

Godelier, M., *The Enigma of the Gift* (Cambridge, 1999).

Godfrey, R.T., *Printmaking in Britain. A General History from its Beginnings to the Present Day* (Oxford, 1978).

Goldman, L., *Science Reform and Politics in Victorian Britain: the Social Science Association, 1857–1886* (Cambridge, 2002).

Goldman, L., 'The Social Science Association, 1857–1886: a context for mid-Victorian liberalism', *English Historical Review* **101** (January 1986) 95–134.

Gooderson, P.J., *Lord Linoleum: Lord Ashton, Lancaster and the Rise of the British Oilcloth and Linoleum Industry* (Keele, 1996).

Goody, J., 'Strategies of heirship', *Comparative Studies in Society and History* **15** (1973), 3–20.

Goody, J., J. Thirsk and E.P. Thompson (eds.), *Family and Inheritance: Rural Society in Western Europe, 1200–1800* (Cambridge, 1976).

Grady, K., 'The provision of markets in Leeds, 1822–29', *Publications of the Thoresby Society* **54** (1976), 122–94.

Gravenson, R.H. and F.R. Crane (eds.), *A Century of Family Law* (London, 1957).

Gray, R.Q., *The Labour Aristocracy in Victorian Britain* (Oxford, 1976).

Gray, R.Q., 'Bourgeois hegemony in Victorian Britain', in J. Bloomfield (ed.), *Class, Hegemony and Party* (London, 1977), pp. 73–94.

Gray, R.Q., 'The deconstruction of the English working class', *Social History* **11**, 3 (October 1986) 363–73.

Gray, R.Q., *The Factory Question and Industrial England, 1830–1860* (Cambridge, 1996), pp. 38 and 53–8.

Green, D., 'Independent women, wealth and wills in nineteenth century London', in J. Stobart and A. Owens (eds.), *Urban Fortunes. Property and Inheritance in the Town, 1700–1900* (Aldershot, 2000), pp. 195–222.

Greg, W.R., 'Why are women redundant?', *National Review* **14** (1862), 436.

Griffin, B., 'Class, gender and liberalism in Parliament, 1868–1882: the case of the Married Women's Property Acts', *Historical Journal* **46**, 1 (2003), 59–87.

Griffiths, A., *Prints and Printmaking. An Introduction to the History and Techniques* (London, 1996).

Gunn, S., *The Public Culture of the Victorian Middle Class. Ritual and Authority in the English Industrial City, 1840–1914* (Manchester, 2000).

Habakkuk, J., *Marriage, Debt and the Estates System. English Landownership, 1650–1950* (Oxford, 1994).

Habermas, J., *The Structural Transformation of the Public Sphere. An Inquiry into a Category of Bourgeois Society*, trans. T. Burger, (Cambridge, 1992), first published in German 1962.

Hall, C., *White Male and Middle Class. Explorations in Feminism and History* (London, 1992).

Hall, C., *Civilizing Subjects. Metropole and Colony in the English Imagination, 1830–1867* (Cambridge, 2002).

Hall, C., K. McClelland and J. Rendall, *Defining the Victorian Nation. Class, Race, Gender and the Reform Act of 1867* (Cambridge, 2000).

Hammerton, A.J., *Cruelty and Companionship. Conflict in Nineteenth-century Married Life* (London, 1992).

Hammond, J.L. and B. Hammond, *The Town Labourer* (London, 1917).

Hannah, L., *Inventing Retirement* (Cambridge, 1986).

Hannah, L., *The Rise of the Corporate Economy* (London, 1976).

Harbottle, S., *The Reverend William Turner. Dissent and Reform in Georgian Newcastle upon Tyne* (Newcastle and Leeds, 1997).

Hardman, M., *Ruskin and Bradford* (Manchester, 1986).

Harrison, B.H., 'The Sunday trading riots of 1855', *Historical Journal* **8**, 2 (1965), 219–45.

Harrison, B.H., *Drink and the Victorians. The Temperance Question in England, 1815–1872* (London, 1971).

Harvey, D., *Social Justice and the City* (London, 1973).

Hastings, A. *The Construction of Nationhood. Ethnicity, Religion and Nationalism* (Cambridge, 1997).

Hayward, Dr J., 'Observations on the population and diseases of Chester in the year 1774', *Philosophical Transactions of the Royal Society of London* (1778).

Hennock, E.P., *Fit and Proper Persons. Ideal and Reality in Nineteenth-century Urban Government* (London, 1973).

Higgs, E., 'Domestic servants and households in Victorian England', *Social History* **8** (1983), 203–10.

Hilton, T., *John Ruskin* (Yale, 2002). Original editions *John Ruskin. The Early Years* (1985) and *John Ruskin. The Later Years* (2000).

Hirsch, P., *Barbara Leigh Smith Bodichon. Feminist, Artist and Rebel*, (London 1998).

Hobsbawm, E.J., *Nations and Nationalism Since 1780* (Cambridge, 1990).

Hobsbawm, E.J. and G. Rude, *Captain Swing* (London, 1969).

Holcombe, L., *Wives and Property: Reform of the Married Women's Property Law in 19th century England* (Toronto, 1983).

Holderness, B.A., 'Capital formation in agriculture', in J.P.P. Higgins and S. Pollard (eds.), *Aspects of Capital Investment in Great Britain, 1759–1850* (London, 1971).

Holdsworth, W.S., *A History of English Law*, 4 vols, (London, 1931, first published 1903).

Hollis, P., (ed.), *Pressure From Without in Early Victorian England* (London, 1974).

Holt, R.V., *The Unitarian Contribution to Social Progress* (London, 1938).

Hoppit, J., 'Counting the Industrial Revolution', *Economic History Review* **43**, 1 (1990), 173–93.

Horstman, A., *Victorian Divorce* (London, 1985).

Houghton, W.E., *The Victorian Frame of Mind* (Yale, 1957).

Hudson, J.C., *The Executors Guide* (London, 1838).

Hudson, J.C., *Plain Directions for Making Wills in Conformity with the Law* (London, 1859).

Hudson, P., *The Genesis of Industrial Capital. A Study of the West Riding Wool Textile Industry, c. 1750–1850* (Cambridge, 1986).

Hudson, P. (ed.), *Regions and Industries. A Perspective on the Industrial Revolution in Britain* (Cambridge, 1989).

Hudson, P., *The West Riding Wool Textile Industry: A Catalogue of Business Records*, (Pasold Research Fund, 1975).

Hunt, E.H., 'Industrialization and regional inequality: wages in Britain, 1760–1914', *Journal of Economic History* **46** (1986), 60–8.

Hunt, E.H., 'Wages', in J. Langton and R.J. Morris, *Atlas of Industrializing Britain, 1780–1914* (London, 1986), p. 68.

Hunt, M.R., *The Middling Sort. Commerce, Gender and the Family in England, 1680–1780* (California, 1996).

Isichei, E., *Victorian Quakers* (Oxford, 1970).

Jackson, R.V., 'Rates of industrial growth during the Industrial Revolution', *Economic History Review* **45**, 1 (February, 1992), 1–23.

Jeffreys, S., *The Spinster and her Enemies. Feminism and Sexuality, 1880–1930* (London, 1985).

Jenkins, D.T., *The West Riding Wool Textile Industry, 1770–1835* (Pasold Research Fund, 1975).

Jenkins, D.T. and K.G. Ponting, *The British Wool Textile Industry, 1770–1914* (London, 1982).

Johnson, T.J., *Professions and Power* (London, 1972).

Jones, A., 'Word and deed: why a post-poststructural history is needed, and how it might look, *Historical Journal* **43**, 2 (2000), 517–41.

Jones, E.L., *Agriculture and Economic Growth in England, 1650–1815* (London, 1967).

Jones, I.G., 'Trollope, Carlyle and Mill on the negro', *Journal of Negro History* **52**, 3 (July 1967) 185–99.

Jordanova, L., *History in Practice* (London, 2000).

Joyce, P., *Work, Society and Politics. The Culture of the Factory in Later Victorian England* (Brighton, 1980).

Joyce, P. (ed.), *Class* (Oxford, 1995).

Kargon, R.H., *Science in Victorian Manchester. Enterprise and Expertise* (Manchester, 1977).

Kiernan, V.G., 'Evangelicalism and the French Revolution', *Past and Present* **1** (February 1952), 44–56.

Klein, L.E., 'Politeness and the interpretation of the British eighteenth century', *Historical Journal* **45**, 4 (2002), 869–98.

Koditschek, T., *Class Formation and Urban Industrial Society. Bradford, 1750–1850* (Cambridge, 1990).

Komter, A.E., (ed.), *The Gift. An Interdisciplinary Perspective* (Amsterdam, 1996).

Lambert, R.S., *The Railway King, 1800–1871* (London, 1934).

Lane, P., 'Women, property and inheritance: wealth creation and income generation in small English towns, 1750–1835', in J. Stobart and A. Owens (eds.), *Urban Fortunes. Property and Inheritance in the Town, 1700–1900*, (Aldershot, 2000), pp. 172–94.

Langton, J. and R.J. Morris (eds.), *Atlas of Industrializing Britain* (London, 1986).

Laslett, P., *The World We Have Lost* (London, 1965).

Lee, C.H.A., *Cotton Enterprise, 1795–1840. A History of M'Connel and Kennedy, Fine Cotton Spinners* (Manchester, 1972).

Lee, T.A.A., 'Systematic view of the history of the world of accounting', *Accounting, Business and Financial History* **1**, 1 (1990), 73–107.

Lee, W.R., 'Robert Baker: the first doctor in the Factory Department, pt. 1 1803–1858, *British Journal of Industrial Medicine* **21** (1964), 85–93.

Lehman, C. and T. Tinker, 'The real cultural significance of accounts', *Accounts, Organizations and Society* **12** (1987), 503–22.

Lester, V.M., *Victorian Insolvency. Bankruptcy, Imprisonment for Debt, and Company Winding up in Nineteenth Century England* (Oxford, 1995).

Lewis, J.P., *Building Cycles and Britain's Growth* (London, 1965).

Leyton, E.H., 'Spheres of inheritance in Aughnaboy', *American Anthropologist* **72**, 6 (December 1970), 1378–88.

Liddington, J., *Female Fortune. Land, Gender and Authority. The Anne Lister Diaries and other Writings, 1833–36* (London, 1998).

Lindert, P.H. and J.G. Williamson, 'Revising England's social tables, 1688–1812', *Explorations in Economic History* **19** (1982), 385–408.

Lindert, P.H. and J.G. Williamson, 'English workers' living standards during the Industrial Revolution: a new look', *Economic History Review* **36**, 1 (February 1983), 1–25.

Lloyd, J.M., 'Raising lilies: Ruskin and women', *Journal of British Studies* **34**, 3 (July 1995), 325–50.

Locke, J., *Two Treatises of Government*, 1st edn. 1690 (Cambridge, 1960), edited with an introduction by P. Laslett.

Lockwood, D. *The Blackcoated Worker*, (London, 1958).

Loudon, I. *Medical Care and the General Practitioner, 1750–1850* (Oxford, 1986).

Lupton, C.A., *The Lupton Family of Leeds* (Leeds, 1965).

Macfarlane, A. *The Origins of English Individualism: the Family, Property and Social Transition* (Oxford, 1978).

Mackie, R., 'Family ownership and business survival: Kirkcaldy, 1870–1970', *Business History* **43**, 3 (July 2001), 1–32.

MacPherson, C.B., *The Political Theory of Possessive Individualism. Hobbes to Locke* (Oxford, 1962).

MacPherson, W.J., 'Investment in Indian Railways, 1845–1875', *Economic History Review* **8**, 2 (1955–56), 177–86.

Marriner, S., 'English bankruptcy records and statistics before 1850', *Economic History Review* **33** (August 1980), 351–66.

Marsh, C., 'In the name of God? Will-making and faith in early modern England', in G.H. Martin and P. Spufford (eds.), *The Records of the Nation* (Woodbridge, 1990), 215–50.

Marshall, A., *Principles of Economics*, 8th edn. (London, 1920), pp. 60–9, 482–505.

Matthews, R.C.O., *A Study in Trade Cycle History. Economic Fluctuations in Great Britain, 1833–42* (Cambridge, 1954).

McAloon, J., *No Idle Rich. The Wealthy in Canterbury and Otago, 1840–1914* (Otago, 2002).

McBride, T.M., *The Domestic Revolution* (London, 1976).

McCartney, S. and A.J. Arnold, 'George Hudson's financial reporting practices: putting the Eastern Counties Railway in context', *Accounting and Business and Financial History* **10**, 3 (November 2000), 293–316.

McCord, N. *The Anti-Corn Law League* (London, 1968).

McCulloch, J.R.A., *Treatise on the Succession of Property Vacant by Death* (London, 1847).

Meacham, S., *Henry Thornton of Clapham, 1760–1815* (Harvard, 1964).

Meacham, S., 'The evangelical inheritance', *Journal of British Studies* **3** (1963–64).

Michie, R.C., *Money, Mania and Markets. Investment, Company Formation and the Stock Exchange in Nineteenth Century Scotland* (Edinburgh, 1981).

Mill, J.S., *The Principles of Political Economy*, first published 1848, D. Winch (ed.), (London, 1970).

Mill, J.S. 'The negro question', *Fraser's Magazine* **41** (January 1850), 25–31.

Mill, J.S., *Autobiography* (London, 1873).

Miller, P. and T. O'Leary, 'Accounts and the construction of the governable person', *Accounts, Organizations and Society* **12** (1987), 235–65.

Millet, K., *Sexual Politics* (New York, 1970).

Mitchell, B.R. and P. Deane, *Abstract of British Historical Statistics* (Cambridge, 1962).

Money, J., *Experience and Identity. Birmingham and the West Midlands, 1760–1800* (Manchester, 1977).

Morgan, K., *Bristol and the Atlantic Trade in the 18th century* (Cambridge, 1993).

Morris, R.J. 'The friars and Paradise: an essay in the building history of Oxford, 1801–1861', *Oxoniensia* **36** (1971), 72–98.

Morris, R.J., 'The rise of James Kitson, trades union and mechanics institution, Leeds 1826–1851', *Publications of the Thoresby Society* **15** (1972), 179–200.

Morris, R.J., *Cholera, 1832 The Social Response to an Epidemic* (London, 1976).

Morris, R.J., *Class and Class Consciousness in the Industrial Revolution, 1780–1850* (London, 1979).

Morris, R.J., 'The middle class and the property cycle during the Industrial Revolution', in T.C. Smout (ed.), *The Search for Wealth and Stability* (London, 1979), pp. 91–113.

Morris, R.J., 'Middle class culture, 1700–1914', in D. Fraser (ed.), *A History of Modern Leeds* (Manchester, 1980), pp. 200–22.

Morris, R.J., 'Samuel Smiles and the genesis of self help: the retreat to a petit bourgeois utopia', *Historical Journal* **24** (1981), 89–109.

Morris, R.J., 'Voluntary societies and British urban elites, 1780–1870: an analysis', *Historical Journal* **26** (1982), 95–118.

Morris, R.J., 'The middle class and British towns and cities of the Industrial Revolution, 1780–1870', in D. Fraser and A. Sutcliffe (eds.), *The Pursuit of Urban History* (London, 1983).

Morris, R.J., *Class, Sect and Party. The Making of the British Middle Class: Leeds, 1820–50* (Manchester, 1990).

Morris, R.J., 'Clubs, societies and associations', in F.M.L. Thompson (ed.), *The Cambridge Social History of Britain, 1750–1950*, vol. III, (Cambridge, 1990), pp. 395–443.

Morris, R.J., 'Externalities, the market, power structures and the urban agenda', *Urban History Yearbook* 17 (1990), 99–109.

Morris, R.J., 'Occupational coding: principles and examples', *Historical Social Research/Historische Sozialforschung* **15** (1990), 3–29.

Morris, R.J., 'Petitions, meetings and class formation amongst the urban middle classes in Britain in the 1830s', *Tijdschrift voor Geschiedenis* **103** (1990), 294–310.

Morris, R.J., 'Family strategies and the built environment of Leeds in the 1830s and 1840's', *Northern History* 37 (2000), 193–214.

Morris, R.J., 'Structure, culture and society in British Towns', in M. Daunton (ed.), *The Cambridge Urban History of Britain*, vol. III, 1840–1950 (Cambridge, 2000), 395–426.

Morris, R.J., 'Civil society, subscriber democracies and parliamentary government in Great Britain', in N. Bermeo and P. Nord (eds.), *Civil Society before Democracy. Lessons from Nineteenth Century Europe* (New York, 2000), pp. 111–34.

Moss, D.J., *Thomas Attwood. The Biography of a Radical* (Montreal and Kingston, 1990).

Neale, R.S., 'Class and class consciousness in early nineteenth century England: three classes or five?', *Victorian Studies* **12**, 1 (September 1968), 5–32.

Neale, R.S., *Bath. A Social History, 1680–1850 or a Valley of Pleasure yet a Sink of Iniquity* (London, 1981).

Neill, C. and J.M. Willoughby, *The Tutorial Prayer Book* (London, 1912).

Nenadic, S., 'Businessmen, the urban middle classes, and the "dominance" of manufacturers in nineteenth century Britain', *Economic History Review* **44**, 1 (February 1991), 66–85.

Nenadic, S., 'The life cycle of firms in late nineteenth century Britain', in P. Jobert and M. Moss (eds.), *The Birth and Death of Companies. An Historical Perspective* (Carnforth, 1990), p. 181–95.

Nenadic, S., 'Middle rank consumers and domestic culture in Edinburgh and Glasgow, 1720 to 1840', *Past and Present* **145** (1994), 122–56.

Nenadic, S., 'The Victorian middle classes', in W.H. Fraser and I. Maver (eds.), *Glasgow, vol. II, 1830–1912* (Manchester, 1996), pp. 283–87.

Norton, J.E., *Guide to the National and Provincial Directories of England and Wales* (London, 1950 and 1984).

Nossitor, T.J., *Influence, Opinion and Political Idioms in Reformed England. Case Studies from the North East, 1832–1874* (Brighton, 1975).

Oke, G.C., *An Improved System of Solicitors Book-keeping* (London,1849).

Paley, W., 'Moral and Political Philosophy', in *The Works of William Paley, D D, Archdeacon of Carlisle* (London, 1851).

Parry, J.L., *Building Cycles and Britain's Growth* (London, 1965).

Parsons, E., *The Tourists Companion: By the Railroad and Steam Packet From Leeds and Selby to Hull* (London, 1835).

Peacock, A.J., *George Hudson, 1800–1871. The Railway King*, 2 vols. (York, 1988–89).

Pearson, J., FRS, *The Life of William Hey* (London,1822).

Pearson, R., 'Thrift or dissipation? The business of life assurance in the early nineteenth century', *Economic History Review* **43**, 2 (1990), 236–54.

Pearson, R., 'Taking risks and containing competition: diversification and oligopoly in the fire insurance markets of the north of England during the early nineteenth century', *Economic History Review* **46**, 1 (1993), 39–64.

Perkin, H.J., *The Origins of Modern English Society, 1780–1880* (London, 1969).

Perkin, H.J., *The Rise of Professional Society. England since 1880* (London, 1989).

Peterson, M.J., 'No angels in the house: the Victorian myth and the Paget women', *American Historical Review* **89**, 3 (June 1984), 677–708.

Pollard, S., *The Genesis of Modern Management. A Study of the Industrial Revolution in Great Britain* (London, 1965).

Poovey, M., *Uneven Developments. The Ideological Work of Gender in mid-Victorian England* (London, 1989).

Porter, G.R., *Progress of the Nation* (London, 1847).

Poynter, J.R., *Society and Pauperism. English Ideas on Poor Relief, 1795–1834* (London, 1969).

Price, R., *Masters, Unions and Men. Work Control in Building and the Rise of Labour, 1830–1914* (Cambridge, 1980).

Price, R., 'Historiography, narrative and the nineteenth century', *Journal of British Studies* **35** (April 1996), 220–56.

Prochaska, F.K., *Women and Philanthropy in 19th century England* (Oxford, 1980).

Ramelson, M., *Petticoat Rebellion* (London, 1967).

Reed, M.C., 'Railways and the growth of the capital market', in M.C. Reed (ed.), *Railways in the Victorian Economy* (Newton Abbott, 1969), pp. 162–83.

Reid, T.W., *A Memoir of John Deakin Heaton MD* (London, 1883).

Reiss, E., *The Rights and Duties of Englishwomen* (London, 1934).

Rimmer, W.G., *Marshall's of Leeds, Flax Spinners, 1788–1886* (Cambridge, 1960).

Robbins, M., *The Railway Age* (London, 1962).

Rodger, R.G., *Housing in Urban Britain, 1780–1914* (London, 1989).

Rodger, R.G., *The Transformation of Edinburgh. Land, Property and Trust in the Nineteenth Century* (Cambridge, 2001).

Rowbotham, S. *Hidden from History: 300 Years of Women's Oppression and the Fight Against It* (London, 1973).

Rowntree, B.S., *Poverty: A Study of Town Life* (London, 1902).

Rubinstein, W.D., 'Wealth, elites and the class structure of modern Britain', *Past and Present* **76** (August 1977), 99–126.

Rubinstein, W.D., 'The Victorian middle classes: wealth, occupation and geography', *Economic History Review* **30** (November 1977), 602–23.

Rubinstein, W.D., *Capitalism, Culture and Decline in Britain, 1750–1990* (London, 1993).

Sanderson, M., *Education, Economic Change and Society in England, 1780–1870* (London, 1983).

Saul, S.B., 'Housebuilding in England, 1890–1914', *Economic History Review* **15** (1962), 119–37.

Savage, G., 'Erotic stories and public decency: newspaper reporting of divorce proceedings in England', *Historical Journal* **41**, 2 (1998), 511–28.

Scammell, L., 'Town versus country: the property of everyday consumption in the late seventeenth century and early eighteenth centuries', in J. Stobart and A. Owens (eds.), *Urban Fortunes. Property and Inheritance in the Town, 1700–1900* (Aldershot, 2000), pp. 26–49.

Schivelbusch, W., *The Railway Journey. The Industrialization of Time and Space in the 19th century* (New York, 1986).

Schofield, R.E., *The Lunar Society of Birmingham. A Social History of Provincial Science and Industry in Eighteenth-century England* (Oxford, 1963).

Scholfield, R.S., 'Dimensions of illiteracy in England, 1750–1850', *Explorations in Economic History* **10** (1973), 437–54.

Schroeder, W.L., *Mill Hill Chapel, Leeds, 1674–1924: Sketch of its History* (Hull, 1924).

Seed, J., 'Unitarianism, political economy and the antinomies of liberal culture in Manchester, 1830–50', *Social History* **7**, 1 (1982), 1–26.

Seed, J., 'Gentlemen dissenters: the social and political meanings of rational dissent in the 1770s and 1780s', *Historical Journal* **28**, 2 (1985), 299–325.

Seed, J., 'Theologies of power: Unitarianism and the social relations of religious discourse, 1800–1850', in R.J. Morris (ed.), *Class, Power and Social Structure in British Nineteenth Century Towns* (Leicester 1986), pp. 107–56.

Seed, J., 'From "middling sort" to middle class in late eighteenth and early nineteenth-century England', in M.L. Bush (ed.), *Social Orders and Social Classes in Europe since 1500. Studies in Social Stratification* (London 1992), pp. 114–35.

Sennett, R., *The Fall of Public Man* (London, 1986 (1st edn. New York 1977)).

Shammas, C., M. Salmon and M. Dahlin, *Inheritance in America from Colonial Times to the Present* (Rutgers University Press, 1987).

Shanley, M.L., *Feminism, Marriage and the Law in Victorian England, 1850–1895* (London, 1989).

Shaw, G. and A. Tipper, *British Directories. A Bibliography and Guide* (Leicester, 1988).

Shoemaker, R.B., *Gender in English Society, 1650–1850* (London, 1998).

Siddle, D., 'Inheritance strategies and lineage development in peasant society', *Continuity and Change* **1**, 3 (1986), 333–61.

Sigsworth, E., *The Brewing Trade During the Industrial Revolution. The Case of Yorkshire*, Borthwick Papers 31 (York, 1967).

Sims, J. (ed.), *A Handlist of British Parliamentary Poll Books* (Leicester and Riverside, 1984).

Sitwell, E., 'Jane Welsh Carlyle, 1801–1866', in *English Women* [sic], (London, 1942).

Smail, J., *The Origins of Middle Class Culture. Halifax, 1660–1780* (Cornell, 1994).

Smart, R., 'Famous throughout the World. Valentine and Sons Ltd., Dundee, *Review of Scottish Culture* **4** (1988), 75–88.

Smiles, S., *The Life of George Stephenson, Railway Engineer*, (London, 1857).

Smith, A. *An Inquiry into the Nature and Causes of the Wealth of Nations*, 5th edn. with an introduction by J.R. McCulloch (Edinburgh, 1849).

Smith, F.B., *The People's Health, 1830–1910* (London, 1979).

Smith, R.M., 'Families and their property in rural England, 1260–1800', in R.M. Smith, *Land, Kinship and the Life Cycle* (Cambridge, 1984), pp. 45–52.

Springett, J., 'Land development and house building in Huddersfield, 1770–1911', in M. Doughty (ed.), *Building the Industrial City* (Leicester, 1986).

Spufford, M., *Contrasting Communities. English Villagers in the Sixteenth and Seventeenth Centuries* (Cambridge, 1974), pp. 230–44.

Stedman Jones, G., *Languages of Class. Studies in English Working Class History, 1832–1982* (Oxford, 1983), pp. 90–178.

Stephens, H.J., 'Sergeant at law', in *New Commentaries on the Laws of England*, 4 vols. (London, 1841).

Stephens, W.R.W., *The Life and Letters of Walter Farquhar Hook* (London, 1885).

Stone, L., *Road to Divorce. A History of the Making and Breaking of Marriage in England* (Oxford, 1995).

Supple, B., *The Royal Exchange Assurance. A History of British Insurance, 1720–1978* (Cambridge, 1970).

Swinburne, H., *A Treatise of Testaments and Last Wills*, 7th edn. with annotations of the late John Joseph Powell. (London, 1803), vol. I, pp. 300–2.

Tadmor, N., *Family and Friends in Eighteenth-Century England* (Cambridge, 2001).

Taylor, R.V., *The Biographia Leodiensis: or Biographical Sketches of the Worthies of Leeds and Neighbourhood from the Norman Conquest to the Present Time* (London, 1865).

Thompson, E.P., *The Making of the English Working Class* (London, 1965).

Thompson, E.P., 'The moral economy of the English crowd in the eighteenth century', *Past and Present* **50** (1971), 76–136.

Thompson, E.P., 'The peculiarities of the English (1965)', reprinted in E.P. Thompson, *The Poverty of Theory* (London, 1978), pp. 35–91.

Thompson, F.M.L., 'Whigs and Liberals in the West Riding, 1830–60', *English Historical Review* **74** (1959).

Thompson, F.M.L. (ed.), *The Rise of Suburbia* (Leicester, 1982).

Thoresby, R., *Ducartus Leodiensis*. T.D. Whitaker (ed.) (Leeds, 1816).

Tilley, C., *Popular Contention in Great Britain, 1758–1834* (Harvard, 1995).

Tosh, J.A., *Man's Place. Masculinity and the Middle-Class Home in Victorian England* (Yale University Press, 1999).

Trainor, R.H., *Black Country Elites. The Exercise of Authority in an Industrialized Area, 1830–1900* (Oxford, 1993).

Trebilcock, C., *Phoenix Assurance and the Development of British Insurance, vol. I, 1782–1870* (Cambridge, 1985).

Trevelyan, G.M., *Illustrated English Social History*, 4 vols. (London, 1942).

Vann, R.T. and D. Eversley, *Friends in Life and Death. The British and Irish Quakers in the Demographic Transition* (Cambridge, 1992).

Vickery, A., 'Golden age to separate spheres? A review of the categories and chronology of English women's history', *Historical Journal* **36**, 2 (1993), 383–414.

Vickery, A., *The Gentleman's Daughter. Women's Lives in Georgian England* (Yale, 1998).

Vincent, J.R., *How Victorians Voted* (Cambridge, 1967).

Wahrman, D., *Imagining the Middle Class. The Political Representation of Class in Britain, c.1780–1840* (Cambridge, 1995).

Wakeman, A., *The Autobiography of a Charwoman* (London, 1900, 2nd edn.).

Ward, D., 'Victorian cities: How modern?', *Journal of Historical Geography* 1 (1975), 135–51.

Ward, D., 'Environs and neighbours in the "Two Nations": residential differentiation in mid-nineteenth century Leeds', *Journal of Historical Geography* 6 (1980), 133–62.

Ward, J.R., *The Finance of Canal Building in Eighteenth Century England* (Oxford, 1974).

Weatherill, L., *Consumer Behaviour and Material Culture in Britain 1660–1760* (London, 1988).

Weber, M., *Economy and Society*, G. Roth and C. Wittich (eds.), (New York, 1968).

Wells, R., *Dearth and Distress in Yorkshire, 1793–1802*, Borthwick Papers 52 (York, 1977).

Wells, R., *Wretched Faces. Famine in Wartime England, 1793–1801* (Gloucester, 1988).

Westergaard, J. and H. Resler, *Class in Capitalist Society. A Study of Contemporary Britain* (London, 1975).

White, H., *The Content of the Form. Narrative Discourse and Historical Representation* (Baltimore, 1987).

Whitehand, J.W.R., *The Changing Face of Cities: A Study of Development Cycles and Urban Form* (Oxford, 1987).

Wicksteed, C., *Lectures on the Memory of the Just, Being a Series of Discourses on the Lives and Times of the Ministers of Mill Hill Chapel*, (Leeds and London, 1849).

Wicksteed, H.M., *Charles Wicksteed, a Biography* (London, 1933).

Wiener, M.J., *English Culture and the Decline of the Industrial Spirit, 1850–1980* (Cambridge, 1981).

Wilberforce, William, *A Practical View of the Prevailing Religious System of Professed Christians in the Higher and Middle Classes in this Country Contrasted with Real Christianity* (London, 1797).

Williamson, J.G., 'The distribution of earnings in nineteenth century Britain', Discussion Paper, Department of Economics University of Wisconsin, December 1979.

Williamson, Jeffrey G., *Did British Capitalism Breed Inequality?* (London, 1985).

Wilson, R.G., *Gentlemen Merchants. The Merchant Community in Leeds, 1700–1830* (Manchester, 1971).

Winstanley, Michael, 'Owners and occupiers. Property, politics and middle class formation in early industrial Lancashire', in Alan Kidd and David Nicholls (eds.), *The Making of the British Middle Class? Studies in regional and Cultural Diversity since the Eighteenth Century* (Stroud, 1998).

Woolf, Janet and John Seed (eds.), *The Culture of Capital: Art, Power and the Nineteenth Century Middle Class* (Manchester, 1988).

Wrightson, Keith, *English Society, 1580–1680* (London, 1982).
Wrigley, E.A., *People, Cities and Wealth* (Oxford, 1987).
Wrigley, E.A. and R.S. Scholfield, *The Population History of England, 1541–1871, A Reconstruction* (Cambridge, 1989 (first edition 1981)).

Unpublished Thesis

Diana E. Ascott, Wealth and Community in Liverpool, 1650–1750 University of Liverpool PhD thesis, 1996.
Ewan Knox, Between Capital and Labour: the Petite Bourgeoisie in Victorian Edinburgh, Edinburgh PhD, 1986.
Stana Nenadic, The Structure, Values and Influence of the Scottish Urban Middle Class, PhD, Glasgow 1986.
Alastair J. Owens, Small Fortunes: Property, Inheritance and the Middling Sort in Stockport, 1800–57, University of London PhD, 2002.

Index